CRITICAL JURISPRUDENCE

Jurisprudence is the prudence of *jus*, law's consciousness and conscience. Throughout history, when thinkers wanted to contemplate the organisation of society or the relationship between authority and the subject, they turned to law. All great philosophers, from Plato to Hobbes, Kant, Hegel, Marx and Weber had either studied the law or had a deep understanding of legal operations. But jurisprudence is also the conscience of law, the exploration of law's justice and of an ideal law or equity at the bar of which state law is always judged. Jurisprudence brings together 'is' and 'ought', the positive and the normative, law and justice.

But after a long process of decay, legal theory is today characterised by cognitive and moral poverty. Jurisprudence has become restricted and academically peripheral, a guidebook to technocratic legalism and a legitimation of the existent. Critical jurisprudence returns to the classical tradition of a general philosophy of law and adopts a much wider concept of legality. It is concerned both with posited law and with the law of the law. All legal aspects of the economic, political, emotional and physical modes of production and reproduction of society are part of critical jurisprudence. This widening of scope allows a radical rethinking of the nature of rights, justice, sovereignty and judgement. A political philosophy of justice today must examine the political economy of law; transitions from Empire to nation; ideological and imaginary constructions through which we understand ourselves and relate to others; ways in which gender, race or sexuality create forms of identity that both discipline bodies and offer sites of resistance. Law's complicity with political oppression, violence and racism has to be faced before it is possible to speak of a new beginning for legal thought, which in turn is the necessary precondition for a theory of justice. *Critical Jurisprudence* offers an ethics of law against the nihilism of power and an aesthetics of existence for the melancholic lawyer.

Critical Jurisprudence
The Political Philosophy of Justice

Costas Douzinas
and
Adam Gearey

·HART·
PUBLISHING
OXFORD – PORTLAND OREGON
2005

Hart Publishing
Oxford and Portland, Oregon

Published in North America (US and Canada) by
Hart Publishing c/o
International Specialized Book Services
5804 NE Hassalo Street
Portland, Oregon
97213-3644
USA

Hart Publishing, Salter's Boatyard, Folly Bridge,
Abingdon Road, Oxford OX1 4LB
Telephone: +44 (0)1865 245533 or Fax: +44 (0)1865 794882
e-mail: mail@hartpub.co.uk
WEBSITE: http//www.hartpub.co.uk

British Library Cataloguing in Publication Data
Data Available
ISBN 1–84113–452–X (paperback)

Typeset by Hope Services (Abingdon) Ltd
Printed and bound in Great Britain by
Page Bros, Norwich

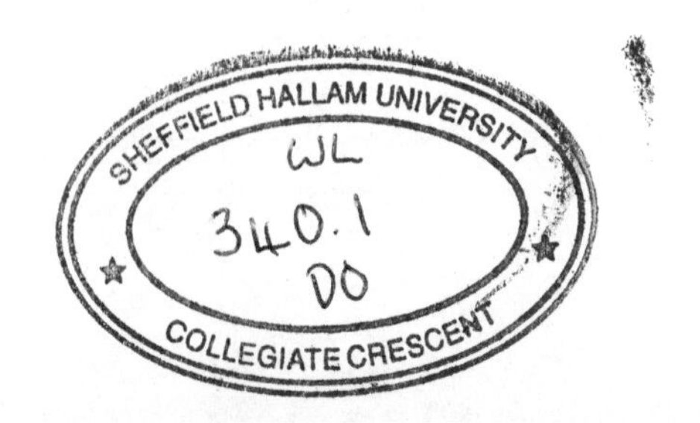

Embarking; Passages

I

This is the logbook of a journey. It started a long time ago, just before the end of the war (Troy had not yet fallen, but Cassandra's oracle had cast a thick shadow over the city).

The first leg was good; the sea was calm, a good northern wind, the cabinets well-stocked with bread, wine and exotic herbs, the crew full of spirit. Then news of Troy's fall reached us. We also heard that Menelaus had sailed. We were not to see him again. Philoktetes' illness started soon after, the pain, the horrible pain he did not want us to know about. How can you share the pain of a friend? Can you take some of it yourself to help him bear it? Or does pain seal them into their own world?

Understanding things does not mean that we can experience them. Knowledge and life are two different worlds. Nothing was the same after that revelation. Philoktetes stayed in Lemnos. We sailed on with his bow. But, separated from its master, it had lost its power. We met the Sirens whose words were even more enticing than their melody. They sang beautifully of how they would give knowledge to every man who came to them; ripe wisdom and a quickening of the spirit. Later, we landed on Circe's island and stayed for a while. The algos (pain) for nostos (day of return) became plain hurt. Ithaca was no longer a destination or even a fantasy, just something immemorial that had to be forgotten. Lethe did not bless us. You can never return home.

Later, the Christians came. They shook things up with new stories.

Other cities fell. We heard of wars in the desert. Tragedies turned to farce. The world seemed to move far faster than our words. Perhaps the best use for books now is purely practical. Texts of philosophy can plug leaks in the hold; bonfires of sonnets keep us warm on dark nights. As for history, pages torn from Thucydides make fine paper hats for clowns.

II

Early plans for a book of this kind were made by Ronnie Warrington, Peter Goodrich and Costas Douzinas. Ronnie's untimely death made it impossible to continue. Peter and Costas also began to move in different intellectual directions. However, Ronnie and Peter's work still remains the keel and ballast of this book. They are both part of this book and indelible parts of Costas' world. Adam joined the project and brought the wisdom of (relative) youth and the élan of style. In this long peregrination through ideas and philosophies, many people served as supporters, crew or chandlers. Shaun McVeigh, Piyel Haldar, Alexandra Bakalaki, Peter Rush, Alison Young and Les Moran have been companions throughout the long journey. Christos Lyrintzis, Maria Komninos, Nicos Douzinas, Kostis Douzinas and Nancy Rauch-Douzina have been the most generous donors of ideas and fortifications. A version of Chapter 7 was published as 'Identity, Recognition, Rights' (2002) 29/3 *Journal of Law and Society* 379–405.

III

We are most grateful to Richard Hart, Mel Hamill, Anna Greer and Rachel O'Dowd whose hard work and vision made this book.

IV

Other influences and voices that speak here: Paul Virr, Robert Cartledge, Ari Hirvonen, Panu Minkinnen, Angus MacDonald, Peter Goodrich, Anthony Farley, Melanie Williams, Maria Aristodemou, Nathan Moore, Louis Wolcher, Thanos Zaratoulidis, Peter Fitzpatrick, Maria Drakopoulou, Karin Van Marle, Johan Van der Walt, Wessel Le Roux and the many friends at Birkbeck and the CLC.

V

Mary, my lode star, thank you. Niamh, little bear, dancing light.

VI

Phaedra Douzinas' life spans the period of this adventure and has inspired some of its finishing touches. Joanna Bourke has been the closest of fellow-travelers for a long time. Her quiet wisdom, natural elegance and unceasing love have convinced me that this trip is worth finishing (if it ever will), even at the time of the tempest.

Contents

Part 1

Introductions

1

From Restricted to General Jurisprudence

JURISPRUDENCE AND MODERNITY

EARLY MORNING PIRAEUS. The city is beginning to wake; workers hurry to the metro, squeeze into buses and the metal shutters of cafés rattle up; already the roads are full of traffic; the smell of petrol and cigarettes. But after London even this air is refreshing. A slight breeze on the quay. Look out to the sea, waiting for the ferry. The surrounding hills emerge from the shadows into the sharpest of outline in the morning sun, becoming intense. The city itself sprawls into a haze of heat. When should I go aboard? Later, azure light on the water. Islands and mountains stand out hard edged in the sun glare.

Reading law books is like eating sawdust.[1] Few of us have escaped the dry taste in the mouth occasioned by the study of jurisprudence. And yet jurisprudence is the prudence, the *phronesis* of *jus* (law), law's consciousness and conscience. What does this mean? All great philosophers from Plato to Hobbes, Kant, Hegel and Weber had either studied the law or had a deep understanding of legal operations. Juristic issues have been central to philosophical concerns throughout history. Well before the creation of the various disciplines, when thinkers wanted to contemplate the organisation of their society or the relationship between authority and the citizen they turned to law. Plato's *Republic* and Aristotle's *Ethics* as much as Hegel's *Philosophy of Right* are attempts to examine the legal aspects of the social bond, to discover and promote a type of legality that attaches the body to the soul, keeps them together and links them to the broader community.

But this first meaning of wisdom (as the consiousness of law) cannot be separated from a second: jurisprudence is the conscience of law, the exploration of law's justice and of an ideal law or equity at the bar of which state law is always judged. As the wisdom of law, jurisprudence brings together *is* and *ought*, the

[1] Franz Kafka, *Letters to Friends, Family and Editors* (1977).

positive and the normative, law and justice. Plato's *Republic* is the first and most extended search for the meaning of justice in the western canon, while his *Laws* were a constitutional blueprint and a complete guide to legislation two millennia before Bentham.

Seen from the perspective of the *longue durée*, the law represents the principle of social reproduction; the passing on of what survives our brief sojourn in this world. Whenever classical philosophy occupied itself with the persistence of the social bond, it turned to law and became legal philosophy—the great source from which political philosophy and then the disciplines, sociology, psychology, anthropology, emerged in the seventeenth and nineteenth centuries respectively.

All major early modern philosophers were jurists. Thomas Hobbes was preoccupied with the common law, *Leviathan* is a clear exercise in jurisprudence. Immanuel Kant, the philosopher of modernity par excellence wrote extensively on legal issues and at the end of his life came up with a blueprint for a future world state based on international law and respect for freedom and rights. Hegel and Marx wrote superb jurisprudential texts but were also well versed in the positive law of their time. Emile Durkheim and Max Weber, the founders of sociology, wrote extensively on law and used types of legality as markers for the classification of different social systems.

But the birth of the disciplines from the womb of legal philosophy led to an impoverishment of legal study and jurisprudence. Two types of poverty accompanied modern legal theory, cognitive and moral. Through its cognitive impoverishment, legal scholarship became an entomology of rules, a guidebook to technocratic legalism, a science of what—legally—exists, and a legitimation of current policies. Edmund Burke called this obsession with reason, rights and codification metaphysical 'speculatism'.[2] Rationalism and positivism, doctrine and dogma replaced the humanistic immersion in the legal text. But rule formalism is a woefully inadequate representation of the legal enterprise even at the descriptive level. As a result, legal scholarship became academically peripheral—an examination and understanding of law unnecessary and uninteresting for the social sciences and disciplines. Legal education took the form of vocational skills training and was treated as such by both students and the rest of the academy. When legal academics complain about students' lack of interest in theoretical or other 'extracurricular' issues we have only ourselves to blame. We have set ourselves up as the purveyors of a technical knowledge that must be condensed, memorised and repeated—the death of the soul and the intellect. But as old Nietzsche said of his own studies, when the only organ addressed by the professor is the ear, it grows disproportionately large by eating away at the brain.[3]

How can we read this story of decline? The history of jurisprudence can be described as the movement from general to restricted concerns. This gradual

[2] E Burke, *Reflections on the Revolution in France*, JGA Pockock (ed), (London, Hackett, 1987) at 51, and see C Douzinas, *The End of Human Rights* (Oxford, Hart, 2000), 148–57.

[3] Nietzsche, quoted in J Derrida, *The Ear of the Other*, P Kamuf (trans), (New York, Schocken, 1985) 53.

diminution of scope and the replacement of thinking about the law of the law by a technical and professional approach have given us the standard jurisprudence textbook. Generations of jurisprudence writers have subdued their readers by obsessively repeating the question 'what is law?' and have presented legal theory as the history of the meaning(s) of the word 'law'. The 'concept' of law, the 'idea' of law, and 'law's empire' are titles of some of the most influential jurisprudence textbooks.[4] This 'ontological' enquiry indicates a certain anxiety about law's proper domain. We have to spend so much energy thinking about the essence of law because it is assumed that the law does have an essence. Once this essence is discovered, glittering like a lost coin, it will allow law to be separated from non-law. But this essence is always under threat, subject to contamination by non-law or pseudo-law—clipped coins and forgeries, which, if admitted to law's empire, may endanger its reason, coherence and systematicity.

Jurisprudence thus sets itself the task of uncovering and pronouncing the truth about law. It approaches the task by following two major approaches, the internal and external. Internal theories adopt the point of view of the judge or lawyer and try to theorise the process of argumentation and reasoning used in institutional discourse. This method often deteriorates into an extended set of footnotes to judicial pronouncements, a practice useful for a certain type of pedagogy but intellectually suspect, and, as tasteless as Kafka's sawdust. External theories, on the other hand, typically the sociology of law and Marxist approaches, treat reasons, arguments and justifications as 'facts' to be incorporated in wider non-legal explanatory contexts. The task here is to identify the causal chains that shape or are shaped by legal practices. External theories could be used as a corrective to the excessive formalism of jurisprudence. They can provide the background and methodology for empirical socio-legal research, which explores the economic and social effects of legal operations and domination. They are interested in behavioural patterns and the motivations rather than the intentions of people; they focus on social structures, on the causes and unintended consequences of action rather than individual agency. But the law is preoccupied with individual choice, will and liability while structural and institutional concerns are secondary. As a result sociological and socio-legal scholarship has remained marginal. Normative jurisprudence has become the standard fare of the law-school curriculum and external theories have been demoted to an occasional supplement for the politically aware, or re-positioned as sociology and criminology courses for those who are bored with the law curriculum or drawn to the romance of scholarship rather than to the cold utilitarianism of legal practice.

Within normative jurisprudence, legal positivism has been the dominant and typically modernist internal approach. Positivism is both the cause and effect of the moral poverty of the jurisprudence of the twentieth century. Positivism

[4] HLA Hart, *The Concept of Law* (Oxford, Clarendon, 1979); D Lloyd, *The Idea of Law* (London, Penguin, 1978); R Dworkin, *Law's Empire* (Oxford, Hart, 1998).

based the legitimacy of law on formal reason and on the consequent decline of ethical considerations. Using the strict distinction between fact and value, positivists excluded or minimised the influence of moral values and principles in law. The effort was motivated by cognitive-epistemological and political considerations. Hans Kelsen and Herbert Hart, the two towering influences of continental and Anglo-American positivism, turned the study of law into a 'science'. A 'science' of law could only be founded on observable, objective phenomena, not on subjective and relative values. Kelsen called his approach a 'pure theory of law', a discourse of truth about norms.[5] The object of study was defined as the logical hierarchy of norms, presented as a coherent, closed and formal system, a legal grammar guaranteed internally through the logical interconnection of norms and externally through the rigorous rejection of all non-systemic normative matter, such as content, context or history. All correct legal statements in legislation and adjudication follow a process of subsumption of inferior to superior norms. No possibility of conflict between the higher and the lower norm exists. At the basis of the pyramid a presupposed *Grundnorm* sets the system into motion but is an abstract imperative, an empty norm with no substantive value.

Herbert Hart, the most prominent English positivist, constructed his theory in a more pragmatic fashion. Hart calls his *Concept of Law* both an essay in descriptive sociology and an analytical jurisprudence. Distinguished both from coercion and from morality, law should be approached as a coherent and self-referential system of rules. As rules refer to other rules, their systemic interdependence determines the existence, validity and values of any particular rule. Hart shifts the question from 'what is law?' to 'what is a modern legal system?' and finds the answer in the combination of primary rules of obligation, such as those of crime or tort, and secondary rules or rule-governed mechanisms which enable primary rules to be enacted, changed and applied. Behind all, a master rule, the rule of recognition, determines whether a particular rule is legal and whether a legal system exists. But when Hart turns from his virulently systemic order to the actual interpretation and application of the rules, a small crack appears in the edifice. In most cases, legal terms and rules have a paradigmatic core of settled meaning, which makes interpretation non-controversial. Occasionally, however, certain terms have a linguistic or motivated indeterminacy—a 'penumbra of doubt'—as to their meaning. In such instances, the interpreting judge and the rule-applying administrator must exercise a degree of discretion. Discretion re-introduces moral, political or policy-based value-choices. But this was the dreaded supplement, the Trojan horse of moralistic naturalism, that positivism had tried to keep at bay.

The political dimension of the attempt to exclude morality from the legal domain should be sought in the modern experience of relativism and pluralism. The fear of nihilism is also important. In the positivist world-view, law is the

[5] H Kelsen, *The Pure Theory of Law* (Berkeley, University of California Press, 1934).

answer to the irreconcilability of values, the most perfect embodiment of human reason. Its operation should not be contaminated by extrinsic, non-legal considerations, lest it loses its legitimatory ability. These claims can be found throughout the law curriculum. Let us list some. Private law turns social conflict into technical disputes, the resolution of which are entrusted to public experts and technicians of rules and procedures. Public law imposes constitutional limits and normative restrictions upon the organisation and exercise of state power. Rules de-personalise power and structure the exercise of discretion by excluding subjective values—they restrict choice in the application of law by administrators and judges. Indeed, the rule of law is presented as the law of rules, the main achievement of which is to rid the law of ethical considerations. We encounter this attitude in the distrust of administrative discretion and of judicial creativity; in the antipathy towards administrative tribunals, legal pluralism and non-judicial methods of dispute resolution; in the insistence on the declaratory role of statutory interpretation and the 'strictness' of precedent; finally, in the emphasis on the 'literal' rule of interpretation which allegedly allows the exclusion of subjective preferences and ideologies.

But the banning of morality from legal operations did not protect the common law from its many shortcomings. On the contrary, the many miscarriages of justice revealed since the Eighties, law's persistent racism and sexism, its aloofness from social reality and its highly unrepresentative personnel indicated that the proclaimed absence of morality lies at the heart of the problem. At this crucial point, jurisprudence turned its attention to hermeneutics, semiotics and literary theory as an aid to the failing enterprise of positivism. The hermeneutic turn was motivated by the urgent need to correct the descriptively inadequate and morally impoverished theory of law. The new hermeneutical jurisprudence insisted that the law is not just a system of rules—that additionally, it contains a huge depository of values and principles and a rich thesaurus of meanings. We may disagree as to the meaning of any particular statute or precedent, we may even accept that judicial reasoning and justification can legitimately lead in conflicting directions, but as a minimum, the law is about the interpretation of its own texts. Law is written to be applied in the future; interpretation is the life of the law. We must abandon, therefore, the *Grundnorm* and the rule of recognition for the meaning of meaning. We must replace or supplement the technical rules of legal reasoning with the protocols of interpretation or with the study of rhetorical tropes and hermeneutical protocols. We must approach the texts of law through the law of text.[6]

The literary and hermeneutical turn gave legal theory a long-lost sense of excitement. Another consequence was to make morality integral to law's operation again and, in particular, to judicial interpretation. The jurisprudence of meaning responded to a highly topical demand and ethics became part and

[6] C Douzinas, R Warrington, S McVeigh, *Postmodern Jurisrpudence: The Law of Text in the Texts of Law* (London, Routledge, 1991).

justification of the newly discovered interpretative character of the legal enterprise. But there is a catch. To take Ronald Dworkin's popular hermeneutical theory, the operation of law is presented as necessarily embodying and following moral values and principles. The law is no longer just about rules in the manner of Hart and certainly it is not the outcome of the untrammeled will of an omnipotent legislator as John Austin, the nineteenth century founder of legal positivism, had argued. Law's empire includes principles and policies; the application of law involves creative acts of interpretation. Judges are asked to construct the notorious 'right answer' to legal problems by developing political and moral theories that would present the law in its best possible light and create an image of the 'community as integrity'. Legal texts must be read as a single and coherent scheme, animated by the principles of 'justice and fairness and procedural process in the right relation'.[7] A similar position can be found in the work of James Boyd White, the most prominent representative of the law and literature movement. Justice must be approached as translation between the values of a community and their incorporation into legal texts.[8]

Morality and moral philosophy are thus correctly acknowledged as an inescapable element of judicial hermeneutics. But the effect of hermeneutical jurisprudence is to justify and celebrate a practice that has long been divorced from the quest for justice by presenting the law as the perfect narrative of a community at peace with itself. Morality is no longer a set of subjective and relative values, as the positivists claim, nor is it a critical standard against which acts of legal power can be judged. If a right legal answer exists and can be found through the use of moral philosophy, even in hard cases, judges are never left to their own devices and judicial choice can be exorcised. The nightmare of positivism has been turned into the noble dream of the hermeneuticians.[9] Hart had reluctantly accepted the dreaded supplement of judicial discretion at the cost of endangering the rational completeness and coherence of the law. Dworkin's hermeneutics presents judicial interpretation as both formally correct and replete with morality. Against the positivist lack of interest in ethics, the interpretative scholars assert that the law is all morality and that judicial interpretation implies or leads to an ethics of legal reading.

Undoubtedly the law is interpretation and interpretation is the life of law. The law may follow principles and further values. But two caveats must be added. First, the values a legal system promotes represent the dominant ideology of society—they are the canonical expressions of its social and political power. The 'others'—the poor, the underprivileged, the minorities and the refugees—can find little solace in rules and principles that sustain and are sustained by their subjection. And there is more to it: before and after the mean-

[7] R Dworkin, above n 3, 404.

[8] JB White, *Justice as Translation* (Chicago, University of Chicago Press, 1990).

[9] N Lacey, *A Life of HLA Hart: The Nightmare and the Noble Dream* (Oxford, Oxford University Press, 2004).

ing-giving act, law is force.[10] Statutes, judgments and administrative decisions act upon people and impose patterns of behaviour, attitudes and, ultimately, violent sanctions. As Marxists have always known, and as Robert Cover has pithily stated 'legal interpretation takes place in a field of pain and death'.[11] Law's meaning coerces and legal values constrain. This all-important aspect of the legal operation, fully acknowledged by the early positivists, was underplayed by Kelsen and Hart and became extinct in recent hermeneutics. In the enthusiasm for principles, rights and creative interpretation, the law is presented as exclusively textual and ethical. In contrast to the moralism of hermeneutics, classical positivism was more realistic when it insisted that sovereign power, which in its very nature is coercive, remains central to the operations of law.

We are thus faced with a new paradox. Power relations and practices proliferate and penetrate deeply into the social, often taking a loose and variable legal form. Their common characteristics are few: an often extremely tenuous derivation from the legislative power; more importantly, their link with the increasingly empty referent 'law' which bestows upon them its symbolic and legitimatory weight. If, for positivism, the 'law is the law'—in the sense of law's certification according to internal criteria of validity—the underlying idea becomes now fully radicalised. Power relations are law if and when they successfully attach to themselves the predication 'legal' or, law is everything that succeeds in calling itself law. But contemporary jurisprudence ignores these accelerating developments and continues to be preoccupied, like classical political philosophy, with sovereignty and right, representation and delegation, integrity and 'right answers'. It examines almost exclusively the case law of appellate courts, the most formal and centralist expression of the legal system, arguably unrepresentative of the rest of the law. If positivism fails to understand the moral substance of law, apologetical hermeneutics becomes even more unrealistic by neglecting power or reducing and subsuming it under the operations of legal *logos*. *Auctoritas est potestas non veritas* (Authority is power, not truth).

It appears, therefore, that the presentation of law as a unified and coherent body of norms or principles is rooted in the metaphysics of truth rather than the politics and ethics of justice. The truth of justice is justice as truth. From this it follows that law is the form of power and power should be exercised in the form of law. Power is legitimate if it follows law, *nomos*, and if *nomos* follows *logos*, reason. This peculiar combination of the descriptive and prescriptive, of *logos* and *nomos*, lies at the heart of modernist jurisprudence. The task of critical jurisprudence is to deconstruct this *logonomocentrism* in the texts and

[10] J Derrida, 'The Force of Law: The Mystical Foundation of Authority' (1990) 11 *Cardozo Law Review* 911. This essay delivered at a Cardozo Law School conference in 1988 became the foundational text of the ethical turn in critical jurisprudence.

[11] R Cover, 'Violence and the Word' (1986) 95 *Yale Law Journal* 1601.

operations of law. The hermeneutical moral turn in jurisprudence was welcome; but the moral substance of law must be argued and fought for rather than simply assumed. Furthermore, any understanding of justice, the legal facet of morality, must make the link between justice and the force of law.

GENERAL AND RESTRICTED JURISPRUDENCE

Now we can understand why the dominant type of legal thinking may be called restricted jurisprudence. By revolving around the question 'what is law?' jurisprudence becomes an endless interrogation of the essence or substance of law. It assumes that there is a number of markers or characteristics that map and delimit the terrain and define what is proper to law. But once the question has been posed as a 'what is' one, the answer will necessarily give a series of predicates for the word 'law', a definition of its essence, which will then be sought out in all legal phenomena. As a result, a limited number of institutions, practices and actors will be included and considered relevant to jurisprudential inquiry and a large number of questions will go unanswered.

General jurisprudence, on the contrary, returns to the classical concerns of (legal) philosophy and adopts a much wider concept of legality. It examines the legal aspects of social reproduction both within and without state law. In this sense, general jurisprudence is concerned not just with posited law, but also with what can be called the law of the law. Interdictions, commands and norms have played a central role in social life from Moses' Decalogue to Freud's superego. They organise religion and animate the ethics and aesthetics of existence. Laws define the political reason through which societies develop their idea of the common good. All legal aspects of the economic, political, emotional and physical modes of production and reproduction are part of a general jurisprudence.

A general jurisprudence addresses all those issues that classical philosophy examined under the titles of law and justice. Today it includes the political economy of law, those global processes and institutions which regulate flows of capital and people from Nairobi to Neasden, privileging some and turning others into refugees without rights; the transitions from Empire to nation which characterise the postcolonial condition; ideological and imaginary constructions and scenarios through which we understand ourselves and relate to others; ways in which gender, race or sexuality create forms of identity that both discipline bodies and offer sites of resistance; the action of rights which allows people both to acquire and to contest identities. And as legality operates both at the level of social being and social existence, a general jurisprudence examines ways in which subjectivity is created as a site of freedom and of subjection.

One major part of this process takes place in families, by means of the law of the father and the mother. For psychoanalysis, the characteristic mode of operation of the unconscious is the desire-inducing prohibition, and our responses to this law contribute our identity. Indeed, from the position of the individual subject of the law, this prolix legality touches all aspects of existence and leads to the modern versions of the classical *ars vivendi*, the art of living, of which law and ethics was a central part. The art of life addresses the question of how one lives and should live one's definition. It has two moments. The first is the raising of one's life into a problem, into a process that needs to be examined. Life choices, even when they are not fully free, require justification. The second moment addresses the way in which one lives the choices, partly forced and partly free; the necessary compromises that are the stuff of life. It is to those defining structures that we now turn.

THE LAW OF SOCIAL BEING AND SOCIAL EXISTENCE

Towards a Communism of the Heart

Modern jurisprudence has neglected the big philosophical questions and has avoided what we will call the 'ontology of social life'. If the law plays a central role in social reproduction, this omission has seriously affected the integrity of the discipline. According to the ontology proposed in this book, social being is not reproduced through the static repetition of an essence or a series of laws but in a dynamic passing on and constant re-constitution of social relations. Social being is always a becoming—its essence is to unravel itself in historical existence—which is another name for the lived experience of people. In this sense, social being represents the 'whole' of social existence and cannot be broken down into neatly arranged regions or instances of autonomous operation. Many Marxists, for example, compartmentalised this wholeness, by creating an architecture of foundations, bases and superstructures, and privileging some level, mainly the economy, against others. This aspect of the Marxist tradition has been widely condemned and, in our opinion, justly so.[12] It represents a particularly impoverished understanding of the complexity of social being. The problem with much Marxism, but also with other 'scientific' approaches, such as evolutionary biology and law and economics, is that they confuse the disciplinary organisation of inquiry with a solid part of social reality. In so doing, they turn what is just a perspective on the world, albeit a necessary one, into a part of the world. To this extent we would agree with Max Weber. The object of the science of economics or of jurisprudence is projected as the 'reality' of the economy or of law—the creations of the history and imagination of the discipline become a thing that circularly justifies its disciplinary predilections.

[12] See E Laclau and C Mouffe, *Hegemony and Socialist Strategy: Towards a Radical Democratic Politics* (London, Verso, 1985).

All philosophers worth reading are sociologists of the imagination.

The economy, politics or law, are not separate solid parts of social reality but the sites where social being presents itself to us. If today the economy and technology are prevalent modes of social life, in pre-modern times religion and authority constituted the dominant structures of being. In this sense, social being is a matrix of overlapping social practices that appear to us in history as different aspects of the world. These practices are necessarily viewed from different perspectives depending on the observer's position. To argue that reality is ultimately economic—or for that matter political or legal—is to confuse one perspective with the manifold structure of the world. At the same time, no standpoint from nowhere is available: one is always in the world, part of its humming, bustling, confusing streams. Economics, politics or jurisprudence are ways through which humanity strives to understand different facets of social being. We use economic or legal theory to understand the social world, but social being is never just economics, just jurisprudence, or just anything else. Social being exists in all the social practices examined by the disciplines, but always transcends them in the way in which the church that Cezanne drew from a number of different perspectives was something different and something more than any one of the sketches.

Marxism reduced social being to the economy and identified social existence with class belonging while, for liberals, existence is defined as individual and as a matter of free will (we would also disagree with Weber's methodological individualism). Both these reductions are too crude or simplistic and cannot understand gender, race, sexuality, or ethnicity as structures and ways of living. Following the analysis offered above, these are different aspects, predications or characteristics through which we are seen by others, assessed and given a place, and through which we, in turn, live in the world. All these aspects of social existence have their own histories and ways of defining lived experience. They invest bodies with relations of power, but they can also empower. They create modes of evaluation, expressed both in formal terms, and in the informal politics of everyday life. An individual, a subject or legal person, is a point of intersection at which all these aspects of existence knot themselves together into a unique and singular being whose life shares many aspects with others, but is always lived uniquely. One could argue that each individual is a world: a unique set of meanings values and experiences, the outcome of contingent genealogy and unavoidable sociality, the point at which social being and social existence come together and create on a ground of necessity what is unique in its uniqueness and different from all difference.

But we would not assert that this leads to a valorisation of a human 'essence'. Subjectivity is no more than a complex knot or fold. There is no soul or human animus that stands behind the conjunctions of force and structure that create consciousness. The soul is no more than a huge prison that various powers have patiently constructed to imprison the body. Attempt this thought experiment. Strip away your personal history, examine your sense of what it means to be 'you'. Repeat your name to yourself until it becomes just a meaningless sound. This is what it always was, a few letters, a couple of syllables, A-dam, Cos-tas, that have no sense or intrinsic value. And yet this arbitrary phoneme or grapheme is what keeps us together, what gives us solidity in space and continuity in time. Does anything survive this realisation? When you awake suddenly from a deep sleep, in that moment of waking, of coming back to consciousness, are you instantly 'you'—or just some force becoming aware of itself again; a certain reflexivity that, over time, through education, repetition and subjection to the law, becomes identifiable as 'me'? You might be unique, but you're nothing substantial. Get used to it.

We may be men and women, gay or straight, black or white, builders, shopkeepers or idlers, skally or chevy, lawyers, policemen or plumbers; these aspects of our existence inscribe us within categories of generality and structure our life. But these necessary predicates of existence are not closed and non-negotiable. We can appreciate the dynamism of existence if we think of the way in which the term of abuse 'queer' has been appropriated by the gay movement and turned into a proud badge of identity. This re-articulation of the offensive into the positive is an instance of what could be called transvaluation, a process in which a negative value is politically co-opted and radically transformed.

We are left with the need to elucidate the relationship between social being and social existence. This relationship forms the core of the process of reproduction. If social existence is the lived experience of people in the world individually and collectively, then it represents the historical manifestation of social being, the way in which its overlapping practices acquire meaning and force in the lives of people. In this sense, social reproduction is precisely this linking of the historical existence of finite humans with ongoing communal life, the way in which our own existence opens up social being for us and becomes one of its manifestations. Law, in its various facets, is the thread that knots together individual existence and social being. As the French legal historian and psychoanalyst Pierre Legendre has put it, the law 'institutes life',[13] it forms the bond which binds the biological, social, and unconscious elements of the human person. The legal institution performs for society the role that the law of the father plays for the subject.

Freud's paternal prohibitions on incest and patricide turn the infant into an independent person; similarly, a social interdiction supports social being. Social reproduction is predominantly a strategy of mediation with the absolute Other that is not given to consciousness or reason: inescapable death, unconscious trauma, absent justice.

The need to accept the finitude of existence and one's mortality calls for a guarantor, a 'sacred' inaccessible place that stages the origin or cause of the

[13] P Legendre, 'The Other Dimension of Law' (1995) 16 *Cardozo Law Review* 943.

subject and explains the limited span of life through a story of origins or destination. In pre-modern societies, this role was played by totems, religions or mythical references to the natural foundations of law. Religion was the first institutional response to the need to link humanity with absolute otherness. The worship of God, the divine statuary of the classics, the incarnation of Christ and the *imagoes dei* of Christianity are all ways of reconciling finite life with death and with the demand that society lives on, survives the pathetic sojourn of any single one of us on earth.

Religion, and later law, staged the totem or the interdiction around the father, more specifically around the image of the father, and its legal expressions: God or Pope, Emperor, Czar or King, nation, state or legislator. In the western tradition, Roman law was the earliest manifestation of the transfer of this function from religion to law. Roman law laid down a way of supporting the functions necessary for the institution of human life and the reproduction of society. It has shown itself to be flexible, adapting to various historical contexts—from its formal use in the development of the common law tradition to the more concrete way in which it provided the axioms for the law of the Holy See. The common law, which has always developed in relation to civil law and has absorbed the ecclesiastical jurisdiction, continues this operation. Admittedly, other discourses, such as technology or managerialism, claim today to offer the main support for social being. But the fundamental need to stage absolute otherness and familiarise humanity with its finitude cannot be performed exclusively by secular discourses of efficiency. The law may no longer play fully the role of its Roman origins. But even today the existence of individuals and societies would remain precarious without mediation with the absolute and frightening Other. The nation-state, irrespective of its constitutional form, has become such a sacred place and, while challenged from various directions, it remains a main guarantor of social reproduction. Democracy and human rights are becoming candidates for the role in late modernity.

Psychoanalytical theory makes certain assumptions about the conditions necessary for bringing body and soul together and linking them to society. But this does not mean that social existence can be totalised and subsumed into social being. Being is not a totality. And yet most modern philosophy and jurisprudence explicitly or implicitly totalises being and turns subjects becoming into essence. The idea of being as totality is associated with the German philosopher Hegel and his progeny. In this tradition, being is animated by a spirit or some other principle, which guarantees the coherence of all in one. This approach has both structural and historical versions. In the former, every aspect of the world replicates the principle found in the privileged domain, such as the economy or political organisation. In the latter, the same principle structures the movement of history towards its final completion and realisation. Following this approach, Hegel claimed that the inherent rationalism of human organisation was destined to produce the modern state and, Fukuyama, in Hegel's wake, suggested that it would lead to the end of history and transformative social conflict in the final victory of capitalism and the western way of life. The proliferating complexities and conflicts of postmodern societies, and the ever-present spectre of war in the twenty-first century, make these theories ring as hollowly as the old shell casings littering the deserts of the Middle East.

Marx followed Hegel's dialectical method and its totalising tendency. Marxism posited being as common in a material sense: a real historical force replaced Hegel's idealistic odyssey of the spirit. Now a social class, a political party, or the leader, became the summation that brings together social being and existence. In this sense, one aspect of existence was turned into the determinant—the causal motor which animated and moved the whole.

The liberal tradition has not had the same propensity to think in terms of totality. Indeed, the idea that the life-world is the foundation of social thinking works against master narratives that interpret the world from a single perspective. It might even be argued that the professionalisation of the law was necessary precisely because the social is no longer an organic community rooted in custom and shared values. The same openness appears in the more explicitly political accounts of the law, where practical reason effectively negotiates between the claims made by the state and the individual's prerogative to determine freely her life. To resist any reduction of diversity reason maintains its vigil. However, despite this resistance to totality, community is ultimately presented as a ground that resolves difference, to the extent that value consensus is posited as the constitutive feature of the social. In the philosophy of Hart and his positivist followers, for instance, social being can be united, its differences absorbed into a greater whole. It may be that the nation does not form an explicit theme in this work, but it is, as we will later argue, the ever present supposition.

The Dworkinian turn to principles and rights has been seen as an abandonment of the positivistic approach in jurisprudence and a turn towards a greater appreciation of morality, ethics and meaning; an appreciation of the openness of the social. But, Dworkin's claim that there is always a right answer to even the hardest of legal cases can only be substantiated through an appeal to a rigorous grammar underlying the legal system and by allowing the formation of correct legal sentences. To this extent, while the legal system appears moral and principled on the surface, it can deliver its answers and solutions only if the social world is unified according to the dictates of a strict code. If we turn to the more hermeneutical humanism of James White and much of law and literature, responsiveness to the other becomes the mark of a new humanism in law. Yet, the ongoing conversation between past and present, which animates the legal tradition, is made possible through faith in the destiny of America, exemplified in the constitution as the embodiment of the spirit of the nation. The Hegelian totalisation of spirit and the Marxist totalisation of class have been replaced by different totalities: community, principle, and text.

Why has thought always tried to explain being as a totality? One reason perhaps is the desire of philosophy to turn being into an object that can be known, being into something, a thing or object, clearly defined, demarcated and frozen as the structure of the knowable. But, this ignores what we take to be the most irrefutable aspect of the world: it passes away. Being is always becoming. It emerges in time, and history is its mode of existence. The drive of disciplines, like law and economics, is to posit a knowable object and then to move towards a totality in which that object is located. But time and history need to be written back into picture. If we return to the example of the Cezanne drawings, the artist's drawings are aspects of the same church, but the church of being is always in the process of being built and falling into ruins, again and again, ad infinitum.

In our view, if being is the matrix of the various overlapping practices through which it presents itself to us, being can only exist in so far as it is being-in-common. To put this somewhat differently: I acquire language because an other has spoken to me; I develop my own values and create meanings because others have acted in principled ways towards me and treated me as a source of meaning. The other is always part of the intimacy of self. Before self comes to being, another has existed and created a repertory of meanings, which I inhabit and enrich. I am only to the extent that others are. To exist is to ex-ist, to move beyond of myself, in ceaseless motion. This is why each of us is a world; every person is a world, because we are the singular embodiment of meanings and values, a knotting of different aspects of existence, always in motion and always becoming. But this is a world that comes into being always and necessarily in relation to others, my world is always an inter-world: my world is created by others and I am in the world of others. Our essence is our becoming in the infinity of encounters with others, encounters that compel us to keep re-interpreting what the world is for us and who we are in the world. In this sense, identity is constituted in social existence as a set of infinite, non-totalisable encounters with others who themselves are different worlds. We could call this a communism of the heart. As communism, it describes our being in common; a being that is embodied and pledged to the love of the other. As a communism *of the heart,* it indicates that our experience of being is, at least in the first instance, emotional rather than intellectual. As in Whitman's poem,[14] our experience of the others in the world always moves between the unique other and the crowd; the anonymous others among whom a face suddenly appears; a glance of recognition. This is neither a romantic solipsism, nor a fear of the faceless mass; merely an acknowledgement that the unique and the general are bound up together like the most intimate of lovers.

If we turn now to state law or institutional legality, general jurisprudence opens a new examination of institutional legality, or, rather returns to the classical tradition in renewed form. Restricted jurisprudence based its empire on the strict demarcation of an inside and an outside, of a clear distinction between a

[14] W Whitman, 'Once I Passed through a Populous City', *The Complete Poems* (Harmondsworth, Penguin, 1986) 144.

pure law and its contexts, social, economic, political etc. However, to the extent that it defines itself through the exclusion of all matter that does not belong to state law, jurisprudence addresses a restricted part of legality's role in social being. General jurisprudence, on the other hand, locates the legal institution with its practices and procedures, its rules norms and rights, in what can be called a legal interzone. The interzone is neither internal nor external to law; it is neither committed to conceptual and normative coherence or systemic closure, nor does it follow and apply the rules and theories of sociological method. It accepts the importance that the context has in understanding the law, but places context within the legal text and reads legal texts and legal history as aspects of social being in which other expressions of sociality, like politics, economics or ethics, will be reflected. In this sense, the interzone exists between law and society as a passage or boundary that both demarcates the two fields and allows movement and communication between them. And while general jurisprudence challenges the separation between normative and contextual approaches, it accepts that fields have their own imaginary integrity, built through the efforts of theorists to construct a 'pure' legal or social field.

More specifically, general jurisprudence carefully reads legal texts and legal history and treats them as a privileged terrain of study. But unlike internal theories, it reads these texts not just for their normative coherence but also for their omissions, repressions and distortions, for signs of the oppressive power and symptoms of the traumas created by the institution. If there is patriarchy or economic exploitation, it will be traced in the text—in its rhetoric and images, in its certainties and omissions—which will then be followed outside the text in the lives of people and in the history of domination. Adopting neither a doctrinal nor a sociological approach, general jurisprudence introduces external and contextual perspectives to the study of law, but these become relevant only if they can find evidence in the texts of law and help us develop our own specific theoretical instruments. Neither just in the text nor only outside it 'in the world', general jurisprudence explores the textual and institutional organisation of the law as a system of signs, as an inescapable pillar of the symbolic order and as a crucial script in the imaginary constitution of self and society. The law is both necessary and fictitious. But law's fictions operate and change the world—they help establish the subject as free and/because subjected to the logic of the institution.

Our field of inquiry is thus occupied by structures and institutions that fill the space of the social and its becoming and by the individuals whose lives animate the structures. We can trace a line that runs from Moses' code, to Plato's republic, to Hegel's and Marx's philosophy of right and Weber's economy and society, to Freud's discontents of civilisation where explorations of legality address all these aspects and treat the legal institution as just one moment of the wider operation of law. This philosophical tradition was lost at the very moment that the claim to the autonomy of the legal system became dominant. At that moment, what was central to the inquiry into legality was dispersed to other disciplines and jurisprudence became an apologetics for the professional practice of law. In opening a general jurisprudence we try to re-connect with the classical philosophy of law, and to remind ourselves that a law without a spirit is like a body without a soul: At best a corpse, at worst a zombie.

GENERAL JURISPRUDENCE—ITS HISTORY AND THEMES

The Promise of Reason

We now turn to examine some of the key strategies that have influenced the writing of this book. Six themes run through this work in various combinations and permutations. Sometimes they appear explicitly, at other times they run just below the surface argument: reason, violence and struggle, justice, emotions, foundations, critique. We will discuss these themes below, but let us first attempt an almost impossible statement of the book's overall trajectory.

The use of reasoned argument, justification and disputation lies at the heart of all attempts to order community and society; all attempts to turn legality into legitimacy and power into authority. But reason has always been followed by disputation and conflict. Societies, as much as families, are animated by passionate antagonism, even violence, as they struggle towards rational agreement and peaceful co-existence. Jurisprudence has neglected the dialectic between reason and the emotions—or between consensus and conflict—and has privileged the reasoned and pacified aspect of social being and existence over the violence of domination. Justice, the absent value of the social, always leads to arguments for change, reform and revolution, and thus exemplifies the inherent conflict that permeates social being. The obsession of jurisprudence with grounds and reasons has led to the claim that reason is the ground of law. But reason and its claims have always been undercut by heretics, relativists, nihilists; similarly, the law has always been accompanied by its critics. The law supports the established order but every order and establishment generates the aspiration for better, more just arrangements and initiates the critical moment. General jurisprudence belongs in this interzone between law and critique, authority and violence, reason and passion, freedom and subjection.

The myth of Prometheus (at its best in Shelley's interpretation) is an imaginative exploration of what it is to become human. Humanity is born in a revolt against the gods. Prometheus steals fire from the gods and gives it to the humans. For this rebellion against the gods—and in particular Zeus, their father and king—Prometheus is punished in all eternity. Yet it is this supreme act of defiance that creates humanity. The world initiated by Prometheus is not so much dependent on the divine as in opposition to and revolt from the divine. Prometheus divides himself from his divine origin when he curses Zeus. As humankind is effectively created in the image of Prometheus, this statement of revolt against the father of the gods suggests that men and women may be capable of a similar defiance. The myth of Prometheus is an expression of humanity's tendency to ask the question of its own being. To overthrow the reign of Zeus is to become aware that the power of the gods is predicated upon differentiation—the distinction between the divine and the human. Zeus is powerful because he is 'on high'; he personifies the potentiality of human imagination. Revolt reinterprets divine absence and haughtiness as a space of immanence, a source of human possibility. Human possibility is imagined and lived in a space opened between the limit-experiences of love and death; experiences that cannot be put into words or reduced to rational discourse. After the fall of the gods, the differences and absences that exist in social life structure our dwelling in the world. The Prometheus myth brings together struggle and reason, the two forces that have defined history.

This opening of the world in rebellion was confirmed by classical philosophy and law. They were born together in acts of resistance against the authority of the ancestral tradition. Philosophy begins when it distinguishes between the truths about a topic given by law, convention or the received opinion (*doxa*) and the truth or the good arrived at through the dialogical critique of received wisdom and the observation of the nature of a thing or entity. For the classical philosophers, nature was not just the physical world, the 'way things are' or everything that exists. Nature was a term of distinction, a norm or standard used to separate the work of philosophical and political thought from what obstructs or hides it. Nature was philosophy's weapon, the unsettling and revolutionary Promethean fire used in its revolt against authority and the law. Its 'discovery' and elevation into an axiological standard against convention emancipated reason from the tutelage of power and gave rise to natural right.

The possibility of judging the real in the name of the ideal can only start when what is right by nature confronts what is considered rightful by custom or past practice. The concept of right, freed from its subjection to history or common opinion, becomes an independent tool for critique. This autonomisation of right was the necessary precondition for the development of a theory of justice and can ultimately be used as a contemporary principle of critique. Nature was used against culture to create the most cultured of concepts. But if nature was a tactical move motivated by the need to combat the claims of authority that ruled early Greek society, its 'discovery' was not so much a revelation or unveiling as an invention or creation. Nature was seen in the classical teleological world as a dynamic concept, never finished or perfected, always on the move. Similarly, natural right—the outcome of the observation of nature and of the dialectical confrontation of opinions—was also provisional and changeable according to new contingencies. Nature must present itself as what was occluded by culture because philosophy could not come into existence or survive if it submitted to ancestral or conventional authority. In this sense, the origins of philosophy and the discovery of nature were revolutionary gestures, directed against the claims to authority of the past and of law-as-custom and giving rise to critique in the name of justice.

If we turn to Greek political philosophy, it is only in the 'best polity or regime' that human perfection and virtue in association with others can be achieved. For

Plato, the Republic must be constructed by the philosopher who, in so doing, clarifies and promotes the requirements of human excellence according to nature but also pays attention to the exigencies and contingencies of the historical situation. The 'best polity' can be developed only in the *polis*, within a political community and through the use of public reason. No polity can survive or acquire legitimacy if it does not acknowledge the importance and take account of the 'unenlightened' opinions of its citizens. The philosopher's Republic is a utopia, it does not exist in the present, and its realisation in the future cannot be guaranteed. Its success depends on the uncertain and always fragile acceptance of the philosopher's reason by his fellow citizens in full and open debate; but also on a large measure of chance.[15] Classical political philosophy asserts that the fundaments of right, of individual virtue and social organisation, transcend the present political order but are accessible to human reason. In this sense, political reason offers an alternative to historical existence and to conventional and authoritative opinion. It refers to a perfect moral order, to an ideal which, because it is critical of what exists, adopts nature for its prescriptions and claims a natural objectivity for its right. But this ideal is not given by God, revelation or even an immutable natural order. It is a construction of thought and its application is deeply political.

These ideas and political gestures became dormant in the medieval transition of natural law, which turned from an active process of political reasoning to a god-given set of commands. By contrast, early modernity defined itself through a return to the classical tradition in which political reason can again be put into the service of resistance against received wisdom and the dominant relations of power of the old order. The Reformation could be described as the re-awakening of political reason in the garb of theology. When Luther nailed his statement of faith to the doors of the cathedral, he inaugurated a period in which the ossified ecclesiastical and political writ of the Holy Roman Church would be increasingly contested. Protestantism links back to the classical tradition by declaring the power of citizens to come together following the dictates of their conscience. Radical Protestantism motivated the English revolution and the Republican tradition of the American Revolution, even when monarchic order, albeit in a more limited form, had returned to England. The Americans, inspired in part by Paine's rewriting of the classical natural law tradition in terms of the rights of man, rebelled against monarchy and the colonial order. The Declaration of the Rights of Man in France, on the other hand, proclaimed the political reason of common humanity against the class and statist order of the *ancien regime*. Similarly, the Bolshevik revolution of 1917 in Russia drew its inspiration from a reworked notion of what it could mean to be a citizen in a just polity. Every major revolution represents a reinvigoration of the power of political reason to radically change the world according to the advice of philosophers and seers.

[15] L Strauss, *Natural Law and History* (Chicago, University of Chicago Press, 1965) 139.

A theme that runs through this history is that of the tragedy of the successful revolution. The need to preserve the new order against its enemies has repeatedly led to the abandonment of the principle of political reason as deliberation and open argument, and the identification of political action with the interests and concerns of one section of society. This process can lead to sedimentations of power and authority similar to those against which the revolution set its face and fist. Indeed, the more recent expressions of the spirit of political reason have been directed against those forms of power that abandoned the revolutionary principle from which they emerged. The liberation struggle in the colonised world, the great social movements in the west, feminism, anti-racism, and the gay movement share in different ways the demand that democracies based on public deliberation and reason honour their promise of equality and liberty. Similarly, the popular uprisings in eastern Europe, in Berlin, Bucharest, Prague and Belgrade, expressed the revolt of those who were told that the communist regimes represented the most rational organisation of political society—only to discover that reason had been subordinated to the logic of the party apparatus and that humanity had been restricted to the few privileged members of the state bureaucracy. Despite their differences, these instances of rebellion and resistance, represent the historical appearance of the same principle that animated classical political philosophy: the belief in the power of reason and deliberation to criticise the existent, imagine the good city or the best polity and act in its name. In this sense, we could argue that revolution is an event of truth and the truth of the event. It forms the essence or meaning of the idea of the event, as it unexpectedly changes the root of history through the close articulation of reason and force. But revolution is also the essence of truth: that which reveals what had been hitherto hidden and that which projects a new way for the future. *Nihil sine ratione* (nothing without reason) was the early modern manifesto. No truth without reason and force would be its late modern emendation.

Force, Power, Law: An Eristics of the Social

While the tradition of public reasoning accepts explicitly or implicitly that the common good exists and can be approached through public reason, deliberation and practice, a different tradition, which can also be traced back to pre-classical times, emphasises struggle as the condition of social being. Classical political reason and natural right set themselves up in conflict with the ancestral—the pre-existing principle of social organisation. Indeed every new form, philosophical, social or political, emerges out of a struggle with the old; a struggle that either destroys the old in a revolutionary affirmation of the new, or adopts and retains its main characteristics, elevating them to a higher stage. The tradition of political reason from which the Platonic dialogues and contemporary dialectics derive, emphasise the exchange of views—dialogue, contradiction and agreement—the discursive organisation of political life. But as Nietzsche insisted, dialectics was not just about a peaceful and civil exchange of views; it also involved angry disagreements, quarrels and even fights. There is an inescapable tendency for verbal disputation to end in brawling—as any Saturday night spent in a bar would suggest to the keen observer.

But our point is far broader. If we return to the notion of social existence that we sketched above, we can remind ourselves that its main characteristic is the encounter with the other. Social existence is the sense we have of ourselves as worlds of meaning and experience, worlds always in flux as they come into contact with the worlds represented by others, in an infinite number of encounters. Encountering others or strangers can lead both to peaceful exchange and to violent contestation. The nature of the social as encounters amongst strangers makes these two opposed positions the very condition of the possibility of experience itself. Violence, as much as debate and agreement, is a possible condition of experience and therefore a necessary eventuality of existence. Indeed, the West has always fought its wars under the promise of future pacification—of a better world that will dawn upon its defeated enemies once they have accepted the wrong of their ways and the superiority of the culture of their victors. The just and god-approved cause of the campaigns of Crusaders and Conquistadores, the civilising mission of imperialists and colonialists and our recent and ongoing humanitarian wars indicate that war has been glossed consistently in the language of justice and the rhetoric of morality and remains an integral part of western life.

As an account of human nature, pacifism describes only one pole of experience. This account has dominated rationalist and liberal philosophy but has always been shadowed by its opposite, an account for which humanity is riven by aggression and conflict, for which its history is a succession of different types of domination. The trope of the state of nature that precedes the entry into society and polity is a good example of this duality. Philosophers such as Kant, Rousseau, Locke and Rawls posit a peaceful human nature that has to be protected in perpetuity through the instrument of a social compact and the institutions derived from it. Hobbes, on the other hand, sees human nature involved in continuous combat—fearful and in need of protection and security—and derives his conception of the compact from those axioms. The common feature of these different stories is to establish a strict division between struggle and peace, violence and fraternity. But these accounts, sensitive as they are to an agonistic part of social being and human identity, in their commitment to construct a peaceful polity through a rational constitution, soon lose or obscure their insight. Social experience is the radical possibility of both love and hate; the two poles are united in the ground that allows them to appear at all. Indeed, the social bond is kept together not just by gestures of love, empathy and legal propriety; struggle, strikes and war are also ways through which social being expresses itself. Societies both understand their bearings through violence and use violence to raise themselves to new heights. This tension can be traced at all levels. Whether or not the diverse worlds of social existence are to be enclosed by violence into a community, a nation or federation, or allowed to develop their own articulations of community through peaceful means, depends on the contingencies of history.

What we have just traced as an historical process also finds its expression in philosophy. One approach associated with Nietzsche would hold that all phenomena are signs and interpretations. Every thing and process is the site of a struggle. The history of a phenomenon is the succession of forces that have possessed it; its meaning is posited by those struggling for its current possession. Every thing, accordingly, has many antagonistic senses that depend on the perspective of the forces that try to dominate it. Nietzsche reminded us that force and violence, the needs and desires of concrete people and groups, as well as unspoken events and coincidences, lie behind the eternal principles and high values of morality and religion. By abandoning the Kantian insistence on eternal, *a priori* conditions of understanding and universally valid norms, Nietzsche developed a new type of history called genealogy, which examines not the ethereal sources and linear paths but the contingent conditions and circumstances out of which values grow.

For Michel Foucault, Nietzsche's successor, power forms the unthought dark side of metaphysics and becomes the prime mover of social, legal and institutional developments. Knowledge, truth and the law are effects and causes of power and of the will to power. The operations of power and of the philosophical system have excluded and silenced the different and the other, and have subjected the singular to the universal and the event to the laws of necessity. The task of genealogy is to recognise their central historical importance. For Foucault, modern man is the product of a contingent and unstable combination of a multiplicity of forces and knowledges, discourses and practices. He is born in a welter of regulations, of meticulous rules and sub-rules, of detailed and fussy inspections and supervisions of the most minute fragments of life and the body that are modelled on the discipline and surveillance of 'total' institutions, like prisons and hospitals. Modern man's birth is accompanied by a new type of normalising judgment, with its own laws, offences and punishments. Discipline thrives on normalisation. The norm, keeping to the norm, being normal, becomes the form of law and morality. Increasingly, more areas of life—too trivial or too local for the law in the pre-modern period—become the object of a petty but all too important intervention. Genealogy draws the map of modernity and us, its subjects, as knowing, willing, desiring and as subjected to the operations of power.

A different approach to that of Foucault is psychoanalysis. This is the cast of thought that has posited the centrality of desire to all social phenomena. In some of its versions, desire is aroused by lack and need. Law is its stimulus: it both bars desire and calls us to pleasure through obedience. In other versions, desire is not based on lack or the need to acquire or dominate. Desire is a force of production; it results from its own differentials, its own tensions and contestations. One example of this would be the psychoanalytical approach to subjectivity.

Psychoanalysis does not imagine a pre-existing human subject 'filled' by the conscious and the unconscious. In one of its typologies, subjectivity is a product of the constant war or opposition of the constituent elements of id, ego and superego. Freud himself became obsessed with positing the relative dominance of these phases. While we do not need to become distracted by technical discussions here, the very model presupposes that subjectivity is a product of contesting forces. If we extrapolate from this a theory of society in the wider sense, we must postulate civilised order as the outcome of submission to certain energies. However, these energies cannot be entirely restrained. The social repressed, like the individual trauma, returns in symptoms, the violence that, as argued above, is the inescapable feature of human society. This is why psychoanalysis has always offered itself as an ally to legal philosophy (although its offer to lend its services has not always been accepted). Freud's vision of the treacherous forces that compose the human has always had a place for law as the force of necessary restraint; the narrow line that separates the human from the animal.

For Foucauldians, this is precisely the problem with psychoanalysis. It is simply another disciplinary technique; another way of damning and controlling the errant forces that striate social being. Whatever the differences between the epigones of Anaxagoras and Nietzsche, they all share an emphasis on struggle and force: they are all thinkers of strife—of what could be called a social eristics.

Justice: The Excess of Reason and Force

The contest between reason and force, which has conditioned the history of western law, opens the thinking of justice. The political reason of the classics was associated with a strong sense of ethics, but reason on its own cannot negotiate the domination that results from the conflict of forces and the victory of the powerful. Indeed, reason has all too often been recruited by the powerful and turned into victors' justice. The sense that justice has miscarried is particularly strong in our time. Justice has been aborted in miscarriages of justice and denials of access to justice, in racial and gender discrimination, in institutional violence and legal dogmatism, and recently in the legal monstrosities of the war against terror. There is much to be done to improve the legal and criminal justice systems and the funding for legal services. It may be that, as far as the common law is concerned, the Human Rights Act is opening up a new era, but this is accompanied by the steady erosion of traditional civil liberties, from the right to jury trial and the presumption of innocence to political asylum and privacy.[16] But for the legal scholar the question is somewhat different. How is it that we came to the point where the legal system appears to be almost divorced from considerations of morality? What is the meaning of justice in our postmodern

[16] H Kennedy, *Just Law* (London, Chatto and Windus, 2004).

world of cognitive and moral uncertainties? Michel Foucault has called the great 18th century civil lawyers, who stood against the autocratic state 'universal intellectuals': 'The man of justice, the man of law, he who opposes to power, despotism, the abuses and arrogance of wealth, the universality of justice and the equity of an ideal law.'[17] Today we have lost our belief in the universality of law or in the ability of an ideal equity to ground its operations. Does that mean that we must abandon morality, and be unable to oppose 'power, despotism, the abuses and arrogance of wealth'? Can we develop contemporary critical and reconstructive yardsticks for our legal system, after the end of the grand narratives of modernity and its attempts to ground the social bond on a principle of universal application?

The Judaic and Greek idea of justice has an ethical and political character which links justice with the idea of the good. Justice, the prime political virtue, is intimately linked with individual moral perfection. In the ancient definition of morality, every animate and inanimate being has a *telos* or aim to become the best specimen of its type. The *telos* of the acorn is to become a mature tree offering a huge shade, that of the soldier is to be the most courageous of all and that of the cobbler is to create perfect sandals. Virtuous action helps them move from what they are to what they ought to be according to their nature and to occupy their proper place in the wider order of *cosmos*. But this can only happen within the political community, and the law, *nomos*, should acknowledge and promote the normative aspects of this purposive order. A just city is the precondition of individual perfection and happiness; conversely, virtuous citizens make the city just.

The Platonic dialogues stand at the beginning of western philosophy. Yet the power of reason in morals and justice appears severely restricted. Behind the meandering dialogues on justice lies Socrates' ultimate argument: his sacrifice on the altar of a justice that cannot be defined or conclusively proven. Socrates represents not so much the triumph of reason, but the first clear formulation of the paradox or *aporia of justice*: to be just is to *act justly,* to be committed to a frame of mind and follow a course of action that must be accepted before any final rational justification.[18] Political philosophy can be described as the history of the intellectual efforts to define justice. These attempts have partially failed, but the sense of injustice has persisted and keeps building and reforming legal and moral systems. Justice is not fully of this world. It is caught in an unceasing movement between knowledge and passion, reason and action, this world and the next, rationalism and metaphysics.[19]

[17] M Foucault, *Power, Truth, Strategy* (Sydney, Feral Publications, 1979) 43.

[18] A Heller, *Beyond Justice* (Oxford, Blackwell, 1987) 54.

[19] The *aporia* or paradox of reason and justice is even stronger in the Jewish tradition. To be just, the Jew must obey the law, without any reason or justification. For Buber, Jews act in order to understand, while Levinas denounces what he calls the western 'temptation of temptation', the—'Greek'—demand to subordinate every act to knowledge and to overcome the 'purity' and 'innocence' of the act. See E Levinas, *Nine Talmudic Readings* (Bloomington, Indiana University Press, 1990) 30–50.

This internal relationship between the ethical and legal elements of justice has been severed in modernity. As Alasdair MacIntyre argued, ours is the era of a profound 'moral catastrophe', of a radical breakdown in ethical agreement and of the systematic annihilation of communities of value and virtue.[20] Modern theories of justice belong to the deontological school of ethics associated with Kant's attempt to reconcile freedom, rationality and morality by concentrating on the form of law and duty. Ethics is identified with universal rules or principles, which are either grounded in reason or, in the writings of contemporary neo-Kantians, are reached through an understanding of the universal preconditions of argumentation and discourse. For Kant, the ancients believed in the concept of the good and derived the law from it. As a result the fundamental moral principle was found outside the self in social demands and expectations.[21] Kant reverses the procedure; it is not the concept of the good that posits the law but the moral law that defines good and evil. Morality meets certain universal preconditions found in the free and rational action of the subject who follows the law of the categorical imperative out of a pure sense of duty and respect: 'Act in such a way that the maxim of your will can always be valid as the principle establishing universal law'.[22] Kant's great discovery was that in modernity morality equals subjection to the law. But subjection to the law and conformity with duty do not give pleasure, but pain—an insight developed by psychoanalysis.[23] Justice no longer communes with the aspirations of the soul; it works through the suffering that reason imposes on desire.

The second characteristically modern attempt to ground morality derives ethical commands and norms from grand theories about the just society, most notably in dogmatic Marxism and utilitarianism. Theory of all types is a form of representation of reality, a description that claims to correspond to its referent, the 'real' world. Knowledge and its object are declared to be equivalent. But theory can never fully occupy the space of ethics. Descriptive and theoretical statements place their speaker and their addressee in a position of equivalence because the referent of the sentence is 'reality'. Moral action, on the other hand, is a response to an ethical stimulus that originates in another person and addresses the self. The ethical response is always still to come, and it places the other who asks and the self who responds in a position of radical dissymmetry. No theory of the good society or account of justice can furnish the final word on ethical action. Theories are descriptions of determinate states of affairs, while

[20] A MacIntyre, *After Virtue* (London, Duckworth, 1981) 1–5.

[21] 'The ancients openly revealed this error by devoting their ethical investigation entirely to the definition of the concept of the highest good and thus posited an object which they intended subsequently to make the determining ground of the will in the moral law', I Kant, *Critique of Practical Reason* (London, Macmillan, 1956) 66–7.

[22] *Ibid*, 30.

[23] J Lacan, *The Ethics of Psychoanalysis* (London, Routledge, 1992); C Douzinas, 'Law's Birth and Antigone's Death: On Ontological and Psychoanalytical Ethics' (1995) 16 *Cardozo Law Review* 1325.

the ethical response is indeterminate, something to be done rather than something said.[24]

As a result of this loss of faith in substantive justice, morality as much as politics must be kept away from law; indeed the main requirement of the rule of law is that all subjective and relative values should be excluded from the operation of the legal system. In formal terms, justice is identified with the administration of justice and the requirements and guarantees of legal procedure. In substantive terms, justice loses its critical character and acts, not as critique, but as critical apology for the extant legal system. As a 'disillusioned radical' barrister put it 'as a lawyer you don't have moral choice because the law makes the moral choices for you. I have no morality.'[25] And a former Chairman of the Bar went further: 'It's easy for the lawyer: there are rules. There are lighthouses all along the route for me and I haven't got to make moral judgements as I go. I am not a social worker. The rules fix my morality for me.'[26] The radical gap in the normative universe created by the strict separation between legality and morality and by the reduction of ethics to the private and subjective is filled by the law as the lighthouse on the way to universal and objective truth. This insulation of law from ethico-political considerations allegedly makes the exercise of power impersonal and guarantees the equal subjection of citizens and state officials to the dispassionate requirements of the rule of rules as opposed to the rule of men. Justice, therefore, loses its ethical character and becomes a device for the legitimation and celebration of the law. As no generally acceptable criteria of justice exist, justice becomes restricted to the more manageable domain of legal procedures.

In postmodernity, justice must be grounded in the ethical turn to the other; justice 'is impossible without the one that renders it finding himself in proximity . . . The judge is not outside the conflict, but the law is in the midst of proximity'.[27] The judge and law teachers are always involved and implicated, called upon by the other to respond to the ethical relationship by the other. We must compare and calculate, but we remain responsible and must always return to the surplus of duties over rights. Injustice would be to forget that the law rises on the ground of responsibility for the other and that ethical proximity and asymmetry overflow the equality of rights. The law can never have the last word. Legal relations are just only if they recognise 'the impossibility of passing by he who is proximate'.[28] We cannot define justice in advance, because that would turn the injunction of ethics into an abstract theory. Justice is not about

[24] See J-F Lyotard, *The Differend: Phrases in Dispute* (Manchester, Manchester University Press, 1988); for an application of these ideas to law see C Douzinas and R Warrington, 'A Well-Founded Fear of Justice' (1991) 2 *Law and Critique* 1.

[25] 'Clean Hands Murky Deals', *The Guardian*, 6 February 1991, 21.

[26] *Ibid.*

[27] E Levinas, *Otherwise than Being or Beyond Essence*, A Lingis (trans), (London, Kluwer, 1991) 159.

[28] *Ibid.*

theories and truth; it does not derive from a true representation of just society. If the law calculates, if it thematises people by turning them into legal subjects, ethics is a matter of an indeterminate judgement without criteria and justice is the bringing together of the limited calculability and determinacy of law with the infinite openness of ethical alterity.

If questions of justice and ethics are to be taken seriously, an understanding of the case law system, as a system of principles that are sensitive to the needs of the individual and the totalities of circumstances in the particular case, has to be brought to the forefront of legal reasoning. We need to develop a secular form of casuistic reasoning for use in the law. The common law has the resources for turning into a form of decision-making that is fully cognisant of the needs of the other, as well as the requirements of principle. There is all the more reason, therefore, to draw out the possibilities implicit in the common law for arguing and acting otherwise. This combination of an ethics of alterity that posits an external entity, whose needs must be respected, with the prudential and concrete casuistic decision-making is the starting and finishing point for the re-ethicalisation of law.

The Sense of Injustice

We are surrounded by injustice, but we do not know where justice lies. This typical statement captures a commonly felt bewilderment. The great paradox of justice is that while the principle has been clouded in controversy, uncertainty and disputation, injustice has always been felt with great certainty and conviction and creates a sense of urgency. We know injustice when we come across it and we immediately feel moved to denounce and attack it with all the powers of our reason and imagination and, occasionally, with action. But when we discuss the qualities of justice, both certainty and emotion recede. What appears most obvious and striking in its absence, becomes unclear and controversial in its positive statement. What engages most emotion and commitment when missing, is reduced to an emotionless and bloodless speculation when present. Justice and its opposite are not symmetrical. Justice exists and moves people in its breach, its absence makes people concerned with its requirements. Injustice is an affair of the heart and of action; justice is a state of affairs belonging to philosophical speculation. Injustice acts on the emotions and leads to action; justice is often just an academic exercise or a piece of rhetoric that fails to convince or enthuse.

Consider for a moment the recent and dominant reduction of justice to fairness. Rawls' theory may have some usefulness in explaining some of the underlying assumptions of western social democracy. But one cannot imagine the banners of revolutionaries bearing drawings of the veil of ignorance, nor the tracts of protesters and reformers carrying popularly translated versions of the two principles of justice as fairness in their lexical order. Justice as fairness may or may not be a fair approximation of western political systems (recently, neo-liberal orthodoxy has been fast moving away from it) but fairness can scarcely become the platform for social change, and unfairness provokes only an emaciated version of the fury and indignation that injustice provokes.

How can we understand injustice? Most philosophers approach injustice, if at all, as the absence of justice in the same way that evil has been seen as the lack or deprivation of the good since Plato. Injustice is a fall from the state of justice, a limitation, privation or imperfection, *privatio justitiae* or *steresis dikes*. Aristotle opens his discussion of justice in *Book V* of his *Ethics* by claiming that a 'state [of affairs] is often recognised by its contrary . . . if bodily soundness is firmness of flesh, then bodily unsoundness must be flabbiness of flesh'. He goes on to examine the 'various senses in which a man is said to be unjust' as preliminary to his attempt to define justice.[29] Aristotle applies his theory of the mean to claim that 'just behaviour is intermediate between doing injustice and suffering it' although he immediately admits that the mean is not used here in the same way as with other virtues. But doing injustice and suffering it are not two different states of the same essence and justice cannot be placed between them. An injustice done to another leads to the other suffering it. Saying that justice is the mean between doing and suffering injustice amounts to no more than the tautology that neither the injustice done nor the injustice suffered is just.

We can see this logical domestication of injustice in the work of John Stuart Mill. Mill claims that 'justice, like many other moral attributes, is best defined by its opposites.' For Mill, injustice is the violation of good laws, the breaking of promises, the refusal to reward deserts and to punish crimes and, finally, partiality in judging.[30] Injustice is therefore the lack and breach of legal justice. Justice and injustice stand opposed, there is a logical symmetry between them and justice is the perfect symmetrical antithesis of injustice. Injustice helps us understand justice, by highlighting those characteristics justice lacks and tries to eliminate. Injustice allows the examination of instances in which the explicit or implied criteria of that justice are missing—as contrast or illustration. As Tom Campbell puts it 'a concept of justice aims to distinguish the just from the non-just, not to take a view on what is just as distinct from unjust.'[31] But in this case, the main benefit of this approach is to confirm the logical principle of non-contradiction: justice is justice and not injustice. If some action violates the—given—criteria of justice then it is unjust. In this sense, injustice is linked with justice in a circular manner, as a 'hasty preliminary to the analysis of justice' and becomes banal and uninteresting.[32]

But what if we do not have a principle or theory of justice; what if we were to recognise many conflicting principles? Have our philosophical problems

[29] Aristotle, *Ethics* (Harmondsworth, Penguin, 1976) 171–2.
[30] JS Mill, *Utilitarianism* (London, Everyman, 1954) 38–60, at 39.
[31] T Campbell, *Justice* (Basingstoke, Macmillan Education, 1988) 20–1.
[32] J Shklar, *The Faces of Injustice* (New Haven, Yale University Press, 1990) 19.

stopped the victims of injustice from rebelling? Is injustice not felt by many who have not read any theory of justice, and have not pondered about the intricacies of the principles of distribution? One commentator finds that 'it is easier to recognise injustice than to define justice'.[33] This is indeed a valuable point. Justice has been presented in most philosophies as a matter of definition and theory, as a matter of seeing the truth. Injustice, on the other hand, is a question of feeling and responsibility, of hearing and responding to the call of the victim. Injustice is felt by our authors and poets, by our priests and revolutionaries, by our dissidents and reformers. Our best literature expresses in the strongest and most moving terms the desperation, the disasters, the large and petty evils of daily life. Most of all, injustice is felt by the oppressed, the excluded, the exploited, the discriminated against. Injustice is felt by its victims. The unjust is not the contrary of the just, and suffering injustice is not the logical opposite of doing injustice.[34] If we do not have a theory of justice we must start from the bottom up, from the perspective of the losers and the oppressed. Injustice exceeds the theory of justice. Thinking starts with justice. Life starts with injustice.

Theories of justice have shown little interest in destroyed, damaged or lowly lives. The interest of philosophy is to find the 'truth' of the matter, its concern is more of a cognitive and less of a moral or political character. Theories of justice start from 'objectively' measurable entities, laws and their application, judicial reason, fairness and impartiality. As Judith Skhlar puts it, 'the judicial mind-set looks only at what is relevant to its social aims, not to everything we should know about misfortune and injustice'.[35] Injustice does not need a theory before it is felt and does not follow universalisable principles. It does not call for dialogue, but for action. Understanding injustice necessarily starts with the victim and her subjective feelings, and involves both empathy and reason. The victim of injustice is not the opposite of its perpetrator, there is no symmetry or reciprocity between them and in many instances there is no clear agent of the injustice visited on the victim. The anger caused by injustice leads to protest and action but often too injustices are forgotten. Injustice easily becomes invisible; its feeling silenced or suppressed. The organ of justice is a specially trained eye; the blindfold and the veil of ignorance are meant to create the right perspective for perceiving certain differences and not others. Injustice addresses the ear; it is about hearing the sufferer and responding to her demands. If justice should be seen to be done, injustice should be heard to be undone. The greatest injustice happens when the victim is not allowed to give evidence of her injury. Injustice then turns into destiny, and the victim feels guilty for her own oppression.[36] But

[33] M Ginsberg, *On Justice in Society* (Harmondsworth, Penguin, 1971) 73.

[34] 'That is what is unjust. Not the opposite of the just, but that which prohibits that the question of the just and the unjust be, and remain, raised', J-F Lyotard, *Just Gaming*, W Godzich (trans), (Manchester, Manchester University Press, 1985) 66–7.

[35] J Schlar, above n 32 at 50.

[36] J-F Lyotard, above n 35 and C Douzinas and R Warrington, above n 24.

there is more: the sense of injustice is always in excess of any possible restitution and circulates endlessly 'according to the ordinance of time' as the first extant text of western thought, a fragment by the Pre-socratic philosopher Anaximander puts it.[37] Injustice is not the opposite of justice but whatever prevents the question of justice and injustice from being raised.

Unbeknown to the philosophy of justice and to history of just institutions, often subsumed or silenced by them, there runs an underground history, which prioritises evil and injustice. It starts with the brutal men who violated *Dike,* the archaic Goddess of the order of the world and doing in so, opened the course of human history. The Anaximander fragment acknowledges this original injustice and becomes the precursor of many heresies and antinomian theories that insisted on the primary character of injustice. The heretic Marcion taught, circa 120 AD, that the vengeful God of the Scriptures could not be a loving father. His justice distributes good and evil and therefore he is the cause of both. Such a God, whose law rewards good with good and visits evil on evildoers, cannot be the father of Christ. Christ has another unknown father, whose justice follows love and not the law of giving each his due. This unknown God does not calculate, reward and punish; he gives without return, *gratia gratis data*. But this God of love is perennially pursued and suffers in the hands of the God of justice. This conflict between the principles of retributive justice and love has been one of the great theological problems, symbolised by the doctrine of atonement propounded by Anselm of Canterbury. The medieval Father distinguished three forms of justice: a divine, a human and a *justitia diaboli,* in which *malum tribuere bonum*, evil compensates the good.

There is a parallel secular history of injustice. Jean-Jacques Rousseau became convinced that the sense of injustice is natural and innate when he saw an infant cry in despair after his nurse hit him to stop crying. His education of Emile, his imaginary pupil, is an attempt both to foster and to direct his natural feeling of injustice. Emile is asked to plant some beans on a fruit plot belonging to a gardener. When the gardener uproots the fruit of his labour, Emile is indignant. He now understands the importance of property as well as the injustice that property and its deprivation can cause. With this experience of injustice, Emile 'has entered society and its rules, and he is no longer an innocent young animal but an intelligent and moral being.'[38] In the same tradition, the philosopher Schelling claimed that evil and injustice have a being and force of their own.[39] Finally, Marx presented the injustices and infamies of capitalism in the starkest light, but did not discuss in detail the requirements of justice. For Marx, the demand for a theory of justice is created by the economic exploitation and political domination of capitalism. But capitalism makes fair distribution

[37] See chapter 4 below.

[38] J Shklar, above n 32 at 88 and J-J Rousseau, *Emile*, A Bloom (trans), (New York, Basic Books, 1979) 97–101.

[39] S Zizek and FWJ von Schelling, *The Abyss of Freedom. Ages of The World* (Ann Arbor, University of Michigan Press, 1997).

impossible. Capitalist societies are condemned to give rise to endless debates on justice but are unable to meet its concerns.[40] Communism, like Plato's *Republic* and Augustine's *City of God,* draws its inspiration from the injustice of existing institutions and the failures of conventional theories, rather than from a clear vision of the utopia to come.

Justice is an economic theory; its principles of distribution try to balance pleasures and pains and to close the social accounts without leaving any remainder. Injustice is uneconomic, because suffering can never be fully accounted for. Its untold history is in excess of law and economics; it violates good order and legal propriety and insists that the authority of institutions is not fully authorised and that the only authority is resistance to injustice. Injustice is always in excess of measure and order. This is why injustice belongs to the passions, to children and to poets. But without the sense of injustice, all discussion of justice would remain useless, a plaything of those who are, on the whole, happy with the world.

Foundations and Their Deconstruction

A key strategy that brings together our various themes and topics is that of anti-foundationalism. Foundationalism is the belief in the existence of a ground, foundation or ideal, discovered or posited by thought, which makes the world into a coherent whole. The belief that being can be totalised, briefly considered above, is one example of this metaphysical thinking. Foundationalists establish their founding axioms and then follow an internal logic that builds propositions from the necessary interconnections between them. But this approach was followed from its very beginnings by an anti-foundational, critical gesture. Indeed, anti-foundationalism is one of the most ancient and noble western traditions of thought. Heraclitus's belief that life is a constant process of becoming and struggle, and Anaximander's claim that injustice and its restitution moves history, predate the Platonic foundation of western philosophy based on the theory of ideal forms. After these classical beginnings history is marked by an ongoing oscillation between the belief in the power of reason to order the world, and those 'heretics' who privileged living, the material and becoming, over the ideal. As much as thinkers would privilege Being over the shifting sands of becoming, a thinking of becoming has always ghosted their endeavours.

Nietzsche, the *enfant terrible* of philosophy, is for us moderns, the anti-foundationalist *par excellence*. Nietzsche was the first to emphasise that while Socrates had been appropriated by the philosophical mainstream as the thinker of reason and ideal forms—the Apollonian moment of thought—Socrates was also a singer, a dancer and a drinker. Those aspects of his embodied life—its

[40] A Buchanan, *Marx and Justice* (London, Methuen, 1982); S Lukes, *Marxism and Morality* (Oxford, Clarendon Press, 1985).

Dionysian excess—were as crucial to his philosophical thought as its reasoned abstractions. Nietzsche unpicked the elaborate tapestry of philosophy and showed that values, morals and law, rather than being the result of a linear progression of ideals and ideas, are often the contingent outcome of a clash of arms, a struggle of forces and an array of coincidences.

Nietzsche's thinking of becoming has been linked to the great disasters of modernity, the collapse of all values into nihilism: do what you will shall be the whole law. But Nietzsche's main point was that nihilism was the result of the transference of morality beyond life and onto a realm of eviscerated ideals, like Kant's categorical imperative, which must be transcended or transvalued, as old Friedrich put it, if we want to take responsibility for our lives. The great Nietzschean imperative is to create value for oneself, to give the law in the absence of any foundation for the law. This moral or legislative moment is the greatest summation of the anti-foundationalist tradition. The problem is that this duty to create a novel morality has been placed predominantly on the sovereign individual. The lonely creator, the superman, rebels against the mass and the sediment of tradition. But this can lead to a kind of aristocratic elitism. However, if we link Nietzsche's injunction to transvalue dead values to the idea of social being as a being-in-common, new possibilities are created. Values must be created anew; this is not the task of the lone individual, but of collective political and cultural action.

We should note parenthetically that Nietzsche's thinking of becoming is inseparable from what has been described as his poetic philosophy. Poetry is, literally, a making. The poet responds to the world with words of passion rather than abstract thought and logic (which is not to say that poetry does not have its own logic of images). Nietzsche shows that philosophy itself follows the ruses of poetry in two ways: first, philosophical texts use the rhetorical, linguistic and semiotic devices of the poetic, and, also, philosophy is open to those urges, drives and desires that have been associated with poetry. Philosophy is not somehow suited to the serious masculine matter of thinking, whilst poetry is flippant and feminine. Nietzsche's lesson is precisely that law and legal philosophy are themselves poetic endeavours. This is not just confirmed to the historical record. Ancient history shows that laws were first given in epics, in the great poems of the tribe. In more recent times, laws were linked to the myths of nation building. Only later does this origin and this truth become forgotten. As the poet Shelley reminds us, poets are the unacknowledged legislators of the world. Shelley offers an insight into the role that poetry plays in the transmission of values, ways of being and living, from mother to daughter, father to son. Shelley, as a classicist, understood the necessity of this operation, and saw it as law's animus.

The restricted jurisprudence of modernity, by focusing exclusively on the form of the law—the logic of the institution, legal texts and the protocols of legal procedure—forgets that law has always been a mode of social being and an aspect of the way in which individual existence is hooked up to the social. In this approach, law's reason can only be thought through the rigours of a language purged of poetic ornament. It is no wonder that jurisprudence offers a partial understanding of eviscerated forms. As we insisted above, law's task—from the tables of Moses to the Human Rights Act—has been to transmit a way of life, a morality of existence; an *ars vivendi*. The legal institution is part of that process, one of its domains, but not the whole. In concentrating exclusively on institutional preoccupations, modern jurisprudence becomes a limited examination of law's place in the social world. We do not, however, mean to essentialise the poetic. Our concern is with those other domains of the social world that are equally essential to the reproduction of a way of being. A general jurisprudence aims to bring back into the picture those other aspects of the legality of existence—aesthetic, ethical and material—which are absolutely crucial to social reproduction. By reminding us that writers and artists have legislated, while philosophers and lawyers (some celebrated, others forgotten) have spoken poetically, we suggest the possibility of new ways of thinking and living the law.

Nihilism has been rejected in jurisprudence as a 'philosophy' according to which if there can be no truth, anything goes. But this is a parody and detracts from nihilism's more radical and challenging aspects. Nihilism has both epistemological and moral aspects; it starts from the premise that reason, the ultimate foundation of modernity, cannot deliver the pacification of conflict and the good society. This recognition forces the question of how one is to live the good life in the absence of rational justification of one's position. One set of answers to this crucial question is provided by pragmatism. Richard Rorty, the best known proponent of American pragmatism, has attacked moral and legal foundationalism.[41] Adopting the Nietzschean position, Rorty argues that that the attempt to ground morality and law on some universal human attribute is bound to fail. Human nature is always changing and no common human characteristics exist which could be used to establish a globally valid moral or legal code. Reason, the faculty commonly proposed as the answer to the question of moral foundations, is important as an attempt to make one's beliefs coherent and perspicuous but rationalists of all kinds have imposed impossible tasks on it.

Rationalism believes that people will be motivated to act morally if they know the truth about the foundations of morality. In this vein, Plato tried to distinguish through reason between true and false versions of self and polity but failed. Kant identified morality with rationality because he thought that reason would motivate moral action and support his claim that an unconditional moral obligation lies at the basis of individual freedom. But as the tragic heroine Phaedra observed, I may know the truth but I will still do wrong. Rorty's conclusion is that we should abandon the search for universal moral truths and rational foundations. Not only is the quest for the common attributes of human nature fruitless, but it detracts from the moral job at hand. Our moral intuitions are the result of our cultural histories and traditions; they speak mostly to the

[41] R Rorty, *Contingency, Irony and Solidarity* (Cambridge, Cambridge University Press, 1989).

emotions. Once we have accepted the truth that knowledge cannot lead to good actions, the question becomes one of efficiency: what is the best way in which a legal system can promote peaceful cohabitation? How can morality best rid the world of prejudice, superstition and brutality. Consistent with his liberal pragmatism, Rorty answers the first question by exalting the American constitution and legal system as embodiments of the highest achievements of the 'conversation of civilisation' and of cultural tolerance. As far as morality is concerned, eschewing the moralism of religion and Kantianism, Rorty suggests a kind of sentimental education in which the telling of sad stories will cultivate moral sympathy towards refugees and the victims of torture and famine. These conclusions may be unconvincing to the American victims of racism or the targets of its foreign policy in many parts of the world, but Rorty's powerful anti-foundationalism shows that the abandonment of the attempt to ground law or morality does not lead to immorality.

An interesting combination of Nietzschean nihilism and Rortyan pragmatism emerged in the American Critical Legal Studies movement. Here, nihilism questioned how it is possible to justify law as a rational system of rules. If, as critical work has shown, reason is itself contradictory, the claim that law can provide a guide to action or a restraint to government can no longer be sustained. Thus, the fundamental premise of nihilism is that reason is unable to adjudicate value conflicts and that legal reasoning provides indeterminate solutions to problems that are not hopelessly compromised by political exigencies. But where does this leave us? Is the conclusion of this argument that, after nihilism, one must accept that might makes right?

According to the American critics, the demolition of the foundations of reason does not necessarily mean that morality and the possibility of justification disappears. On the contrary, weakening the rational grounds for action increases our responsibility to the other, making it the most important moral prerogative. It is when rules run out and no longer offer simple instructions for living that acting towards the other morally through our own resources becomes the strongest imperative. Furthermore, once one accepts that the old stories no longer have a hold, then the possibility of thinking about the world anew becomes possible. After nihilism, one need not be trapped in the polarities of reason and emotion, law and politics, objectivity and subjectivity. In the field of legal theory, the wake of reason is over and still mourning its death is a sign of bad faith. Reason's passing allows the conceptualisation of legal reasoning as a form of conversation in which value claims are made and contested in the absence of right answers. As the American critics have insisted, the conversation itself presupposes that no discussant has a privileged claim, but that all must be weighed up in coming to a pragmatic conclusion. Restraint does not come from belief in reasons, procedures or foundations, but from groundless passions, that are then subjected to the tribunal of debate.

To conclude, the antifoundationalism we pursue in this project is both epistemological and 'normative'. It makes no claim to a universal truth, but in pursuing the moral responsibility towards the other it opens the possibility of a different justice that is both within and beyond the law.

The Interminable Tango Between Law and Critique

This project belongs to a long history of radical exploration and critique of the legal institution. Law and its contestation, doctrine and critique, are born together. Critique has always followed the law, as its twin, its shadow or ghost. It could not be otherwise. The law divides between the lawful and the unlawful, the permitted and the prohibited, it marks those who obey it from those who don't. But the gesture that instantiates what is permitted and acceptable also posits crime and the forbidden, law's creatures and legality's companions. Borderlines are always challenged and border guards always come under attack. St Paul wrote that without the law we would not have sin; we can paraphrase, that without the law, critique would not exist, and vice versa. If law finds its destiny in its contestation, critique is bound constantly to become law. This is the dilemma of both the critic and the apologist for the orthodoxy. The melancholia of the lawyer, often commented upon, must be partly attributed to a certain schizophrenia that attends the legal thinker.[42] One is always caught in an endless seesaw, a dance between the justice of the institution, that must be mobilised despite its limitations to protect the powerless, and the dream of higher justice which will found the good city and transcend the injustices of the present. We cannot survive without the justice of the law but we cannot live without the hope of another justice. This oscillation has been repeated throughout the history of the west and is the only non-foundational ground of our laws and institutions.

The first exploration of justice in the western world, Plato's *Republic* was both a critique of the polity of Athens and a utopian constitution for a polis to come in the future. Cicero celebrated the achievements of Roman law but spoke in the same breath of a natural law or justice, against which the edicts of the consuls must be judged. In England, the common law was born out of a continuing struggle of adoption and rejection of Roman law and its embodiment in French civil law. Today, our ambiguous attitude towards Europe repeats this gesture. We cautiously welcome some European legal ideas but we emphatically reject the European political and constitutional process. More recently our turn to rights, the only values left in a godless age, is a further example of the reluctant, often forced, marriage of law and critique in late modernity. The positivist insistence that the law consists just in state-posited rules which can match society fully and plan all aspects of life, was a kind of dumb show and a prelude to the great catastrophes of the twentieth century; all of them extrava-

[42] P Goodrich, *Oedipus Lex* (Los Angeles, University of California Press, 1995); 'The Critic's Love of the Law' (1999) 10 *Law and Critique* 343.

gant megalomanias of total social engineering. It was against those ethically impoverished and descriptively inaccurate presentations of law that the turn to rights in political, moral and legal thinking repeated the moves of Plato and Cicero. The rigidity of the common law constitution has now been supplemented by the Human Rights Act, modeled on European concepts and human rights treaties. But the many safeguards have been introduced to the scheme ensure that the Englishness of sovereignty and the commonality of tradition are not surrendered to exalted moral claims and unbritish federal schemes.

When we move from philosophy to religion, and from the Greek to the Judaeo-Christian, the same concerns are apparent: the old and the new law are inseparable. The moment that the law tables are engraved is the moment that they are smashed. Religion was traditionally the mode of the reproduction of social life, and of transmission of the mores that need to be passed on for community to live on. The dialectic of old and new that colours the history of western and eastern Christian and Judaic tradition has been passed on to law, the institution which largely replaced religion as the repository and archive of our communal being.

Let us now turn to the modern critical tradition. Kant's *Critiques*, the foundational document of modernity, start by posing the question '*quid iuris*'—by what legal right.[43] The link between law and critique is a central feature of modernity. 'In the eighteenth century, history as a whole was unwittingly transformed into a sort of legal process . . . the tribunal of reason, with whose natural members the rising elite confidently ranked itself, involved all spheres of activity in varying stages of its development. Theology, art, history, the law, the State and politics, eventually reason itself—sooner or later all were called upon to answer for themselves.'[44] Critique brings reason to a tribunal of law, and asks reason and its faculties to justify themselves according to legal protocols. In the original Kantian sense, critique means the exploration of the transcendental presuppositions, the inescapable conditions of possibility of a discourse or practice. Kant saw critique as setting limitations to speculative reason, imposing strict borderlines that reason cannot cross without losing its explanatory power. To use human rights as an example, we could say that an examination of the transhistorical conditions of the emergence of human rights requires a critical appreciation of humanism and of the concept of right as it emerges from the western legal tradition.

The aim of critique is to introduce a limit attitude, to 'dare people to know', but also to delineate what ought to remain off limits to knowledge because it does not belong to its kingdom. Critique is therefore also a policing operation; its judgement establishes boundaries while its border guards police the line between inside and outside, a function that appeared from the beginning to be

[43] I Kant, *Critique of Practical Reason* (London, Macmillan 1956); J Rose, *The Dialectics of Nihilism* (Oxford, Blackwell, 1984) 11–49.

[44] R Koselleck, *Critique and Crisis* (Cambridge, Mass, MIT Press, 1988) 9–10.

excessively and essentially negative. Critique's business is to prohibit and exclude, to keep ideas safe and protected. As with all judgement and setting of limits, critique both prohibits and enables. Critique comes before the law and is shaped according to legal protocols, peculiarities and procedures. It finds in law its essence and form, it becomes law-like, the critic becomes a judge or a guard, something not far removed from the Freudian conception of the law-like character of conscience or the superego. The critic is either the judge who makes distinctions, passes judgment and sets limits, or the policeman who guards those limits and ensures that the judicial fiat is translated into daily practice. We are well aware of these two positions in intellectual life and their expressions in the legal academy. Critique takes its severe and austere stance from the protocols of legal propriety and sobriety.[45]

But *krinein* means also to cut; critique is a diacritical or cutting force, a critical separation and demarcation. It aims to distinguish between the just manifestations of a phenomenon and their inauthentic counterparts. Bringing dialectical thinking to bear on political economy, Marx's critique undercut 'bourgeois' philosophy to the extent that the categories and suppositions of thought concealed true operations. Economics was posited as the key to the social world. What mattered was who controlled the means of production, as this determined the political and intellectual structure of any given society, or, indeed, an 'epoch' of history. Marxist critique argued that material history could be divided on the basis of the predominant modes of economic organisation. As a thesis on European (and possibly even world history), this traced a development from feudalism to capitalism. The tensions that made the movement from the former to the latter inevitable, would lead, by the same logic of contradiction, to the eventual coming of socialism. Socialism reconciled the tensions between ownership and control of economy, and could thus be the realisation of 'true' social organisation. The critical gaze thus saw operations of inequality and power where philosophy had seen only logic or the unproblematic development of the tradition. To return to the example of human rights, the classic Marxist tradition would see these ideas as a fiction of a particular political order that attempts to preserve its hold on power by offering minor concessions, or blinding people with ideologies of the 'rights of man'; for a Marxist, the rights of man include the rights of some to live in luxury, and the rights of the many to starve. The key to just social organisation was imagined not as catalogues of rights, but as the masses taking control over the state mechanisms that had been used to oppress them

Marxism is thus irreducibly marked by a utopian moment. The later manifestations of the tradition, for instance, the celebrated Frankfurt School, continued and intensified both the analytical and utopian elements of this body of thought. In post-Marxist theory, the critic places much greater importance on social fantasies and bears witness to the gaping cleavage between the real and its

[45] C Douzinas, '*Oubliez Critique*' (2005) 16(1) *Law and Critique*.

idealised, ideological representations. This type of critique was developed by the Frankfurt School. Max Horkheimer proposed an immanent, dialectical critique and emphasised that 'true theory in a period of crisis is more critical than affirmative'.[46] Critique has society as its object and investigates it through the dialectical tool of political economy. For Horkheimer, critical theory tries to 'take seriously the ideas by which the bourgeoisie explains its own order—free exchange, free competition, harmony of interests and so on—and to follow them to their logical conclusion [a process which will] manifest their inner contradiction and therewith their real opposition to the bourgeois order.'[47] For this type of critical theory there is no outside, there are no factors that remain external to the production of knowledge. While traditional theorists separate their scholarship from their life, the critical approach rejects the division between 'value and research, knowledge and action' and unites theory, politics and action.[48]

Critique has the whole of society as its object and emancipation as its aim. Otherwise the critic becomes victim of ideology:

> The thinking subject is not the place where knowledge and object coincide or consequently the starting point for attaining absolute knowledge. Such an illusion about the thinking subject under which idealism since Descartes has lived, is ideology in the strict sense, for in it the limited freedom of the bourgeois individual puts on the illusory form of perfect freedom and autonomy.[49]

If we replace the 'thinking subject' with the 'legal person', Horkheimer's axiom could become the defining motto of a critical legal ontology upon which the radical critique of society could be based.

Within jurisprudence, this line connects with Critical Legal Studies, particularly its British version. Although it would be wrong to say that early British CLS was primarily Marxist, it did contain a strong political orientation and an affinity to this school of thought and practice. The 'Crits' saw themselves as a counter-movement; they were radicals, demanding the impossible. The social was to be re-imagined. Notions such as the 'intersubjective zap' the intense moment when people perceive that there is a possibility of their coming together, were a provocation, a utopian urge for a better world.[50] Its borrowings from Marxism are also apparent in its deployment of theories of ideology and alienation.[51] The legitimacy of the social world is sustained by 'overpowering' symbols that extend over the whole operation of the law.

[46] M Horkheimer, 'Traditional and Critical Theory' in *Critical Theory: Selected Essays* (New York, Continuum, 1995) 218.

[47] *Ibid*, 215.

[48] *Ibid*, 208.

[49] *Ibid*, 211.

[50] See P Gabel, 'Ontological Passivity and the Constitution of Otherness within Large Scale Social Networks' cited in 'Roll Over Beethoven' (1984) 32 *Stanford Law Review* 24. 'Intersubjective zap' is also drawn from this piece. It is defined as: 'a sudden, intuitive moment of connectedness. It is a vitalising moment of energy (hence "zap") when the barriers between the self and the other are in some way suddenly dissolved' (at 54).

[51] See Z Bankowski and G Maungham, *Images of Law* (London, Routledge, 1976).

In this sense, critical legal theory is intimately associated with the practice of philosophy and with emancipatory and radical politics. In equal measure, a critical movement is theoretical and political, and a critical legal movement addresses the institutional and doctrinal politics of law and the politics of law's self-understanding in the form of jurisprudence and legal theory. If one is not aware that legal concepts are reified and abstracted, they appear to have some kind of foundational substance, a kind of autonomy or independent being. Law presents the social order as if resting upon itself. This loses sight of the fact that the law manufactures its own conditions of legitimacy and then attempts to legislate them as *a priori* universals that have a legitimising effect through their appeal to reason. Reification is a corruption of the very process of reasoning in that it passes off one thing as another: it gives coherence and substance to things that can have no independent being, like those fetishes that attribute human powers and capacities to objects and constructs. This book attempts what we could call a political philosophy of justice. It attests to the political nature of philosophy, in that philosophy should be a practical guide to action; and the philosophical nature of the political. No social organisation is a 'given'—it is a cultural construction, where ideas have gone into action. Over time, these ideas take a solid form, and the sheer contingency of the events that have constituted an order become forgotten. Behind every social organisation there is thus a philosophy, even if this has become fetishised, unquestioned common sense, forgotten.

If there were major themes that run through this book, we would sketch them as follows. It is necessary to regain a sense of political wisdom as a way of thinking about the law. Our concern with natural law and justice relates to an Aristotelean theme: *phronesis*, or practical reason. This is a form of reason that escapes 'grand' theory: it cannot be reduced to an abstract set of principles or goals because it recognises that each situation calls for a different response; a different assessment of the forces that are playing themselves out, of strategic possibilities and limitations.

We relate *phronesis* to a second practical, ethical concern: we are all hostages to the other. This demands that we respond to the sufferings of the other with political action. The demand placed upon us by the other also escapes conceptualisation. It does not make for any particular programme, indeed, it is primarily a thinking of the response as the grounding of the social world, as the very opening of the political. It is not possible to remove this ethical substratum from *phronesis*, as the latter raises the question of the precise nature of our response.

These concerns underline an attitude to law, but do not, as such, describe the law. Law is always a trauma. Law attests to the inherently conflictual form of social life. We approach the law, and the way that it creates legal subjects and structures the social, through a variety of 'methodologies'. We borrow from psychoanalysis, Marxism, hermeneutics and mythology to allow a conceptualisation of law's role in the social imaginary. This might also once have been described as the ideological role of law, but, we would prefer to see the desire that law organises as part of a social fantasy; an essential fantastical investment of the world.

This melange of theory is, ultimately, not synthesised into an argument that there is one school, philosopher or position, or even a combination of positions that adequately presents the world. If this means that there is a sense of incompletion about this book, so much the better. This is not a finished structure. We prefer to build, if we build at all, incrementally like the Mediterraneans. We can pour the concrete, lay the foundations one year—build the walls the next, and the roof when time and money allows. We are indeed much happier when our views are not inhibited by walls; the path from the door leads directly to the sea.

We operate as *bricoleurs*, borrowing what appears to be useful at the time, and discarding what would slow us down or impede our progress. So, this is a book of passages: from A to B, from jurisprudence to philosophy, from philosophy to history and to politics, from law to justice. How do we move from law to justice? What traffic connects these places? We know them well but they are also beyond understanding—the great unknowns. People have lived by the law and have died for justice. But the route that connects the two remains uncharted.

So, are you ready to embark? Are you prepared to come aboard? Listen, they are shouting for you to look sharp—quick before the ropes are cast off.

PASSAGES

We are setting off, hopes high, maps to the ready. We know that the maps are fantastical, their co-ordinates match those of another world; we will probably never find what we are looking for, nor be able to return home. The itinerary of justice: a long journey, full of hope and expectation. We have sailed into important ports on the way. They made us believe that the maps were right after all: 1789, 1917, 1945, 1989. But then the path is lost again and again—justice a horizon that recedes the more the good boat 'Law' appears to come close to it. We are left with the voyage; with an unknown or no destination, but always prepared to load the boat quickly—letter, spirit, beads 'to soothe the evil eye'—and sail again.

You are to share a cabin with the professor. That first evening, during the indifferent dinner, you watch him pushing the food around his plate. Later, when the storms hit, he proceeds to lecture you in the pitching cabin lit by the mad, swinging light:

> The tempest is the time of truth. You may not believe in truth, although by saying that, you reveal your obsession with its existence. But truth is not something we can prepare for, it is not a destination but something that happens to us, a revelation or visitation, the dread and exhilaration in the midst of utmost danger, when our defenses are battered and the vessel of self—or the spirit of history—is thrown around like a child's toy.

On other occasions, kinder waves caress the boat. Standing on deck, in the balmy air, you survey the distant grey line of the coast, your hand over your brow against the strong light. Have we arrived? The waves push us forward now, not too fast but not in a straight line either. After the frigid winds, the gentle air and the rhythm of the waves lull you half asleep; and in a sweet delirium your thoughts return to themselves; outlines become clearer only to dissipate, moving from this to that. Suddenly coming to, the professor is standing beside you:

> The promise of the destination sets us sailing each time and the failure to arrive bitterly disappoints us but also prepares us for the next departure . . .

Is he apologising for this non-voyage? Already the engines have stopped idling and have struck up their monotonous rhythm; the boat swings away from the land, pointing back towards the ocean. You walk to the stern and watch the distant coast recede as night falls. Interminable voyage; in the passage without beginning or end. How can you avoid this madman's eyes; his questions, the search for the truth in which you now seem to be inadvertently implicated? You return to the cabin down the dark corridor that stinks of engine oil.

The professor's tattered manuscript is on the table by the bunk. There is nothing else to do. You pick it up and start reading:

Socrates starts the quest for justice in the *Republic* on his way to Pireaus, the great port city, the place from which Theseus' boat will sail for Crete and the labyrinth of knowledge. But the passage to truth is not easier than that to justice. The linguistic root **pir* or **par* signifies passage by sea, movement from one port to another, from London to Pireaus or Porto, Paris or Paros. Thought too is like a passage . . .

2

Law's Others: Poststructuralism and Law

The Greek wise man, the Jewish prophet, the Roman legislator are still models that haunt those, who today, practice the profession of speaking and writing. (Foucault, *Telos*, 161)

WHAT IS METAPHYSICS?

MIDNIGHT, AND THE owls are hunting. Minerva is yawning. The fire dies down; the philosopher spits into the grate, leans back and, half hidden by the shadows, starts to talk:

'Enlightenment is born of fear':[1] The belief in reason's power to explain the world and the assumption that law can regulate our lives are psychological defences against the horrors of chaotic existence. Humanity is faced with a multiplicity of psychological, social, and environmental forces, which make life without external guidance and support a bewildering prospect. This basic vulnerability, so obvious in the young of the species, has been the reason for a number of institutions and structures whose function is to introduce an element of normality and predictability into the blooming, buzzing confusion of things. Humankind strives to 'construct a conscious world that is safe and manageable in that the laws of nature hold in it the place that statute law has in the polity.'[2] Law turns chaos into order. In this endeavour, law stands alongside religion, morality and social institutions like the family and the state. Behaviour becomes regulated; the main rudiments and structures of the social bond are passed on from generation to generation. Humanity survives the inescapable demise of its individual members. But from Homer's time onwards, philosophers have understood that law as a practical operation is subject to the contingencies of existence and the exigencies of the world, and can scarcely create a perfect tapestry out of the ragged threads of human life.

[1] C Jung, *Modern Man in Search of a Soul* (London, Routledge and Kegan Paul, 1966) 187.
[2] *Ibid*, 187–8.

The fear of the unknown and the urge for order and law has followed all facets of human endeavour. In philosophy, the multifaceted, unpredictable and conflictual condition of life has led to a school of thought known as metaphysics. Metaphysics—*meta ta physica* or beyond nature—is a way of thinking beyond the sensible and immediate experience of things. Metaphysics posits the existence of an ideal, transcendent world over against which everyday reality must measure itself. In our ordinary lives, we are immersed in streams of unrelated, incoherent, criss-crossing streams of people, events and emotions that invade our world in unpredictable, uncontrollable ways. Death is the only certainty, the inescapable destination of our limited earthly sojourn. Behind metaphysics lies a simple and urgent desire: to make sense of the disorder that surrounds us, to master finitude.

The foundation of metaphysics was laid in classical Greece. Perhaps it was something to do with that clear, clean light. You can see into the heart of things. You can see beyond seeing. The great philosophers, from Anaximander to Plato, claimed that the world of the senses was a distraction, a phantasm. The world that could be reached only through the mind was the true one. Plato completed the reversal between the sensible and the intelligible: the phenomenal world is only a series of shadows on the dark wall of a cave, while the world of ideas and forms is the sunlit empire of true reality. The supra-sensible domain, unlike chaotic nature, is united, harmonious and coherent. Phenomena and appearances are many, but the truth is one and can be approached through reason. Truth begets reason (*logos*) but conversely we can reach truth only through reason and language (*logos*). The philosopher's task is to guide us to this ideal world, in which the reason of things that 'rule the world' resides. The metaphysical urge creates ideal, unified, logically harmonious worlds and calls them reality.

Properly metaphysical concepts do not have immediate purchase upon the world. The main characteristic of metaphysical systems such as materialism and idealism' is that they follow their own internal logic and build their propositions from the necessary interconnections between their founding axioms. For the later Greeks, as for the German philosopher Martin Heidegger who charted the history of western metaphysics, the main metaphysical urge is to ask 'what' questions: what is an entity, what is 'its' essence, what does it means for a being to be such? These questions inevitably led to the master question: what does it mean to be, what is the essence of Being itself? The various answers offered in the history of metaphysics take the form of a series of 'words for being'; a number of predicates, determinations or theses about the meaning of Being in general or about the being of particular entities. The metaphysical operation thinks through principles, asserts the primacy of a value or origin and then proceeds to arrange entities and experiences according to their distance from this prior ground. The principle is assumed to exist beyond language, immediate and immediately present to consciousness. This way, unity is privileged over plurality, and sameness over difference. Aristotle called this ground concept *hypokeimenon*, 'that which lies under'. It is the substance or essence upon which all other entities are predicated but which is itself not predicated by anything else.[3] The Latin *subjectum*, or substratum, translated the Greek *hypokeimenon* and became the word for the foundation, the grounding principle of Being and thought.[4] The *subjectum* is that which persists through time, the matter, content or substance upon which form imposes type and change.

Many names have been given to this origin and ultimate value throughout history. The Greeks saw the cosmos as nature, *physis*: Being that arises and opens itself in the manifold of beings. The Medievals interpreted their world as *ens creatum:* divine creation. Modernity was announced by Descartes whose *cogito ergo sum* (I think therefore I am) removed the metaphysical foundation from (Aristotelian) substance, (Platonic) form or (Christian) God, and placed it on Man understood as subject, the centre of the world. Metaphysics has developed by inventing and systematising these metaphors, these different names given to Being. These metaphysical determinations are supposedly present in all beings and animate the world. Metaphysics reduces Being to a word or value, and the temporality of becoming—the motion of existence—is erased and turned into permanent presence.

The subject in its various forms, as self-identical, as ego, consciousness or the Cartesian thinking thing, is now the ultimate ground of all that exists. After the turn to the subject, metaphysics became obsessed with the relationship between empirical individuals and subjectivity—the universal transcendental ground or principle that endows humans with identity, reason and morality. But according to Heidegger, the enlightenment quest for human emancipation and happiness has gone terribly wrong; a combination of arrogance and the forgetfulness of Being. After the destruction of classical teleology, reason became instrumental, a means to ends set elsewhere.[5] The malady of modern rationalism was both unmasked and perpetuated by Nietzsche. Nietzsche's 'will to power' revealed the self-seeking action of modern will. At the same time, Nietzsche's will aims at nothing beyond itself. It is a will to will and glorifies its own mastery. An unconditioned will no longer has any given aims. It becomes a quest for mastery for its own sake. This was of course the great project of modernity enunciated by the French philosopher Descartes: humanity should acquire absolute ownership of the world and control everything: the natural environment, the social world, even the human psyche. The reverse side of this megalomania is that humanity itself turns into an object, like all objects, a plaything to be manipulated by the

[3] S Critchley, 'Prolegomena to any Post-Deconstructive Subjectivity' and U Guzzoni, 'Do We Still Want to be Subjects?' in S Critchley and P Dews (eds), *Deconstructive Subjectivities* (New York, SUNY Press, 1996) 13–46 and 201–16.

[4] Aristotle, *Metaphysics*, 1028b33–1029a33.

[5] The attacks on 'instrumental reason' and technology link Heidegger with the left-wing Frankfurt critical school of Adorno, Horkheimer and Marcuse. T Adorno and M Horkheimer, *Dialectics of Enlightenment*, J Cumming (trans), (London, Verso, 1979); T Adorno, *Negative Dialectics*, EB Ashton (trans), (London, Routledge, 1990); H Marcuse, *Eros and Civilisation* (Boston, Beacon Press, 1966).

subject. The metaphysics of subjectivity keeps 'objectifying whatever is' by 'a setting before, a representation that aims at bringing every particular being before it in such a way that man who calculates can be sure of that being'.[6] Metaphysics has always been a political strategy. Positing an ideal and measuring everything against it is an attempt to manipulate the world. Metaphysics is knowledge obsessed with mastery and control.

The will to mastery through truth has reached its most extreme and self-destructive stage in modern science and technology. This represents the latest turn in the metaphysical quest to name and interpret the meaning of Being. Indeed, the essence of contemporary metaphysics is technology. But technology is not an instrument or means—its aims, purposes and methods are not set outside itself in public debate and moral argument, as the apologists of scientific reason claim. From this perspective, technology is not the tool of science or politics but the culmination of the modern 'will to power' which, once turned upon itself, becomes an infinite and aimless will to will.

When the world is emptied of meaning, humanity becomes homeless. Losing any sense of the place of humankind in the world is the price of technological mastery. 'Subjectification' turns everything into a representation for the subject and affects humanity as much as the world. Man, in his narcissism, forgets that Being is something other than the totality of beings. As a result of this forgetfulness, a totally misleading and catastrophic idea about the centrality of the subject is propagated. But, at the same time, this apparent humanism creates the necessary preconditions for turning man—the proclaimed centre and foundation of the world—into the final object of his objectifying intervention. We see this catastrophic tendency all around us. Nothing is immune from humanity's intervention, no thing or being enjoys or is accepted in its integrity. The reification of the world in the name of progress, development and productivity started with the degradation of the natural environment and has inexorably led humanity to the precipice of natural catastrophe. Society has become the target for various types of social engineering. Some may have been inspired by the best possible motives. But there is a connection between these attempts to change social conditions and the Gulags, the ghettos, and the untold wealth and obscene poverty of our epoch. Finally, humanity turned its own soul into an object of intervention, the target of various psychologists, psychiatrists and other doctors of the psyche, but ended up in the wholesale and cynical manipulation of marketing, consumerism and the media. When the subject becomes the centre of the world and everything, including humanity, is objectified, nothing can stop the will to control and the mastery that eats away at nature, society and self. All there is left to do is shop.

[6] M Heidegger, 'The Age of the World Picture' in *The Question Concerning Technology and Other Essays* (New York, Harper and Row, 1977) 127.

JURISPRUDENCE AS METAPHYSICS

Jurisprudence is a profoundly metaphysical exercise. The subjective turn, which characterises the metaphysics of modernity, is apparent in the organising dichotomies of jurisprudence; the distinctions between public and private, fact and value, principle and policy, subjective choices and objective truths. Both in its positivist and moralistic versions, 'law's empire' is presented as internally coherent and 'pure', the precondition for its task of regulating the world. Jurisprudence is obsessed with foundations, grounds and origins, organising principles and with determining policies, rights and norms. Its task has been to present law as a system that follows a strict logic of rules or a disciplined and coherent arrangement of principles—a procedure that would hopefully give law identity, dignity and legitimacy. The corpus of law is presented, literally, as a body. It must either digest and transform the non-legal into legality, or it must reject it. God's law in naturalism, the *grundnorm* and rule of recognition of the positivists, the principles and the right answers of the hermeneuticians' are the topics of order, identity and unity. It is not surprising that when the question of law's legality becomes dominant, the various answers will offer a definition of essence; they will construct a system of essential characteristics and will inscribe legality within a history conceived exclusively as the unfolding of meaning. The effort to distinguish the legal from the non-legal progresses from the search of an exhaustive list of markers that map out the whole field to the stipulation of a single law of the genre, the law of law. Law's empire is founded on its claim that it can demarcate the properly 'legal' from the terrain of its operation: the social. But according to the forceful deconstructive 'principle', which receives its most compelling application in law, a field is self-sufficient only if its outside is distinctly marked so as to frame and constitute what lies inside. The exterior—morality, politics, economics—is as much part of the constitution of the field as what is proper to it.

Postmodern legality defies the jurisprudential image. Two complementary processes are radically altering the classic ideal of the rule of law. A creeping juridification and legalisation of social and private spaces of activity, on the one hand, and a mushrooming privatisation and deregulation of hitherto public areas of provision, on the other, have turned the public/private divide into an elastic line of passage, communication and osmosis. The regulatory colonisation of the social world does not seem to represent or pursue any inherent logic, overarching policy direction or coherent value system. Policy considerations differ between family law and planning or between criminal justice and the regulation of official secrecy, privacy and data protection. Even worse, contradictory policies appear to motivate regulatory practices in each sphere.

Both sides of this extension and mutation in the governance of society have profoundly affected the nature of legal rules. Rules as normative propositions are supposed to prescribe general and abstract criteria of right and wrong, to anticipate and describe broad types of factual situations and to ascribe legal entitlements and obligations to wide categories of (legal) subjects. Regulatory practices on the other hand are detailed, specific and discretionary. They follow the vagaries of the situation and the contingencies of administrative involvement; they distribute benefits, facilities and positions according to policy choices rather than entitlement; they construct small-scale institutions, assign variable and changing roles to subjects, plan local and micro-relations and discipline people and agencies by arranging them along lines of normal behaviour. Normalisation by reference to the requirements of statistical distribution is more important than norms, principles and values.

Legal language games have proliferated and cannot be presented as the embodiment of the public good, the general will, the wishes of the sovereign people, or of Parliament or some other coherent institution, system or principle. The distinctions between public and private and between rule and discretion, the hallowed bases of the rule of law ideal, are gradually becoming anachronistic as rule-makers couch their delegations of authority to administrators in wide terms, while administrators adopt policies, guidelines and rules to structure the exercise of discretion and protect themselves from challenge. Legislative and regulatory systems are adopted to promote transient, provisional and local policy objectives with no immediate or obvious link with wider social policy. Policy has become visible throughout the operation of law-making and administration; in many instances policy and rule-making are delegated to experts, who fill the gaps according to the latest claims of scientific knowledge. The condition of postmodernity has irreversibly removed the aspiration of unity in law. The law does not have essence; only operations. And yet jurisprudence presents the law at its most imperialistic at the precise moment when it has started losing its specificity. The metaphysical desire is at its strongest when the empirical world denies its claims and norms.

We start the process of unpicking the metaphysics of jurisprudence by introducing the work of three philosophers of 'suspicion'. Friedrich Nietzsche, Michel Foucault and Jacques Derrida have made seminal contributions to the deconstruction of the metaphysical urge in philosophy and law. Their work has helped critical theory move away from the essentialist metaphysics of jurisprudence.

NIETZSCHE

The Genealogy of Morals

Nietzsche's 'madman' marks the beginning of the post-metaphysical era. His impassioned and poetic soliloquy is an epitaph for metaphysics:

> 'Where is God gone' he called out. 'I mean to tell you! We have killed him—you and I! We are all his murderers! But how have we done it? How were we able to drink up

> the sea? Who gave us the sponge to wipe away the whole horizon? What did we do when we loosened the earth from its sun? Has it not become darker? Shall we not have to light lanterns in the morning? Do we not hear the noise of the grave-diggers who are burying God? God is dead! God remains dead! And we have killed him.'[7]

According to Hegel 'the owl of Minerva spreads its wings with the falling of the dusk.'[8] Philosophy and thought are always late in catching reality, condemned to develop their theories as an afterthought to the changes of the world. As the madman insists, darkness has now spread into the day and the night of values is upon us. It is we, the moderns, who killed God, the personification of the metaphysical principle. But in so doing, we have also undermined all attempts to posit an origin, an *arche* or a centre that can stabilise interpretations and become the foundation of meaning.

It is at this point that we enter the era of 'nihilism'. In Nietzsche, nihilism does not refer to one idea or epoch and it is not simply good or bad. Nihilism is an open and plural concept, both a condition of degeneration and decadence and a joyful affirmation of life; the possibility of re-evaluation and regeneration of values. To understand nihilism, let us look, briefly, at genealogy, Nietzsche's philosophical method of approach.

Genealogy and Plurality

Genealogy interprets and evaluates. While the metaphysicians try to gain access to the essence of things, for Nietzsche, phenomena are signs and interpretations. Every thing and process is the site of a struggle. The history of a phenomenon narrates the succession of forces that have possessed it; its meaning is determined by the forces struggling for its current possession. There can be no revelation of a pure 'essence' that 'exists' beyond the play of forces. Every phenomenon, accordingly, has many antagonistic senses that depend on the perspective of the powers that try to dominate it. Pluralism in concepts and perspectivism in interpretation are the properly philosophical approaches.

The force that takes hold of a thing does not encounter an empty space. No phenomenon is free of domination, since all things are the manifestations of forces. In other words, forces are always related to each other, locked in a struggle to make the others obey. Genealogy first accepts the plurality of interpretations and then proceeds to evaluation. It questions all things for their values, and returns them to the beginnings that determined their value. Traditional philosophy is not particularly interested in value or the way in which values have developed historically. For Kantian philosophy, universal principles and rational moral rules are the bedrock of moral action and criticism, while values

[7] F Nietzsche, *The Joyful Wisdom*, in O Levy (ed), *Complete Works* (New York, Macmillan, 1910) 167–8.

[8] G Hegel, *The Philosophy of Right*, TM Knox (trans), (Oxford, Clarendon, 1942) 12–3.

are considered to be subjective and of low moral significance. Utilitarians, on the other hand, are content with creating uncritical inventories of value, deduced from the 'facts' of human behaviour.

Genealogy distrusts both these types of valuations. For Nietzsche, values have no value of their own. They serve as instruments of the will to power. The task of the genealogist is to follow this 'differential element of values from which their value derives. Genealogy thus means origin or birth but also difference or distance in the origin. Genealogy traces nobility and baseness, nobility and vulgarity, nobility and decadence in the origin.'[9] The starting point is the hierarchy between a dominant and a dominating force or forces. The will to power is the struggle of forces as they come into conflict, partial pacification and back into battle again. Genealogy goes back to this polemical origin and difference, not to discover the foundation or to reveal the original identity of the phenomenon, but in order to trace and unravel the threads of the forces, ancient and modern, that have crystallised as values.

Nietzsche and the Law

A Nietzschean approach to law is part of the strategy for overcoming Kantianism. The novelty of Kant's philosophy was to conceive critique as immanent to reason.[10] To examine reason, to understand its operation and uncover its secrets, we need to use reason's own procedures. One must avoid using criteria external to reason, such as the senses, passions, the body or power. Critique took the form of a legal procedure in which both judge and judged were one and the same: reason. But this internal and self-referring procedure lacks the means and the desire for thinking and evaluating the genesis and the genealogy of the law.

Nietzsche poses a completely different set of questions to reason and the law, interrogating its origin and raising the question of the forces that support the law. Kant's answer was that the law comes from reason. We are free and moral, only insofar as we become our own legislators and follow the commands of reason that emanate from our own rational faculties. As modernity stops obeying tradition, God or the King, reason intervenes. Reason asks us to continue obeying because we are autonomous and give the law (*nomos*) to ourselves (*autos*). But this split subject, both legislator and subjected, both free and under strict orders, is a belated theological creature. As priests and penitents, subjects and subjected, we are supposed to be the hinge that unites the phenomenal and the transcendental world. The secular theology of the three *Critiques* clearly sets out the figure of the modern man: although labelled the legislator, he must internalise current values and fully obey the law. Kant's prescription for the ' "proper

[9] G Deleuze, *Nietzsche and Philosophy* (London, Athlone, 1983) 2.
[10] C Douzinas, 'Oubliez Critique' (2005) 16 *Law and Critique*, forthcoming.

usage of the faculties" mysteriously coincides with established values: true knowledge, true morality, true religion.'[11]

Genealogy turns to the long history of the faculty of reason and questions reason's values. Kant excluded values from critical analysis because he presupposed the value of the truth, the right and the good. Nietzsche, on the other hand, proposes to make the history and critique of values the basis of philosophy. The value of the true and the good must be judged according to the kind of life that they promote. Nietzsche attributes the obsession with truth to Plato's distinction between the worlds of appearances and essence. Equally to blame is Plato's method of collecting and ordering sensuous diversity under the unity of an essence. Objective knowledge is either an insight into the essence of things or is the accurate representation of opinion and it acts like law.

Knowledge is belief; truths are expressions of the will to power—of the human need and desire to control. By reducing multiplicity to simplicity, unity and totality and by inventing causality, logic allows us to predict occurrences and to act. Knowledge is normative; not only is it the outcome of the play of forces, it also organises and classifies and world. However, our world is never static; it is always in flux, incessantly shuffled. The multiple and conflicting forces that stage the theatre of the world are given their polyvalent meaning by the will to power. Bodies, consciousness and the self are created through the confrontation of a plurality of forces, the dominant (*active*) and the dominated (*reactive*). In such a world of force and confrontation, no identity is ever stable and no value system complete. But knowledge suppresses this experience, codifying and simplifying the world. Knowledge imposes spurious uniformities and reduces what exists to the ideal.

Truth's obsession with a stable, fixed world, without conflict and contradiction reveals a moral prejudice. Truth as 'the one,' the coherent, the fixed, is also conceived as the *good*. In this sense knowledge becomes law. But as Nietzsche and Deleuze remind us, that part of our experience that is intensity, flux, becoming, the contact and transmission of force, can neither be theoretically represented nor can it be reduced to a law. Intensity and force are neither words nor things; theory cannot transform them into meaning nor can the law transform them into regularity or value. This force 'is what underlies all codes, what escapes all codes, and it is what the codes themselves seek to translate, convert and mint anew.'[12] Nietzsche is the first philosopher who does not attempt to codify force, but celebrates becomings and the world as a play of wild energies.

Nietzsche also gives us another reason why the Kantian method adopts a legal procedure. The law is seen as either external to force or able to translate force to its own register:

[11] G Deleuze, *Nietzsche and Philosophy*, above n 9, 93.
[12] G Deleuze, in D Allinson (ed), *The New Nietzsche* (Cambridge, MA, MIT Press, 1986), 146.

> [T]he question of the concept of law remains quite distinct from and anterior to the question of its force or its compulsive power. Law understood as purpose or purposiveness, value or validity, remains the question of law as concept and standard of judgment; a question which can only arise from within its authoritative domain.[13]

But law's 'outside', its violence, evident and active whenever the law is en*forced*, is what establishes and maintains the law. We can briefly trace these themes in Nietzsche's work.

Just as Islam finds in its jurisprudence the most elaborated expression of its philosophy, Nietzsche hoped that a jurisprudence would be the most perfect embodiment of his own work. This might be suggested by the concluding sections of a late text, *The Antichrist*—a coda, a last set of meditations before madness and silence. We have been unable to read Nietzsche as a legal thinker for the same reason that we have been unable to understand Islam:

> Christianity robbed us of the harvest of the culture of the ancient world, it later went on to rob us of the harvest of the culture of Islam. The wonderful Moorish cultural world of Spain, more closely related to us at bottom, speaking more directly to our sense and taste, than Greece and Rome, was trampled down.[14]

To unpack this strange statement would mean drawing attention to a number of strands of thought. Nietzsche's legal thinking is inseparable from his thinking of religion, or more precisely, the great and monstrous critique of Christianity and Judaism. From these traditions the notion of the law as a total ordering of life is found; and also the law as the force that demarcates, that hides a fear of the 'foreign, strange, uncanny, outlandish'.[15] Thus, the law is defined by the separation it allows between an 'us' and a 'them'—a foreigner that must be resisted. Law thus betrays a logic of opposition, a force of valuation that precedes any organised notion of a people or an identity. The example is the Wahhabis—an eighteenth century Muslim sect that claims a pure form of Islam:

> Thus the Wahhabis know only two mortal sins: having a god other than the Wahhabi god, and smoking (which they call 'the infamous way of drinking'). 'And what about murder and adultery?' asked an Englishman who found this out, amazed. 'God is gracious and merciful,' replied the old chief.[16]

Wahhabi religious identity rests on the prohibition of activities that would identify them with their neighbours, to such an extent that certain acts do not appear to be criminal (at least to the foreigner).

We can follow these meditations through the consideration of 'the Manu law book' in *The Antichrist*. Manu is representative of 'every good law book' because it is an archive, a summary of centuries of experience. It 'creates nothing new'. This is because the 'preconditions' for legal foundation are an author-

[13] N Rose, *Powers of Freedom* (Cambridge, Cambridge University Press, 1999) 27.
[14] F Nietzsche, *The Antichrist* (Harmondsworth, Penguin, 1968) 196.
[15] F Nietzsche, *The Gay Science* (New York, Vintage, 1974), 109.
[16] *Ibid.*

ity acquired over centuries. A book of law can only state and catalogue the law. It cannot account for the law or elaborate the reason for the law, because this would detract from the imperative that the law must be obeyed: a 'thou shalt' that does not allow reasoned investigation. Behind the foundation of a legal order is the power of a class that has the authority to mandate a body of rules that prescribe a way of living. Once this code has been established, there can be no further experimenting or questioning of the values that have been fixed in law.

This is further strengthened by the ascription of divinity to the origin of the laws. Laws are the work of gods, not of men. Laws appear in the world complete and perfect—a communication from beyond. An argument from divinity does not, however, erase the role of tradition. The law is doubly sacred for not only is it a divine gift, it has been lived by the ancestors. This sacred source is still not sufficient for a complete account of the law. For the law to operate successfully, it must infest the everyday to such an extent that it becomes unconscious: the law must ultimately become culture. The 'art of living' is an art of remaining true to the law in the activities of daily life. Presupposed is the need for mastery of the laws, the need to achieve a perfect realisation of law in life. The ordering of society, its hierarchies and rituals have to be seen as 'the supreme law of life itself'.[17] For the language of 'right' to make any sense at all, this hierarchical structure must be preserved; indeed, the foundation of the social is inequality; and this is written in being itself.

Nietzsche's jurisprudence thus returned to law's sacred sources, and to the insistence that law is synonymous with a culture defined through values held in place by religious faith. We can also appreciate that Nietzsche's critique of Kant's presentation of reason operated at an epistemological level: to understand modern law, one had to see it as bound up with a certain metaphysics. These two strands of thinking were continued and intensified by a philosopher who can be seen as writing in a Nietzschean 'tradition', Michel Foucault.

FOUCAULT AND LAW

The Genealogy of Man

Michel Foucault called his approach genealogical after old Friederich,[18] and adapted Nietzschean insights to provide a rethinking of the operations of law and power. How can we understand Foucault's genealogical research? Foucault set out to criticise historicism.

Historicism is a type of evolutionary progressivism: the present is always and necessarily superior over the past. History is the forward march of all-

[17] F Nietzsche, *The Antichrist*, above n 14 at 196.

[18] We concentrate mainly on Foucault's analysis in *Discipline and Punish: The Birth of the Prison* (Harmondsworth, Penguin, 1979) and *The History of Sexuality* (Harmondsworth, Penguin, 1981).

conquering reason, which erases mistakes and combats the prejudices of intellectual positions and political movements. In history, values unravel inexorably towards their perfection in the future. The seed of a value is sown at some point in the past, grows through generations, inspires people who fight for its realisation and, after many trials and tribulations, philosophical potentiality becomes historical actuality. The standard history of human rights is a typical example of this type of historiography. The idea of a law higher than state legislation entered the stage in the 'unwritten laws' of Antigone and the writings of Aristotle on natural law. These were then taken up and generalised by the Stoics and Cicero. The idea of a natural law mutates into the natural rights of individuals in liberal political philosophy. Natural rights are then institutionalised in the great declarations of the American and French revolutions and, as human rights, in the recent international covenants and treaties. In this version, the international recognition of human rights marks the end of a long trajectory, which overrides the ignorant past while retaining and realising its hidden kernel. History moves one way; it is the linear process of gradual disclosure of essences or values: the becoming-realised of the values of freedom, equality or rights.

The genealogist denies this kind of history and diagnoses it as a particularly sycophantic type of story telling. History does not progress triumphantly towards the present in a march in which ignorance, arbitrariness and war are gradually replaced by science, law and democracy. For Foucault, the term genealogy alludes to a 'dirty', uneven view of the historical process, full of clashes of forces and successions of dominations, in which fortunate and unlucky events, coincidences and bad turns, combine in unexpected ways to create some of our most hallowed institutions and values. This approach takes our own personal genealogy as its model. Each individual has come to life through a series of contingent events: the unpredictable encounter of our parents and the chance act of procreation. This aspect of luck, unpredictability and randomness, dignified in its mysteries as *fata*, destiny or fate by the ancients, has become, for us moderns, a source of anxiety to be regulated and controlled. In modernity, social engineers, policy makers and planners try to excise randomness, contingency and emotion in favour of reason, planning and control. But the non-rational part of life cannot be exorcised.

Foucault's genealogy is a history of the present. Nietzsche had reminded us that force and violence, the needs and desires of concrete people and groups, as well as unspoken events and coincidences, lie behind the eternal principles and high truths of morality and religion. By abandoning the Kantian insistence on eternal, *a priori* conditions of understanding and universally valid norms, Nietzsche developed a new type of history which examined not the ethereal sources and linear paths but the contingent conditions and circumstances out of which values grow. Foucault followed the same approach for the crucial period between the madman's announcement of the death of God and our age of modernity and postmodernity. This is the period of the rise of man and humanism, and Foucault became the genealogist of modern subjectivity. Man as *subject*, as source of all meaning and the centre of the world, is the latest appearance of the highest value of western metaphysics. Man entered the stage in Descartes's *Meditations* and became Kant's protagonist. Nietzsche traced the appearance of the modern subject to the theological split between world and afterworld. Foucault follows the double process in which a shifting combination of power relations and developing knowledge, of legal discourses and institutional practices, led to the creation of the modern subject through its submission to power. Following the Nietzschean tradition of devaluation of supreme values, a fate that has befallen all metaphysical values, Foucault made his (in)famous wager: '. . . man would be erased, like a face drawn in sand at the edge of the sea.'[19] In drinking the sea, in destroying the transcendent ground of value and meaning, we have made everything, including ourselves, shifty, unstable and transient—sand running through history's hourglass.

For Foucault, power retains an essential reference to the Nietzschean idea of force. Power forms the unthought dark side of metaphysics and becomes the prime mover of social, legal and institutional developments. Knowledge, truth and the law are effects and causes of power and of the will to power. Philosophy and jurisprudence have excluded and silenced the different and the other, have subjected the singular to the universal, and the unique event to the laws of necessity. The task of genealogy is to return the unique to its dignity and place. In the Foucaultian genealogy, modern man is the product of a contingent and unstable combination of a multiplicity of forces and knowledges, of discourses and practices. He is born in a welter of regulations, of meticulous rules and sub-rules, of detailed and fussy inspections and supervisions of the most minute fragments of life and the body. These are modelled on the discipline and surveillance of 'total' institutions, such as prisons, hospitals and barracks. The birth of the modern man is accompanied by a new type of normalising judgment, with its own laws, offences and punishments. Discipline thrives on normalisation. The norm, keeping to the norm and being normal become the form of law and morality. Increasingly areas of life considered too trivial or too local for the law in the premodern period, become the object of a petty but all too important intervention. Genealogy draws the map of modernity and of us, its subjects, as knowing, willing, desiring and as subjected to the operations of power.

Law and Power

Michel Foucault took a great interest in law and, in particular, in the history of criminal law and criminology. But he was also concerned with liberal political philosophy and jurisprudence, and one of his plans, cut short by his untimely

[19] M Foucault, *The Order of Things* (London, Tavistock, 1974) 387.

death in 1984, was to establish a centre for research on the philosophy of law.[20] In his early work, Foucault was interested in examining ways in which difference types of truth and strategies of 'truth-telling' developed historically. In a series of lectures in the 1970s, he argued that judicial practices, criminal law and technique were constantly modified in the course of history and are 'one of the forms by which our society defined types of subjectivity, forms of knowledge, and, consequently, relations between man and truth.'[21] Foucault's epistemological argument was that legal practices are closely related to the dominant forms of the search for knowledge in each epoch. Between the fifteenth and eighteenth centuries, philosophers and scientists followed a form of reflection—the inquiry—developed by criminal law in the middle ages. This kind of interrogation was initially used in order to clarify the conditions and components of particular crimes and to discover their perpetrators. Juridical procedures, such as testimony, witnesses, reconstructions of events or thoughts, soon became dominant throughout the disciplines and the Kantian *Critiques* confirmed them as the main mode of truth seeking.

A new type of power and knowledge emerged in the nineteenth century and led to profound change in the priorities of social control: 'disciplinary society'. Prisons proliferated throughout Europe, and the criminal was seen in a new way. No longer considered a sinner transgressing natural or moral law, the criminal became pathological, someone disturbing the social compact. The dangerous potential of delinquents and criminals meant that the social response was no longer preoccupied with questions such as 'Was a crime committed?' or 'Who did it?' Power was now concerned with individual behaviour, whether subjects obey the rules or not. Ensuring that people follow the norm—being normal—became the preoccupation of this form of power, and a new type of knowledge developed out of the close supervision, observation and examination of populations and individuals.

A number of specialised institutions such as factories, hospitals, schools, barracks and prisons emerged aimed at disciplining and shaping bodies to make them economically productive and socially pliant. These institutions enabled the creation of knowledge from individuals subjected to continuous observation, classification and disciplining. This new knowledge led to the creation of the human sciences, such as psychiatry, psychology and criminology. Knowledge and truth emerged out of this clash of power relations and petty dominations.

Knowledge is power but not in the banal way that knowledge leads to power and vice versa. It cannot be gained prior to, or independently of, the uses to which it will be put as a function of power relations. When the administrative machinery of the great monarchies started measuring the wealth, fertility, death

[20] C Gordon, 'Introduction' in JB Faubian (ed), *Essential Works*, Vol 3 (London, Penguin, 2000) *xxxii*.

[21] M Foucault, 'Truth and Juridical Forms' in *The Order of Things*, above n 19 at 4.

rate and movement of populations for the purpose of its own aggrandisement, it created at the same time the sciences of demography and epidemiology. Statistics, the method that allowed the development of scientific approaches to social policy, acknowledges its debt by calling itself the science of state. The great incarceration of delinquents and criminals in the nineteenth century led to the creation of criminology. But even these expressions do not fully capture the point. These knowledges and sciences were both the cause and effect of power relations and cannot be distinguished from them. The object of the Foucaultian analysis is this complex construct of power/knowledge.

If we turn to law and government, their internal organisation does not follow the protocols of rationality, nor does it apply singular principles and essences. On the contrary, the genealogist shows that instead of an ascending succession of rules, the rule of law is the contingent outcome of a succession of competing types of domination, all of which back their law with violence. The post-medieval world based domination on the absolute power of the Sovereign over his subjects. This was replaced by a regime of disciplining and 'bio-power' in which power in close collaboration with knowledge and law is exercised on the body. This power/knowledge/law construct creates the modern individual as both free and subjected. The modern person is subjected in that he is 'subjectified', created in schools and workshops, factory floors and barracks, in ways that serve the functional needs of economic, military and administrative systems of power. Rather than a consistent system of norms, the modern legal system resembles an experimental machine 'full of parts that came from elsewhere, strange couplings, chance relations, cogs and levers that aren't connected, that don't work, and yet somehow produce judgements, prisoners, sanctions and so on.'[22]

But while this ill-fitting but productive machine worked in the shadows shaping the bodies and souls of the modern subject, the theories of sovereignty and right which emerged from the natural law tradition were read onto the disciplinary technologies, and concealed the way in which they reproduced domination. The discourse of right was transferred from the Sovereign to the rights of subjects who became the 'collective' Sovereign of democracy. Democracy extended certain limited protections and guarantees to its subjects. But as the disciplines themselves were constituted and propagated by legal and administrative practices, rights offered limited protections against the power of the machinery of the state. In an elaborate hall of mirrors, legal rights promised protection against domination and subjection, but rights themselves had come to existence and were supported by the very disciplinary technologies, which acted as the dark side of the brilliant pronouncements of freedom, equality and the rule of law. Constitutions, legal rights and the rule of law legitimised this new form of power. This justificatory role was particularly evident in legal and political philosophy, which focused on rights and neglected the fact that they were only

[22] Quoted in C Gordon, 'Afterword' in *Power/Knowledge* (Brighton, Harvester, 1980) 257.

the surface of a much deeper penetration of power into the social and individual body.

From the perspective of genealogy, the disciplinary operations of law and their representation by jurisprudence are separated by an abyss. Jurisprudence is preoccupied with the 'question of law', as formulated by Kant. How can we reconcile freedom and coercion, value and fact? What are the normative sources that create a valid duty of obedience? The various answers to these questions from Hobbes to Kant and Rousseau claimed that a social compact lay at the foundation of society and state, protecting basic individual rights by enshrining them in constitutions and bills of rights. In this picture, the role of law was to control the exercise of power and guarantee that the Sovereign, in its monarchical or democratic guise, would not transgress the parameters of the agreement. The eighteenth and nineteenth centuries became the classical age of jurisprudence. Grand theories of the state and sovereignty, of the social contract and the rule of law, of freedom and equality, proliferated. The ideal of the universal intellectual dominated, based on the jurist, the man of law who opposes despotism and wealth and champions the universality of justice and an ideal law.

For liberal political philosophy and jurisprudence, power follows a contractual model and works through punishment and repression. Power is a thing possessed by some and used against the majority that has no access to it. In democratic states, power becomes the object and reward of economic and political competition, in which the powerless try to accede to the position of powerholders. Foucault calls this dominant concept of power, juridico-discursive. Juridical, because its definition of law is that of commands backed by sanctions; discursive, because the best defence against the abuse and excesses of power is the truth of knowledge and the justice of the law.[23] Power lays down the law, which constrains, bans, censors, punishes. All those who oppose it in the name of the ideal believe that there is 'a form of justice linked to a form of knowledge which presupposes that truth is visible, ascertainable, and measurable, that it responds to laws similar to those which register the order of the world, and that to discover it is also to possess its value for purification.'[24] But this agreement between the rulers and their critics meant that power was approached as a substantive and free-floating entity, which is independent of its terrain of operations and of the relationships in which it is exercised.

Foucault argues that this structure of power is linked with the emergence of the modern state out of a motley collection of warring feudal power factions. The first task of modern forms of power was to bring peace and to break down local custom in favour of a centralised state machinery. To achieve this, power used the symbolic order of a common law. The law came to be seen as the

[23] See, for example, J Finnis, *Natural Law and Natural Rights* (Oxford, Clarendon, 1980); R Dworkin, *Law's Empire* (Oxford, Hart, 1998).

[24] M Foucault, *Language, Counter-Memory, Practice* (Ithaca, Cornell University Press, 1977) 204.

emblem of the sovereign and as the sign of abolition of local jurisdictions. As justification of the present or as appeal to a future ideal rule, the law has been both the language of power and of opposition to power, since the late Middle Ages. Moreover, the juridico-discursive paradigm of power has come to dominate because of its ability to conceal the effects and operations of power. The 'question of law' is seen simply as one of obedience to, or transgression of, the code. This simplistic version has suited perfectly the expansion of power's hold.

For Foucault, power must be approached as a positive and productive arrangement of forces. Power produces reality; it creates new objects of intervention and investment, like sexuality or human rights. It gives birth to the individual and to the knowledge we have of him. Power, knowledge and the law are not external to each other. All previous theories of power were based on the great subjects, the King, the State, the ruling class, capital. However, power is not an object of possession but a multiplicity of shifting relations. It is exercised from innumerable points, 'furrowed across individuals, cutting them up and remoulding them, marking off irreducible regions in them, in their bodies and minds.'[25]

But the preoccupation with the legitimacy of power, with sovereignty and right prevented jurisprudence from examining how power confers rationality and acceptability to its practices, how it becomes the 'conduct of others' conduct'.[26] The great theories of sovereignty and right were shadowed by disciplinary technologies of surveillance and control and by local 'capillary' networks of power that spread throughout the body politic. The general legal forms and rules allegedly founded systems of rights and constitutions that restrained the power of the state. But their protective action was supported by those tiny everyday physical mechanisms, the myriad micro-powers of supervision and bodily manipulation, which distributed the subjects in positions of inequality. As analysed in Foucault's classic *Discipline and Punish*, disciplinary technology, the techniques of coercion and subjection of bodies and through them of souls, was the underside, the dark side of societies proclaiming the rule of law, constitutionalism and civil liberties.

This limited understanding of power based on state sovereignty as the ultimate concentration of power and as supreme legislator over a defined territory has been gradually disintegrating. The claims of minority nations and cultures have led to an internal explosion that has undermined the authority of the ethnically defined sovereignty of modernity. Internationally, federal groupings such as the European Union and global institutions—the United Nations, the WTO, the World Bank and the IMF—have weakened the sovereignty of the developing nations and have accelerated the displacement of the classical juridical concept of sovereignty/right with that of power/domination. At the

[25] M Foucault, *The History of Sexuality*, above n 14, 96.

[26] Preface to M Foucault, *The Uses of Pleasure: The History of Sexuality*, Vol 2 (London, Penguin, 1989) 203.

domestic level, the society of discipline has developed towards a bio-political form in postmodernity. According to Michael Hard and Antonio Negri, the practices and institutions of normalisation identified by Foucault have proliferated and intensified to such an extent that every aspect of social relations is now subjected to the operations of power. Disciplinary technologies defined those behaviours considered normal and those seen as deviant, marked the boundaries of acceptable thought and practice and, through the exclusion of the abnormal and alien, policed bodies and souls. But the new form of bio-political power extends its hold to the whole of life. 'Power is thus expressed as a control that extends throughout the depths of the consciousnesses and bodies of the population—and at the same time across the entirety of social relations.'[27] These changes make the pre-occupation of legal philosophy with the extent, scope and effectiveness of legal controls over state power even more anachronistic. To paraphrase Foucault, jurisprudence needs to 'cut off the head of the King'—to change its focus from sovereignty to structures of domination.

But what is the critical purchase of this approach? According to Foucault, the job of the critic is to 'reveal the historicity and the contingency of the truths that have come to define the limits of our contemporary ways of understanding ourselves, individually and collectively, and the programmes and procedures assembled to govern ourselves. By doing so, it is to disturb and destabilise these regimes, to identify some of the weak points . . . where thought might insert itself in order to make a difference.'[28] At the origin of all order, social, scientific or institutional, lies an exclusion. Orders establish and perpetuate themselves by rejecting, silencing, and banning certain 'others' as mad, 'deviant' or criminal, but in all instances she is both inside and foreign to dominant culture. The other is excluded either because she is cognitively unthinkable, beyond the ability of current knowledge to comprehend her difference, or because her existence is inimical to the systematic nature and political claims of dominant power relations.[29] But this position of the 'enemy within' turns her into the great threat that must be incarcerated and silenced, or subjected to the objectifying gaze of science in order to yield her secrets and allay the danger she poses to order. In jurisprudence, the other becomes the unthought, that which must be forgotten or translated into the—alien and hostile—terms of the legal system in order to protect law's coherence and systematicity. In this sense, metaphysics and jurisprudence become synonymous. Metaphysics lays down the law of order and the same—policing its boundaries strictly—while jurisprudence abandons the examination of the actual operations of power in favour of de-materialised principles, values and rights.

[27] M Hardt and A Negri, *Empire* (Cambridge, Mass, Harvard University Press, 2000) 24.

[28] N Rose, *Powers of Freedom*, above n 13, 277.

[29] For the place of the other in western thought and the implications for law and jurisprudence see C Douzinas and R Warrington, *Justice (Mis)carried: Ethics and Aesthetics in Law* (Edinburgh, Edinburgh University Press, 1994) and chapter 5 below.

Similarly with the law; productive power cannot be reduced to its laws, nor does it accept law as its sole limit. The rule of law does not replace earlier forms of force and warfare with the abstract law of rules. Humanity translates successive types of violence into systems of rules and moves from one type of domination to another. Society remains a field of antagonism and struggle, and injustice thrives even in those 'rule of law' states that claim to be just. War and violence were at the basis of modern sovereignty. All modern states, sovereigns and legal systems were the products of war, revolution and strife. Whatever the alleged basis of sovereignty, contract, free will or right, power enforces violence. As the form of power changed in the eighteenth century from a centralised power around the sovereign towards its contemporary disciplinary form, rights super-imposed on disciplinary technologies tried to hide the operation of domination. But the attempt of jurisprudence to dissolve power into constitutional theory and to conceal the reality of violence is doomed to fail.[30]

THE GRAMMATOLOGY OF LAW

Belonging and Transgression

Late modernity is associated with the recognition that the values used to ground Being and the principles rehearsed as the ultimate foundations of meaning—God, truth, reason, spirit, man—have been weakened.[31] The eternal laws of western metaphysics are revealed to be contingent, the unconditional determinations determined, the absolute truths relative interpretations. Postmodernism started at this point and philosophy entered its post-metaphysical and post-structuralist phase.

Michel Foucault took us on an unconventional historical tour of the excluded. Jacques Derrida returns to philosophy, ethics and their unthematised concepts. Derrida addresses the traditional themes of metaphysics—consciousness, reason, the sign, self, the other. But Derrida's thinking is located at the edge of metaphysics; a 'deconstruction'; a reversal or a confounding of an order that presented itself as settled. If there is such a 'thing' as deconstructive philosophy, it is an approach to the concepts, strategies and topics that metaphysics has marginalised, excluded and repressed in order to present its empire as closed, unified and coherent. Derrida insists, however, that the deconstruction of metaphysics cannot succeed fully.[32] Every attempt to think the outside can be

[30] Foucaultian genealogy appears as the most political of the poststructuralist canon and has led to many types of critical analysis of legal institutions. See N Rose, *Governing the Soul* (London, Free Association Books, 1999); D Garland, *Punishment and Modern Society* (Oxford, Clarendon, 1991); D Garland, *The Culture of Control* (Oxford, Oxford University Press, 2002); A Hunt and G Wickam, *Foucault and Law* (London, Pluto, 1994); A Hunt, *Governance of Consuming Passions* (London, Palgrave Macmillan, 1996); A Hunt, *A Social History of Moral Regulation* (Cambridge, Cambridge University Press, 2000).

[31] G Vattimo, *The End of Modernity* (Cambridge, Polity, 1988), chapter 1.

[32] J Derrida, *Positions* (Chicago, University of Chicago Press, 1981) 3–14.

co-opted by the system and become one more regional moment in the history of reason. The relationship between metaphysics and deconstruction is circular.

> There is no sense in doing without the concepts of metaphysics in order to shake metaphysics. We have no language—no syntax and no lexicon—which is foreign to this history; we can pronounce not a single destructive proposition which had not already had to slip into the form, logic, and the implicit postulations of precisely what it seeks to contest.[33]

Both belonging and transgression, both law and its violation must be seen as part of the great metaphysical enterprise. They cannot be easily distinguished as both idealists and materialists have attempted to do in their different ways.

For Derrida, the great unthought of metaphysics has been writing. Writing is both the material practice of inscription and notation, and a metaphor for communication and those themes excluded and marginalised by metaphysics. A post-metaphysical philosophy will be a *grammatology*, an examination of the history and operations of *graphe*, writing and the text. *Of Grammatology,* Derrida's early programmatic text, examines the work of philosophers who have privileged the voice (*phone*) over writing.[34] The voice appears to be close to consciousness: when I speak I assume that I am in full control of my thoughts and ideas. Writing, on the other hand, has been approached throughout western philosophy as dangerous, fallen speech that, severed from its meaning-giving author, circulates without the guarantee of the speaking self. At most it is a *supplement,* a secondary addition to speech that assigns it to notation and aids the memory.

> When I speak not only am I conscious of being present for what I think, but I am conscious also of keeping as close as possible to my thought, or to the concept . . . Not only do the signifier and the signified seem to unite, but also, in this confusion, the signifier seems to erase itself or to become transparent.[35]

This is the case with legal interpretation. The law as natural, divine, as the law of reason or the Constitution is presented as transparent and full of meaning. But both its interpretation and transmission are caught up in the uncertainties of writing. The figure of a divine text establishes the literal meaning given to writing: 'a sign signifying, a signifier itself signifying an eternal verity, eternally thought and spoken in the proximity of a present logos.'[36] The point is not just that limited, human writing has been given the dignity of the divine speech. It is rather that the meaning of words such as 'literal', 'divine', 'natural' and *logos* (speech and reason) acquire their meaning through a process that follows the rules of writing. The 'literal' or 'proper' meaning of writing makes it metaphorical, open to re-writing and re-interpretation.

[33] J Derrida, *Writing and Difference* (Chicago, University of Chicago Press, 1978) 280–1.
[34] J Derrida, *Of Grammatology* (Baltimore, Johns Hopkins University Press, 1974).
[35] Derrida, above n 32, at 22.
[36] *Ibid,* at 15.

Deconstruction is post*structuralist* thought because it shares with classical structuralism the turn to language. According to structuralist linguistics, meaning is created in the interstices of language as a result of the differentiation or 'structural value' of sounds and graphic images (signifiers). These differentiated sounds ('cat' sounds different from 'mat' or 'pat') are then combined with concepts or signifieds (the idea or image of a cat) to create the sign or word 'cat'. Such simple linguistic signs are then joined together to create sentences, paragraphs, texts. For Saussure, the father of structuralism, there is always one signifier attached to one signified and the resulting sign has the same meaning and the same referent in each instance of repetition and use. Signs transmit a content, a thought, representation or meaning which, as the kernel of the communication process, precedes and governs it.

Deconstruction argues that language does not mime reality, and thought does not come in neatly packaged units, which are then put into words. No thought or consciousness exists in pre-linguistic form. Signs, words and images come into existence and acquire meaning by being differentiated from other signs. But if this is the case, a sign does not refer just to itself. To become itself, the sign must take a detour through all the other signs from which it is distinguished. This spatial distinction is accompanied by a temporal deferral. The sign or signs must leave the present and sink into the past to let the next sign present itself, so that the now past sign can acquire its identity through its differentiation from the present one. Derrida has called this process of necessary spatial and temporal differentiation *différance*.[37] In the philosophy of *différance*, every element of a system is constituted through the traces of all the others. Nothing is ever just present or absent. Language is the effect of differences and traces as is the subject, consciousness and all the other privileged terms of metaphysics. 'All the conceptual oppositions of metaphysics (signifier/signified, sensible/intelligible, writing/speech, passivity/activity etc) to the extent that they ultimately refer to the presence of something present (for example in the form of the identity of the subject who is present for all his operations . . .) become nonpertinent.[38]

A related critique addresses the problem of the repetition of the sign. In the representational model of language, a sign transmits an idea or concept under the assumption that it has the same meaning in each instance of use. The act of transmission leaves the content unaffected and passes it from the mind of the sender to the mind of the receiver. But a sign can act as a sign only if it can be repeated. A private language or sign is meaningless to those who are not privy to its rules. Each repetition differentiates spatially and defers temporally. The

[37] '*Differance is the systematic play of differences, of the traces of differences, of the spacing* by means of which elements are related to each other. This spacing is simultaneously active and passive (the *a* of *différance* indicates this indecision as concerns activity or passivity, that which cannot be governed by or distributed between the terms of this opposition) production of the intervals without which the "full" terms would not signify, would not function': J Derrida, *Positions*, above n 32, 27.

[38] *Ibid*, 29.

first and the second usage of a sign, sentence or text are separate and occur at two different points in time. Repetition is the absolute prerequisite for the sign's function, the production of meaning. But the nature of iterability is such that meaning can never be fully controlled by either speaker or listener.

> The reason that allows what I say to mean something, is at the same time the reason that frustrates the expectation of fully matching saying and meaning. Iterability inscribes otherness in the self and difference in the same.[39]

Let us now turn briefly to three strategies, adopted by poststructuralist jurisprudence, in order to deconstruct the concepts, argumentation, textual organisation and inter-textual character of legal texts.

Concepts and Conceptual Chains

The first approach focused on major jurisprudential and doctrinal concepts and through close reading showed that legal texts cannot deliver the conceptual homogeneity or doctrinal coherence they promise. One strategy popular with critical legal scholars in the United States was to show that legal texts followed a quasi-structuralist arrangement animated by conceptual juxtapositions and bipolarities. The public/private divide, for example, underpins the idea of the rule of law and supports areas of individual autonomy free of state intervention. The rule/policy opposition permeates tort and contract, while the opposition between universalism and cultural relativism or communitarianism has dominated the debate on human rights. The distinction between fact and value becomes the is/ought distinction of legal positivism, while that between form and substance—and its double between principles and policies—expresses the faultline of legal hermeneutics. These bipolarities in theory and doctrine are presented as markers of two distinct and antagonistic forms of legal reasoning, doctrinal organisation or theoretical argumentation.

Consider for example, the 'grand' and 'normal' styles of judicial reasoning. The former emphasises policy and discretion—it claims to follow the intention of the legislator and the purpose of the rule and examines the wider social desirability of alternative outcomes. The latter proposes strict adherence to the rules, interprets literally and promotes judicial abstinence when 'gaps' appear in the legal edifice. Again, consider the juxtaposition between rules and policy. Rules are said to make for certainty, predictability and fairness, while policies and discretion make for substantive justice and purposefulness in interpretation. The terms of the opposition are presented as external, but each one is constituted through its differential rather than positive value, and its identity depends on its difference from its opposite. As a result, neither can be properly constituted without a trace of its opposite inhabiting it and barring its closure. The concept

[39] J Derrida, 'Limited Inc' (1977) 2 *Glyph* 162 at 199–200.

is not opposed to its other, rather it is intertwined with it, and, in this sense, legal concepts are non-identical at their core. These bipolarities represent the dream of legal unity—totality and order—but are undermined by what Derrida has called a 'regulated incoherence within conceptuality'.[40]

Doctrinal construction presents a part of law as a closed structure of norms that cohere according to formal principles of non-contradiction. Contract law, for example, or a particular doctrine, such as mistake or misrepresentation, is separated, and the chosen sources, case reports or statutory provisions, are treated as the vessels of a special type of rule, the *ratio decidendi* or reason for the decision. The conceptual opposition—form/substance, rule/policy etc—is then presented as the organising principle of the structure and one of its poles is presented as the dominant centre. But the operation of extracting norms and *rationes* from complex texts, such as law reports, is unavoidably controversial. Rule extraction is the result of judicial institutional power rather than of textual or normative closure. Furthermore, doctrinal structures are decentred and doubly open: first, towards their outside—those areas of law excluded in the determination of the materials to be treated as relevant—and, secondly, because of the differential value that allows the opposition to operate.

Duncan Kennedy has demonstrated, for example, how common law doctrinal categories fail in their attempt to mediate a 'fundamental contradiction' between self and others. This contradiction pervades the whole law and acts as the deep structure of surface doctrinal oppositions, condemning legal texts to endless and fruitless repetition.[41] Kennedy's work was followed by more specific studies. Gerald Frug's analysis of administrative law concluded that the pervasive objective/subjective opposition cannot hold: 'The facets of organisational life that need to be subjective have become so constrained by objectivity that they cannot convincingly represent the expression of human individuality. Similarly the facets that need to be objective have become so riddled with subjectivity as to undermine their claim to represent common interest.'[42] Similarly, for Clare Dalton, 'within the discourse of doctrine [in contract law] the only way we can define form, is by reference to substance, even as substance can be defined only by its compliance to form . . . Each supposed 'solution' to one of these doctrinal conundra, each attempt at a definition or line-drawing, winds up mired at the next level of analysis in the unresolved dichotomy it purported to leave behind.'[43] These studies popularised the 'indeterminacy thesis', a legal expression of deconstruction's 'undecidability'. The indeterminacy of doctrine is logically and formally unavoidable because 'there will remain in any legal

[40] J Derrida, *Of Grammatology*, above n 34 237–8.

[41] D Kennedy, 'Form and Substance in Private Law Adjudication' (1976) 89 *Harvard Law Review* 1685; 'The Stuctures of Blackstone's Commentaries' (1979) 28 *Buffalo Law Review* 209.

[42] G Frug, 'The Ideology of Bureaucracy in American Law' (1984) 97 *Harvard Law Review* 1277, 1287.

[43] C Dalton, 'An Essay in the Deconstruction of Contract Doctrine' (1985) 94 *Yale Law Journal* 997, 1002.

dispute a logically and empirically unanswerable formal problem, that granting substantially greater discretion or limiting discretion through significantly greater rule-boundedness in the formation of the prevailing legal command is always perfectly plausible.'[44]

These problems cannot be avoided by using the 'context' of the rule or text. Indeterminacy is not resolved by adopting a constructive approach to interpretation and attending to the intention of the legislator or the context of the judgment. While legal interpretation takes place in the context of a particular conflict, every 'context' in itself is a text that needs further interpretation. Authorial intention, particularly when the author is a collegiate body, like the Framers of the Constitution or Parliament, is even more inscrutable than the meaning of the text. Opening the text to its context is a necessary hermeneutical operation but, if anything, it multiplies interpretative difficulties. Reading a law report in terms of its politics, as critical legal scholars tend to do, is a valuable process. But this, in turn, opens to further and often inconsistent readings of the law in terms of its economic function, as the school of law and economics does; its ideological operation, as Marxists do; or its aesthetic organisation and psychoanalytical layers in a law and literature reading. Legal texts are bound by their context but the context itself is boundless.

Argumentative Inconsistencies

A second level of deconstruction moves from conceptual paradoxes to the arrangement of arguments in legal texts. Motivated by the desire for clarity, rigour and coherence, legal argumentation moves to its conclusions in an effortless manner, in which argumentative development and closure follow naturally from the premises, and any embarrassing evidence is treated as insignificant exception. Yet a close reading of the texts often reveals contradictions, disparities and conflicts within and between argumentative lines that frustrate the promises of the text's closure and open possibilities that the textual surface ignores.

Take for example the well-known rules on offer and acceptance in the law of contract that have become a *cause celèbre* of postmodern jurisprudence.[45] An offer becomes binding when the offeree has accepted all the important terms of the offer and has expressed this acceptance to the offeror in a clear and unequivocal way. Contract law assumes a representational model of language, accord-

[44] M Kelman, *A Guide to Critical Legal Studies* (Cambridge, Mass, Harvard University Press, 1987) 16 and 245–61.

[45] P Goodrich, 'Contractions' in A Carty (ed), *Postmodern Law* (Edinburgh, Edinburgh University Press, 1990) and *Oedipus Lex*, 198–222; C Douzinas and R Warrington, 'Posting the Law: Social Contracts and the Postal Rule's Grammatology' (1991) 4 *International Journal for the Semiotics of Law* 115; S Gardiner, 'Trashing with Trollope: A Deconstruction of the Postal Rule in Contract' (1992) 12 *Oxford Journal of Legal Studies* 170.

ing to which ideas, thoughts and the acceptance of the offer are first formed in the mind of the contractors and then communicated in linguistic form. Once the minds have 'met' through the assent of the offeree the contract has been completed and is binding on the parties. When the contractors are present, the requirement of a separate communication of the acceptance is deemed unnecessary. Under the prevalent cultural phonocentrism,[46] in face to face negotiations, the voice, the best expression of consciousness, will clarify intentions and prevent future disagreements as to the meaning and terms of the contract. When however negotiations are conducted *inter absaentes*, by means of a letter, fax, telex or email, communication is an indispensable element for the acceptance of the offer and the conclusion of the contract.

One would expect that in such cases, an offer would be turned into a binding contract upon the delivery of the letter of the offeree and its perusal by the offeror. However, according to the 'postal rule', a hallowed part of contract law introduced in the case of *Adams v Lindsell* in 1818, an acceptance is binding from the moment of its posting by the offeree. It remains binding upon the unsuspecting offeror even if it is lost, destroyed or never delivered—an eventuality all too real for those living within the jurisdiction of the Royal Mail. Contract law accepts that the moments of circulation and communication of letters and acceptances are distinct and may be temporarily or permanently disconnected. If that happens, circulation takes precedence over the 'meeting of minds' and creates binding effects. This precedence is not just temporal. There is always a possibility—therefore a necessary possibility—that the letter may not arrive. In this case, the principle of the postal rule, according to which the circulation of letters and signs creates effects although there has been no communication or agreement between the parties, turns into the principle of the main rule with its demand for clear communication. These 'exceptional' cases help us understand the norm.

The standard contract law textbook expresses surprise at the postal rule because it completely undermines the metaphysics of contract. It appears strange that the requirement of communication, which is 'devoid' of all practical content in face-to-face contracts is not applicable 'in the most important arena of its application.'[47] It proceeds to explain the anomaly through the history of the rule. '*Adams v Lindsell* was the first offer and acceptance case in English law and, in 1818 there was no rule that acceptance must be communicated. As so often happens in English law, the exception is historically anterior to the rule.'[48] The cornerstone of the law, which regulates the communication, verification and validity of a contract, is grounded on its exception. The law of communication and agreement relies on interference and disagreement. And as the textbook states, this is a common occurrence in common law. The exception, the law of the letter and of writing, puts the law and contract into

[46] J Derrida, *Positions*, above n 32, chapter 1.

[47] Cheshire and Fifoot, *Law of Contract*, 10th edition (London, Butterworths, 1981) 46.

[48] *Ibid.*

circulation. The letter (the structural effect of writing) comes before the *phone* (the belief in the unmediated presence of consciousness and intention in the voice and in the possibility of uninterrupted agreements) and indicates that semiotic circulation takes precedence over semantic communication. This is the case in agreements between both absent and present contractors and throughout the written archive of the law. Writing, the privileged mode of legality, with its difference, deferral and repetition, both facilitates and frustrates law's promise of order and closure.

Intertextual Possibilities

A third type of heterogeneity results from the intertextual character of legal texts. Legal documents are full of discrepancies and inconsistencies. These arise from the fact that their various elements, parts and layers, with their different roles, functions and operations, are brought together with quotes and grafts from other texts. These admixtures must survive in uneasy and unstable combinations and become authoritative in various unpredicted and unpredictable new contexts. Judgements and law reports are a case in point. The evidence offered in trials and recorded in the reports is not constructed and evaluated against some 'hard' external reality. On the contrary, the construction of the relevant law (the major premise of the legal syllogism) and fact-finding (the minor premise) follows standard and coherent narrative frameworks drawn from the stock of specialist and common knowledge. Events, contradictory evidence and conflicting witness statements must be constructed into a narrative framework, which carries tacit evaluations within it.[49] Adjudication involves the choice of one coherent and plausible narrative for the emplotment of the facts of the case from those on offer, which is then 'matched' with the narrative pattern of the legal rule. But there is more; the relevant law may come from many different sources and, at common law, it involves, as we saw, the extraction of an authoritative legal rule from the narrative of precedent cases and law reports. This again means that the different layers that have gone into the writing of the judgment may lead to different formulations of the rule, from the most abstract and general to a concrete statement that stays close to the narrative of the earlier case. The potential for multiple formulations of the facts and law of both present and previous cases and the continuous dialogue of legal texts with non-legal contexts, creates a fertile ground for alternative readings. These discursive discrepancies do not amount to formal contradictions and cannot be weeded out by the protocols of legal reasoning. As a result, they have largely remained hidden and have become a privileged terrain for postmodern jurisprudence.

[49] B Jackson, *Law, Fact and Narrative Coherence* (Liverpool, Deborah Charles Publications, 1985).

One strategy concentrates on the discrepancy between the surface arguments of the text and its rhetorical organisation. Legal texts, like a certain type of philosophy, have always aspired to a state of linguistic transparency in which the clarity and rigour of argument will not be contaminated by the 'irrational' and devious figures of speech. Plato fired the opening salvo in this campaign by expelling poets from his Republic. John Locke and the early Wittgenstein followed suit by trying to imagine a fully logical language not dissimilar to mathematics. But this is both impossible and undesirable. Legal and philosophical texts, as linguistic constructs and repositories of meaning, are rhetorical like all texts. Indeed, the texts that most stubbornly deny their rhetorical construction are best suited to their deconstruction.

Take, for example, John Finnis' *Natural Law and Natural Rights*, an influential contemporary restatement of the naturalist tradition. Finnis attempts to ground his list of eternal and absolute goods on intuition and practical reasoning rather than on traditional or divine authority. A central trope in this endeavour is the figure of the 'sceptic', who throughout the text challenges its insights and is juxtaposed to 'clear-headed and wise men'. These two figures are used to cajole and put pressure on the reader to accept the 'self-evidently' true character of the argument. The sceptic is presented as slightly dim and villainous; he cannot grasp the meaning of self-evidence and instead uses rhetoric and flowery language in his attempt to mis-direct the reader. The operation of self-evidence as a method of proof is not discussed, because it would have to be 'embarrassingly complex'; but the sceptic who doubts it is 'disqualified from the pursuit of knowledge' and becomes coherent only 'by asserting nothing'. Seductions and promises are the terrain of literature; threats and sanctions the domain of the law. Against its claim to propose a contemporary natural law argument, the rhetorical organisation of the text shows it to be the opposite—a legal positivism. As in all positivism, a sovereign power (the author) commands the subject (the reader) using rewards (self-evidence) and punishments (putting to silence). At the end, the text admits inadvertently that its claims are 'plays on meanings and references'—in other words rhetoric.[50] The elaborate attempt to ground the good on the denial of rhetoric can only be conducted in a highly rhetorical fashion, which undermines the jurisprudential claims.

Law and Violence

In a talk given to a conference at the Cardozo Law School in 1989, Derrida turned to political philosophy and jurisprudence and associated his work with the critical legal studies movement.[51] This lecture was of great importance for

[50] J Finnis, *Natural Law and Natural Rights* (Oxford, Clarendon, 1980) 67, 69, 75, 408.

[51] J Derrida, 'Force of Law: 'The Force of Law: "The Mystical Foundation of Authority" ' (1990) 11 *Cardozo Law Review* 919–1046.

the so-called 'political turn' of deconstruction. Early deconstruction had been criticised for excessive formalism, aestheticism and scant recognition of political realities. Derrida's (in)famous statement that 'there is nothing outside of the text' was a rare philosophical sound bite aphoristically stating his position that language, communication and social interaction cannot avoid, as commonly assumed, the uncertainties and ambiguities of the written text. But it was often misinterpreted by opponents of deconstruction to signify extreme idealism, disregard for the real world and literary and philosophical reductionism. But the 'Force of Law' signified a clear turn towards political and ethical engagement, symbolised by the discussion of law and justice. From that point, deconstruction has become engaged with questions of ethical responsibility, the meaning of friendship and the complex relationship with the other. In recent years, before his death in 2004, Derrida wrote a number of essays on contemporary political events. He denounced the Kosovo and Iraq wars and devoted a book to 'rogue' elements and states, in which he attacked the United States as the greatest rogue.[52] Derrida became preoccupied with the concept of sovereignty as the basis of all tragedies and abuses of modernity. It is to this political and ethical type of deconstruction that we now turn.

The critical traditions associated with Marxism, Nietzsche, realism or feminism have consistently asked the question: 'whose interests are served by law?'; what extralegal power imbalances and asymmetries—class, gender or race—are reflected in the operations of an institution which claims to be neutral, natural, above politics and the contingencies of everyday life? Deconstruction does not refute these critiques. Deconstruction de-sediments 'the superstructures of law that both hide and reflect the economic and political interests of the dominant forces of society.'[53] But Derrida is concerned to go beyond that well-established critique in order to explore two crucial relationships that have determined the life of the institution: that between law and force and that between law and justice.

Law is intimately connected with force. There is no law if it cannot be potentially enforced, if there is no police, army and prisons to punish and deter possible violations. In this sense, force and enforcement are part of the very essence of legality. Modern law, coming out of the endless feuds of princes and local chiefs, claimed a monopoly of violence in the territory of its jurisdiction and used it to protect the ends and functions it declared legal, but also to protect the empire of the law itself. This violence that follows the law routinely, and forms the background against which interpretation can work, is called 'law preserving' by the German philosopher, prophet and *flanneur* Walter Benjamin. It guarantees the permanence and enforceability of law. There are two aspects to the violence that conserves the law.

[52] J Derrida, *Voyous* (Paris, Galilée 2003).
[53] J Derrida, 'The Force of Law', above n 51, 923.

'Every juridical contract . . . is founded on violence' says Derrida and the legal academic Robert Cover agrees: 'Legal interpretation takes place in a field of pain and death'.[54] Legal judgments are statements and deeds. They both interpret the law and act on the world. A conviction and sentence at the end of a criminal trial is the outcome of the judicial act of legal interpretation, but it is also the authorisation and beginning of a variety of violent acts. The defendant is taken away to a place of imprisonment or of execution—acts immediately related to, indeed flowing from, the judicial pronouncement. Again as a result of civil judgments, people lose their homes, their children, their property or they may be sent to a place of persecution and torture.

The recent turn of jurisprudence to hermeneutics, semiotics and literary theory has focused on the word of the judge and forgotten the force of the word.[55] The meaning-seeking and meaning-imposing component of judging is analysed as reasoned or capricious, principled or discretionary, predictable or contingent, shared, shareable or open-ended according to the political standpoint of the analyst. The main if not exclusive function of many judgements is to legitimise and trigger past or future acts of violence. The word and the deed, the proposition and the sentence, the constative and the performative are intimately linked.

Legal interpretations and judgments cannot be understood independently of this inescapable imbrication in violent action. In this sense legal interpretation is a practical activity, other-orientated and designed to lead to effective threats and—often violent—deeds. This violence is evident at each level of the judicial act. The architecture of the courtroom and the choreography of the trial process converge to restrain and physically subdue the body of defendant. From the defendant's perspective, the common but fragile facade of civility of the legal process expresses a recognition 'of the overwhelming array of violence ranged against him and of the helplessness of resistance or outcry'.[56] But for the judge too, legal interpretation is never free of the need to maintain links with the

[54] R Cover, 'Violence and the Word' (1986) 95 *Yale Law Journal* 1601.

[55] The linguistic and interpretative aspects of the law were always a part of legal theory. They were somewhat neglected during the heyday of legal positivism, but they have been reinstated within jurisprudence. Law is often now seen as an exclusively linguistic and meaningful construct and various types of hermeneutics and literary theory have been adopted to explain and justify the operations of the 'prison house of language'. Within orthodox jurisprudence, R Dworkin, *Law's Empire*, above n 23; S Levinson and S Mailloux, *Interpreting Law and Literature: A Hermeneutic Reader* (Evanston, Northwestern University Press, 1988) and S Fish, *Doing What Comes Naturally* (Oxford, Clarendon, 1989) are examples of the linguistic turn. More critical approaches can be found in P Goodrich, *Reading Law* (Oxford, Blackwell, 1987) and *Languages of Law* (London, Weidenfeld and Nicholson, 1990); P Fitzpatrick, *The Mythology of Modern Law* (London, Routledge, 1991) and C Douzinas and R Warrington with S McVeigh, *Postmodern Jurisprudence* (London, Routledge, 1991). Whilst the importation of literary theory and the welcome recognition of the fact that law is, at least in part, a linguistic construct, has done much to revive jurisprudence, this chapter is particularly concerned to stress the violent nature and unjust action that characterises much legal action—something often missing from literary theory's analysis of law.

[56] R Cover, 'Violence and the Word', above n 54, 1607; A Sarat and T Kearns, *Law's Violence* (Ann Arbor, University of Michigan Press, 1992).

effective official behaviour that will en-*force* the statement of the law. Indeed, the expression 'law enforcement' recognises that force and its application lies at the heart of the judicial act. Legal sentences are both propositions of law and acts of sentencing.

Legal interpretation then is bonded, bound both to the deeds it triggers off and the necessary conditions of effective domination within which the sentence of the law will be enforced. Without such a setting that includes a formidable array of institutions, practices, rules and roles—police, prison guards, immigration officers, bailiffs, lawyers, etc—the judicial word would remain a dead letter. All attempts to understand legal judgments and judicial decision-making as exclusively hermeneutical are incomplete. Legal interpretations belong both to horizons of meaning and to an economy of force. Whatever else judges do, they deal in fear, pain and death. If this is the case, aspirations to coherent and shared legal meaning are liable to flounder on the inescapable and tragic line that distinguishes those who mete out violence from those who receive it. Legal decisions lead to people losing their homes or children, being sent back to their persecution and torture: legal interpretation leads to people losing their lives.

But there is also the violence of language itself. The law is full of examples in which people are judged in a language or an idiom they do not understand. This is the standard case with asylum-seekers who are routinely asked by immigration officials to present their case and to recount the brutalities and torture they have suffered in a language they do not speak. 'The violence of an injustice has begun when all the members of a community do not share the same idiom throughout' states Derrida.[57] For Jean-Francois Lyotard an extreme form of injustice is that of an *ethical tort* or *differend*, in which the injury suffered by the victim is accompanied by a deprivation of the means to speak about it or prove it.

> This is the case if the victim is deprived of life, or of all liberties, or of the freedom to make his or her ideas or opinions public, or simply of the right to testify to the damage, or even more simply if the testifying phrase is itself deprived of authority . . . Should the victim seek to by-pass this impossibility and testify anyway to the wrong done to her, she comes up against the following argumentation, either the damages you complain about never took place, and your testimony is false; or else they took place, and since your are able to testify to them, it is not an ethical tort that has been done to you.[58]

When an ethical tort has been committed, the conflict between the parties cannot be decided equitably, because no rule of judgment exists that could be applied to both arguments. In such instances, language reaches its limit because no common language can be found to express both sides. The violence of injustice begins when the judge and the judged do not share a language or idiom. It continues when all traces of the particularity of the person before the law are

[57] J Derrida, 'Declarations of Independence' (1986) 15 *New Political Science* 18.
[58] J-F Lyotard, *The Differend* (Manchester, Manchester University Press, 1988) 5.

reduced to a register of sameness and cognition mastered by the judge. Indeed all legal interpretation and judgment presuppose that the other, the victim of language's injustice, is capable of language in general—man as a speaking animal. But as the Scottish poet Tom Leonard put it:

> And their judges spoke with one dialect,
> But the condemned spoke with many voices.
> And the prisons were full of many voices,
> But never the dialect of the judges.
>
> And the judges said:
> 'No one is above the Law.'[59]

But force has another important role in law's life: force institutes and founds law. Most modern constitutions were introduced against the protocols of constitutional legality that existed at the time of their adoption, as a result of defeat in war, popular uprisings or colonial occupation. Revolutionary violence suspends the law and constitution, and justifies itself by claiming to be founding a new state, a better constitution and a just law to replace the corrupt or immoral system it rebels against. At the point of its occurrence, violence will be condemned as illegal, brutal, evil. But when it succeeds, revolutionary violence will be retrospectively legitimised as means to the end of social and legal transformation. Most legal systems are the outcome of force, the progeny of war, revolution, rebellion or occupation. This founding violence is either re-enacted in the great pageants that celebrate nation and state-building or forgotten in acts of enforcement of the new law and of interpretation of the new constitution.

The French revolution has been retrospectively legitimised by its *Declaration des droits de L'homme*, as has the American revolution by the Declaration of Independence and the Bill of Rights. But these founding documents will carry in themselves the violence of their foundation, as they move from the original act to its representations. The American Bill of Rights is an obvious example. The violence of the militias, so important in the war of independence, is perpetuated in the constitutionally protected right to bear arms, which some two centuries after the revolution, still keeps the United States in a state of war. Similarly, capital punishment reproduces the founding violence of war in every execution, accompanying legal operations as the dark and empowering side of legal normality. But these repetitions of the traumatic genesis of the new law are reinterpreted as demands of legality, and the original violence is consigned to oblivion. Indeed one of the most important strategies in this politics of forgetting is the creation of a dominant approach to legal interpretation. Once victorious, revolutions or conquests produce 'interpretative models to read in return, to give sense, necessity and above all legitimacy to the violence that has

[59] T Leonard, 'Situations Theoretical and Contemporary' quoted in W Maley, 'Beyond the Law: the Justice of Deconstruction' (1999) 10 *Law and Critique* 49, at 59–60.

produced, among others, the interpretative model in question, that is, the discourse of its self-legitimation.'[60] For Derrida, therefore, the founding and conserving violence of law cannot be separated as Benjamin and Cover tried to do. The two types of violence are intertwined and contaminate each other, as contemporary acts of legal 'conservation' or interpretation repeat and re-establish the original law-making violence which establishes the new law.

Even within well-established and democratic legal systems, popular violence shadows that of the state and moves the law in unpredictable and, for the powerful, undesirable, ways. The law accepts a limited right to protest and strike, and in this sense acknowledges, in a reluctant and fearful manner, that violence cannot be written out of history. Driving the public disorders and protests in the miners strike, the poll tax riots and the anti-globalisation demonstrations, many commentators condemned the protesters by calling them undemocratic. The argument was that in western democratic and rule of law states, people have sufficient instruments to put pressure on governments and change policies and laws through the available democratic channels. And yet, the history of Britain and the West is replete with protests and riots and strikes that, condemned as they were at the time, contributed hugely to the freedoms and rights we take for granted. The Diggers and Levellers, the Gordon riots and the Reform protests, the suffragettes and the civil rights movements, the protesters in East Germany, Prague, Bucharest and Belgrade, to name only a few obvious cases, have changed constitutions, laws and governments.

Protests mostly challenge the conserving violence of law, breaking minor public order regulations in order to highlight greater injustices. As long as protesters ask for this or that reform, this or that concession, however important, the state can accommodate it. What the state is afraid of is the 'fundamental, founding violence, that is, violence able to justify . . . or to transform the relations of law and so to present itself as having a right to law.'[61] But the characteristic insecurity that the law feels in the face of its own foundation makes it portray radical protests and desperate attempts to bring about reform by unconventional means as challenges to its founding authority, as acts of revolutionary upheaval. The American civil rights marchers were often painted as communists, the striking miners were called the 'enemy within' and the protesters of Eastern Europe were called agents of the CIA. This exaggerated response to popular protest shows, however, that 'for a critique of violence—that is to say, an interpretative and meaningful evaluation of it—to be possible, one must first recognise meaning in a violence that is not an accident arriving from outside law.'[62]

[60] J Derrida, 'Force of Law', above n 51, 993.
[61] *Ibid*, 990.
[62] *Ibid*, 993.

Justice and Law

There is no law without enforcement. But the force necessary for law's operation is commonly exercised in the name of justice. Indeed the force of law can be interpreted as necessary or violent intervention through an act of judgement. Force is the morally neutral application of pressure upon an entity. The application of force can be evaluated according to moral criteria, highest amongst them justice. Violence is a morally condemned application of force. There is no natural or physical violence despite phrases like 'violent earthquake'. Violence is an unacceptable use of force and belongs to the symbolic order of law and morality. Law and justice are not opposed; they are linked in a paradoxical way. When law violates its established procedures and harms someone; when it does not recognise or uphold rights which have been given already or are reasonably expected; when it breaches basic principles of equality and dignity—in all these cases the law acts unjustly according to its own internal criteria of justice. We can call this first type of justice, legal justice; it is internal to the law and operates when the law matches its own standards and principles.

But legal justice is only one facet of justice. A different conception of justice starts from the statement of the philosopher Emmanuel Levinas that justice exists in relation to the other person.[63] The other is a singular, unique finite being with certain personality traits, character attributes and physical characteristics. But to me, she is also an infinite other, this finite person puts me in touch with infinite alterity. As phenomenology has argued, I cannot know the other as other, I can never comprehend fully her intentions or actions, I can never have an appropriate adequation or presentation, because no immediate access or perception of otherness exists. The otherness of the other means that she is never fully present to me; I can approach her only by an analogy of the perceptions, intentions and actions available to my own consciousness. As a result, while I have to be just to the other as a finite being with specific demands and desires, I can never be fully just, because the infinity of the other makes the giving of justice impossible. We need criteria in order to be just to the other, but these do not correspond to the demands of justice. Indeed any attempt to turn justice into a theory (as some Marxists did) or a series of normative statement sand commands (as Kantians do) is necessarily a violation of justice. Theories and laws need to be applied; but every application would turn the uniqueness of the other into an instance of the concept or a case of the norm, and would immediately violate their singularity. The only principle of justice is respect for the singularity of the other. This principle takes the form of a universal imperative, an absolute command, but this is a strange law—indeed law may be a misnomer—because unlike other theories of justice, it gives no advance instructions or advice except to say 'be unique in your encounters with singular others'.

[63] See chapter 5 below.

The infinite dwells in the finite, justice dwells in the law, but justice also challenges the law since the law must forget the infinity of the other. The law has to deal with many others and it must compare and contrast them. To do that it puts them on the same scale, it compares them by using tools like rights, duties—common denominators that will allow the different to become similar and the other, the same. Justice is immanent to the law but this immanence means that law is unequal to itself—it contains within itself that which opens to a new law, a new politics, a new place or non-place (utopia). Justice lies within the law as a gap, a chasm, which judges specific instances of injustice and violence and also the overall direction of the law. Both inside and outside, justice is the horizon against which the law is judged, both for its routine daily failings and for its forgetting of justice. Whether we see the law as an historical institution or as a system of rules and decisions, its operations can be subjected to deconstruction, which either discovers the violence of origins in law's daily operations or unravels its ordered bi-polarities (fact-values, public-private, objective-subjective) and shows that they cannot stabilise the legal system. But this deconstructive operation is precisely the work of justice of which we cannot say 'here it is', in front of us, full and fully revealed. Deconstruction is justice.

The room is full of light. The fire is ashes. All the bottles are empty.

Part 2

Classical Jurisprudence

3

Natural Law, Resistance and Utopia

The problem was so baffling that I decided to put myself in the hands of our so-called philosophers and tell them that I didn't mind what they did to me, as long as they taught me some simple and reliable rule of conduct. With this object in view I started studying philosophy, only to find that I had inadvertently jumped out of the frying pan and into the fire—for the more I had to do with philosophers, the more I became aware of their ignorance and helplessness, until finally the ideas of the man in the street began to seem positively brilliant by comparison. (Menippus Goes to Hell)

These fragments saved from the more general ruin

THE TRADITION OF natural law was exhausted well before our times. Recent jurisprudence examines it as part of the history of ideas, as an intellectual movement and political doctrine that came to a deserved end in the Enlightenment's assault upon myth, religion and prejudice. Standard textbooks start the examination of natural law with Antigone's 'unwritten laws', and then move to the Stoics for whom natural law embodied the 'elementary principles of justice which they believed to be apparent to the "eye of reason" alone.'[1] Cicero enters briefly: 'there is a true law, right reason, in accordance with nature; it is unalterable and eternal.' He is accompanied in cameo appearances by Aquinas, Grotius and Blackstone. Blackstone's statement that 'natural law is binding all over the globe; no human laws have any validity if contrary to it' is explained in a rather embarrassed fashion.[2] All these writers agree that the right and the natural coincide, although they differ in their definition of nature or of nature's creator—who has mutated from the purposive cosmos to God, then to reason and finally to human nature. The transformation of natural law into natural rights during the seventeenth century is hailed as the first victory of modern reason over the medieval witches, superstition and the old order. Locke and Bentham, the English contributors to the debate, are acknowledged as the early precursors of human rights. Locke is the modern revitaliser of the moribund tradition while Bentham is the definitive debunker of

[1] M Cranston, *What are Human Rights?* (Oxford, Bodley Head, 1973) 10–11.
[2] *Ibid*, 11.

any remaining 'nonsense on stilts'. This potted history of natural law ends with the introduction of the Universal Declaration of Human Rights in 1948, which turned naturalistic 'nonsense' into hard-nosed positive rights. For the first time in history, these unwritten, unalterable, eternal, God-given or rational fictions need no longer be embarrassed. Natural rights have been fully recognised and legislated and enjoy the dignity of law, albeit of a somewhat soft kind.

Like all simplified history, this standard presentation of natural law has some elements of truth, but also many gaps and misrepresentations. Its unspoken ideological premise is historicism, namely, the assertion of the superiority of the present over the past—the claim that our contemporary intellectual and political positions are an immense improvement on past ideas and political movements. The history of natural law is a typical example of Whig historiography, in which every idea moves forward towards our present, guided by the inexorable march of reason that erases mistakes and combats prejudices. In this version, international human rights mark the overcoming of the ignorant past while retaining, and at the same time realising, its potential for individual freedom and equality.

We want to refuse this type of historicism and present an alternative history of natural law in which its promise has not and cannot be completed. The premise behind this brief history is not the superiority of the present but the promise of the future. Young Marx wrote that the task of philosophy is to achieve 'a humanised nature and a naturalised humanity'. This is also the unfulfilled potential of natural law and human rights, which to use Ernst Bloch's evocative phrase, express the 'forward-pressing, not-yet-determined nature of human being.'[3] This retelling of the history of natural law tries to follow Bloch's impulse and exhume from the darkness of tradition the concealed concern for a justice that is to come.

THE INVENTION OF NATURE

For Greek philosophy, nature (*physis*), and its law, are born together in an act of resistance against traditional authority. In pre-classical Greece, law and convention, right and custom were identical and as a result the development of a critical approach towards traditional authority was impossible because no principle external to community existed. This attitude is well represented by the Presocratic philosopher Heraclitus, according to whom justice and injustice are human creations. God does not care about either. The philosophical 'discovery' of the idea of nature brings this claim to an end and makes justice the most contested concept in classical Greece. Nature is a critical concept; it must be discovered, because it is occluded by a combination of convention and law and by

[3] E Bloch, *Natural Law and Human Dignity*, DJ Schmidt (trans), (Cambridge, Mass, MIT Press, 1988) *xviii*.

the claims of ancestral authority. By discovering nature, Plato and Aristotle departed radically from that tradition. For the classical philosophers, nature is not just the physical world, the 'way things are' or everything that exists. Nature is a term of distinction, a norm or standard used to separate the work of philosophical and political thought from that which obstructs or hides it, namely the combination of customary law and conventional opinion. As Leo Strauss has elegantly argued, 'originally, the authority par excellence or the root of all authority is the ancestral. Through the discovery of nature, the claim of the ancestral is uprooted; philosophy appeals from the ancestral to the good, to that which is good intrinsically, to that which is good by nature.'[4]

The creation of philosophy and natural law are Promethean acts of rebellion. Philosophy begins when it distinguishes between the truths given by custom, convention or law and the truth or the good arrived at through the reasoned critique of received wisdom. Nature is philosophy's tool, the incendiary and revolutionary Promethean fire used in revolt against authority and the law. Nature's 'discovery' and elevation into an evaluative standard and weapon against convention emancipates reason from the tutelage of power and gives rise to natural right. But if this philosophy of nature is used as a tactical move motivated by the need to combat the claims of authority that ruled early Greek society, its 'discovery' is not so much a revelation or unveiling as an invention, a creation. Nature presents itself as what was hidden by culture because philosophy cannot come into existence or survive if it submits to ancestral or conventional authority. Philosophy and nature are born against the law. To this day, when knowledge and reason are subjected to authority, they are called 'theology' or 'legal learning', but they cannot be the philosophy practised by the Greeks.[5] In this sense, turning nature into norm—into the standard of right—was the greatest early step of rational civilisation, but also a cunning trick against priests and rulers.[6]

Nature as a critical concept acquired philosophical currency in the fifth century, when the Sophists used it in arguments against custom and law. Socrates and Plato, in turn, deployed nature in arguments against the Sophists. They sought to combat the moral relativism of the Sophists and to restore the authority of reason. The Sophists represented the privileged youth of Athens, who despised the old religious taboos and the training for war in equal measure. In setting nature (*physis*) against law (*nomos*) and individual opinion against tradition, they gave *physis* a normative meaning, in which 'to reason' meant to 'criticise'.[7] The Sophists argued that the *nomoi* are social conventions and laws,

[4] L Strauss, *Natural Law and History* (Chicago, University of Chicago Press, 1965) 91.

[5] *Ibid*, 92.

[6] Luc Ferry and Alain Renaut, *From the Rights of Man to the Republican Idea*, Franklin Philip (trans), (University of Chicago Press, 1992) 32–4 present Strauss's naturalism as a rather sterile authoritarianism which cannot be rescued from Aristotelian cosmology. This critique however totally misses out this aspect of Strauss' analysis. For a poetical account of this same history, see Shelley's *Ode to Liberty*.

[7] Bloch, *Natural Law and Human Dignity*, above n 4, 7–9.

and not part of natural order. Nature as the highest norm justifies, in a rather eclectic way, whatever the instincts lead humans to desire.[8] Callicles in *Gorgias* and Thrasymachus in the *Republic* anticipated Nietzsche when they argued that human laws were invented by the weak in order to protect themselves from the strong. Their conception of nature combined the savage with the universal, and stood both for the right of the strongest and for equality for all. With the Sophists, the critique of law and the figure of the naturally free and self-serving individual entered the historical scene.

Plato's response to the Sophist challenge was to re-establish the normative character of nature by showing that, far from contradicting law, it sets the fundamental norm of each being. Plato's late dialogue, *The Laws*, extended the concept of *physis* to include the whole cosmos. But this was not a return to the pre-classical *dike,* the order of the world. This was the order of the soul and of the transcendent spiritual world it inhabits; it was the highest and most natural of orders and animated the empirical cosmos.[9] The distinction between the two spheres, an otherworldly spiritual world and a historical fallen one, and between the two types of nature, those of the soul and of the flesh, acquired political significance much later, when Christianity adopted these philosophical themes and turned them into its dominant ideology. As Luis Dupré put it, the separation of the two worlds 'laid the philosophical basis for the later attempts to integrate the classical concept of nature with that of a Hebrew-Christian Creator beyond nature.'[10]

But our story runs ahead of itself. We must remain, for the moment, with the Greeks. The significance of the debate between Plato and the Sophists was that by juxtaposing *physis* and *nomos* in their various meanings, the debate opened the whole basis of classical civilisation and institutional existence to radical questioning and innovation, and gave rise to political philosophy and jurisprudence. Classical natural right was radically anti-historicist—or to use a term anachronistically—it had something 'objective' about it. But as the radical split between the subject and object—a mainstay of modernity—had not yet occurred, the right reason revealed in nature had none of its modern characteristics. Unlike 'objective' statements, natural right was neither static, nor certain, nor did it mirror an inert nature. To understand its meaning, we need to bracket our contemporary assumptions about nature and culture and place natural light within the teleological cosmos of antiquity.

[8] The classical treatment of *nomos* in Greek thought is J de Romilly, *La Loi dans la pensée Grecque: des origine à Aristote* (Paris, Les Belles Lettres, 1971); see also M Nussbaum, 'The Betrayal of Convention: A Reading of Euripides' *Hecuba*' in *The Fragility of Goodness* (Cambridge, Cambridge University Press, 1986) 397–421.

[9] Plato, *The Laws*, TJ Saunders (trans), (London Penguin, 1988): 'When [the ignorant] use the term 'nature', they mean the process by which the primary substances were created. But if it can be shown that soul came first, not fire or air, and that it was one of the first things to be created, it will be quite correct to say that soul is preeminently natural' 892 c.

[10] L Dupré, *Passages to Modernity* (New Haven, Yale University Press, 1993) 17.

Classical ontology believed that the cosmos, the world and its 'contents', animate or inanimate, has a purpose, *telos* or end. The Greek cosmos included the *physis* of beings, the *ethos* of social mores, the *nomos* of customs and laws and, most importantly, the *logos* or rational foundation of all that exists, which founded the cosmos as a closed but harmonious and ordered universe. Entities were arranged in a hierarchical way, each holding its unique and differential place within the overall scheme according to its proper degree of perfection, 'at the top the incorruptible imponderable luminous spheres, at the bottom, the heavy, opaque material bodies'.[11] The end or *telos* of an entity or being is a state of existence at which disposition or potency reach fulfilment or perfection. The nature of the acorn, for example, is to become a mature oak tree, the purpose of the vine is to produce sweet tasting grapes.

The teleological nature of the cosmos means that all entities have their unique purpose and end. But these purposes do not exist in isolation; they are always in conjunction with the purpose of other things and beings. The end of persons could be pursued and achieved politically, in the city (*polis*). In this sense, the good life is lived according to nature and there is no separation between is and 'ought'. This natural teleology, with its purposeful nature, provided a strong ethics of virtue and value. Right according to nature is what contributes to the being's perfection, what keeps it moving towards its end; wrong or unjust is what violently removes a being from its place, disrupts its natural trajectory and 'prevents it from being what it is.'[12] Natural right, therefore, both transcends reality as an 'ideal', and can be confidently discovered through observation and reasoning. Nature itself, unlike the inert matter of modern science, represents the principle of motion in a purposeful cosmos, in which acorns, lambs and infants can only be understood as a developing order of meaningful and future looking interrelations. Being is always on the move, in a journey that will never end, because perfection is always a step too far, a state always still to come.

The natural constitution of man, his ability to speak and reason, makes him live in the city and to construct his life politically—to be what Aristotle called a *zoon politicon* or political animal. Pleasure can be achieved only in association with others. Love and affection, pity and friendship form the natural kernel of natural right. Justice, the social virtue *par excellence*, is the necessary accompaniment of natural law. Individual happiness is to achieve one's 'standards of excellence' and political activity aims to facilitate individual perfection and the realisation of virtue. A citizen can become excellent only in a just city and a city can become just only if its citizens live a life of virtue. Accordingly, personal morality and political ethics have the same end, peaceful activity in furtherance

[11] B Barret-Kriegel, *Les Droits de l'homme et le Droit Naturel* (Paris, PUF, 1989) 46. It should be emphasised here that this cosmology is intrinsically linked with the inegalitarian nature of classical natural right and of its societies. For Aristotle, slavery was natural and therefore not an affront to natural right.

[12] L Fery and A Renaut, above n 6, 34.

of virtue. Human life according to nature is a life of human excellence or virtue in community with others.

Classical natural law can be described as an ethical and political doctrine, the theory of the 'best polity or regime' in which human perfection and virtue in association with others can be achieved. But as we move from Plato to Aristotle and then to Cicero, the blueprint of the 'best polity' becomes increasingly tempered with pragmatic and circumstantial considerations. For Plato, the right way of life is disclosed by reason against convention, in an ascent from the unreflective opinions of the many to the truth of philosophy. For Aristotle, on the other hand, the terms justice and natural law are attributed mostly to concrete decisions. It is cognitively and morally preferable to judge the justice of particular acts rather than to state general rules, because while nature arranges a hierarchy of ends, no universally valid rules of action exist. In every case or conflict, the just decision will be dictated by the situation and the relevant circumstances. Right according to nature refers precisely to such timely, prudent, just decisions and is obviously mutable.

Right according to nature is particular or legal justice. It opens a wholly new way of looking at legal relations. Its nature is strange to the modern mind. To understand justice in its classical conception, we must examine the end and nature of law. Justice today is a principle or an ideal towards which societies aspire, the (absent) soul of the body of laws. For Aristotle, however, this distinction between law and justice did not exist. The same word *dikaion* was used to express an intimately connected cluster of ethical, legal and political concepts. The *dikaion* or *jus* in Latin means the right or just state of affairs in a particular situation or conflict, according to the nature of that case. Particular justice is achieved in contests between two parties in which a third disinterested person, the *dikastes* or judge, intervenes. His judgement is also called *dikaion,* meaning both the lawful and the just solution.

The *dikaion* is therefore the most polysemic of terms: it is the object of judicial decision-making, the action of the just man and, finally, the end of law. It is a state of affairs in the world—the distribution or share of things decided by the judge—and, as the object of justice—the aim of human acts and the outcome of judicial consideration. The *dikaion* as the art of judging aims at the right proportion between things—it is 'an external relation to be established between persons on the basis of things.'[13] The rightful judgement distributes things to people proportionately, gives them their fair or just share according to the pattern of right relationships. The jurist is not concerned with upholding individual rights or entitlements but with observing the cosmic and civic order, from which he derives guidance. The way of the world teaches patterns of proportionate distribution that the judge must respect and promote. The idea of

[13] R McInerny, 'Natural Law and Natural Rights' in *Aquinas on Human Action* (Washington, DC, Catholic University of America Press, 1992) 217.

proportion is crucial; it brings justice close to the aesthetic beauty immanent in the harmony of the world.

Aristotle's description of the judicial art is detailed, practical and follows the method of natural right. A just distribution involves two elements: a recognition of a state of affairs—of an equitable proportion subsisting amongst things—and a distribution of the disputed things according to this arrangement. First, observation: for classical philosophy, the source of natural law was the natural organisation of the cosmos. The just outcome is already inscribed in the nature of things and relationships, in the cosmic order of interrelated purposes and ends, and awaits its judicial recognition and pronouncement by the judge. The cosmos and everything in it, including the *polis*, are part of a universal harmony—when the various parts and constituents are properly balanced. To be sure, the city does not enjoy perfect justice. But families, social groups and cities—which have come into being spontaneously—gradually develop their political relations, values and constitutions as pre-figurations of the future perfect order. They can serve as models because the belief in perfect justice presupposes that we can extract its idea immanently from existing approximations. Observing reality is the first step to the discovery of the just solution.

The judge acts like a botanist or anthropologist: he observes the connections and relations amongst his fellow citizens, the way in which they arrange their affairs, and in particular the way in which they distribute benefits and burdens. But the just decision is always provisional and experimental, transient and dynamic. In the same way that human nature continuously adjusts to changes, the just decision must take into account new circumstances and contingencies. Finding the *dikaion* is the aim of the classical jurist, but this task is never fully and finally achieved. The *dikaion* always remains a step ahead, full justice is deferred, not here yet and never fully done. In this sense, seeking the just involves the observation of the objective world as well as a futural or transcendent element. 'If we understand the word law as synonymous to a formulated rule, there is no natural law' writes Michel Villey.[14] Natural right is a methodological principle: it helps the discovery of the just solution which lies, not in our conscience or on some strict set of rules, but is part of the external world of human relations. Natural law is unwritten law, its content is never fully known; it has nothing to do with the idea of a positive rule or commandment prevalent in modernity.

Finding the just solution is a practice of argumentation and a political act. The judge considers all the circumstances of the case and the conditions pertaining at the time.[15] He discovers the *dikaion* by using the *ars juris*. Its key principle is *audem alteram partem*: there are always at least two conflicting arguments that must be heard. This style of argument is rhetorical and the

[14] M Villey, *Lecons d'Histoire de la Philosophie du Droit* (Paris, Dalloz, 1962) 240.

[15] 'One cannot know in advance the content of positive justice; it depends on the free decision of the law-giver': Aristotle, *Nicomachean Ethics*, JAK Thomson (trans), (London, Penguin, 1976) VII 61.

method is dialectical. The dialectical approach was an integral part of classical thought and the main scholarly method in theology, philosophy and law until the Renaissance. The dialectically just solution is not deduced from a general rule, nor is it the outcome of a logical exercise but is discovered by the application of knowledge about the nature of things. It will be discovered in reality, through a consideration of arguments, examples and by observation of the relations amongst the parties. The judge considers the pleadings and compares their conflicting and contradicting opinions, seen as partial expressions of reality. Thus, by putting terms and arguments to debate, judges arrive at their decisions dialectically: the dialectical decision is not the only or the truthful opinion but it is the best in the circumstances.

The final ingredient of the just decision is political: in decision-making, the legislator or judge supplements the observation of nature—the dialectical confrontation and the rational justification with an act of will which cannot be fully theorised. Dialectics is always provisional, open to new arguments, experiences and concerns. Legal judgment—conducted in the realms of *praxis* and *techne* rather than science, (*episteme*) is always accompanied by a degree of uncertainty, which is brought to an end by the decision. The *dikaion* is therefore an act of judicial will which, starting from a combination of natural observation and argumentative confrontation, adds a precise meaning and determination (the punishment for such a tort is the sacrifice of two goats) and brings the issue to a close.

Within this broad framework, the various schools of classical philosophy interpreted nature differently. For the Sophists, *physis* was the essence of things—that which endures through change and remains constant behind diversity. The Cynics fought tradition, artifice and institutions and attacked luxury, family and the city-state equally as unnatural inventions. Against the simplicity of the 'dog-life' of the body preached by Diogenes the Cynic, the Hedonists taught and practiced a life of pleasure. Aristippus lived in luxury and preached that the natural is what contributes to happiness; and that happiness is the only criterion for judging the value of institutions. To this day, the Cynics and the Hedonists have remained the forefathers of revolutionary movements; situationists *avant la lettre*. It should be noted that preaching the universal right to pleasure for all is more dangerous to ruling elites, and harder to fulfil, than the message of meagre frugality of the Cynics.[16]

Many times in the history of natural law, an initially revolutionary idea was co-opted by the established powers, tamed and domesticated. Indeed, the final and most dramatic mutation in the early relationship between *physis* and *nomos* was introduced by the Stoics. They preached a private life of tranquillity and reflection and practised *ataraxia* (imperturbability) and self-control over passions and the irrational. The Sophists had set *physis* against *nomos*; the Stoics turned *nomos* into a universal bond and identified the two concepts. The

[16] E Bloch, above n 3, 9.

new natural law was universal and even divine. This divinely sublime nature governed by necessity was raised over positive society and became the sole criterion of valid law. The Stoics were not particularly interested in jurisprudence but they made a lasting contribution to legal thought. Their notion of universal humanity based on the rational essence of man, and equal rights for all was a dramatic departure from the Greek world of freemen and slaves, Hellenes and barbarians. But these revolutionary ideas were initially confined to the inward looking and austere gaze of the philosopher. Their more concrete application would have to wait for the law of the Roman Empire and the political declarations of early modernity.

THE NATURAL LAW OF THE STOICS

Aristotelian concepts of legal justice survived and thrived in Rome where the Stoic ideas of natural law, simplified and transformed by Cicero, were also applied for the first time. As the Roman Empire grew in strength, the idea of a law common to all imperial subjects, of a *jus gentium*, started to take hold. The Stoics had stayed away from direct political involvement, but the morality of universal humanity based on the norms of rational human nature could be used to promote a new cosmopolitanism. The Stoic Chryssipus, for example, described universal humanity as a nation, while for Posidonius, the world was 'the commonwealth of gods and men'.[17] But it was Cicero, an eclectic Stoic and a pragmatic lawyer and politician, who turned the rational universality of Stoicism into the legal ideology of Rome.

Cicero rationalised Roman law and claimed that many of its central tenets could be traced back to universal rational norms. When the Roman jurists spoke of *jus naturale* or used nature to explain or qualify legal concepts, their terms had less of an Aristotelian tint and more of a practical import: 'For "natural" was to them not only what followed from physical qualities of men and things, but also what, within the framework of that system, seemed to square with the normal and reasonable order of human interests and, for this reason, not in need of further evidence.'[18] Still, the Roman *jus* continued to signify a set of objective relations in the world and, like Greek law, did not have a concept of individual rights. And while Aristotle and universal legality may have pragmatically coincided for a brief period through the needs of the Roman Empire, they soon diverged again. Aristotelian justice made its last grand appearance in the writings of Thomas Aquinas and then gradually descended into positivism. The natural right tradition, on the other hand, influenced by Stoicism and Christianity, moved towards a command-theory of law and a subject-based interpretation of right and prepared the modern conception of human rights.

[17] *Ibid*, 14.

[18] E Levy, 'Natural Law in Roman Thought' *Studia et Documenta Historiae et Juris* 15, 949 at 7.

Let us examine more closely some of the main elements of Stoic thought which, mis-digested and eclectically revised by Cicero, exerted such immense influence on later political and legal thought.[19]

The Stoic teaching radically changed the classical method of arguing about natural right as well as the content of nature, the source of law. Nature became the source of a definite set of rules and norms, of a legal code, and stopped being a way of arguing against institutional crystallisations and common opinions. The Stoics were the first pagans to believe that natural law was the expression of a divine reason that pervades the world and made human law one of its aspects. Cicero's famous quotation from the *Republic* is worth quoting at length:

> The true law, is the law of reason, in accordance with nature known to all, unchangeable and imperishable it should call men to their duties by its precepts and deter them from wrongdoing with its prohibitions . . . To curtail this law is unholy, to amend it illicit, to repeal it impossible; nor can we be dispensed from it by the order either of senate or of popular assembly; nor need we look for anyone to clarify or interpret it; nor will it be one law in Rome and a different one in Athens, nor otherwise tomorrow than it is today; but one and the same law, eternal and unchangeable will bind all people and all ages; and God, its designer, expounder and enacter, will be the sole and universal ruler and governor of all things.[20]

This God-given, eternal and absolute natural law had little to do with the natural right of the Sophists or of Plato and Aristotle.

Next, the idea of nature. The Aristotelian *physis* was a normative concept that combined the essence of a thing with its potential for growth and perfection, the efficient and final end of all beings and things. Stoic nature was much more static. Its normative character was retained but became an omnipresent and determining spirit, the *logos* or reason found as seedling in everything. This omnipotent *logos* unites man and world; in humans, it begets and sculpts the body and assembles its components.[21] Nature became the creative spirit or life principle, which, in its pure state, is God. In man, nature resides in the soul. The soul is an internal force that unites humanity with divine *logos* and makes it possible to discern the law of nature, which it is necessary to obey.

The laws, institutions, rules and order proceed from nature, the sole *fons legum et juris*[22] and reason discloses them. Nature commands men to obey the sovereign *logos* that rules history. Natural right became a matter of introspection and revelation rather than of rational contemplation and dialectical confrontation, and led to the abstract morality of precepts, anticipating the moralism of Kant. As a result, two possibilities were opened. In the first, nature, with its principles of human dignity and social equality, was retained as a cate-

[19] M Villey, *Histoire de la Philosophie du Droit*, 4th edn (Paris, PUF, 1965), 1975, 428–80.
[20] Cicero, *Republic*, N Rudd (trans), (Oxford, Oxford University Press, 1998) *III*, 22.
[21] *Ibid*, *II* 11.29; *II* 22.58.
[22] Cicero, *De Legibus*, N Rudd (trans), (Oxford, Oxford University Press, 1998) *I*, 5.

gory of social and legal opposition and as the content of right. The second and more dominant, however, equated natural with positive law and the real with the rational, and anticipated the historicism of Hegel and positivism. This approach privileged the private morality of the happy soul and sanctioned existing institutions, social hierarchies and inequalities. *Physis*, which had started its career in opposition to *nomos*, came finally to be identified with the established order.

The Stoics were the first to express a philosophical and ideological position, that could be called 'logonomocentrism'.[23] This identifies the *logos* (language and reason) with the law and presents rational rule as the foundation and spirit of community. Being is equated with what is present in individual consciousness and with the primacy of reason in the form of law. Rationalism, the cult of the legislator and of rules, and the celebration of individual rights that derive from human nature, all appear in late Stoic thought and in the writings of Cicero. But the Stoic view also promotes human dignity, social equality and an, admittedly abstract, fraternity of all humankind.

THE CHRISTIANISATION OF NATURAL LAW

The main force moving the law towards a theory of natural rights was its gradual Christianisation. Jewish cosmology did not possess an inclusive and purposive concept of the cosmos. For the Jewish religion, the universe is the creation of God. It displays his omnipotence and presence precisely through his absence and as such it cannot acquire the autarcy and normative weight of the Greek *physis*. Similarly, Christianity claimed that the world had been created *ex nihilo* through the free act of God. Nature, the invention of Greek philosophical imagination, was turned into the creation of an all-powerful being. The cosmos was reduced to the natural universe. The natural ends given to all things and beings were turned into their providential position in the plan of salvation, and teleology became eschatology. Nature retained a limited normative character 'expressing in time what from all eternity resides in God' and confirming and complementing divine law.[24]

The seeds of Christian natural law could be found in the statement of Saint Paul, perhaps inspired by Stoic teaching, that God has placed a natural law in our hearts (Romans 11.15). This was the beginning of the idea that conscience is the rule of God ingrained in the heart. With the development of Christianity, *jus* became intertwined with morality and took the form of a set of commandments or rules, the paradigmatically Jewish type of legality. Eventually, the Christian Fathers, commenting on the Bible, started using the term *jus* to mean divine command and natural law to signify the Decalogue. Gratian's *Decretum*,

[23] C Douzinas and R Warrington with S McVeigh, *Postmodern Jurisprudence* (London, Routledge, 1991) 25–8.

[24] L Dupré, *Passage to Modernity*, above n 10, 30.

published in the twelfth century, stated that the natural law is contained in the Gospels and is 'antecedent both in point of time and in point of rank to all things. For whatever has been adopted as custom, or prescribed in writing, if contrary to natural law is to held null and void . . . Thus both ecclesiastical and secular statutes, if they are shown to be contrary to natural law, are to be altogether rejected.'[25] This usage was adopted by the medieval canonists and, finally, in the fourteenth century, *jus* came to mean individual power or subjective right.

A crucial link in the Christianisation of law must be sought in the theology of Augustine and Thomas Aquinas. The most important contribution to jurisprudence by Thomas Aquinas was the fourfold distinction between eternal, natural, divine and human law, with its religious overtones. Here the law has none of the cosmic flexibility and transience associated with Aristotle and the classical tradition. Natural law is definite, certain and simple. No doubt is expressed about its harmony with civil society and the 'immutable character of its fundamental propositions', formulated by God the lawgiver in the 'Second Table of the Decalogue.'[26] These principles of divine law suffer no exception and their universal validity is emphasised by their inscription in human conscience. At the same time, the natural law revealed in the Decalogue presupposed a fallen humanity and a sinful nature and, as a divine remedy against sin, natural law became flexible and relative. Natural law cannot be legislated in rules or canons and does not accept a rigid or fixed formulation. It offers only general directions as to the character of people and the action of the law. These are supple and flexible, imprecise and provisional. This god-ordained and newly-found flexibility allowed state authorities a large degree of discretion.

Aquinas integrated law and state into the divine order through the mediation of relative natural law: while the state was the result of the original sin, it was also justified because it served the hierarchical celestial order as its human part. State law and its coerciveness were the necessary punishment and indispensable remedy for sins (*poena et remedii peccati*) and were open to criticism only if they did not follow the edicts of the church. At the same time, the state was responsible for the well-being and security of its citizens and the Decalogue, the 'compendium of relative natural law', furnished it with the necessary rules. Thus in equating the Decalogue with natural law, Thomas helped turn natural law into a 'technical, rational canon of positive law',[27] a way of interpreting and justifying reality, an almost experimental method.[28]

And while Thomas separated natural and eternal law and ascribed them respectively to the here and the hereafter, he also linked them through a series of hierarchised divine mediations. 'Now, all men know the truth to a certain

[25] *Decretum*, D 8, 2, 9.

[26] L Srauss, above n 4, 144.

[27] E Bloch, above n 3, 27.

[28] M Villey, '*Abrégé du Droit Naturel Classique*' in (1961) 6 *Archives de Philosophie du Droit* 27, 50; *La Formation de la Pensée Juridique Moderne* (Paris, Monchretien, 1968) 126–30.

extent, at least as to the common principles of natural law . . . and in this respect are more or less cognisant of the eternal law.'[29] Justice is the canonical form of this mediation and a principle of gradual participation in the divine order. 'Even an unjust law, insofar as it retains some appearance of law through being framed by one who is in power, is derived from the eternal law, since all power is from the Lord God, according to Romans.'[30] Natural law and justice came together again and justice 'in giving to each his due—whether that be a requital in the form of punishment or reward, or distributive according to merit—[it] expressed a gradation, namely, that architectonic hierarchy which Thomism had erected as the mediation between earth and heaven, heaven and earth.'[31] In this way, Thomism justified fully the medieval order, once its rulers and masters had accepted the dominance of the church.

But the greatest problem with Aquinas, from the perspective of classical natural law, lies in his definition of justice. Justice turned into a category of law that expressed the supremacy of church and feudal hierarchy; its demands were satisfied as long as the law was administered without prejudice and exception. This type of justice represented the inauthentic and relative natural law that repressed sins and atoned for guilt. Classical natural law, by contrast, was not about the just application of existing laws. It used reason and dialectics to confront institutional and political common sense. Thomism combined the classical and Old Testament conceptions of justice in a way that retained both Greek class hierarchies and the Judaic patriarchal principle, itself alien to social divisions.

The Jewish philosopher Maimonides brilliantly combined severity of form and relativity of content in his definition of justice: 'Justice consists in granting his right to everyone who has a right, and in giving to each living being that which he should receive according to his rights.'[32] This justice is the highest virtue and ideal relative natural law, but differs greatly from its classical antecedent. Freedom, communal property and abundance ruled the Stoic edenic age; for the Church Father, the original sin and the fall turned natural law into the law of retribution, necessarily accompanied by courts, punishments and the authority of the Bible and the sword. The Church abandoned the Stoic beliefs in rational freedom and human dignity and 'in this way the worst *embarrassment* of natural law, namely, oppression was founded upon natural law itself as something that had been relativised.'[33] The law was handed down from above; it was based on inequality and domination and underpinned and promoted social inequalities. It was a hierarchical justice that legitimised an unjust rule. It was represented throughout medieval Europe in the form of *Justitia,* a severe woman whose scales weigh each person's dues, whose sword decapitates the enemies of

[29] Aquinas, *Summa Theologiae*, ST *I–II*, Q 93, 3d Art (38).

[30] *Ibid.*

[31] E Bloch, above n 3, 28.

[32] *Guide for the Perplexed*, III, Chapter 53.

[33] E Bloch, above n 3, 26.

order and Church and whose blindfolded eyes, added in the late Middle Ages, symbolise an impossible impartiality.[34] As Bloch pithily observed, this is not 'a category that thought, justifiably dissatisfied, could consider its own.'[35]

The religious re-definition of natural law profoundly undermined the political and prudential character of the classical doctrines of justice and the critical emphasis of natural law. The ideal city of the future, which for the Greeks and Romans would be built through rational contemplation and political action, was replaced by the non-negotiable other-worldly city of God. God, the law-giver, infuses his commands with absolute certainty; natural law is no longer concerned with the construction of the ideal moral and political order and the just legal solution but with the interpretation and confirmation of God's law. After Aquinas, justice largely abandoned its critical potential for jurisprudence. With its pathos vacated and its role as primordial standard gone, it turned into a 'cold virtue.' The word survives but 'its supremacy in natural law disappears, and above all, the undeniable moment of condescension and acquiescence, inherent in the severity that the word confers upon itself, disappears.'[36] Rousseau defined it as 'the love of man derived from the love of oneself'.[37] This formulation eventually matured into the concept of social justice, and migrated from law to the discipline of economics and the ideology of socialism. Freedom and dignity, not justice, became the rallying cries of modern natural law.

FROM NATURAL LAW TO NATURAL RIGHTS

There is one final and crucial piece in the genealogical jigsaw of human rights, without which we cannot understand the jurisprudence of modernity. This is the process through which the classical and medieval tradition of *jus* and right turned into that of subjective rights and led to the birth of the modern individual. John Finnis has argued that the transition from Aquinas' *jus* defined as 'that which is *just in a given situation*' to that of Suarez as 'something beneficial—a *power—which a person has*' as a 'watershed.'[38] It re-defined the concept of right as a 'power' or 'liberty' possessed by an individual, a quality that characterises his being.[39]

The birth of modern man and of individual rights passes through the theology of Catholic scholasticism, which discovered the principles of natural law in the way God created human beings. The essential nature of man and all

[34] M Jay, 'Must Justice be Blind' in C Douzinas and L Nead (eds), *Law and the Image* (Chicago, University of Chicago Press, 1999) chapter 1.

[35] E Bloch, above n 3, 38.

[36] *Ibid*, 43.

[37] JJ Rousseau, *Emile or on Education*, A Bloom (trans), (London, Penguin, 1991) *IV*.

[38] J Finnis, *Natural Law and Natural Rights* (Oxford, Clarendon, 1980) 207.

[39] R Tuck, *Natural Rights Theories* (Cambridge, Cambridge University Press, 1979); M Villey, *La Formation*, above n 28; B Tierney, *The Idea of Natural Rights* (Atlanta, Scholars Press, 1997) chapter I.

the essentials of natural law can be deduced from the morality of the Commandments. Moral and political obligations derive from revealed truth and, as a result, Christian love and providence replaced the quest for the best polity. The first radical step in this direction was taken by the Franciscan nominalists Duns Scotus and William of Ockham. They were the first to argue, in the fourteenth century, that the individual form is not a sign of contingency and the human person is not the instantiation of the universal. On the contrary, the supreme expression of creation is individuality, as evidenced in the historical incarnation of Christ; individuality's knowledge takes precedence over that of the universal forms of the classics. Nominalism rejected abstract concepts and denied that general terms like law, justice or the city represented real entities or relations. For William, collectivities, cities and communities, are artificial. The term 'city', for example, refers to the sum total of individual citizens and not to an ensemble of activities, aims and relations, while 'law' is a universal word with no discernible empirical referent and has no independent meaning. Society, as Mrs Thatcher a contemporary nominalist would say, does not exist, only individuals do. Science started avoiding totalities and systems and concentrated on particulars because, according to the nominalists, all general concepts owe their existence to conventional linguistic practices and have no ontological weight or empirical value. Meaning and value became detached from nature and were assigned to separate atoms or particulars, opening the road for the Renaissance concept of the genius artist, God's disciple and partner—and—later, for the sovereign individual—the centre of the world.[40]

The legal implications of nominalism cannot be overstated. William argued that the control exercised by private individuals over their lives was of the type of *dominium* or property and, further, that this natural property was not a grant of the law but a basic fact of human life.[41] The absolute power of the individual over his capacities—an early prefiguration of the idea of natural rights—was God's gift to man made in his image. At the same time, the nominalists based their ethics on divine commands and deduced the whole law from their prescriptions. The law was given by the divine legislator whose will is absolute and obligatory for humans *per se* and not because it accorded with nature or reason. Indeed, Duns Scotus argued that God's will has priority over his reason; the good exists because the omnipotent wills and commands it and not on account of some other independent quality. In this way, the source and method of the law started changing. It was gradually moved from reason to 'Will, pure Will, with no foundation in the nature of things'.[42] Similarly, the jurist's task was no longer to find the just solution but to interpret the legislator's commands for the faithful subjects.

[40] E Kantorowicz, 'The Sovereignty of the Artist: A Note on Legal Maxims and Renaissance Theories of Art' in *Selected Studies* (New York, JJ Augustin, 1965) 352–65.

[41] M Villey, *Histoire de la Philosophie du Droit*, 4th edn (Paris, PUF, 1965) 157–265; *Le Droit et les droits* (Paris, PUF, 1981) 118–25; R Tuck, above n 39, 15–31.

[42] H Rommen quoted in JM Kelly, *A Short History of Western Legal Theory* (Oxford, Oxford University Press, 1992) 145.

The separation of God from nature and the absolutisation of will prepared the ground for God's retreat and eventual removal from earthly matters. The celebration of an omnipotent and unquestionable will was both the prelude for the full abdication of divine right and the foundation stone of secular omnipotent sovereignty. Legal positivism and untrammelled state authoritarianism found their early precursor in those devout defenders of the power of God. And in a move that was to be repeated by the political philosophers of the seventeenth century, the Franciscans combined absolute legislative will with the nominalist claim that only individuals exist. The combination 'led pretty directly to a strongly individualistic political theory which had to undergo only a few modifications to emerge as something very close to the classic rights theories of the seventeenth century.'[43] The mutation of objective natural law into subjective individual rights, initiated by William, amounted to a cognitive, semantic and eventually political revolution. Villey describes it as a 'Copernican moment', emphasising its theoretical and epoch-making affinities with the new scientific world. From that point, legal and political thought placed at the centre of its attention the sovereign and the individual with their respective rights and powers.

The theological influence was still evident in the work of all the great philosophers of the seventeenth century. *Omnia sub ratione Dei* was their principle, a slogan destined for a temporary but all-important existence. It destroyed the medieval world-view by linking God's will with reason's discoveries, but it soon succumbed to its internal humanistic tendencies and led to the 'death' of God. Descartes explicitly linked new physics with theology, Hobbes and Locke organised their civil state under the auspices of God. All the great philosophers wrote a kind of political theology and believed that God underwrote their systematic efforts. But soon a laicised deism replaced Christ with the God of Reason and, eventually, with Man become God. At the same time, the great Enlightenment writers, despite their differing conceptions of natural right and social contract, were the vanguard of reason's rebellion against the theocratic organisation of authority. The modern natural rights tradition, which turned violently against ancient cosmology and ontology and redefined the source of right, was a reaction to the co-optation of natural law by religion and the accompanying loss of juridical flexibility, political latitude and imaginative utopianism which characterised the classical tradition. The secular theology of natural rights placed the abstract concept of man at the centre of the universe and transferred to him the adoration offered to God by the medievals. While the forward looking and prudential aspects of the theory of the 'best polity' were undermined, the openness of classical natural law became a potential horizon of individual identity and right.

Medieval constitutional theories and utopias had been organised around the ideas of the fall and the divine legislator. But the early modern undermining of

[43] R Tuck, above n 24.

the secular power of theology meant that the relative natural law, which regulated humanity in a state of sin, could no longer be used to justify oppressive social and political regimes. The grace of divine authority and the aura of its earthly representative could not captivate the soul of the people and, in its place, modern natural law attempted to re-construct the constitution using reason alone. Epicurean ideas, according to which the *polis* was the outcome of an original contract, as well as the Stoic belief that the law should be in harmony with the reason of the world, acquired renewed importance. But this was the natural law of modern merchants and not of ancient sages; legal and social arrangements were attributed to a fictitious bourgeois assembly and an equally fake but freely-entered contract.

The idea of an original compact was accompanied by a pre-contractual state of nature in which men lived before entering society or the state. Against the ancients, for whom nature was a standard of critique transcending empirical reality, the nature of Rousseau, Hobbes and Locke was an attempt to discover the common elements of humanity—the human essence behind the differing individual, social and national characteristics and idiosyncrasies. This quest for the permanent, universal and eternal had to deduct from empirical people whatever historical, local or contingent factors had added to their 'nature'. The natural man or *noble savage* was not a primitive forefather of the patrons of Parisian salons or of London merchants but had similarities with both. As species representative, man *qua* man, he was an artificial construct of reason, a naked human being endowed only with logic, strong survival instincts and a sense of morality. According to John Rawls, who famously repeated the mental experiment, natural man toils and contracts behind a 'veil of ignorance'.[44] The fiction drew its power from the importance that contract had acquired in early capitalism. It was only in an emerging market society that important institutional and personal questions could be addressed through the putative agreements of rational individuals. But despite assurances to the contrary, the man of nature was not totally naked: his 'natural' instincts and drives differed widely from one natural lawyer to the next. For some, natural man was competitive and aggressive, for others peaceful and industrious, for others both. Eternal nature seemed to follow current social priorities and political concerns, and to be quite close to the preoccupations, hopes and fears of the contemporaries of the theorist.

The fictional contract became a device for philosophical speculations about the nature of the social bond and political obligation, the model constitution and the rights of empirical men in London and Paris. Abstraction, the removal of concrete characteristics, was seen as logically necessary. The contractual fiction justified attacks on feudal society and absolutist government. Its revolutionary and unprecedented termination clause authorised the overthrow

[44] J Rawls, *A Theory of Justice* (Oxford, Oxford University Press, 1972). The veil conceals all the major individualising characteristics from the contractors.

of government when it was not performing its contractual obligations. At the same time, the contract acted as the blueprint for modern constitutional arrangements. In this second function, the contractual device introduced the rationalism of the Enlightenment into the constitution. Legal norms and social relations were shamelessly deduced from axiomatic normative propositions (original evil and desire for security, original goodness and sociability, individual freedom and the need to restrict it, etc).

The various schools of modern natural law, despite their differences, shared a number of characteristics.[45] First, they all believed that social life and the state are the result of free individual activity. We can detect here the heavy influence of legal mentality. It is deeply pleasing to a lawyer, steeped in the doctrine of contract, to believe that legal forms and free agreements lie at the basis of society. Social contract theories adopted the contract doctrine of 'constructive knowledge': the contractors willed all reasonable consequences of their agreement, while what could not have been rationally willed was not willed at all. (Restrictions on property and capital accumulation, for example, were unreasonable and a political system that enforced them brought the contract's termination clause into operation.) Secondly, the legal and social order emerging from the original agreement was realised through the power of reason and logic to deduce a complete and gapless system of rules from a few axiomatic principles. The essence of the state was to be rationally reconstructed from its valid elements and justified only by means of reasoned argument, based on its founding principles in the contract; indeed reason was declared the essence of the state. The prestige of the natural sciences was transferred to political philosophy and, natural law became a pure discourse of deduction modelled on mathematics.

The natural sciences, in their quest for predictability and certainty, discarded irregularities, and natural law followed suit. The methodological purity of mathematics complemented perfectly the belief in universal homogeneous concepts and eternal laws, which became a central tenet of natural law. The iron laws, strict necessity and homogeneity of Newton's mechanical nature were reinterpreted as a normative universality and were co-opted in the fight against the hierarchical society of feudal privilege. Rational natural law and natural rights became the discourse of revolution. The liberal version of Thomas Paine inspired the Americans, the democratic vision of Jean-Jacques Rousseau encouraged the French. No political philosophy or version of natural law was worthy of the name if it was not grounded on universal principles or did not aim at universal ends. The great discoveries, the marvellous inventions and the triumph of the mercantile and urban economies, aided by the levelling exchange-value of money, combined to increase the *cachet* of the universal.

But the discourse of the universal soon became the companion of capitalism and the upholder of the market, the place where, according to Marx, human rights and Bentham reign supreme. The rationalism of natural law too, having

[45] E Bloch, above n 3, 53–60.

consigned the classical conception of politics and the search for the 'best polity' to the history of ideas, became the legitimatory discourse of utilitarian governments and was used against the emerging socialist and utopian movements. A side-effect of this rampant rationalism was the intellectual impoverishment of jurisprudence: the violence at the heart of law and of public and private power, which had helped re-organise the world according to the new political and economic orthodoxies, was written out of the texts of law, which became obsessed with normative questions, with the meaning of rights, sovereignty or representation. Much of the unrealistic rationalism that still bedevils jurisprudence hails from this golden age of natural law. This idealism not only totally obfuscates law's role in the world, it also distorts our understanding of legal operations because

> it serves no purpose to pick out partial relations and even partial tendencies in real life and insert them into the head as an arithmetical problem . . . in order to come up with a logic that formally is like iron, but remains weaker and unreal form the point of view of content . . . formal necessity, that is, the absence of contradiction in the deduction and from of a proposition, is hardly a criterion of its truth in a dialectical world.[46]

But alongside this law-abiding and sombre nature, which accorded with the bourgeois interests in calculability and certainty, another conception of a *natura immaculata* lurked, in the pure and harmonious nature of classicism, the edenic visions of romanticism and the perfectibility of utopian socialists. This marginal conception of a purified and perfect nature linked with the classical tradition of nature as standard, and provided a critical and redemptive perspective against the injustices and oppressions that the social system, justified by rational natural law, tolerated and even promoted. This concept of nature would eventually combine with the idea of social utopia and provide the radical side of human rights.

UTOPIA AFTER THE 'END OF HISTORY'

> A map of the world that does not include Utopia is not worth even glancing at, for it leaves out the one country at which humanity is always landing. (Oscar Wilde)

What is the use of natural law today after its limited positivisation in the law of human rights? In a strange way, it is the method rather than the source or content of natural law that seems to retain its relevance. Classical natural law was a weapon of rebellion against priests and rulers. It combined reason and emotion, knowledge and passion. These aspects are shared by utopianism. Indeed, natural law was perfectly complemented by the great social utopias of

[46] *Ibid*, 191.

the nineteenth century. More, Campanella, Bacon, Owen, Fourier and St Simon wrote their utopias casting an eye to natural law ideas. But while the natural lawyers derived their schemes of rights from axiomatic principles about human nature drawing on mathematical deductions and scientific proofs, the utopian imagination used narratives, images and allegories to project the future society. Natural law draws its power from the great thinkers of the past, while utopias are imaginary projections of the future. More importantly, natural law aims to abolish degradation and uphold human dignity while social utopias aim to reduce suffering and promote human happiness, to bring about the *eu zein* or living well of the Greeks. Dignity and happiness—freedom and equality have been the twin aims of the great revolutions of modernity, particularly those inspired by the different versions of Marxism.

It would not be inaccurate to say, however, that our epoch has witnessed the demise of utopian hopes and that, additionally, the utopian motif has been suspended in critical thought. The concept of utopia was dealt the first debilitating blow in the Fifties and Sixties when the Soviet gulags and mental asylums became widely known. It was deleted from the political dictionary with the collapse of communism. In this anti-utopian climate, Francis Fukuyama earned world-wide fame when he stated that 'today, we have trouble imagining a world that is radically better than our own, or a future that is not essentially democratic and capitalist . . . We cannot picture to ourselves a world that is *essentially* different from the present one, and at the same time better.'[47] As the individual and his rights became the universal religion, collective imagination seems to have dried out—the principle of hope either realised in liberal capitalism or extinguished.

Russell Jacoby, in his aptly named *The End of Utopia*, recently addressed the loss of nerve on the left and concluded that 'at best radicals and leftists envision a modified society with bigger pieces of pie for more customers. They turn utilitarian, liberal and celebratory. The left once dismissed the market as exploitative; it now honours the market as rational and humane.'[48] The statement accurately charts the way from Clause Four to new Labour. But it also alludes to the wider cultural moment of the *fin-de-siècle*, in which grand theories and meta-narratives have been discredited and the politics of multiplicity, difference and pluralism have replaced the promise of a perfect future. The demise of communism has created a grudging respect on the left for liberalism and its (failing) attempts to create a rational scheme for negotiating individual conflict.

And yet no century has been more murderous and genocidal than the twentieth; the 'end of history' has not signalled the end of genocide. Jacques Derrida has helpfully catalogued the limitations of the 'new world order' and of the discourse on human rights that will remain

[47] F Fukuyama, *The End of History and the Last Man* (London, Penguin, 1993) 46.
[48] R Jacoby, *The End of Utopia* (New York, Basic Books, 1999), 10.

inadequate, sometimes hypocritical, and in any case formalistic and inconsistent with itself as long as the law of the market, the 'foreign debt', the inequality of techno-scientific, military and economic development maintain an effective inequality as monstrous as that which prevails today, to a greater extent than ever in the history of humanity. For it must be cried out, at a time when some have the audacity to neo-evangelise in the name of the ideal of liberal democracy that has finally realised itself as the ideal of human history: never have violence, inequality, exclusion, famine, and thus economic oppression affected as many human beings in the history of the earth and of humanity.[49]

As the millennium draws to a close, Fukuyama's complacency makes Jacoby's diagnosis too painful for everyone who wants to deny the infamies of the present in the name of the future. Does that mean that we are left with no hope, that we are condemned both individually and collectively to tinkering with the margins of the social system, private and privatised by the forces of global culture? This was always the advice or threat of the apologists of power and of the common sense pragmatists, against whom natural law consistently rebelled. The 'end of history' thesis, the celebration of the present for its presence, has accompanied every historical period, more as a warning of imminent change than as celebration of stability—usually surfacing at the point at which history was about to enter a radically new phase. What is interesting about our present prophesies of the 'end' is that, unlike previous periods, they are accompanied by the powerful utopian imagination of human rights which the new order has positivised, tamed and co-opted to a large extent, but which retains a huge creative and explosive potential. While theories of justice are the longest failure of western thought, symbolic attempts to appease the discontent of civilisation created by the symbolic order,[50] the sense of injustice and the utopian hopes associated with it, have always acted as a social imaginary domain, as if societies have an imagination of well-being and wholeness comparable to that of individuals.

It is here that the grandiose and eloquent utopianism of Ernst Bloch,[51] steeped in central European Jewish culture and German romantic values, can become a critical resource for our postmodern cynical times. Bloch represents a genuine advance on Marx; he retains the main elements of his critique of rights but discovers in the tradition of natural law and right the historically variable but eternal human trait, the determination to resist domination and oppression and to imagine and fight for a society in which 'man will walk upright'. There can be no real foundation of human rights without an end to exploitation and no real end to exploitation without the establishment of human rights.

[49] J Derrida, *Spectres for Marx*, P Kamuf (trans), (New York, Routledge, 1994) 85.

[50] See below, chapters 4 and 12.

[51] Bloch's combination of utopianism, interest in natural law and qualified support for the socialist regimes meant that he did not feature in the pantheon of western Marxists, despite his great interest and affinity with Walter Benjamin and the Frankfurt School. The only offerings in English are V Geoghegan, *Enrst Bloch* (London, Routledge, 1996) and JO Daniel and T Moylan (eds), *Not Yet: Reconsidering Ernst Bloch* (London, Verso, 1997).

Bloch argued that nature, albeit constituted in different ways, from the Sophists and the Stoics to the moderns, provides a category that confronts existing social relations as 'a fetish against social defaults.'[52] But the struggle between this ever-changing nature and the sedimented world of positive law was always lost until Rousseau and Marx 'invented' democracy and socialism. Rousseau resolved the problem of how to protect individual freedom by establishing an immediate relationship between citizens and the general will, thus turning natural law from a philosophical or religious construct into a historical institution. Natural law became the law legislated by popular sovereignty, and the general will ensured that the principle of individual freedom could only exist in a human rights community. In this sense, politics and rights were indissolubly connected, and guaranteed the achievements of the revolution by subjecting the government to the constant control of citizens. Natural law was no longer deduced from the abstract rule of reason and axiomatic propositions about human nature, but was the outcome of the concrete reason of people. For the first time in history, right or *jus* became synonymous with the rights of the people, politics adopted the idea of equality for all and the triptych of liberty, equality and fraternity acquired normative weight. But property counted as one of the inalienable rights and, as a result, equality was restricted to politics—and even there to white males; the potential of rights was not allowed to materialise. 'This was the high point of natural law, but the epoch in which it flourished was an illusion, for out of the *citoyen* there came the bourgeois; it was a foreshadowing, for the bourgeois was judged by the *citoyen*.'[53] Expanding Marx's distinction between man and citizen, Bloch saw the latter as a pre-figuration of future socialised freedom. Although the idea of citizenship had been damaged by its bourgeois misuse, it did not represent 'a barrier to freedom as it does in the egotism of the *droits de l'homme* . . . indeed, as the German poet Holderlin pointed out, it always possessed the capacity of self-purification.'[54]

The foreshadowing of a future not-yet and not-ever present helps the self-purification of moral ideas contaminated by the powerful. The triptych of the French revolution shows this strategy at work. Freedom as ethical and political, as personal and public, as freedom of choice and of action, is the ability to 'act *contra fatum*, thus in a perspective of a still *open* world, one not *yet determined all the way to the end*.'[55] Oppression and domination are obvious violations of freedom, because they turn political power and economic conditions into inescapable destinies. But freedom is also irreconcilable with a fully determined and closed world, in which the only possible personal intervention is a judicious adjustment to dominant ideas and the exploitation of given and inescapable structures to the subject's advantage; an advantage whose contours have been

[52] E Bloch, *Natural Law and Human Dignity*, above n 3, 192.
[53] *Ibid*, 65.
[54] *Ibid*, 177.
[55] *Ibid*, 162.

well demarcated and whose boundaries are strictly policed. In this sense, freedom is enhanced by the ability of rights to extend the limits of the social and to expand and re-define self and group identities. It operates only if as yet unclosed possibilities remain in the world, and is extinguished when the double determination of the subject as free and subjected moves towards the pole of subjection. But in a regulated world, in which little margin of play is allowed outside the parameters of global capitalism and authoritarian order, freedom might come to mean resistance to the 'freedom' to own and control ever more objects as the ultimate sign of self-expression, or to the 'freedom' to define and shape life according to a closed list of rights defined by 'moral experts'. Freedom cannot be defined in advance, except as the 'human comportment in the face of objective real possibility'.[56] Its every exercise opens in turn a new vista, which, if petrified, itself becomes an external limitation that must be overcome again. Freedom is an ambiguous concept that starts from past determinations and crystallisations and continuously defies them in the name of an ever elusive and deferred future.

The openness of the concept of freedom has allowed its co-optation by ideologies and movements hostile to its essence, like those of de-regulated market capitalism or of neo-liberal law and economics. This cannot happen with its twin concept of equality. Its meaning may be restricted to equality before the law, or obscured as the equality of souls in God's plan of salvation, but its obvious and gross violations cannot be concealed. The huge gap between North and South, between rich and poor or, in its postmodern version, between the satisfied middle classes and the disenfranchised underclass, cannot be falsified. The life threatening consequences of poverty exemplify the fact, well-known for over a hundred years, that there can be no freedom or dignity without economic equality. The first task of freedom as liberation from oppressive determinations is therefore to eliminate economic deprivation. Freedom not linked to equality is a chimera. Equality's work to this day, some one hundred and fifty years after the first socialists identified its internal link with freedom, is about giving a minimum of freedom to the great majority of people in the world. While their action differs, the aim of equality and freedom coincide: they are both inclined towards 'the *human identity* that has yet to arrive; namely, that identity which always threatens, always glimmers like the harmony of men with the image they have of the *humanum*.'[57]

This identity that is 'not yet' draws its inspiration from the past and the best traditions of radical natural law. Bloch's humanism presents Marxism as an heir of rebels and reformers who replaced faith in gods and loyalty to kings with human dignity and equality. But as reality is always incomplete and the present is pregnant with future possibilities, all realism has utopia at its core. Utopia is the name for the great power of imagination that finds the future latent in every

[56] *Ibid*, 163.
[57] *Ibid*, 167.

cultural product and preserves the kernel of radical enthusiasm in every ideology it criticises. Natural law, despite its many religious and reactionary formulations, emerges from this revisionist history as the unwavering passion to save the dignity of the *humanum.* While Bloch's criticisms of the illusions of 'bourgeois natural law' are devastating, he concludes that 'men were in agreement in the intention of freeing themselves from oppression and installing human dignity, at least since the time of the Greeks. But only this will is immutable, and not . . . "man" and his so-called eternal right.'[58]

Bloch's principle of utopia does not coincide with the various grand places and schemes of that name. His magnum opus, *The Principle of Hope,* is not restricted to formal plans but encompasses under the utopian moment daydreams and private reveries of ordinary everyday life, the apocalyptic vistas of religion and mysticism, the sublime tableaux of literature and art and also the fairy-tales, folk songs, carnivals and pagan traditions of popular culture. 'A free-flowing utopian energy' is pursued in high and low history, 'channelled into a multiplicity of forms, some reactionary, some progressive; utopianism is therefore not confined to "the Utopia." '[59] Utopianism is a dream of the future, fuelled by the past and immanent in the present.

Happiness and dignity have marched separately during the ages (and we are repeatedly told that their definite separation is also the greatest achievement of liberalism). But 'there can be no human dignity without the end of misery and need, but also no human happiness without the end of old and new forms of servitude.'[60] This dialectical relationship between dignity and happiness or between rights and utopia permeates the work of Ernst Bloch. But his main argument is that the Enlightenment promise remains unfulfilled: 'We are concerned with a peculiar heritage. Its best remains in abeyance and is still to be appended. What is past does not return, especially not in an out-of-date way but it can be taken at its word. It is just as urgent *suo modo* to raise the problem of a heritage of classical natural law as it is to speak of the heritage of social utopias.'[61]

Bloch's narrative did not involve a simple appropriation or repetition of the past. The radical impetus of natural law had been implicit from the Stoics until early modernity and the task, started but still incomplete, is to redeem a past not present to itself and re-activate moments that 'remained dormant in the margins of illusionary excess.'[62] For the utopianist, tradition does not follow linear time and is not a direct descent from the past. It is rather a retrospective recreation of the past reminiscent of the psychoanalytical interpretation of a contemporary symptom as the effect of an unknown but active unconscious cause. And as this

[58] E Bloch, *Natural Law and Human Dignity*, above n 3, 191.

[59] V Geoghegan, *Ernst Bloch* (London, Routledge, 1996) 145–6.

[60] E Bloch, *Natural Law*, above n 3, 208.

[61] *Ibid*, *xxix*.

[62] D Kaufmann, 'Thanks for the Memory: Bloch, Benjamin, and the Philosophy of History' in JO Daniel and T Moylan (eds), above n 51, 41.

past is put in the service of an undetermined future, utopia can be defined as the remembrance of the future. In this, we are reminded of the theses on history of Walter Benjamin, the other great messianic Marxist, for whom all hope lies in a memory of past defeats and resistances: 'The danger affects both the content of the tradition and its receivers. The same threat hangs over both: that of becoming a tool of the ruling classes. In every era the attempt must be made anew to wrest tradition away from a conformism that is about to overpower it.'[63] It is precisely this conformism which threatens when it becomes a tool of states, governments and international organisations.

For Bloch, natural law and human rights are given priority over utopia. While a state law that supports oppression and domination has no place in the society of the future, human rights will be at the heart of socialism and will ensure that the 'pathos of the free individual seems like a warning against any confusion or mixing up of collectivity with the herd or herd character.'[64] The 'stipend' of human rights takes the concrete form of a promise, which anticipates a real humanity still to come. 'Freedom, equality, fraternity, the *orthopaideia* of the upright carriage, of human pride, and of human dignity point far beyond the horizon of the bourgeois world.'[65] This 'principle of hope'—according to which all relations in which man is a 'degraded, enslaved, abandoned or, despised being' should be overthrown—remains as valid today as it has ever been. As the new millennium opens, with a promise of satisfied uniformity for some and oppressive domination for many, the principle of utopian hope is one of the few hopes left.

While Bloch blended together utopia and natural law, Theodor Adorno in a more melancholic mood, emphasised the central paradox of all utopian hope. On the one hand, 'the only philosophy which can be responsibly practiced in the face of despair is the attempt to contemplate all things as they would present themselves from the point of redemption. Knowledge has no light but that shed on the world by redemption. All else is reconstruction, mere technique.' On the other, utopia is 'also an utterly impossible thing, because it presupposes a standpoint removed, even though by a hair's breadth, from the scope of existence . . . the more passionately thought denies its conditionality for the sake of the unconditional, the more unconsciously, and so calamitously it is delivered up to the world.'[66] Utopian thought is caught in a double bind: by denying the determined character of thought, 'even by a hair's breadth', in order to raise itself above the infamies of the present, it risks forgetting the determinations of thought or the subjection of the subject, thus letting the impositions of power

[63] W Benjamin, 'Theses on the Philosophy of History' in *Illuminations*, H Zohn (trans), (New York, Schocken, 1969) 255.

[64] E Bloch, *The Principle of Hope*, N and S Plaice and P Knight (trans), (Oxford, Blackwell, 1986) 547.

[65] E Bloch, *Natural Law and Human Dignity*, above n 3, 174.

[66] T Adorno, *Minima Moralia: Reflections from Damaged Life*, E Jephcott (trans), (London, Verso, 1991) 247.

work undetected. We cannot stop criticising the present, and we cannot do that without adopting the position of the future; but, similarly, we can never remove ourselves sufficiently from our here and now to adopt the redemptive position. Utopian hope is necessary and impossible; a general utopian plan, if imposed on people, risks becoming a blueprint for worse oppression and domination. As Thomas Nagel argued in a more prosaic style, the problem with utopia is that 'it presents an ideal of collective life, and it tries to show people one by one that they should want to live under it'—that it forces people to be free.[67]

It is here that Bloch's combination of natural law and social utopia can be developed in a postmodern perspective. If a fantasy of integrity, supported by the discourse of human rights, helps construct our radically inter-subjective social identity, this fantasy is inextricably bound with the desire of the other. Existential completeness, the negation of dependence and subjection, impossible as it is, helps build our sense of uniqueness—which can exist only in relation to unique others. Similarly, if all human activity is relational, our actions address—directly or indirectly—another, before becoming objectified into events, facts or rights. A just relationship does not attack the ontological constitution or undermine the existential integrity of the related entities. The utopia projected by the human rights imaginary would be a social organisation that recognises and protects the existential integrity of people expressed in their imaginary domain. The postmodern utopian hope has ontological importance: it protects the integrity of unique beings in their existential otherness, by promoting the dynamic realisation of freedom. While the individual imaginary helps build an other-dependent identity, the social imaginary supports a social organisation in which human relationships respect and promote the uniqueness of the participants.

In the social imaginary, memories of fear, tales of pain and suffering and the experience of oppression have a key role. During the Yugoslav wars, when people were presented with images which brought to the surface the memories and emotions of the Nazi concentration camps, the reaction was immense horror and willingness to act. Although most people today do not have first hand experience, the Holocaust has formed a central part of our moral imagination and these communal resources can be mobilised by the utopian hope. The imaginary domain of each society is partly constructed as a reaction to specific injustices and multiple instances of major and petty dominations and oppressions, and draws its force from the *a priori* pain of human life. When the struggle against injustice takes the form of human rights, they become invested with the energy and creativity of this imagination.

The postmodern utopia promises to shelter human relations from reification, from being turned into the non-relation of subjection, dependence and the mastery of one over others. Subjection makes a relationship unavoidable and therefore destroys the existential freedom of the participants, of both master

[67] T Nagel, *Equality and Partiality* (New York, Oxford University Press, 1991) 23.

and subjected. The utopian hope promotes social relations in which the people experience their lives as if they were free from necessity. But unlike theories of justice, which go for the high ground and top-to-bottom reform, utopian thought has always been filled with suppressed popular images and reminiscences, untold dreams and stories, lowly memories and emotional affects projected into an adorable future. In this sense, the utopianism of human rights is the opposite of the classical utopias which hoped to create a 'new man' to fit the collective plan. Like classical utopianism, it is the prefiguration of a future in which people are not degraded, despised or oppressed, the anticipation of a completeness in which the desire of the other would be erotic and not just competitive and destructive. And while, like all utopias, its realisation is always deferred, turning human rights from governmental triumphalism and diplomatic somnambulism into utopian hope would be the greatest contribution of our political culture to the new millennium. Human rights can fill the non-place of the postmodern utopia: they generate a powerful political and moral energy, unlike any other ideology; they draw their force from past memories and future hopes; their promise exists hidden beyond conventions, treaties and bills in a variety of inconspicuous cultural forms. Human rights, based as they are on the fragile sense of personal identity and the—impossible—hope of social integrity, link integrally the individual and the communal. Like all utopias, they deny the present in the name of the future, which means that they paradoxically deny the rights of laws and states in the name of the plural humanities yet to come.

But Adorno's warnings are justified. The hope of the future must not conceal the infamies of the present, and the distance necessary for critique must not become the gap of detachment. The postmodern principle of hope as represented by human rights is perhaps aporetic rather than utopian: caught between the dismembering action of law which splits the body physical and politic (the work of the symbolic) and the redeeming future of existential integrity (the work of the imaginary), human rights are both the malady and its cure, both the poison and its antidote, a veritable Derridean *pharmakon*.[68]

At the end of this historical journey, it is important to be reminded that classical natural law was built on the intrinsic connection between natural right and justice. The same terms, *dikaion* and *jus* connoted both the just and the law, and the business of the classical lawyers was to discover the just solution to a conflict. This linguistic link survives today in the double meaning of the word justice, as the transcendent ideal of law and as the administration of the judicial system. But classical right was not a moral law that lurks in the human conscience as a universal superego and places all under the same moral commands. It was rather a methodological principle that allowed the philosopher to criticise sedimented tradition and the jurist to discover the just solution in the case in hand. Classical natural law contained a passion for justice but it did not

[68] J Derrida, 'Plato's Pharmacy' in *Disseminations,* B Johnson (trans), (London, Athlone Press, 1981) 61–171.

coincide with it. Natural right enters the historical agenda, directly or in disguise, every time people struggle 'to overthrow all relations in which man is a degraded, enslaved, abandoned or despised being.'[69]

Classical justice, on the other hand, has a political and a legal aspect. Political justice explores the overall organisation of the *polis* and tries to imagine the perfect constitution, the most beautiful and harmonious arrangement of the social bond. But justice or the just is also the end, both the aim and outcome, of legal action. Justice as an ideal is never fully of this world; it forms the horizon against which current practices are judged and found lacking. The just as the outcome of the juridical process is both present- and future-looking. The concept of justice is therefore split: an ideal or general justice which promises a future perfection and judges reality in its name, and a legal or particular justice which upholds and redresses proportional equality in the everyday dealings of citizens but which also reproduces the existing balance between free citizens and slaves, men and women, Greeks and barbarians. Legal justice could also face both ways—its provisional judgments reached against the horizon of a purposeful order and a perfect justice always deferred to the future.

Whenever justice lost this future-looking aspect it became associated with a moralistic, patriarchal attitude, in which distributions and commutation protect the established order and perpetuate the inequalities and oppression natural law tries to redress. In these cases, a gap opens between the utopian function of natural law and this conservative version of justice. As Ernst Bloch put it,

> Genuine natural law, which posits the free will in accord with reason, was the first to reclaim the justice that can only be obtained by struggle; it did not understand justice as something that descends from above and prescribes to each his share, distributing or retaliating, but rather as an active justice of below, one that would make justice itself unnecessary. Natural law never coincided with a mere sense of justice.[70]

The Greeks were indebted to philosophers, tragedians and dissidents, rather than judges, for upholding natural right against the justice from above. They remain powerful voices, warning that one should not confuse received opinion and truth. These voices speak to our present, and urge us not to forget our future.

PASSAGES

We are sitting under the fig trees in the shadows; far too hot to sit in the sun. A light breeze from the sea. The racket of the cicadas against the clump of the typewriter. Work all day until the night falls, dark as wine. Later, leaving the island on the airport bus, I go through the suitcase. Pressed between towels, the travelling library: The *Republic* and the *Inferno*. The only two books you need.

[69] J Derrida, 'Plato's Pharmacy' in *Disseminations,* B Johnson (trans), (London, Athlone Press, 1981), *xxvii–xxix*.

[70] *Ibid*, *xxx*.

4

Justice: A Short History of (a Long) Failure

One can only laugh at the narrowness of spirit of those who believe that the power of the present can extinguish the memory of future times. (Tacitus)

THE CLASSICS

THE MOST PAINFUL WITNESS of our time is the widely-felt belief that justice has miscarried. Outside the law, justice has been aborted in African famines and inner city ghettos, in the victims of economic blight and domestic violence, in genocide, ethnic cleansing and imperial conquest. Within the law, justice has been aborted in miscarriages of justice and denials of access to justice, in race and gender discrimination, in institutional violence and indifference to ethics.

Yet justice has miscarried in the midst of a prolific explosion of theories about its nature. No topic has been debated more passionately by some of the greatest minds of our civilisation and no rallying cry has moved more revolutionaries and reformers. From Plato to Kant, from Aristotle to Marx and from Augustine to Rawls, justice has been the single most debated topic of philosophy, the ultimate aim of social thought and political action. According to David Hume, no human association could subsist without justice.[1] Justice is the primary political virtue that a society pursues, an 'overall standard of social rightness [and] logically no other value can stand prior to justice since all relevant values are subsumed under its umbrella.'[2]

Most theories of justice start from the classical precept of *suum cuique tribuere* or giving each one his due. In its ancient version, this maxim states that 'injustice arises when equals are treated unequally and also when unequals are

[1] D Hume, *An Enquiry Concerning the Principles of Morals* (Oxford, Clarendon, 1998) 165.
[2] T Campbell, *Justice* (London, Macmillan, 1988) 7–8.

treated equally'.[3] Its modern interpretation makes justice the just distribution of social resources. But deciding what is 'due' to someone is highly contentious. It is closely linked with determinations about which classifications count as legitimate and which count as offensive and irrelevant discriminations. In America, for example, both the 'separate but equal' principle of racial segregation and the later prohibition of segregation were accepted as equally valid interpretations of the equality and due process clauses of the Fourteenth Amendment of the Constitution by the Supreme Court, in two radically opposed decisions separated by some sixty years.[4]

Equal treatment made sense in the classical *polis* with its teleological concept of nature. But modernity destroyed classical *dike*. It undermined communities of virtue and value, and turned individual freedom into the cornerstone of community. The theory of justice became preoccupied with the proper criteria of social distribution and has, been rehearsing for some 300 years, various irreconcilable tests such as desert, ability, entitlement or need. Others, faced with the inherent difficulties of these principles of distribution, equate justice with some other value such as equality,[5] fairness,[6] or procedure.[7] Yet others have insisted on a linguistic analysis of the uses of the word 'justice' or 'fairness', hoping to discover behind linguistic variations and idiosyncrasies a common kernel or quality that will enable us to understand the concept.

A survey of these theories and approaches confirms the impression that justice is blessed or cursed with a bewildering number of conflicting conceptions and interpretations. Justice is praised as the highest virtue of social and legal institutions but its study is clouded in uncertainty and disputation. Despite the ferocity of the rhetorical affirmations and polemical denunciations, theory offers little agreement as to its nature and action. If justice is the name of the social bond,[8] the various theories of justice look like so many masks or fronts for a diverse array of deeply antagonistic conceptions of the good society. Every theory of justice seems to offer conclusive arguments to its critics for its refutation, every law or constitution applying a model of justice is soon found wanting and is portrayed as a sad or brutal repository of injustice. If there is a common characteristic to theories of justice, it is their unceasing tendency to attack and replace earlier ones, before themselves becoming obsolete. After centuries of thought, justice seems as remote as ever. 'The resigned wisdom applies' argued Hans Kelsen, 'that man cannot find a definitive answer, but can only try to improve the question'.[9] The only service that philosophy and jurisprudence

[3] Plato, *Laws*, TJ Saunders (trans), (London, Penguin, 1988) Bk *VI*, 757.

[4] *Plessy v Ferguson* 163 US 537 (1896); *Brown v Board of Education of Topeka* 349 US 294 (1955).

[5] A Buchanan, *Marx and Justice* (London, Methuen, 1982); H Collins, *Marxism and Law* (Oxford, Clarendon, 1982); S Lukes, *Marxism and Justice* (Oxford, Clarendon, 1985).

[6] J Rawls, *A Theory of Justice* (Oxford, Oxford University Press, 1971); 'The Law of Peoples' in S Shute and S Hurley (eds), *On Human Rights* (New York, Basic Books, 1993) 1–82.

[7] A Heller, *Beyond Justice* (Oxford, Blackwell, 1987).

[8] JR Lucas, *On Justice* (Oxford, Clarendon, 1980) chapter 1.

[9] H Kelsen, *What is Justice?* (Berkeley, University of California Press, 1971) 1.

can offer is 'to provide means for a more accurate and informed definition of disagreement rather than for progress toward its resolution'.[10]

The recognition that theories of justice provide a 'definition of disagreement' points to the most striking characteristic of justice: this self-proclaimed quality of every political and legal system has been something of a philosophical failure. No society or ideology has developed an acceptable theory of justice, and it is fair to assume that no such theory can be developed this late in the day. Theories of justice are repeated recognitions of the failure to define justice or imagine the conditions under which a just society can come into existence.[11] There can be no greater evidence of the magnitude of this failure than the fact that the foundational texts of classical civilisation, Homer and Plato, the prophets and the Bible, are prolonged meditations on justice, and yet from the perspective of us latecomers, us postmoderns, no generally acceptable principles, ideas or values have been agreed.

But there is a reasonable refutation of this argument: while the various conceptions of justice emerge historically and are bound to their place and time, the idea or the essence of justice transcends them all and is not restricted by the vagaries of historical circumstance or the limitations of concrete formulations. Indeed, Rawls starts his celebrated theory by claiming that 'justice is the first virtue of social institutions as truth is of systems of thought.'[12] The analogy between justice and truth, first used by Plato, is apposite: most analytical philosophers assume that justice is a concept with universal validity. In the same way that truth is seen as cognitively independent of particular theories of knowledge, justice too, it is claimed, is not normatively bound by its environment.

But the concept itself, the idea of justice, is as controversial as its conceptions. The philosophical failure is so radical that one could argue that the problem does not lie with particular theories or conceptions of justice but with the idea itself. No theory of justice seems capable of leading the way to the just society or the new Jerusalem. Every theory on offer has, therefore, failed. It may be that the ability of language is limited in this regard or that the scope of theory fundamentally differs from the operation of justice; or again, it may be impossible 'to produce a learned discourse upon what justice is' because justice has no theory or model.[13] Despite the failure, justice has always been the *deus ex*

[10] A MacIntyre, *Whose Justice? Which Rationality?* (London, Duckworth, 1988) 3. Lyotard and Rorty agree with MacIntyre's diagnosis but conclude that the problem lies not with particular conflicting theories but with the theoretical enterprise itself. J-F Lyotard, *Just Gaming* (Manchester, Manchester University Press, 1985); R Rorty, 'Human Rights, Rationality and Sentimentality' in S Shute and S Hurley (eds), *On Human Rights*, above n 6, 111–34.

[11] Formal and procedural theories of justice start from the recognition that people have different conceptions of the good life and therefore there is no common or generally acceptable pattern of cooperation. They therefore concentrate their efforts on creating the formal conditions which will allow people to pursue their antagonistic projects. Rawls's theory of justice as fairness is such a theory. It is a recognition of the failure of those philosophies of justice which tried to specify what a good society would be.

[12] J Rawls, above n 6, 3.

[13] J-F Lyotard, *Just Gaming*, above n 10, 26.

machina of political and moral philosophy: an all-encompassing but elusive principle, the sanctuary for the messianic, the utopian or simply the pragmatic element of ethics.

But are there any common elements in these failed visions of justice? What is the relationship between the theory of justice and the sense of injustice? The fervour and indignation that the denunciation of injustice can still muster in our apathetic societies indicate a new direction: justice acts as a horizon that transcends our political and legal institutions. If this is the case, our traditional enquiries about justice may have been asking the wrong question. When one asks 'what is justice' the answer will take the form of a definition of the essence and characteristics of justice. But if justice does not belong exclusively to the order of being, truth is not its proper value. As Jean-Francois Lyotard put it, the only certainty is that 'no one can say what the being of justice is'.[14] It may be that justice cannot be known or understood fully, and its exploration resembles the quest for God in negative theology.[15]

For negative theology, God cannot be described through positive or negative statements because he transcends human thought so radically that language cannot signify his essence or the attributes of the divine source. The negative theologian constantly points to the poverty and failures of the discourse on God and tries to shift attention from the various orthodox representations of divinity to a God, who cannot be conceptualised. Negative theology is a discourse of absence.[16] But the great mystics are not just prophets of the absolute absence of a *deus absconditus*. The relationship between God's transcendence and his ever-present representations takes the form of a double bind. Every icon or *imago* of divinity, every description of the marvels of the world, refers back to a prime cause and an ultimate *representatum*; God's absence is present in the endless proliferation of his representations and creations. In this sense, God belongs to being and presence as an absence. But God also transcends the realm of being. He is before being, outside of its force, the condition of possibility of all being. God's command is both 'represent me' and 'do not—you cannot, represent me'.

By analogy, there is not much we can say about the attributes and characteristics of a transcendent justice. Yet justice is the theme of the oldest and most prolific enterprise of thought. A negative jurisprudence examines the positive discourse on justice and points to the causes of its failure and to the emotions, passions and action that injustice gives rise to. We will examine, in turn, some of the major classical and contemporary theories of justice for the signs of their failure. But we start with an examination of the mythological roots of justice. What is striking is the decisive importance they place on injustice.

[14] J-F Lyotard, *Just Gaming*, above n 10, 66.

[15] See Philo, *Allegorical Interpretation, III lxxiii* 206 and K Hart, *The Trespass of the Sign* (Cambridge, Cambridge University Press, 1989).

[16] K Hart, *ibid* 184.

The Origins of Justice and Injustice

The western origins of the thought on *dike* or justice take us back to the Greek pre-Socratic philosophers. Heracleitos believed that things commonly regarded as opposites are in fact united and cannot exist without their opposite. There is no upward path without the downward (fragment 69), there would be no heat if there were no cold (fragment 39), justice would be unknown were it not for injustice (fragment 60).[17] In his most famous fragment, Heracleitos tells us that 'war is universal and justice is strife'. If justice means strife, its cessation would be the end of the world.

The oldest extant text of western thinking, a fragment by Anaximander on justice, has led to a fierce philosophical debate.[18] The fragment reads: 'but where things have their origin, there too their passing away occurs according to necessity; for they are judged and make reparation (*didonai diken*) to one another for their injustice (*adikia*) according to the ordinance of time'.[19] According to Anaximander, an archaic original injustice (*adikia)* comes before time and imposes a debt on beings and things for which they must make reparation in time and in law. Beings must be judged and give endless restitution for their primordial injustice. But what is this injustice?

The German philosopher Martin Heidegger has offered a powerful interpretation of the fragment. According to Heidegger, our form of life and destiny are not of our making. We found ourselves thrown in *medias res* in the middle of an ancient river. The destiny and truth of being is the way a people 'dwells'. This dwelling comprises their knowledge, art and political arrangements as well as a people's understanding of the world, of Gods and of themselves. Its force lies in the 'demand placed on the individual to assume his place within his society, to answer the call of Being in his time'.[20]

[17] Hayek believes that Heracleitos is the earliest philosopher to emphasise the primary character of injustice. However this is inaccurate as the Anaximander fragment is earlier. FA Hayek, *Law, Legislation, Liberty*, Vol 2 (London, Routledge and Kegan Paul, 1976) 162, n 9. See J Burnet, *Early Greek Philosophy*, 4th edn, (London, A & C Black, 1930) 166.

[18] M Heidegger, 'The Anaximander Fragment' in *Early Greek Thinking*, DF Crell and F Capuzzi (trans), (New York, Harper and Row, 1975).

[19] This translation is ours. It combines elements from a number of translations offered in the extensive literature and emphasises the legal character of the fragment. Heidegger's essay is about the various (mis)translations of the fragment. Nietzsche in his early but posthumously published *Philosophy in the Tragic Age of the Greeks* translates it as follows: 'Whence things have their origin, they must also pass away according to necessity; for they must pay the penalty and be judged for their injustice according to the ordinance of time'. The classical translation by Herman Diels in *Fragment of pre-Socratics* states that 'but where things have their origin, there too their passing away occurs according to necessity; for they pay recompense and penalty to one another for their recklessness, according to firmly established time', quoted in M Heidegger, above n 18. Finally JM Robinson, *An Introduction to Early Greek Philosophy* (Boston, Houghton Mifflin, 1968) 34 translates it as 'Into those things from which existing things have their coming into being, their passing away too, takes place according to what must be; for they make reparation to one another for their injustice according to the ordinance of time'.

[20] J Caputo, *Radical Hermeneutics* (Bloomington, Indiana University Press, 1987) 247.

But how does history unfold and what connects the destinies of beings? Heidegger's answer is found in his superb reading of the *Ode on Man*, the famous choral song in Sophocles' tragedy *Antigone*.

> *polla ta deina kouden anthropou deinoteron pelei* (332).
> Numberless wonders (*deina*), terrible wonders walk the world
> but none more wonderful and terrible (*deinoteron*) than man.

Deinon, the key word of the song, has two meanings: it is first man's violent power, evident in knowledge, art and law (*techne).* But it is also the overpowering power of *dike,* the proper order and structure of Being. *Techne,* human knowledge—language, law and institutions—confronts *dike,* the overpowering order of things man finds himself in. In this struggle between *techne* and *dike,* man stops being at home, in the tranquillity and security of his abode. Both the idea of home and of the alien are disclosed in this confrontation. Through naming and acting, violent word and deed, the manifold of beings and humanity's own historical being is made manifest. But this opening of being and history is pursued by the disaster that lurks behind every achievement as its existential precondition: death. The essence of being human rises on the breach into which the overwhelming power of Being bursts, 'in order that this breach itself should shatter against being'.[21] Man cultivates and guards the familiar, home, city and hearth only 'to break out of it and let what overpowers break in'.

Heidegger follows the same approach when he reads the 'fundamental words' of the Anaximander fragment, *dike, adikia* and *tisis* (restitution), to present his ontology. Being appears when beings 'gods and men, temples and cities, sea and land, eagle and snake'[22] come to presence—appear out of their earlier state of non-being—and linger awhile with each other, arranged according to the order of things. Beings appear when Being discloses itself to Man in its many manifestations. The proper presence of beings is this lingering awhile which—against the standard interpretation of the fragment—cannot commit injustice. 'How is what lingers awhile in presence unjust? What is unjust about it? Is it not the right of whatever is present that in each case it lingers awhile, endure and so fulfils presencing?'[23] When they present themselves, beings cannot be out of joint (*adikia*); on the contrary, they are joined with others in the order of their being and care for them. But as it reveals itself in beings, Being withdraws, it becomes concealed and keeps to itself. In this process of unconcealment/concealment beings are cast adrift, Being withdraws and, 'history unfolds . . . Without errancy there would be no connection from destiny to destiny: there would be no history'.[24]

The violence through which history opens is the original injustice of the world. It is linguistic (naming and classifying beings) and proactive (opening

[21] J Caputo, *Radical Hermeneutics* (Bloomington, Indiana University Press, 1987) 163.
[22] M Heidegger, above n 18 at 40.
[23] *Ibid,* at 41.
[24] *Ibid,* at 26.

paths and setting boundaries, creating laws and institutions, mastering the earth and the sea).[25] The opening of history and every 'connection from destiny to destiny' through which history unfolds is the outcome of violence and injustice.[26] Heidegger thinks this violence is necessary and heroic. Ethics cannot be made to measure, and philosophy has little to say about justice. But Anaximander calls this violence unjust, and Heracleitos reminds us that the order and disorder of things—their justice and injustice—are closely related. Heidegger forgets injustice; but his reading confirms the link between justice, strife and violence. History and law come into being through violence and shattering; they persist through catastrophe and death's imminence. Violence is the midwife of the law and injustice the foundation of justice. This is an 'aboriginal injustice in which we share, to which we belong. Older than time, than measure and law, it owns no measure of justice of equality or inequality'.[27] Our sense of injustice, which has established and overthrown institutions, governments and laws, is history's judgement, and reparation for its original and continuing violence. Violence and (resistance to) injustice form the tragic destiny of beings.

But what is the role of this original or 'aboriginal' injustice in the foundation of laws and institutions? This is a question that turns us from archaic cosmology to tragedy and philosophy.

Aeschylus's trilogy, *The Oresteia*, is a myth of origins.[28] Orestes is ordered by Apollo, the male god of light and reason, to avenge the murder of his father Agamemnon by his mother Clytemnestra. Orestes kills his mother and is set upon by the Furies, old and dark goddesses, who protect the earth and the bloodlines of the tribe. The last play of the trilogy, *The Eumenides*, or the Good-Fortuned ones—a euphemism for the Furies—revolves around the trial of Orestes before the Athenian court. The Furies demand Orestes's punishment, while the god Apollo defends him. Apollo is a relatively recent arrival to the pantheon and a novice in relation to the Furies, the daughters of *Gaia* and representatives of the old matrilineal order. The trial ends with a majority of judges finding against Orestes. But Goddess Athena's casting vote for the defendant ties the outcome, and as a result of procedural rules Orestes goes free. The Furies wail and threaten terrible punishments. Victorious Athena sets up a supreme court, the *Areos Pagos*, as symbol of the new secular legal order. But she also consoles the Furies. The tied vote was in no way a humiliation. They

[25] See Heidegger's discussion of the *Ode on Man* in *Introduction to Metaphysics*, R Mannheim (trans), (New York, Doubleday Anchor, 1961) 155 ff and C Douzinas and R Warrington, *Justice Miscarried* (Edinburgh, Edinburgh University Press, 1995), chapter 2.

[26] 'Does Heidegger repeat a tradition that persists in knowing nothing of its injustices, nothing of others' suffering, nothing of its own subjections, that knows nothing of these in the name of truth, hopes to pay no penalty for that truth?' S Ross, *Injustice and Restitution: The Ordinance of Time* (New York, State University of New York Press, 1993) 4. J-F Lyotard in *Heidegger and the 'Jews'*, A Michel and A Roberts (trans), (Minneapolis, University of Minnesota Press, 1990) also ascribes Heidegger's forgetfulness of the Holocaust to a certain structure of his theory of 'unconcealment' (*aletheia*) of Being.

[27] S Ross, *Injustice and Restitution*, above n 26, 10.

[28] Aeschylus, *Oresteia*, R Lattimore (trans), (Chicago, University of Chicago Press, 1953).

will continue to be revered and every newborn child will be given to their protection. As a myth of origins, *Eumenides* relates the foundation of law to reason, force and justice.

The Athenian political and legal system, with the court of law at its centre, rises out of two conflicts: between the divine and the chthonic and between female and male. Law emerges out of a profound and unpunished crime, Orestes's matricide. Oedipus's patricide was the result of an ancient curse. Orestes too was the victim of forces beyond his control; but his crime, unlike that of Oedipus, is only partly the result of past events; its commission looks to the future. His crime is the necessary precondition for the establishment of the law-court as the key institution of the new democratic Athens. As Kuhns put it, 'Orestes cannot know that he is directed to act on behalf of a further purpose; he does not know that the crime is committed in order that he may be judged', so that the law can come into existence.[29] The crime begets the law that will judge it and the newly-established court asserts itself by twice committing violence against women: first, against Clytemnestra, the murdered mother whose death will not be avenged and, secondly, the Furies, the ancient goddesses of earth and kinship, whose justice is presented as blind, 'childish and barbarous',[30] irrational, vindictive and regressive. Apollo, the counsel for Orestes, is described, on the contrary, as new, progressive, civilised, rational and enlightened.[31] The court founded as a result of the success of this first trial, will judge through argument and 'holy persuasion' and not through force (970).

Apollo's arguments in court are quite revealing. Clytemnestra's murder by her son is less heinous than her killing of her husband as revenge for the sacrifice of their daughter, Iphigenia. Furthermore, matricide does not call for the harsh punishment that the Furies want to visit on Orestes, because the 'mother is not the true parent of the child; she is the nurse who tends the growth of young seed' (658–61). The new law is founded on an attack on motherhood and womanhood. 'To break the binding force of the symbiotic force between mother and child, Apollo needs a new forum, namely a law court, the city's device, which admits the use of logical argument and debate'.[32] The law court is founded on violence and uses reason to commit further violence. The Furies express the injustice of this new justice well:

> Now true and false must change their names,
> Old law and justice be reversed,
> If new authority put first
> The wrongful right this murderer claims (490–2).

[29] R Kuhns, *The House, the City and the Judge* (Indianapolis, Irrington Publications, 1962) 35.

[30] R Lattimore, 'Introduction' to the *Oresteia*, fn 28 at 30.

[31] See JP Euben, *The Tragedy of Political Theory* (Princeton, NJ, Princeton University Press, 1990) 77ff and, for the various distinctions and hierarchies of value, F Zeitlin, 'The Dynamics of Misogyny in the Oresteia' in J Peradotto and JP Sullivan (eds), *Women in the Ancient World: The Arethusa Papers* (New York, State University of New York Press, 1984) 181–2.

[32] Zeitlin, *ibid* at 178.

and in response to the acquittal, they add

> The old is trampled by the new
> Curse on you younger gods who override
> The ancient laws and rob me of my due (778–80).

If the Furies represent the old law of revenge or *lex talionis*, their original justice is overthrown in an act of violent injustice to their just claims. For law to come into existence, a previous justice is destroyed and untold violence is committed. The law commits the crime it condemns. And yet the justice of the Furies is not totally forgotten by Athena, when she draws the constitution of her court:

> For fear, enforcing goodness,
> must somewhere reign enthroned,
> And watch men's ways and teach them,
> Through self-inflicted sorrow,
> That sin is not condoned (516–8).

Athena offers the Furies a place opposite Zeus' *agoraios,* (Zeus of the forum), and makes them part of the new legal institution. *Philia* and *peitho*, persuasion through argument and the mean between extremes (528–30), are the principles of the new law. *Dike* becomes *techne*, argument, calculation and measure. But the *techne* of the orator and the balancing of the court are not enough. 'Fear and terror (the *deinon*) should not be driven from the city' (690–9). At the end, Athena herself, the wise androgynous maiden born out of the head of Zeus, comes to praise the Furies who have the power to rule among men and give songs to some and tears to others (930, 954–5). They are renamed *Eumenides,* the Kindly Ones.

In the eyes of the court, old *dike* is terror and injustice. But the terror of injustice must be domesticated and turned to good use. Law and political authority will be based on violence and rational argument, on force and gentle persuasion, on emotions, passions and fear. 'There is advantage in the wisdom won by pain' (529–31). Athena hopes that the domestication and rational use of the Furies will help pacify the conflict between reason and emotion, justice and violence. But these hopes are denied in almost every tragedy and most clearly in Sophocles' *Antigone.*

Creon is the representative of the enlightenment, Apollo's partner. His laws aim to increase the happiness of citizens and to promote the common good, presented as an internally coherent set of values. Creon's practical wisdom and civilising temper have no limit: good judgment, *phronesis*, is the most precious gift and its lack, *me phronein,* Antigone's affliction, the worst curse (1050–1). Godly and human reason do not differ; to know man is to know god and fate. Creon abhors the prospect that women might acquire public power and categorically refutes the claim that a distinct form of female rationality exists, except perhaps madness. Neither religious nor family ties should make any difference in the way rational men conduct their affairs. Creon's favourite word is *symmetros*; the concept of symmetry permeates the discourse of rationality. It is a juridical harmony of higher and lower principles, where reason triumphs over madness, male over female, age and experience over youth, right over wrong (281; 719ff; 1088).

Antigone's justice in contrast does not calculate or balance.

> It wasn't Zeus, not in the least,
> who made this proclamation—not to me.
> Nor did that Justice (*Dike*), dwelling with the gods
> beneath the earth, ordain such laws (*nomous*) for men.
> Nor did I think your edicts had such force
> that you a mere man, could override
> the great unwritten and certain laws of the gods
> *(agrapta kasphale theon nomima).*
> They are alive, not just today or yesterday:
> they live forever, and no one knows
> when they were first legislated (446–57).

Antigone juxtaposes the divine proclamations of Zeus and of chthonic *Dike* to the laws of the city. Divine law is unwritten, certain and eternal; as unwritten law it is felt and acted upon by those who receive its call. It lives in the actions of people rather than in public proclamations. Its certainty calls, not for interpretation, but for immediate action that does not weigh advantage and deficit. Antigone's calculus is an assault on rationalism: to die before her time carrying out her duty is, for her, a 'gain' (464). Finally, *ta theon nomima,* the laws of the gods, are *everlasting*; they exist before and beyond the time of political institutions and human devices like writing. In Antigone's world, Heaven and Hades intrude upon history as disturbances of temporality and rationality. The timelessness of their commands stands a as permanent challenge to the timeliness of the laws and institutions that establish the boundaries of the city.

At the end, Antigone chooses death out of love for her dead brother, while Creon is destroyed because of the folly of his wisdom. Antigone is the revenge of the Furies over Apollo and Athena. But her death, like that of Socrates, marks the history of law and shows its inescapable association with violence and injustice. The philosophers will try to cleanse the remnants of ancient injustice from the law and make justice fully calculable, an almost mathematical operation. But injustice and its horror have been entombed in the institution. Death and violence are launched in law from its beginnings, its foundation is the burial stone of Antigone. This sepulchral quality makes Benjamin say that 'there is something rotten in law.'[33] There is a darkness at the heart of law, an injustice for which the institution will be paying its restitution in the fullness of time. It is this original injustice that has made the task of the philosophy of justice almost impossible.

[33] W Benjamin, 'Critique of Violence' in P Demetz (ed), *Reflections* (New York, Schocken Books, 1978) 286.

Classical Theories of Justice

The classical formulation of the problem of justice, both in the Old Testament and in Greek philosophy and tragedy, involves the denunciation of a double *in*justice: 'the world is regarded as *unjust*, as the very negation of justice, and this negation of justice must itself be negated . . . men are unjust because they are corrupt and wicked, rather than righteous, and society (or the body politic) is unjust because it puts a premium on wickedness and allows the righteous to be trampled upon and perish'.[34] The striking characteristic in this *ethico-political* idea of justice is its identification of justice with righteousness and of injustice with wickedness—in other words—the close link between justice and the good. In ancient natural teleology men have an aim in life, which places them in the order of the world. Virtuous action helps them move from what they are to what they ought to be. The law is a recognition and statement of the normative aspects of this purposive cosmos. It exists in the order and law of the city, as Socrates argued in *Crito,* but it is also a future projection, the promise of an unknown and constantly deferred utopian perfection.

These two aspects are represented by Plato and Aristotle. Plato's *Republic* remains the earliest and most sustained discussion of justice. Both in form and substance, *The Republic* has framed the parameters of subsequent debates and has launched a thousand attempts to arrive at a rational definition of justice. The quest is conducted in the form of a dialogue between Socrates, the defender of justice as righteousness, and various Sophists and other purveyors of commonsensical wisdom. The dialogue proceeds through the refutation of various definitions that Socrates shows to be wrong because they describe injustice rather than justice.[35] Socrates aims to explore the meaning of injustice, hoping that this will unlock the universal and absolute nature of justice. He searches the truth about justice, a search that must be conducted by reason alone. The Socratic quest for justice is a refutation of injustice through reason.

Socrates starts by dismissing conventional theories. Justice is not about giving people their due; or telling the truth and paying one's debts; nor, finally, doing good to friends and harm to enemies. He then turns to the main challenge—Thrasymachus's cynical view that what passes for 'justice' is the expression of the interests of the rulers, the wealthy and the strong. From this perspective, the truly righteous man will always lose out.[36] It is in the interest of the virtuous, therefore, to act unjustly and to promote their own benefit since injustice gives more strength, freedom and mastery than the misnomer 'justice'. Thrasymachus's challenge goes to the heart of the rationalist dialectic. He

[34] A Heller, *Beyond Justice*, above, n 7, 54.

[35] See FA Hayek, *Law, Legislation, Liberty*, above n 17, 162, n 2.

[36] The Sophist Callicles in *Gorgias* had argued, in a proto-Nietzschean manner, that men are divided by nature into the strong and the weak, and that law and convention are the creations of inferiors who use the talk of justice to drag their superiors to their own low level.

admonishes Socrates to stop 'playing to the gallery by refuting others . . . It's easier to ask questions than to answer them. Give us an answer yourself, and tell us what you think justice is.'[37] Socrates repudiates this view vehemently; it is most dangerous because it is convincing to the philosophically naive. But despite his long denunciation, Socrates admits at the end that he cannot define justice. He insists, however, that justice is good and injustice evil, and that doing justice is always more advantageous than committing injustice.[38] Reason commands that it is better to suffer injustice than to commit injustice.

But Socrates soon realises that while philosophy is committed to the rule of reason, reason alone cannot win the argument. Reason cannot prove that it is better to suffer injustice than to commit it. Socrates knows that, as Ovid put it, *video meliora proboque; deteriora sequor* (I know the good and approve of it, but I follow evil). To win his audience over, Socrates supplements his arguments with a number of non-rational assertions. Righteousness should be practiced because it brings happiness—an argument that can be empirically ascertained only by those who are already righteous. Although he explicitly dismisses the theory of justice as retribution, he reminds his interlocutors of the religious myths of Radamanthus and Er who threaten retribution for evil deeds in the afterlife. Finally, Socrates admits that while philosophy is the best teacher of conscience and the city, the authority and discipline of parents and legislators may be the only realistic way for the instruction of virtue to the many.

Socrates offers no definition of justice. Justice is first replaced by reason, later, by the idea of the good—presented as its substance and ultimate value. The good of the individual and of the *polis* provide the necessary criteria for choosing between competing courses of action, but the good itself is not accessible to reason. Similarly with justice: Socrates follows various routes in his quest and repeatedly re-affirms that justice and the good exist and are the highest values. But all attempts to define or describe their content are soon abandoned, and the dialogue circles from justice to the good, and back. The closest we come to the essence of justice is when Socrates compares the constitution of ideal city and citizen. They both follow the principle of 'doing one's own and proper task', *suum agere*. The right constitution leads to a balanced relationship between the three classes of citizens and between the three parts of the soul. But *suum agere* is a formal principle and gives no guidance as to what is to count as proper and due to each. In any case, after the tripartite division has been presented, Socrates draws back; if the comparison of state and soul is not fruitful we will have to move on.[39] The most sustained attempt to describe the characteristics of justice is abandoned.

Every time the discussion appears to move to a conclusion the position is abandoned and the search starts again. The good is finally declared to be

[37] Plato, *The Republic*, D Lee (trans), (London, Penguin, 1974) 336c.
[38] *Ibid*, 354b.
[39] *Ibid*, 435.

epekeina ousias, beyond Being and essence, at the other side of knowledge and reason. As Plato admits in his seventh Epistle, we can never fully know the good 'for it does not admit of verbal expression like other branches of knowledge.'[40] Justice too, the political expression of the good, cannot be discovered in laws and in written treatises. It has no essence or, its essence lies in the 'city in the sky'. The quest for justice exemplifies the paradox of reason, formulated by Socrates 'in the most extreme manner: reasoning leads to unreason. Faith surfaces three times and in three forms: faith in other-worldly justice, faith in authority, and faith in revelation'.[41] Socrates's ultimate argument overshadows reason and faith: he sacrifices himself on the altar of a justice that cannot be defined, nor its superiority proven rationally, but which must be acted upon, even at the greatest of costs. Socrates's death is the strongest argument about the inherent injustice of the law. After his death the burden of proof lies with those who believe in law's justice.

The Republic is the first attempt to raise justice into a universal ethical idea, completely independent of its historical context. People must leave the cave or prison of empirical existence and enter the world of ideas or forms before they can grasp the operation of the good and of justice. *The Republic*'s unrelenting attack on conventional and traditional views is coupled with its inability to define justice. The truth about justice may not be accessible at all, in which case we must remain silent in these matters.[42] Philosophy's contribution is to refute the falsehoods of the common sense. Socrates represents not the triumph of reason but the first clear formulation of what can be called the *aporia of justice*: to be just is to act justly, to be committed to a frame of mind and follow a course of action that must be accepted before conclusive rational justification. From Anaximander to Socrates, early philosophy claimed that men have a sense of injustice that constantly moves them to seek justice by building legal and moral systems. But justice is not fully of this world. Justice is caught in an unceasing movement between knowledge and passion, reason and action, this world and the next; rationalism and metaphysics.

Aristotle takes the rational quest for justice further.[43] Against Plato's attack on convention he defines justice as giving everyone his due. The Aristotelian moral agent is the prudent man, who acquires his moral sense and discrimination in the course of a life of practical experience. His judgement is always situated in the concrete circumstances of the case at hand. Moral knowledge becomes sensitive to context and circumstance and practical judgements involve calculations, tempered by experience and prudence and guided by the aims

[40] Plato, Epistle VII, in *Phaedrus and Epistles VII and VII*, W Hamilton (trans), (London, Penguin, 1973) 341c. For a full discussion of the Platonic search for the meaning of justice and the good and his admission of defeat see H Kelsen, *What is Justice?* above n 9.

[41] A Heller, *Beyond Justice*, above n 7, 73.

[42] Plato, Epistle VII, 337.

[43] For a discussion of Aristotle's ethics see JO Urmson, *Aristotle's Ethics* (Oxford, Blackwell, 1988) and WFR Hardie (Oxford, Oxford University Press, 1980).

inherent in persons and things by their nature. But the links between justice, righteousness, ethics and the city remain. Man is a political animal and it is only in a just *polis* that the individual becomes a virtuous citizen; conversely just men make the city great.

Aristotle distinguished between a general and a particular justice. General justice is the 'moral disposition which render men apt to do just things, and which causes them to act justly and to wish what is just'.[44] Justice belongs to the virtues, but it is not just one more virtue; it is the whole of virtue, complete righteousness as it regards others. Justice is virtue addressed to the 'good of others', *allotrion agathon*. We saw in chapter 3, how the just and the lawful coincided in classical Greece. The 'unjust' man is a law-breaker and someone who takes more than his due. But Aristotle adds, in an early corrective to formalism, that illegality is unjust only if the law is 'rightly enacted'.[45] The prime case of an unjust law is one that does not promote the good as it regards others.

Particular justice is concerned with distribution and retribution. A just distribution of 'honour, wealth and other divisible assets of the community' follows the principle of proportionality, of 'equal shares for equals and unequal for unequals'. The *dikaion*, just and lawful distribution, will be determined by the nature of the object and the claimant's merit, and desert will be proportionate according to the decisive quality—equality in democracy, birth in aristocracy, virtue in oligarchy. Corrective justice, on the other hand, restores equality between the parties by returning them to their position before the act disturbed their equilibrium.

But Aristotle's theory of justice cannot be understood outside of its intricate connection with his approach to practical wisdom and judgement, *phronesis*. Ethics aims to achieve the good life. But the good is always situated; it is good for us. It involves an ongoing dialogue and adjustment between our actions and our overall 'life plan', which makes us believe that our life through its various successes, despite its frequent mishaps, is a fulfilled, good life. Against this background, *phronesis* is the method of deliberation followed by the prudent. While science (*episteme*) examines general principles and the formal connections between phenomena, practical knowledge as *phronesis* deals with the changing and the variable, with the 'ultimate particulars' of each situation in its singularity.[46] Practical judgements, unlike theoretical statements, do not deal with truth, essences or necessary and immutable relations. They have a timely and circumstantial character and they depend on a full and detailed understanding of the facts. Indeed Aristotle goes as far as to compare the singularity of practical judgement to that of sense perception, *aisthesis*.[47]

[44] Aristotle, *Nicomachean Ethics*, Bk V, *i*, 3.
[45] *Ibid*, at 14.
[46] *Ibid*, 215.
[47] *Ibid*, 219–20.

For Aristotle, equity (*epieikeia*) is the rectification of legal justice (*nomos*), insofar as the law is defective because of its generalisations. While laws are universal, 'the raw material of human behaviour' is such that it is often impossible to subsume under general terms. Thus 'justice and equity coincide, and both are good, [but] equity is superior'.[48] Because people and life have an 'irregular shape', the law should resemble the leaden rule used by Lesbian masons: 'just as this rule is not rigid but is adapted to the shape of the stone, so the ordinance is framed to fit the circumstances'.[49] There is no model or blueprint to guide the judge—his true vocation is to give justice in the absence of set criteria or rules. Each case is unique and the judge must develop and fine-tune the art (*techne*) of evaluating the forces, relations and arguments involved. Justice is the outcome of the just judgement, but whether the judge is just or not cannot be judged in advance of the judgement. Particular justice, the art of distribution, of evaluation and calculation must be conducted against the horizon of general justice, the 'whole of virtue', which demands the 'good of the other' but cannot be theorised outside its context. Aristotle is preoccupied with the method of arriving at just decisions, but his approach indicates that it may be 'impossible to produce a learned discourse upon what justice is.'[50]

Augustine's theory of justice combines the failures of Plato's metaphysical quest and Aristotle's rationalism. Aristotle believed that a non-sacral version of *dike*, the order of the world, still existed in his time, and that just laws and constitutions were part of its nature. His identification of law with justice was, therefore, a way of strengthening the authority of law while retaining the dynamic character of justice according to nature. Augustine, on the other hand, equated the two in order to undermine the authority of the still pagan Roman Empire. His definition of justice followed Aristotle: *tribuere suum cuique*, to give each his due. But while for Aristotle, a man's due was determined by the *ethos* of his *polis* and the judgements of the practically prudent, the Christian Bishop believed that man's due is to serve God. The virtue of justice was defined as *ordo amoris*, the love of order: by attributing to each his proper degree of dignity, justice leads men to an ideal state in which the soul is subjected to God and the body to the soul. When this order is absent, man, law and state are unjust. Justice is therefore the love of the God as the highest good.

Unjust law is no law and an unjust state is no state. Without justice, states become great robberies. 'Where there is no true justice there can be no law. For what is done by law is justly done, and what is unjustly done cannot be done by law. For the unjust inventions of men are neither to be considered nor spoken of as rights.'[51] But while injustices are denounced, the earthly city is called the *civitas diaboli*. Its laws come into existence and are called just out of necessity.

[48] *Ibid*, 199.
[49] *Ibid*, 200.
[50] J-F Lyotard, *Just Gaming*, above n 10, 26.
[51] Augustine, *De Civitate Dei*, M Dods, J Smith and G Wilson (trans), (New York, Random House, Modern Library, 1950) at Bk *XIX*, ch 21.

Augustine's denunciation of the injustice of the pagan state and its law is only one consequence of his deep pessimism about the human condition. The fall and original sin make it impossible for secular law and justice to redeem people from evil. Justice is an attribute of God and does not belong to this world. We can never know God's wishes, justice will remain a promise that cannot be fulfilled in this life. Indeed, ignorance is such that we cannot even fully understand fellow humans. Christian princes and judges, despite good intentions, cannot expect, therefore, to know people well enough to pass correct judgments. Secular justice is a misnomer and a poor approximation of the justice of God and, while necessary, its success will always be limited and its lamentable judgments based on cognitive and practical ignorance. As Judith Shklar puts it, 'injustice embraces more than those social ills that justice might alleviate. The State's is the sum of our moral failures as sinful people, which from the outset dooms us to being unjust.'[52] The function of states and laws is to coerce men, to restrain their *cupiditas,* their insatiable desire and to keep the peace. The state has no intrinsic legitimacy and the nations are certain to decline and fall. Its limited utility is to meet internal and external violence with violence.

Against the classical tradition, Augustine argued that 'the removal of justice [not only does] not lead to the breaking up of a state, but in fact there never has been a state that was maintained by justice.'[53] Those few predestined to be saved will live in *the civitas terrena* as *peregrini*, itinerant foreigners, until they join the realm of true justice in the city of God in the hereafter. Agreeing with Plato, Augustine argued that we can neither fully know nor achieve justice in this world. Justice identified with God's love does not belong to this world; injustice becomes the condition of humanity. The Stoics had placed their utopia in a mythical past, while the city of God belongs to an unknown but pre-determined and certain future. Augustine is the first political philosopher who both accepted and legitimised the might of the state, and proposed a higher divine justice that state law flagrantly violates. Augustine's Christian peregrines were asked not to contrast the two but 'to tolerate even the worst, and if need be, the most atrocious form of polity.'[54] But the juxtaposition between heaven and earth, and their sharp separation, had created the conditions for their eventual comparison and combination. As the two-world metaphysics was gradually weakened, the time came when the principles of heaven were made to justify the infamies of earth.

In this long trajectory, justice was finally identified with God's love and was made transcendent to this world, while injustice became the condition of humanity. We are thrown into this world of archaic *adikia;* our theories of justice cannot save us from its ravages. One way around this problem is to refute or downgrade the significance of injustice by turning justice into a pragmatic

[52] J Shklar, *The Faces of Injustice* (New Haven, Yale University Press, 1990) 26.

[53] D Bigongiari, 'The Political Ideas of St Augustine' in H Paolucci (ed), *St Augustine, The Political Writings* (Washington DC, Gateway, 1962) 346.

[54] Augustine, *De Civitate Dei*, above n 52, *XVIII*, 2.

theory of little consequence or by identifying it with the law of the state. This is the dominant approach of modern philosophy.

MODERN THEORIES OF JUSTICE

The classical *ethico-political* idea of justice identified justice with righteousness and injustice with wickedness and brought together justice and the good. But for the jurisprudence of modernity this internal relationship has been severed. Justice has been broken up into its legal and social components, into legalism and principles of distribution. But legal justice, the impartial application of rules, has nothing to say about the content or the nature of the rule as 'just' or 'right'. Strangely, this denuding of legal or formal justice of all ethical concerns has been hailed as its greatest moral accomplishment.[55]

'Now laws remain in credit not because they are just but because they are laws. That is the mystic foundation of their authority; they have no other. And that is a good thing about them' wrote the French essayist Montaigne.[56] Blaise Pascal agrees:

> Nothing according to reason alone, is just in itself; all changes with time. Custom creates the whole of equity, for the simple reason that it is accepted. It is the mystic foundation of its authority; whoever carries it back to first principles destroys it. Nothing is so faulty as those laws which correct faults. He who obeys them because they are just, obeys a justice which is imaginary, and not the essence of the law; it is quite self-contained, it is law and nothing more.[57]

The law is just because it is the law, in other words, law's justice derives from its force and longevity. According to Pascal, a philosophy of justice that goes back to first principles or attributes justice to law's reason is not just wrong, it is dangerous. But this is precisely the philosophy of Plato, which the Romans continued and which is today expressed in the jurisprudence of rights. For Cicero, law is the highest reason and its commands are always just.[58] This is exactly the claim, warns Pascal, which will destroy law's force. The law repeats in its punishments the crimes it commits. But if the law lacks any moral qualities, where does its force come from—what is the authority of law's authority? If law's force is partially the result of time's passage, if law is timely and all changes with time, we must assume that law's 'mystic' foundation must be found before time or outside the time of the institution. Finally, if the justice of the law is imaginary, and if there is no non-imaginary justice, we must explore the relationship between justice and the social imaginary. These questions will be addressed in chapter 12.

[55] See C Douzinas and R Warrington, *Justice Miscarried*, above n 25.

[56] M de Montaigne, 'Of Experience' in the *Complete Works of Montaigne*, DM Frame (trans), (Stanford, Stanford University Press, 1958) 821.

[57] B Pascal, *Penses*, WF Trotter (trans), (New York, EP Dutton, 1932) 84.

[58] Cicero, *Republic*, N Rudd (trans), (Oxford, Oxford University Press, 1998) *III*, 22.

Montaigne's question reminds us that legal systems have tried to collapse the question of law and justice, or of social order and social imagination. But 'only the blindest of dogmatisms could prevent the recognition of how much injustice there is in the juridical history of mankind.'[59] To understand the way in which the relationship between law, justice and violence is understood in modernity, we must turn to the 'deontological' school of ethics, which was initiated by Immanuel Kant and has dominated moral and legal philosophy. Kant's aim was to reconcile individual freedom with morality and rationality.

According to Kant, classical philosophy made the mistake of positing a conception of the good first, and deriving the (moral) law from this concept. 'The ancients openly revealed this error by devoting their ethical investigation entirely to the definition of the concept of the highest good and thus posited an object which they intended subsequently to make the determining ground of the will in the moral law'.[60] But in so doing 'their fundamental principle was always heteronomy and they came inevitably to empirical conditions for a moral law'.[61] Kant reversed this procedure. Morality is not grounded in some pre-existing idea of the good, nor does it derive from an external source. It is not a given conception of the good that posits the law; rather the moral law defines what is good and evil. Moral action meets certain universal or 'transcendental' preconditions found in the free and rational action of the subject who follows the law out of a pure sense of duty and respect. The most general form of the law, the categorical imperative states: 'Act in such a way that the maxim of your will can always be valid as the principle establishing universal law'[62] or, in its more Christian formulation, 'act so that you treat humanity, whether in your person or in that of an other, always as an end'.[63]

This law is imperative, but it commands the will to follow a pure form (the maxim or principle of action should always take the form of a universal norm). For Kant, the standard Christian principles of marriage, family and promise-keeping are strict requirements of reason and, purged of all 'pathological' elements, such as feelings, passions and emotions, meet his stringent formal criteria.[64] Secondly, this law that obligates the will emanates from the will itself. Man becomes an autonomous subject in a double sense: he is free—the subject who gives the law to himself—and, he is also the legal subject, subjected to the law. The law commands universality—a pure form and a requirement of reason. But as reason is found in the subject, the subject is free because he finds all determinations in himself. The moral law hurts; we must follow its injunctions disinterestedly, out of a pure sense of duty, abandoning all feeling, emotion and

[59] G Del Vecchio, *Justice: An Historical and Philosophical Essay*, edited with additional notes by AH Campbell (Edinburgh, Edinburgh University Press, 1952) 131.

[60] I Kant, *Critique of Practical Reason*, WL Beck (trans), (London, Macmillan, 1956) 66–7.

[61] *Ibid*, 66.

[62] *Ibid*, 30.

[63] *Ibid*, 47.

[64] At around the same time, Hume bases his moral principles, which are similar in content to those of Kant, on desire and the passions.

desire. Modern justice is the total and painful subjection to the law. No longer does justice commune with aspirations of the soul. It works through the suffering that reason imposes on desire.

Duty and respect are equally important for morality and legality. Moral action follows the universal law of reason, legality is obedience to the laws of the state. Autonomy dictates that laws, to be just, must be prescribed by those who have to obey them. This is the function of the social contract, which, as a requirement of reason, lies behind state law. This contract commands the legislator to introduce laws as if they emanated from the will of the people—as if people had participated in the formation of the law. But this way, Kant seriously weakened Rousseau's concrete democratic demands by accepting that the laws of the autocratic Prussian state meet his formal criteria. 'The Penal Law is the categorical imperative' he enthuses, it 'is the right of RETALIATION'.[65]

The conflict between universal reason and Prussian legislator is conveniently sidestepped. Reason's authority is logically unquestionable and questioning law's authority is prohibited. 'The Origin of the Supreme Power is practically inscrutable by the People who are placed under its authority. In other words the Subject need not reason too curiously in regard to its origin in the practical relation, as if the Right of the obedience due to it were to be doubted.' The law is threatened by any examination of its 'inscrutable origin' and does not take to 'curious subjects' kindly: 'For, should the Subject, after having dug down to the ultimate origin of the State, rise in opposition to the present ruling Authority, he would expose himself as a Citizen, according to the Law and with full Right, to be punished, destroyed or outlawed.'[66] This form of legality leaves no room for resisting the injustices of law. While the law must be followed through the passionless sense of duty, its injustice and violence must be protected through the fear of total outlawry.

Recent deontological theories have turned the categorical command into a methodological principle. A moral principle or law is valid if it would be generally accepted, on rational and non-coerced grounds, by all those affected by it. The moral point of view is identified with a rule or procedure which helps establish how morally relevant principles of action can be judged impartially. Furthermore, Kant's emphasis on duty has been replaced by legal rights and entitlements. A just legal system constructs, distributes and protects a coherent structure of individual rights.

Contemporary theories of justice have two components: formal or legal and economic or legislative. The former is usually presented as equality under the law, the latter as equality through the law. Formal criteria of justice refer to the right operation of primary rules, which regulate social conduct and entitlements. Economic principles are concerned with the right disposition of the primary rules and the distribution of economic resources. Various criteria of fair

[65] *Ibid*, 257, 258.
[66] *Ibid*, 256.

distribution have been proposed, with desert, entitlement and need the most prominent amongst them. Considered as universal principles of distribution, these criteria are incommensurable and mutually exclusive. Rather than providing answers to the problem of distribution, they are evidence of its intractability.

We should add, parenthetically, that the importance that Marx and the socialist tradition placed on economic need and the suffering caused by capitalist exploitation has been invaluable for contemporary explorations of justice. 'From each according to his ability to each according to his needs' has been a powerful statement of the ethics of revolution. But the emphasis on justice as distribution gives a false image of the social bond and leaves the law empty of ethical substance. Despite their increasing sophistication and their apparent differences, liberal theories of justice reach broadly similar conclusions about the principles of justice. In most cases, the theory confirms, with some corrections or permutations, the broad parameters of current social distribution and consequently defines injustice as the absence of the attributes posited by theory.

From this perspective, people are seen exclusively as appropriators and consumers. All aspects of the social bond, including power, emotions and passions, love and desire, are treated as commodities to be owned distributed and exchanged. Justice becomes lawful possession,[67] while the psychology of justice takes the form of an extreme individualism. People inherit, create or in some other way acquire their conception of the good and their value-system, and nothing more can be said about it. All values are equally valid or invalid, and the only acceptable limits are those that are there to protect the essence of liberalism. Values and preferences belong to sociology and market research, emotions, commitments and passions to psychology and psychiatry—but not to philosophy. This equivalence of values, which makes them equally indifferent, is the essence of nihilism: when no value is valued for itself, values have lost their value and their validity is a matter of calculation and manipulation.

The most celebrated neo-Kantian theory is that of John Rawls. Let us follow this type of nihilism in the Rawlsian moral agent. Rawls distinguishes between teleological and liberal approaches to justice. A society is just if it promotes a common and commonly held good in its laws and institutions. Liberal justice, on the other hand, accepts that people follow a plurality of opposing and irreconcilable conceptions of the good. As a result no rational, non-coerced and meaningful agreement as to the content of the good can be attained. Social institutions must be based, therefore, on a theory of justice that is independent of, and prior to, the various conceptions of the good. This is the gist of justice as fairness; it provides a framework of action and distribution of resources, that both allows and limits the conceptions of the good to be pursued. Justice is the

[67] IM Young, *Justice and the Politics of Difference* (Princeton, NJ, Princeton, University Press, 1990) chapter 2.

outcome of the operation of right; what is right is determined by law and the right has priority over the good.

Under these constraints, the procedure offered by Rawls for arriving at the principles of justice as fairness is rather strange. In a further impoverishment of social contract theory, these principles are contractually agreed in what Rawls calls the 'original position'. This 'original' person is blindfolded by a 'veil of ignorance', like the artistic representations of justice. She does not know her class, status, fortune and ability, her intelligence and strength—nor does she have any conception of the good or a rational plan of life. Behind this absurd hypothesis lies the modern concern with, and fear of, the other person. Classical philosophy saw personality as a part of the order of things. Self belongs to history and culture, which determine its aim in life in conjunction with others. But the modern self is a rational egotist. The temporary and heuristic destruction of identity in the original position attempts to place self in a position of reversibility with others: while the agent remains a rational egotist—the model for all modern individuality—she must consider the interests of others, since she cannot predict her exact state in life. Such a huge abstraction from what a real self is, and from how moral argument operates, is necessary in order to sustain the Kantian claim of the universality of the moral law. The subject of moral philosophy is not a real life person but a 'generalised other'; someone we come across and relate to through public and institutional norms of formal equality and reciprocity. The other is a representative of abstract humankind.

We must formulate laws, writes Rawls, 'without the use of what would be intuitively recognised as proper names or rigged definite descriptions.'[68] The other person, the litigant who comes before the law, is stripped of what makes her a real self. Law silences her pain and anger, turns her into the instance of a rule or the example of a principle. Moral philosophy, in its ontological imperialism, needs and creates the generalised other. The law on the other hand, sharing the preoccupation to abstract and universalise, turns concrete people into generalised legal subjects. In existential terms, the subject of legal and contractual rights stands at the centre of the universe and asks the law to enforce his entitlements without great concern for ethical considerations, and without empathy for the other. If the legal person is an isolated and narcissistic subject that perceives the world as a hostile place to be either used or fended against through the medium of rights and contracts (s)he is also disembodied, genderless, a strangely mutilated person.[69] The other as legal subject is a rational being with rights, entitlements and duties like ourselves. We expect to be treated equally with the other, and reciprocity of entitlement and obligation is placed at the basis of the legal mentality. Formal justice as fairness reduces the concreteness of the other, minimises differences of need and desire, and emphasises the

[68] J Rawls, *A Theory of Justice*, above n 6, 131.

[69] For a more detalied discussion see C Douzinas, *The End of Human Rights* (Oxford, Hart Publishing, 2000) chapters 8, 9 and 13.

similarities and homologies between the subjects. The moral worth of the other's demand is to be sought more in what self and other share than in those differences and specificities that make the other a concrete historical being.

But the legal subject, too, is a fiction, and the natural (legal) subject is infinitely more fictitious than the corporate. The difference between the fictions of Rawls and those of the law, is that the legal subject is a persona, a mask, a veil or blindfold put on real people who—unlike the abstractions of moral philosophy—hurt, feel, pain and suffer. The law proceeds by abstraction from 'proper names' and subsumption to the rule. A perfect justice, if such a thing exists, would return to the name and give it its due—would be a judgment from case to case, a perfect casuistry of unique individuals and unrepeated events and moments. It is doubly important in law and jurisprudence, therefore, to remove the mask from the face of subject and the blindfold from the eyes of justice.

As Sheila Benhabib notes, the persons sketched by Rawls may have the capacity of agency but they are defective, unreal human selves.

> Identity does not refer to my potential for choice alone, but to the actuality of my choices, namely to how I, as a finite, concrete, embodied individual, shape and fashion the circumstances of my birth and family, linguistic, cultural and gender identity into a coherent narrative that stands as my life's story . . . The self is not a thing or substrate but the protagonist of a life's tale. The conception of selves that can be individuated prior to their moral ends is incoherent.[70]

The proper moral standpoint of the 'concrete other', by contrast, is based on norms of 'equity and complementary reciprocity: each is entitled to expect and to assume from the other forms of behaviour through which the other feels recognised and confirmed as a concrete, individual being with specific needs, talents and capacities'.[71] The veil of ignorance and all such generalising devices, by obscuring the concreteness of the other, destroy her identity and, because such devises lack the necessary criteria for individuation, they cannot distinguish between self and other.

Rawls' theory is a rare example that utilises the sense of justice. Rawls arrives at his principles by two distinct routes. The contractual method involves disinterested negotiations and agreements between people in the 'original position'. But the same principles can be reached independently, through a systematic reflection based on the moral person's intuition and sense of justice. This second method of contemplation leads to a 'reflective equilibrium' about justice. It consists in selecting some of our strongest moral convictions and trying to discover the most consistent set of principles that can justify them. This set is then refined and adjusted to match and explain other beliefs and intuitions, some of which are revised or abandoned in the process if they are found to be distorted or 'irregular'. Eventually this palindromic movement will yield the most complete

[70] S Benhabib, *Situating the Self* (Bloomington, Indian University Press, 1992), 161–2.
[71] *Ibid.*

and persuasive set of judgements, justifications and principles at a state of equilibrium. 'It is an equilibrium because at last our principles and judgments coincide; and it is reflective since we know to what principles our judgments conform and the premises of their derivation.'[72]

This process allegedly finds a fit between our sense of justice and the better principles of justice available in our culture. Its outcome is compared with the contractual agreements in the 'original position' and after some further adjustments the principles of justice will emerge. The sense of justice therefore has a central role in arriving at a theory of justice. But what is this sense of justice, where is it grounded and what types of emotions and judgements does it lead to? Rawls is quite explicit as to the scope of his theory: it applies only in liberal democratic societies and, even there, it is restricted to the distribution of wealth, benefits and burdens in relation to their basic institutions. In these 'well-ordered' societies, law and the institutions impose their sense of justice on people: '[G]iven that a society's institutions are just and publicly known by all to be just (sic), then a person acquires the corresponding sense of justice as he recognises that he and those for whom he cares are beneficiaries of these arrangements'.[73] The same basic intuitions and emotions about justice, which have been inculcated by the institution, become the starting point and confirmation of the justice of the institution.[74] This rather tight and self-validating circle has no place for intuitions about the injustice of the law and does not understand pain and suffering. Against the classical theories of justice, the concept of Rawls starts and ends with the conventional, the institutional and the commonsensical.

Justice as fairness therefore offers the framework for pursuing incommensurable goods, but in a deeper sense it betrays a total agnosticism—if not hostility—to anything other than a non-procedural morality. All conceptions of the good have been banned from moral philosophy. Not only justice, but morality too, is a thin version of fairness. But this extension of the distributory model to non-material goods objectifies social relationships and underestimates the oppressive potential of the legislative, judicial and administrative institutions that carry out social distributions. Foucault has called this model of power contractual and economic. It assumes that power is a thing that may be possessed and exchanged, owned and disposed of, a zero sum game between individuals. But oppression and domination are not simply effects of one-to-one relations. They are the name for asymmetrical relationships of power; institutions and patterns of distribution are their main expressions.

When justice becomes an economic theory it is pre-occupied with fair shares and good book-keeping, reciprocal exchanges and correct accounts; morality is reduced to a profit and loss account. It is no wonder that justice is seen as a cold virtue. Calculating the value of people through some universal exchange

[72] J Rawls, *A Theory of Justice*, above n 6, 20.
[73] *Ibid*, 491.
[74] M Hardt and A Negri, *Labor of Dionysus* (Minneapolis, University of Minnesota Press, 1994) 228–33.

mechanism, balancing their credit and debit sides on a ledger book of rights and wrongs may satisfy the demand for retribution and may lead to some just returns. But the pain, suffering and oppression of injustice is unaccounted for and ignored. The dominant modern conception of justice, obsessed with investments and returns, is a 'shabby remnant only of the "sum total of virtues" that was once called "justice". On the plane of socio-political justice, only *minima moralia* remain'.[75]

Dominant theories of justice have often been used to defend established distributions and institutional patterns, and to legitimise extreme injustices. As Ernst Bloch put it 'justice is not a category that thought, justifiably dissatisfied, could consider its own.'[76] There are many reasons for this. Classical theories were obsessed with the aristocratic justice of rulers and nobles and neglected the concerns of the 'justifiably dissatisfied' victims. Dominant conceptions of justice have been predominantly patriarchal. God the Father in the Bible, Plato's 'philosopher-kings', Aristotle's just old men and Hegel's masters with their long experience and practical wisdom are venerable representatives of male justice.

Furthermore, theories of justice give greater prominence to the unjust than to the lowly victims of injustice. In Plato, the unjust is a victim of his own defiance of reason, often caused by a disturbed psyche or by madness. By choosing injustice and harming his soul, the unjust is as unfair to himself as to others and deserves greater pity than his victims. Aristotle did not regard the unjust as victims of their own actions but he could still summon sympathy. While the unjust initially choose their injustice, they cannot change later and choose otherwise even if they want to.[77] As a result, being the victim of injustice is a lesser evil than acting unjustly.[78] Slaves and non-citizens did not have any stake in the books of just distribution. The Christian view takes this position to extremes. For Augustine, the slave is better off than the master because he is not exposed to as many temptations and can expect a better judgement in the afterlife. The real victim is not the sufferer but the perpetrator of injustice.[79] Rawls 'original position' belongs to this tradition: by bracketing all reference to the real characteristics of people, it forgets the gender and race of the victims. The rich, the powerful and wise are at greater risk than the poor, the oppressed and the simple. *Dike* is a female deity and Justice, a statuesque woman, but the philosophy and theology of justice are more concerned with the patriarchal notions of social propriety, authority and fairness than with the plebeian emotions of suffering and exploitation or the feminine emotions of empathy and care.

[75] A Heller, *Beyond Justice*, above n 7, 93.

[76] E Bloch, *Natural Law and Human Dignity*, DJ Schmidt (trans), (Cambridge, Mass, MIT Press, 1987) 38.

[77] *Nicomachean Ethics*, Bk *III*, 1114a, 124.

[78] *Ibid,* Bk *V*, 1138a, 292. For the importance of the sense of injustice as a corrective to the failures of justice, see above p 28–32.

[79] Augustine, *De Civitate Dei*, above n 51, 694–8.

Our public justice, despite its democratic legitimacy, remains a justice from above. Laws and institutions express the dominant relations of their times; their justice is an apology of the established relations of power. A theory of 'just war' is not likely to appeal to its Serb or Iraqi victims, a theory of 'just wages' has rarely given rise to major economic redistribution and, a theory of 'just laws' has always been used to discredit disobedience. For democratic theory, the law is just if it is made by the citizens themselves or through their representatives. Without entering the controversy about the meaning of 'representation', it is obvious that there is no better method for weakening the sense of injustice than the claim that legal rules are just because they were legislated by 'us', the citizens. The democratic principle makes the law just without anything else and disobedience to the rule of law becomes the greatest injustice. There is always the theoretical possibility of changing some particular rule but, while it remains valid, it is accorded the full legitimacy of the 'law' and of its democratic justice. Democratic institutions give an extremely restricted answer to the deeply felt offence of injustice. Justice as lawful conduct, or as redress for injustices according to the law, is too tame to heal the wound opened by the desperation of the victim.

Theory has turned its face away from injustice. The only element we can rescue from classical philosophies of justice is, perhaps, their despair about the inability of normal conceptions to deliver justice and about the inevitability of injustice. What unites Plato's rationalism with Augustine's deism is what separates them from the jurisprudence of modernity: their equally strong opposition to the conventional views of their time. The classical writers knew that justice often turns into injustice perpetrated in the name of justice. Injustice has not been eliminated by law, society or individuals. But its consideration is absent from modern jurisprudence. Injustice (*adikia*) has survived this jurisprudential forgetfulness.

The Justice of the Law

The classical writers presented justice as the prime, albeit missing, virtue of the polity and as the spirit and reason of law. A just constitution is a legitimate constitution and a just legal system has a valid claim to the obedience of its citizens. From Aristotle to contemporary political philosophy, justice has been related to the law and legal decision-making. 'Law exists among these between whom there is a possibility of injustice', writes Aristotle.[80] But he immediately adds that legal justice is only one aspect of particular justice. 'Legal justice is different from justice in the primary sense . . . actions prescribed by law are only accidentally just actions. How an action must be performed, how a distribution

[80] Aristotle, *Ethics*, JAK Thomson (trans), (London, Penguin, 1976) 291.

must be made to be a just action or distribution [is a much harder task].'[81] For the Romans, law and justice come together in the order of right reason (*orthos logos*), which is also the order of nature. 'Law is the highest reason implanted in nature, which commands what ought to be done and forbids its opposite' writes Cicero.[82]

We find many similar ideas in the writings of the common lawyers. Justice is cumulatively the foundation, the spirit and the end of the law. As law's immemorial and unwritten foundation, justice links the common law with divine will and its expressions in nature and reason. After the Reformation, justice as equity is explicitly associated with the divine order and becomes law's spirit: 'The chief end or lost mark of the law . . . is God's glory. But the next and immediate end which is allotted to it, is to administer justice to all, and in that sense it may be called the rule of justice: for religion, justice and law do stand together.'[83] Justice is the expression of divine epiphany and law's foundation. It comes before and stands above the human artifice of law and acts as a corrective to its harshness. When law and justice, in the form of equity, are in conflict, the law must give way to higher reason. In all these formulations, justice is seen as the 'primitive reason'[84] of law, its virtue and ethical substance, an ideal or principle that gives rules their aim and limit, and remedies their defects. But justice is also something outside or before the law, a transcendent principle that gives it overall direction, a higher tribunal or reason to which the law and its judgments are called to account. In this sense, a law without justice is a law without spirit, a dead letter—it can neither rule nor inspire.

Contemporary jurisprudence has travelled a long way from these classical formulations. Today justice is identified fully with the law. Legality, the rule of law, the impartiality of the judiciary and the correct following of formal procedures are the main topics in the discourse of justice. Decisions should be made according to general rules, impartially applied according to general criteria, which should exclude personal interests or considerations. Far from being the spirit and the reason of the law, justice has become conformity with the law, and is identified with the administration of justice. We find the symbol of legal justice outside our civic buildings and courts of law: It is a blindfolded goddess holding the scales of justice and a sword. There is something chilling about the austere image of the scales accurately balancing actions and the sword threatening the punishment of the unlawful. Justice is presented as a 'cold virtue, sometimes even a cruel one'.[85] The world of legal justice 'lacks the warmth' of morality.[86]

[81] Aristotle, *Ethics,* JAK Thomson (trans), (London, Penguin, 1976) 311.

[82] Cicero, *The Laws,* N Rudd (trans), (Oxford, Oxford University Press, 1998) *I, VI.*

[83] W Fulbeck, *Direction or Preparative to the Study of the Law* (London, 1599, 1829 edn) 2–3.

[84] H Finch, *Law, or, A Discourse Thereof in Four Books* (London, Society of Stationers, 1627) at folio 57, quoted in P Goodrich, 'Review of JB White *Justice as Translation*' (1990) *Anglo-American Law Review* 90.

[85] A Heller, *Beyond Justice,* above n 7, 11.

[86] JR Lucas, *On Justice,* above n 8, 263.

The standard explanation of the blindfold is that for justice to be impartial and impersonal, she should not be able to see those she judges. The law should be declared, and the wrongdoers punished, without fear, prejudice or any consideration for charity, pity, or the individual characteristics of the litigant. The judgement of Justice must not be corrupted by the senses and must be discovered wholly within herself, in her bosom.[87] Retribution shows no emotion, and distribution has the feeling of the grocery check-out. Public legal justice is a conservative justice that serves entrenched expectations and vested interests. The natural company of law is order, and not justice. As Anatole France memorably put it, the law in its majesty forbids both rich and poor to steal bread and to sleep under bridges. *Fiat justitia et pereat mundus*. But a blind justice can be an uninformed, uncaring—an unjust justice who, as Thrasymachus argued, can be hoodwinked by the wealthy and powerful. It is not the justice of the classical or the common lawyers. What are the reasons for the blindfold? How did such a radical change come about?

Political philosophy and jurisprudence see law as the main answer to the weakening of authority and the moral polyphony of modern society. Liberal philosophy, as interpreted by Rawls, for instance, assumes a wide variety of incommensurable, even opposed conceptions of the good (life) and tries to create a framework of co-operation within which conflict can be constrained and individuals can pursue their private aims. There is too little common ground and there are too many causes of conflict in this social vision. In the absence of any widely shared vision of the good life, liberalism relies on formal procedures: on positive law and general criteria of distribution. Law excludes considerations of value from its domain and limits the quest for, or the application of, any substantive criteria of justice. The law becomes the main substitute for absent ethics and the emptied normative realm. The signs of this depletion of justice from the body of the law are all too evident. For jurisprudence, the law is public and objective; its posited rules are structurally homologous to ascertainable 'facts', which can be found and verified in an 'objective' manner, free from the vagaries of individual preference, prejudice and ideology. Its procedures are technical and its personnel neutral. Any contamination of law by value will compromise its ability to turn social and political conflict into manageable technical disputes about the meaning and applicability of pre-existing public rules. Morality—as much as politics—must be kept at a distance; indeed, the main requirement of the rule of law in its contemporary version of legality is that all subjective and relative value should be excluded from the operation of the legal system. This insulation of law from ethico-political considerations allegedly makes the exercise of power impersonal and guarantees the equal subjection of citizens and state officials to the dispassionate requirements of the rule of rules, as opposed to the rule of men. And as adjudication is presented in common law jurisdictions as the paradigm instance of law, the demand for justice is equated

[87] J Shklar, *The Faces of Injustice*, above n 52, 46–9.

with the moral neutralisation of the judicial process. In formal terms, justice becomes identified with the administration of justice and the requirements and guarantees of legal procedure, and the 'interests of justice' are routinely interpreted as the interests of adjudication.[88]

In more substantive terms, justice loses its ethical character and becomes a device for the legitimacy and celebration of the law. This tendency, most evident in legal positivism, permeates the whole of jurisprudence. Positivism starts from the recognition that no generally acceptable criteria of justice exist and proceeds to argue that, as justice cannot be generally defined, it should either be abandoned or its application should be restricted to the more manageable domain of legal justice. Law is technical reason, a poor remnant of the right reason of the classics, while justice is associated with emotions and non-rational passions. To assert that a legal system is unjust, says Ross, is an 'emotional expression . . . To invoke justice is the same thing as banging on the table: an emotional expression that turns one's demand into an absolute postulate.'[89] Non-formal conceptions of justice are 'illusions which excite the emotions by stimulating the suprarenal glands.' There is no hope of a rational foundation of justice, because the concept is ideological and 'biological-emotional' and the science of law should abandon it.[90] When 'someone says "that thing is unjust" what he means is that the thing is offensive to his sentiments.'[91]

Appeals to justice are not only emotional and irrational, they are also mischievous. Chaim Perelman, one of the foremost theorists of justice, claims that, 'an attempt to judge the law in the name of justice is . . . confusion . . . We must not say that the law is condemned in the name of justice, unless that is, we want to create confusion advantageous only to the sophists.'[92] Justice is a confusion cultivated by sophists and dissidents. Plato has been totally reversed: his rational theory of justice was the tool to defeat the common sense of the Sophists. For the positivist, all claims to justice are dismissed as sophistry in the name of a common sense, which mobilises in its arrogant defence, the modern form of rationality, (pseudo) science. But this institutional and formal conception of justice cannot act as critique, but solely as critical apology for the extant legal system. Its distaste for those emotional 'sophists' who criticise the justice of the law is evident. Interestingly, the gender of justice in artistic representations remains female. As Hegel reminds us in his readings of *Antigone*, the feminine principle is not associated with the cold logic of legal reason nor with the uncaring character of a blind calculation.[93] Positivists are right in emphasising the emotional character of appeals to justice but they reach the wrong conclusion.

[88] See C Douzinas and R Warrington, *Justice Miscarried*, above n 25, chapters 4 and 6.

[89] A Ross, *On Law and Justice* (London, Stevens & Sons, 1958) 274.

[90] *Ibid*, 275.

[91] FA Hayek, *Law, Legislation and Liberty*, above n 17, 168, n 30.

[92] C Perelman, *Justice, Law and Argument* (Dordrecht, Reidel, 1980) 26.

[93] C Douzinas, 'Law's Birth and Antigone's Death: On Ontological and Psychoanalytical Ethics' (1995) 16 *Cardozo Law Review* 1325.

What makes justice indispensable is exactly her caring for the victims and her passionate denunciation of injustice in law and outside law.

The 'legal scientist' has nowhere to turn but the law. 'If nobody can ascertain what is just, somebody must determine what shall be legal'.[94] Justice becomes internal to the legal system, its principle identified as conformity with the law. For the 'science of law', the normative universe is now exclusively inhabited by the prescriptions of the legislator and the decrees of the institution. Consequently, justice is not directly involved with ethics. As Lucas puts it, justice is 'set in a somewhat low moral key . . . I can be just, and yet lack many moral virtues'.[95] Hart, too, accepts that wicked and bad laws are not necessarily unjust, nor good laws necessarily just.[96] According to his now classical formulation, justice has two parts, 'a uniform or constant feature, summarised in the precept "Treat like cases alike" and a shifting or varying criterion used in determining when, for any given purpose, cases are alike or different'.[97] Its core is found in the administration of law, where justice is identified with formal equality before the law and the application of the same general rule to the various cases without prejudice or interest. And while conformity to the law is the key to legal justice, the concept also includes a limited 'dynamic' element that allows the critique of those rules determining the relevant resemblances and differences that the law must recognise if it is to treat like cases alike. Justice is the combination of legal procedure and social or distributive justice. But legal justice is the central instance, while social justice, since it deals with groups rather than individuals, is not the concern of jurisprudence.

In this respect, Perelman identifies the only common element of the various theories of justice as the purely formal idea that 'beings in one and the same essential category must be treated in the same way.'[98] Hart, too, concludes that 'justice constitutes one segment of morality primarily concerned not with individual conduct but with the ways in which *classes* of individuals are treated'.[99]

Hayek takes the argument further: justice has nothing to do with the distribution of resources and the balancing of interests. It is not concerned with ethics or equality; it does not try to alter or bring about a general state of affairs; nor does it look to the consequences of a particular act. 'Justice is thus emphatically not a balancing of particular interests at stake in a concrete case, or even of the interests of determinable classes of persons, nor does it aim at bringing about a particular state of affairs which is regarded as just.'[100] For Hayek, justice is not concerned with the consequences of any action or distribution, but solely with the application of just rules of conduct. Lucas thinks that the exclusive

[94] Radbruch quoted in FA Hayek, *Law, Legislation and Liberty*, above n 17, 90.
[95] J Lucas, *On Justice* (Oxford, Oxford University Press, 1980) 262, 263.
[96] HLA Hart, *The Concept of Law* (Oxford, Clarendon, 1961) 153–4.
[97] *Ibid*, 156.
[98] C Perelman, *Justice, Law and Argument*, above n 92, 16.
[99] HLA Hart, *The Concept of Law*, above n 96, 163.
[100] FA Hayek, *Law Legislation and Liberty*, above n 17, 39.

association of injustice with the positive responsibility of named individuals 'a little too stringent'.[101] A state of affairs may be unjust, even though it has not been brought about intentionally, if people have not amended or ameliorated it. But in all instances, injustice requires concrete human responsibility, which is to be judged according to the established rules, entitlements and obligations. 'Contrary to the opinions of many, it is not inherently unfair if someone has more than anybody else, but only if other are done out of their due.'[102] It is always easier to turn injustice into bad luck, misfortune, the victim's mistake or responsibility.

Justice simply means treating all under the same general rules. Its action is purely negative: just rules are always negative, they enjoin certain types of harmful action; more generally, the justice of the law is negative. Indeed, legalism appears as a principle of negativity. From Hayek to Fuller, from Hart to Nozick, jurisprudence has argued that the business of legal justice is say nay, to prohibit and prevent.[103] As Lord Atkin put it 'the rule that you should love your neighbour becomes in law you should not injure your neighbour.'[104] Hayek equates the 'primary character of injustice' with legal prohibition and the principle of negativity.[105] But Hayek's rather facile passage from injustice to legal negation reminds us that a non-articulated sense of absence or lack has remained at the heart of the social. Injustice may have become a simple negation of justice but the latter is still haunted by a crack, a social faultline or a primary injustice, which the law acknowledges but can never fully address.

Western legal systems, in their gradual and organic evolution, have arrived at the 'negative' principle of Kantian universalism. Justice as generality is the genius of the common law. Negativity and universality are not creations of the philosophical imagination but the result of an interstitial and principled historical evolution threatened by social democratic distributory mechanisms and positivistic limitless sovereigns. Hayek's jurisprudence is a solitary reminder of the lost spirit of the law. His non-rationalist conception of formal justice may be compared to natural law. But its demands are minimal. The spirit of the law has been hollowed, turned onto a pure negation with no ethos, substance or principle—a ghost that never appears. Formalism has become the only substance of the law.

Legality may bestow authority on the law either through its origin in the organised power of the state or through its emanation from a long historical and

[101] J Lucas, *On Justice*, above n 95, 5, n 8.

[102] *Ibid*, 8.

[103] FA Hayek, *Law Legislation and Liberty*, above n 17, chapter 8; L Fuller, *The Morality of Law* (New Haven, Yale University Press, 1969) 42: 'In what may be called the basic morality of social life, duties that normally run towards other persons generally . . . normally require only forbearances, or as we say, are negative in nature'; HLA Hart, *The Concept of Law*, above n 96: 'The common requirement of law and morality consists for the most part not of active services to be rendered but of forbearances, which are usually formulated in negative form as prohibitions', 190.

[104] *Donoghue v Stevenson* [1932] AC 532.

[105] 162 n 9.

'spiritual' process. In both cases, however, legality, as the nineteenth century liberals explained, operates through external coercion. The morality of legality is totally heteronomous and acts through the fear of sanctions or the utilitarian calculation of rewards and punishments. But the paramount task of suppressing human wickedness endows coercion with the ethereal attributes of morality. Moral values may not be the provenance or contribution of legal transactions or judgements, but the operation of the law as a whole is the only expression and guarantee of ethical power and public virtue that can tame private vice. The very absence of ethical value—the flight of justice—ensures the morality of the law. This is the basis of the jurisprudential claim that unjust laws should be obeyed because the morality of legality overrides any local injustice.[106] Moral content may have been abstracted from law but the legal enterprise as a whole is blessed with the overall attribute of morality. On the surface, the transition from status to contract is supplemented by a parallel passage from value to norm and from good to right. The foundation of meaning and value has been firmly transferred from the transcendent to the social, and in this transition, normativity has forfeited its claim to substance and value, and has replaced them with blanket certifications of source, and of conformity with form. In the world of law, 'justice' and 'injustice' refer to fairness—the restoration of balance and proportion and the redress of the *status quo* between individuals. But this is a very limited conception of justice.

The most extreme and unrealistic celebration of the morality of the law is found in the writings of Dworkin. The law does not consist exclusively of rules, as Hart claimed—nor is it the outcome of the unlimited will and power of the omnipotent legislator *a la* Austin. Law's empire includes principles and policies and its operation involves the interpretative acts of judges, who are invited to construct the 'right answer' to legal problems creatively. To do so, judges must develop and apply political and moral theories about the legal system that should present the law in the best possible light and create an image of the community as integrity. Morality (and moral philosophy) now enters the law and is properly recognised as an inescapable component of judicial hermeneutics. But its task is to legitimise judicial practice by showing the law to be the perfect narrative of a happy community. Morality is no longer a set of subjective and relative values, nor is it a critical standard against which acts of legal and judicial power can be judged. The law is assumed to possess an internal integrity and coherence that allows the construction of public and quasi-objective principles of morality which can then be used as its underlying grammar and help resolve 'hard cases'.

Law's morality as found by the judge with the help of moral philosophy becomes the guarantee that the law never runs out. If a right answer exists it can be discovered in every case through the mobilisation of the morality that law's

[106] L Fuller, *The Morality of Law*, above n 103; J Finnis, *Natural Law and Natural Rights* (Oxford, Clarendon, 1980).

internal criteria of coherence yield. Judges are never left to their own devices; the dreaded supplement of judicial discretion (in other words the individual morality of the judge) that Hart had reluctantly admitted at the cost of endangering the rational completeness, coherence and closure of law—is firmly kept outside. Dworkin seems to reintroduce moral considerations into law. But his theory is the last step in the juridification of morality and in the assertion of the moral legitimacy of legalism—both common symptoms of the de-ethicalisation of the law. The radical gap in the normative universe created by the strict separation between legality and morality, and the reduction of ethics to the private and subjective, is filled by the discourse of law as the lighthouse on the way to universal and objective truth. But for those who want to challenge the dominant political theory; for those unrepresented, unrepresentable and excluded from the 'integrated' community; for those who experience the law not as rationality, rights and justifications but experience it as victims of the exercise of power and as the targets of legal force; for all those 'others', law's empire has no place.

At the end of this long detour, we return again to the failure of theories of justice and the inescapable sense of injustice. Our recent 'just wars' have put violence, conquest and occupation at the service of justice. They offer a further twist in the story. In its various guises, justice has been a 'gift' given from above. It was excessively patriarchal, it forgot its lowly victims and it has supported institutions and distributions that abandoned people and races and nations in the name of 'fairness' or right procedure. The quest for justice has been the oldest failure of thought and philosophy. But despite its persistent misconceptions and miscalculations, despite the violence and war committed in its name, the feeling of injustice keeps coming back holding law and power to account. Anaximander wrote that we must pay restitution for our original injustice. It may be that this endless cycle of hope and failure, of struggle and disappointment, of revolution and betrayal, is the price we have to pay. But this endless dialectic between despair, thought and action; between emotion, philosophy and politics, is what opens temporality and creates history. The quest for justice—or rather the denunciation of injustice—has always been the animus of humanity.

PASSAGES

A friend stands before his friend's coffin. Tears pour from his eyes. 'It is so unjust'. He curses fate. The love for the friend becomes stronger now he is not there. The feeling of loss leads to a sense of injustice; the dead friend was not given his due, he was not given the time he deserved, and this deprivation of time deprives the world. He was not allowed to develop in his own way and offer to the world what only he could. Mourning is emotion released by injustice. The sense of injustice is heightened by impotence before death. There is nothing the friend can do to bring his dead friend back. Death is irreversible, death is inevitable. The friend's death reminds him of the inescapability of his own. Death is destiny, a destiny both known and strange, and yet, the destiny of the friend, his inevitable fate, fires a sense of injustice. The injustice of the friend's death, the sense of loss and lack, stem from the love of another and deprivation of the love object. He did not deserve death here and now, although he could not have escaped or avoided it in the future. Justice is time, and injustice the deprivation of time. Injustice links in strange ways with a sense of destiny or fate, the ability to control and avoid, or to accept and love, fate. The sense of injustice is a powerful *emotion* of *loss or lack*, linked to the *deprivation another has suffered* and heightened by the *unavoidable but untimely* character of the deprivation. Time, lack, suffering for the other and inevitability or fate are all part of the sense of injustice.

5

England's Dreaming: The Spirits of Positivism

NEVER AND ALWAYS

POSITIVISM AS A SCIENTIFIC school has been associated with the careful elucidation of the canons and protocols of knowledge. Linked with empiricism, scientific positivism privileges experience, observation and perception over speculation, abstract theorising and idealism. For the legal positivist the only law that counts is the law posited by the legislator, a law which can be recorded and dated and, in application, observed and measured.[1] In law, positivism is linked with the rise of the secular, modern state and the dispelling of illusions associated with theories of natural law and natural right. Not only is positivism linked inexorably to the defence and celebration of state law, but it repudiates any strong links between law and ethics, and presents a morally impoverished view of the legal universe. Positivism has been considered the philosophy of the 'enemy' by critical legal thinkers.[2] It was no surprise, therefore, that critical scholars rejoiced when positivism appeared to suffer something of a mauling at the hands of the 'rights' theorists, the hermeneuticians and postmodernists. When Dworkin argued that principle and morality form an integral part of the law or when the school of law and literature read legal texts as literary, rhetorical and semiotic constructs, they drew on well-established critical resources.

Positivism has, however, shown great resilience; although its epistemology and politics have been repeatedly criticised, it keeps coming back like Marley's ghost. Furthermore, like the *Alien* or the *Body Snatchers* it has the ability to imitate its opponents' characteristics, take over their bodies and turn them to its own ends. It is precisely, these energies of positivism that we want to examine in this chapter.

[1] But for a norm to be called law it must also be backed by the might of the state. Other types of law, such as morality or custom, are not laws properly called, since they miss one or both of these tests of legal pedigree.

[2] See P Goodrich, *Languages of Law* (London, Weidenfeld and Nicolson, 1990).

The dominance of positivism in jurisprudence throughout the twentieth century has led to a huge and proliferating literature. We do not have the space to deal with the rather repetitive exegesis of positivism's Greats. Rather than reading Positivism as a statement of law in its general form, we will read it as a particularly English engagement with history and the conditions of its own production. To do so, we will draw on the writings of the three father figures of English positivism: John Austin, Jeremy Bentham and Herbert Hart. In re-reading their philosophies, we do not want to re-stage old debates, or review the hoary arguments about their relationship to each other. In particular, we will not discuss here the opposition between natural law and positivism. We will argue that positivism is resilient because, despite its apparent secular and modern nature, it manages to co-opt and incorporate theories about the sacral or poetic nature of law. Whilst these concerns sit rather unhappily with positivism's scientific approach, their presence allows this school of legal philosophy to put forward a more rounded view of the law than is often assumed. Positivism's success is partly to be found in this unacknowledged adoption of mytho-poetic themes.

We will begin with Austin. Austin's thought can be read as an attempt to re-found jurisprudence as the scientific study of the common law. In presenting this beginning, Austin had to separate the law from its association with the obscurities of the past and to reaffirm the clarity of Roman law. However, despite the surface claims, the spirit of a sacral conjunction of the divine and history returns and occupies an essential presence in Austin's system. Turning to Bentham, we will see that his work also tries to write a history of the English common law. However, so radical is his account of the social, and law's place within it, that he describes a universe where spirit is almost entirely replaced by the materiality of the world. 'We' are momentarily cohering measures of pleasure or pain. Law is merely a mechanism, a means of manipulation. The spirit has been transubstantiated into an ever-present matter. It is as if this vision can be seen as a particularly accurate exemplum of the Nietzschean thesis of the death of God. Finally, we will read Hart as writing a jurisprudence that attempts to mediate between these two extremes by positing another spirit: the spirit of England. Hart's England—and the spirit of English history—provide the ultimate foundation for a philosophy that turns out, finally, to have more to do with an engagement with the tensions of English history than a desire to posit a general theory of law. Hart's positivism is an attempt to re-write the positivist tradition as a refusal of extremism, and as the celebration of a spirit of compromise that is inexorably English; or, rather, as a kind of poetic-philosophy that articulates, rather than resolves, the strange spirits of positivism.

DIVINE UTILITY

Modern positivism has been understood as founded on a distinction between the divine and the human. If we turn to Austin, however, we find that rather than separating these two discourses, his jurisprudence incorporates theology into itself. Let us examine this argument in outline. To determine the province of jurisprudence, Austin developed a principle of utility rooted in the idea of God, a dark God who does not show himself. Furthermore, when Austin goes on to develop the key positivist concept of sovereignty, he explicitly models the state on the Godhead itself. To elaborate this argument, we now need to place Austin's jurisprudence in the context of his 'moral' theory.

'Nothing without reason, nothing without cause' is the motto of modernisation. Austin's jurisprudence proceeds in this spirit by providing clear foundations and principles for law. He begins from the central tenet of positivism: 'every possible law, or rule of law . . . emanates . . . from a sovereign or subordinate source.'[3] One must then approach posited law in an ordered manner, through careful demarcation and division. This is achieved through the extrapolation of the terms of Roman jurisprudence. Austin uses Roman law to determine how the common law should be organised. Indeed, the very expression '*fons juris*' (the source of law) is explicated by reference to Roman law and an account of origins: it refers to the documents that provide us with knowledge of the law. This reinterpretation of origins allows Austin to position his own work in a line that stretches from the earliest documents of Roman law, through the classical writers to the medieval Glossators and Commentators. From these sources of legal knowledge, an explicit link is made to the writers on the common law from Bracton through to celebrated figures such as Hale and Blackstone. Austin presents his legal philosophy as the realisation of the past. His work is not just part of this tradition, it represents its apotheosis, its latest flowering.

Roman law may be able to provide categories that reveal the true shape of English law, but these categories need to be revised in their application. Language must be used with precision. Consider, for example, the Roman distinction between the law of persons and the law of things. Austin considers the distinction meaningless, because both these divisions of law relate to 'rights and duties which are incumbent upon men.'[4] Once this notion of rights and duties is clarified, we can appreciate that the distinction is not absolute, but rather a question of the best organisation of the *corpus juris*. But a deeper logic is operative here. For Austin, the distinction between the law of persons and the law of things rests on a concept of the person meaning 'status' or 'condition.'[5] If this is the case, the law of persons can be 'subtracted' from the law of things, which ought to precede the law of persons.[6] The law of things must take precedence because it contains the most general exposition of the law, while the law of persons is more specific. The divisions of the law should follow an order that moves

[3] J Austin, *Lectures on Jurisprudence or The Philosophy of Positive Law*, R Campbell (ed), Volume Two (London, John Murray, 1885) 533.
[4] *Ibid*, 687.
[5] *Ibid*, 696.
[6] *Ibid*, 727.

from the general to the specific. In this structure of order, public law can be seen as a limb of the law of persons while private law can be divided by reference to a distinction between relative and absolute rights and duties, correlating to a second distinction between primary and sanctioning rights and duties.[7]

Why should this complex division and classification detain us? Methodologically, jurisprudence becomes linked with the epistemological systems that characterise modern science, Law's meaning can thus be found in an elaborate system of classification. But if these complex and detailed classifications offer a map of the surface of the legal edifice, what is the principle or grammar that lies beneath and determines law's functioning?

It is the modernist impulse. The need to define a secular legal order. Indeed, at first glance, Austin clearly separates the human from the divine. The very idea of a positive jurisprudence, of a study of law as posited by a human source, must distinguish the *ius gentium* from the *ius civile*. The *ius gentium* is general and universal, based on 'laws coming from God' or 'rational Nature.'[8] It lacks the precision of the *ius civile*—of the rules of specific, earthly communities. Divine law may have been revealed in the scriptures, but an important part of divine law remains unrevealed. These laws are not known by reason, but by feeling. The signs of unrevealed laws are attested by the universal feelings of sadness or disgust that accompany certain wrongful acts.[9]

So, there remains something dark or inchoate about divine law. Indeed, it is this obscurity that ultimately makes divine law unsuitable as a guide to human conduct. In this sense, secular positivism has to supplement the failures of divine law. However, when Austin turns to his main principle of utility he cannot articulate it without returning to divinity. As his account develops, it become apparent that the obscurity that affects divine law comes to compromise the very principle of utility:

> In so far as they [the laws of God] are not revealed, we must resort to another guide: namely, the probable effect of our conduct on that *general happiness* or *good* which is the object of the Divine Lawgiver in all his laws and commandments.[10]

Note how this argument switches between the human and the divine. Utility is the 'index' to our duties, but these duties are based on God's commands and the sanctions that flow from their breach. These commands are not 'abstractions', but 'proceed' from what we are: 'living and rational beings.'[11] Utility rests upon God's commands, but God's commands remain obscure. It would thus appear that the 'index to his will is imperfect and uncertain', 'signified obscurely'[12] and 'subject to inevitable and involuntary misconstruction.'[13]

[7] *Ibid*, 761.
[8] *Ibid*, 41.
[9] *Ibid*.
[10] *Ibid*, 45.
[11] *Ibid*, 45.
[12] *Ibid*, 77.
[13] *Ibid*.

The best a theory can do is to present a kind of calculus, an account of a 'tendency.' The starting point is again the unqualified beneficence of the creator who desires the 'greatest happiness of all his sentient creatures.'[14] God requires that our actions contribute to the sum of human happiness. However, precisely because the ways of the creator remain dark, we have to ascertain the 'sum of [the] possible consequences' of an act by noting the results of general classes of acts, and asking whether an act would increase or decrease the general 'sum' of happiness. Certain acts are 'pernicious' in general, and their repeated commission would decrease the sum of human happiness.

But, why should there be a human urge to act perniciously? There is an innate propensity to revel in transient and selfish pleasure. If God is the general lawgiver who speaks through rules addressed to fallen human nature, the nature of appetites appears in the inability to follow the rule, to create exceptions that accord with habitual inclination. However, it is not as if human nature is profoundly flawed. It is possible to speak in general of a human propensity to avoid the mischievous and to act usefully. There is an innate appreciation that some actions lead inexorably to negative consequences. Austin cites Locke; these 'natural inconveniences, operate without a law.' In this sense there is a tendency of human nature that is not law, but gives the mark of law to the law:

> [t]o grasp at present enjoyment, and to turn from present uneasiness, is the habitual inclination of us all. And thus, through the weakness of our judgements, and the more dangerous infirmity of our wills, we would stretch the exception to cases embraced by the rule.[15]

Austin effectively makes the principle of utility the point at which the divine and the human correspond, and diverge. It is precisely at this level of ontology, when Austin comes to define the properly human, that we can most clearly appreciate that his jurisprudence has to bring together the divine and the sacred. It cannot maintain a separation. The problem of human appetite is both what gives rise to the law, and means that there is forever a divergence between divine perfection and flawed humanity. It is this interzone, this profound gap at the heart of Austin's thought, that causes his jurisprudence of utility to appear like so many wild sparks that arc between God and man. If this differential gives rise to the force that runs through Austin's thinking, then it is perhaps closer to the poetic urge to mend the ruptures and pain of a humanity forever fallen from divinity, than it is to the sound foundation of scientific endeavour.

Austin's notion of sovereignty continues this strange disjunction. Austin would like to demarcate sovereignty from any association with divinity.[16] Let us

[14] J Austin, above n 3, 41.

[15] *Ibid*, 44.

[16] Already, in the formal definition of rules and commands, there is a way in which divinity and secular power is held together. Thus, all rules can be seen as commands. Secular laws are commands in the same way that divine laws are commands. A command is the expression of a desire that a certain act be performed or not performed. Behind all forms of rules as law there is thus an imperative. If the person or persons to whom the command is addressed do not comply, then there

begin with the determining features of the secular. Rules reside in an aggregate or complex edifice that must correlate with political sovereignty. A political superior posits these laws. They are not the commands of divinity. The 'mark' of positive law[17] is 'sovereignty" a term that must be understood in conjunction with 'subjection' and 'independent political society.'[18] These terms combine in the following definition of sovereignty: The bulk or 'generality'[19] of a population must, by habitual obedience, obey a common superior, who is dependent on no other, thus making the population dependents or subjects. Sovereignty is a relationship of inferiority/superiority. The independent element of political society is thus most properly the sovereign. A society could remain in the 'state of nature' if it does not have this ongoing relationship of obedience to a determinate sovereign.[20] Law as command must, then, be thought of as an ongoing ability to command generally and not as a single instance of command. There is thus a temporal constant to law as command. Power, expressing itself as law, presupposes a political structure with a certain degree of permanence. Constitutional lawyers following Austin, such as AV Dicey and Walter Bagehot, distinguished between political and legal sovereignty. The former belongs to the electorate and has only ideological significance. Legal sovereignty by contrast is presented as perpetual, indivisible and illimitable and resides in the 'Queen in Parliament'.

The paradox of an 'indivisible and illimitable' sovereignty, which is divided into two parts has been repeatedly commented upon.[21] But this bifurcation has both historical provenance and a prospective function. The formal division remains the distinction and bond between the divine and secular spheres that permeates the modern theory of sovereignty. The anaemic 'political' sovereignty of the 'electorate', on the other hand, hides the fear of democracy and the looming entry of the masses into politics. For Maine, 'the gradual establishment of the masses in power is the blackest omen for all legislation founded on scientific opinion';[22] for Bagehot, 'the common ordinary mind is quite unfit to fix for itself what political questions it shall attend to';[23] while Dicey dreaded 'the passing of laws, and still more the administration of the law, in accordance . . . with the immediate wishes of a class, namely the class of wage earners.'[24] The dangerous electorate is accorded a higher but ethereal 'sovereignty', while the

will be a sanction that applies. The very ability to apply a sanction is one way in which power is bound up with the very notion of a rule; terms such as duty and obligation clearly signify that there is a power that can command others to perform or desist from performing certain acts. In this root sense, there would be no difference between the command of God, and the command of a secular authority.

[17] *Ibid*, 165.
[18] *Ibid*.
[19] *Ibid*, 167.
[20] *Ibid*, 169.
[21] M Loughlin, *Public Law and Political Theory* (Oxford, Clarendon Press, 1992) chapter 7.
[22] H Maine, *Popular Government* (London, John Murray, 1885) 98.
[23] W Bagehot, *The English Constitution* (London, Keegan Paul, 1965) 274.
[24] Quoted in M Loughlin, *Public Law and Political Theory*, above n 21, 143.

real principle of power is concentrated into the combination of Monarch and Parliament (for which today read the Executive). The real attributes and powers of *Deus* (the power to create *ex nihilo* for example) have been passed to the political institution (Parliament can make and unmake any law whatsoever)—while its nature as *Absonditus* has been passed on to the people—declared supreme in their submission. The idea of popular sovereignty, so popular (and unrealistic) elsewhere, never took root in England.

Sovereignty can thus be understood as that which defines itself. The power to determine itself is also the power to create and sustain a relationship of dominance and subservience. Moreover, sovereignty separates the civilised from the uncivilised. Politics marks that which comes into the light and can be determined. The similarity between this conception of sovereignty and Christian divinity is striking. The mark of God can be found in his power to 'know himself': that which cannot be divided, and remains self present to itself. As the unmoved mover, political sovereignty recalls this feature of the Godhead. At the same time, divinity can divide itself; it can become man. It is as if this is the mark of the political; that aspect of the sovereign that marks community as of sovereignty, but as a fallen and inferior form, forever subordinate. In precise opposition to the fallen world, divinity sustains itself: it is continuing. Power, then, in a secular political sense, is the earthly version of the very notion of the perpetuation of divinity.

Political society, when it appears, 'exists' to the extent that it incorporates and expresses the truth of sovereignty. It is defined by a spirit of sovereignty that transverses it. This is evident in Austin's 'relations of sovereignty'. The fact of sovereignty means that members of a society are in a 'state of dependence'[25] to the determinate 'superior'. It is this 'habit of obedience' that allows us to talk of an independent political society. Independence, is, then something of an 'ellipsis' (it is not surprising, then, that we have to read Austin elliptically) because it is only the sovereign 'portion of society' that is, in reality, independent. Independence is an elliptical phenomenon, because an independent society is marked by something that is both part and not part of it. In this sense, sovereignty both marks the social, but must be the mark that is strictly separate and 'independent' from that which it marks.

This is an irredeemably theological model of political society. Austin's power of sovereignty operates in terms of a secularised divinity that both marks the world, and is separate from it. We encounter here, of course, the paradox of God become man; the mystery of the divine nature that can separate itself from itself, but return to itself. Austin's social is sacral. This mystery of divine substantiation can be revealed still further if we consider the examples that Austin uses to illustrate his thesis on sovereignty.

[25] Quoted in M Loughlin, *Public Law and Political Theory*, above n 21, 194.

First, the example of 1815 and Napoleon's defeat at Waterloo. For someone educated in the Hegelian tradition, this reference to the aftermath of Napoleon's reign cannot be irrelevant. Hegel had called Napoleon 'the spirit on horseback'. Although perhaps not directly theological, and relating more to Hegel's idea of a world rational spirit that works through history, this reference raises similar issues to those discussed above. Austin's example reminds us that the defeat of Napoleon brought to an end a certain coordination between a people and the person who represented them. The 'commands' of the occupying allied armies were too 'rare and transient' to 'constitute the relations of sovereignty and subjection.'[26] Behind the ostensible sense of this passage, a real concern lurks about the separation of the mystical bond that binds a ruler and his people. Rather than merely showing that commands were too transient to constitute authority, Austin suggests that once the animating spirit has been extinguished, sovereignty dissolves.

Other examples suggest related aspects of the same dynamic. While the absent presence of the spirit defines society, this does not mean that the social body is at peace with itself. Indeed, the social body is marked by conflicts over the interpretation of the divine truth that constitutes it. European history, riven by conflict over religious truth, intrudes into Austin's second example of sovereignty. He is attempting to illustrate the claim that sovereignty can come about if a state that finds itself under the sovereignty of a more powerful state is able to resist that sovereignty, or—as in the example of the French nation—if the more powerful nation is in fact unable to exercise its sovereignty practically: 'Such, for instance, is the position of the Saxon government and its subjects in respect of the conspiring sovereigns who form the Holy Alliance.'[27] It is intriguing that this thesis is illustrated by reference to the conflict between the Catholic and the Protestant powers of Europe. Again, contrary to Austin's conscious intent, we find within this theory of sovereignty, a more profound hidden history of conflict over religious truth.

Austin's discourse on sovereignty turns at this point to one of the scenes that haunts English positivism, the Civil War. We shall see that Hart himself grapples with this moment as perhaps the most intractable problem of jurisprudence. Within the terms of Austin's argument, though, we are still concerned with a fractured social body marked by the spirit. At this point, the conflict that divides Europe is seen to be at the heart of English history. During the Civil War, and at 'the height of the conflict between Charles the First and Parliament, the English nation was broken into two distinct societies.'[28] Each of these fragments may be thought of as both politically and independently sovereign. However, the English example is not just one of conflict; it is one of resolution: '[a]fter the conflict had subsided, those distinct societies were in their turn dissolved; and the nation was

[26] *Ibid*, 196.
[27] *Ibid*, 197.
[28] *Ibid*, 204.

reunited . . .'.[29] What this account of resolution conceals is the sacrifice that makes the reuniting of the nation possible. The execution of Charles I in 1649 allowed a unified nation to be re-created. With the Reformation, an even more bizarre sacrifice is asserted. Cromwell is exhumed and 'executed'. Austin's analysis indicates that the social bond is based on a primordial sacrifice. Underlying sovereignty, underlying the social, is the ruined part, the accursed share. In the same way that the sovereign is part—but not part—of the social, the sacrifice is its foundation—present and not present. The sovereign is a secular God incarnate, his real or Eucharistic sacrifices are necessary for society to come together and become the political ecclesia. The sacrifice guarantees the coherence of social being. This analysis is shared by both the anthropological and theological accounts of social being that lie at the centre of this most positivist description of social life.[30]

[29] Quoted in M Loughlin, *Public Law and Political Theory*, above n 21, 204.

[30] See C Schmitt, *Political Theology, Four Chapters on the Concept of Sovereignty* (Cambridge, Mass, MIT Press, 1985). For Schmitt, political theology is the symptom of a return to theology as a means of thinking modern politics and law. Schmitt's own genealogy would run through Leibniz, who rejected mathematics and preferred theology as a model for jurisprudence, as both disciplines worked with concepts of inherent reason and a text that contains positive prescriptions (38). One of the central claims of this thinking is that the 'omnipotent state' functions in its executive, legislative and pardoning role as an institution whose model is a theological notion of divinity. Furthermore, in the modern period 'personalistic' and 'decisionistic' elements that were associated with God become linked with the people. American political thought reveals this trope in the idea that 'the voice of the people is the voice of God.' To try and develop this thinking, however, is not to subscribe to the other elements of the Schmittian project. Schmitt was attempting to produce a systematic sociology of the concept of sovereignty that would be able to penetrate through to the specific consciousness of different eras and trace the juridical concepts that emerged. It must remain open to question, for example, whether this could be founded on a study of metaphysics as 'the most intensive and the clearest expression of an epoch' (46). More importantly, political theology is a kind of analogue to Nietzsche's political thinking. Schmitt describes a response to democracy in Catholic theologians that is comparable with Nietzsche's. If the notion of legitimacy has shifted to a notion of positive power founded and justified on the 'voice of the people'—then the response of thinkers such as Donoso Cortes was that the era of royalism was over. If there could no longer be kings, the best solution was 'dictatorship' (52). Nietzsche's will to power, in one way, would communicate with the thinking of the counter reformation that asserted the complete corruption of the human being, as that which lived only for its own self perpetuation. See Schmitt on Cortes and De Maistre, 58–9. Schmitt's problematic has been most recently taken up by Giorgio Agamben. See, in particular, *Homo Sacer* (Standford, Stanford University Press, 1998). Agamben is concerned with the figure of *homo sacer* in Pompeius Festus' treatise *On the Significance of Words. Homo sacer* is a paradoxical figure. He has been found guilty of a criminal act. He can thus be killed, but he cannot be sacrificed. This is peculiar. One would have thought that the *homo sacer*, the sacred man, would be precisely one who could not be killed, and whose sacred quality would allow him to be offered as a sacrifice to the gods. To understand the *homo sacer*, it is necessary to see that he is excluded from both the *ius humanum* and the *ius divinium* (74). Homo sacer is excluded from the former in that he can be killed, and his murderer will suffer no penalty; and from the latter as he is not a worthy sacrifice for the gods; 'a double exclusion' (82). Thus, in Agamben's argument, the '*nomos*' of law is thus not simply the power to divide up and lay claim to territory. Law's *nomos*, law's own order, is a 'taking of the outside'. To exemplify this structure, we can refer to the ancient German term '*ban*'. *Ban* refers to the subject who is banished from the lawful community; as such the banned subject is both marked by the law and abandoned by the law to the forest; the wilderness. This can be described as the paradox of the exception. The sovereign power of the law exercises itself by excluding from its order. The excluded is marked and banished. If the 'force of law' that traces this line 'includes through its exclusion' (18), then Agamben's work perhaps indicates what could be described as a divinity that is both immanent and absent to the world. Law is founded on this paradox.

To summarise the argument: The theological moment remains central to Austin's jurisprudence. This is perhaps why it provides such a problematic starting point for positivism, and why it was necessary for Bentham to try and purge, or purify, Austin's terms of this compromising character. The next section suggests that although this operation was successful, it created a new set of problems while opening a truly modern way of looking at social relations.

THE DARK CHAOS OF THE COMMON LAW

Jeremy Bentham, preserved forever to our gaze in the foyer of University College, is the modern demystifier *par excellence*—the social scientist committed to the bringing to light the true foundations of the social. If Austin seems too theological, Bentham is emblematic of the radical separation of the modern from the ancient, and of the belief in secular law as opposed to the dark musings of the sacred:

> For my part, I know not that we owe any . . . deference to former times that we owe not to our own. I know not that we owe them any such deference as to suppose a reason for what they did, when none is visible . . .[31]

This is the motto of the newcomer who will not be bound by the past. With this statement of intellectual autonomy, Bentham declares himself a critic of the common law tradition. He is the less deceived, unwilling to be taken in by a 'reasoning' that owes more to mysticism than to scientific logic. Bentham objects to the language of 'debt' owed by the present to the past. For Bentham, the present is a break, the coming of a new day with its illuminations and its sweeping away of cobwebs.

Bentham aims to set the philosophy of the common law on its feet, to save it from the uncertainty in which it had fallen and to clear the mist from its eyes—and this attitude provides the motivation for the attacks on Blackstone. Blackstone had traced law's form to its own development—its peculiarities as manifested in its history—and had tried to write the great epic of the *lex non scripta*. He was less concerned to compile a rigorous statement of its principles; he even thought this an impossible task because one could not separate principles from their history. For Blackstone, the scholar must patiently trace the spirit of the law through its organic growth. The metaphors Blackstone used can illustrate this process. He described precedent as the location and discovery of a hidden logic, a debt of 'deference to former times'. Precedent was the depository of the customs of the tribe articulated by judges from a time so remote as to be 'out of mind'. Those who come latterly must not depart from these earlier decisions 'without a breach of [their] oath and the law.'[32] It was this process which made the common law, according to the famous metaphor, 'an old Gothic

[31] J Bentham, *A Commentary on the Commentaries* (London, Athlone Press, 1977) 203.
[32] *Ibid*, 203.

Castle'[33] whose battlements and towers have been neglected; but whose 'interior apartments' are now adapted to 'daily use', but accessible only through 'approaches which may be winding and difficult'. No architect's plan determines the modifications of the common law, rather, as the metaphor suggests, the process was one of ongoing adaptation to exigencies through prudential judicial practice.

Bentham's criticism of the irrationality of precedent is well known. It is part of his wider attack on all forms of mystification and of the various types of obfuscation, such as natural law and 'the fallacy respecting natural rights.'[34] We are more interested here in the way that a certain spirit of the law, or of common law philosophy, is exorcised. We can consider a set of strategies that recur throughout *A Comment on the Commentaries* and can best be represented by the following approach. Bentham is considering case reports, 'Books of authority', but, more broadly, a whole structure of the common law. Here are the 'venerable sages of the common law'[35] 'named as "Glanville and Bracton, Britton and Fleta, Littleton and Fitzherbert".'[36] Common law is presented as a history of names; authority preserves a truth laid down by the ancestors. At the same time, names are nonsense. For the list to make sense, one already has to have been inculcated into the culture and know what the names mean. This is no way for a scientific study of law to proceed. As cultural history, jurisprudence lacks scientific rigour. This is what is at stake in Bentham's attack on Blackstone's own veneration of the tradition. Blackstone is celebrating the 'ancient customs' that 'are as old as the primitive Britain, and continued down, through the several mutations of government, unchanged and unadulterated.'[37] For Bentham, this is an emblem of all that is wrong with this scholarly spirit. The veneration of authorities is no more than a repetition of error. Blackstone fails to bring a sufficiently critical regard to bear on his sources, a problem perpetuated in the fetishisation of custom as good by virtue of its longevity. For Bentham, customary norms are submerged in the mess of time and the dark chaos of the common law.

Against this obfuscation, Bentham proposes a new beginning. For we live in a 'busy age . . . where knowledge is rapidly advancing towards perfection.'[38] Just as science is exploring and classifying the natural world, it is necessary to approach law in a new spirit. Indeed, these two endeavours proceed side by side. Scientific learning determines the way. If it is possible to comprehend the 'principles' of the natural world, then the principles of the law should similarly reveal themselves. This is not to reject history or the historical study of law, but to

[33] W Blackstone, *A Commentary on the Laws of England*, 3 Comm 267–8 (this was a description that Bentham found particularly objectionable: *ibid*, 410).

[34] J Bentham, *A Commentary on the Commentaries*, above n 31, *xx*.

[35] W Blackstone, *A Commentary on the Law of England*, above n 33 (3 Comm 267–8).

[36] *Ibid*, 207.

[37] *Ibid*, 178; 1 Comm 64. This observation is based on the authority of an earlier statement by Selden (itself a comment on Sir John Fortescue's *De Laudibus Legum Angliae*).

[38] *Ibid*, 178; 1 Comm 64.

understand history in a different manner. Historical study offers a dispassionate and objective representation of the law in its stages of development. Demonstration can then be undertaken to show what the law is at any given time. Jurisprudence must focus on the working through of a logical typology that orders the law and names its constituent parts. Jurisprudence, then, is systematic; it 'mark[s] out and denominate[s] the principal heads', it makes for 'a technical arrangement.'[39] If this sounds somewhat dry, it is necessary to remember that the re-ordering of law is geared towards a greater goal—a much broader philosophy of self and community. Jurisprudence as 'technical arrangement' is the path that leads towards human 'happiness.'[40]

A PNEUMATICS OF POWER: BENTHAM'S ACCOUNT OF COMPLETE LAW

It is only correct then, that this most celebrated of legal theories should begin with what is most visible and most shared amongst us. In defining his notion of political community, Bentham strips Austin's terms of their theological echoes. Law takes the form of a language, a demotic; a way of speaking and acting:

> A law may be defined as an assemblage of signs declarative of a volition conceived or adopted by the sovereign in the state, concerning the conduct to be observed in a certain case by a certain person or class of persons, who in the case in question are or are supposed to be subject to his power: such volition trusting for its accomplishment to the expectation of certain events which it is intended such declaration should upon occasion be a means of bringing to pass, and the prospect of which it is intended should act as a motive upon those whose conduct is in question.[41]

Bentham is attempting to create a language that can reduce the operation of law to a form of algebra and achieve a precision that will allow society to appear as an object of knowledge that can be categorised, measured and explained. This operation has nothing to do with the dark operations of the sacred. There is no address of the inner voice, no secret mark or inherited sense of belonging that creates the community of the faithful. Everything is in the open. Authority can be observed, it has its 'signs' that make its volitions visible. The effect of these signs, the obedience shown to them, can be observed in the same way that we would deal with any empirical data. The motivation for obedience to the law is coeval with (and can be defined as) the expectation of the occurrence of some event. You act from the fear of a certain consequence. Behaviour can be predicted, arranged and improved.

Our argument will proceed as follows: Bentham may be able to move away from the theological spirit of Austin's work, but only by reintroducing a

[39] J Bentham, *A Commentary on the Commentaries*, above n 31, 415.
[40] *Ibid*, 415.
[41] J Bentham, *Of Laws In General* (London, Athlone Press, 1970).

different idea of spirit. Bentham conceives of law, utility and society as varieties of force. They appear often in mechanistic terms as the division and re-articulation of different factors or components, but they ultimately relate back to pressures and forces. The distinguishing characteristic of this jurisprudence of force is the rigour with which law and society are approached as inter-linking machines. Like a watchmaker, Bentham breaks the complex mechanism down into its components. Long before Wittgenstein's narrator gazed on the controls of a locomotive, and seized upon the levers and dials as illustrative of the operations of meaning and language, Bentham himself gained an insight into the meaning of words by looking at the whirring wheels and gears of a machine. To understand, stop the mechanism; take the machine apart, and then put it back together.

For Bentham, a law is an assemblage of factors that brings something about or achieves an end. Law is a tool or an enabler. Law's 'being' is connective—it relates or links together certain effects, creating, literally, chains of command. Law itself 'may be considered in eight different respects.' What holds these factors together? The first of the eight facets of difference is source. The 'will of a sovereign in a state' is the source of law; law must enable a sovereign to achieve the ends of government. Law thus has its 'subjects' and 'objects' to which it applies; an 'extent', a temporal reach and its own internal workings, its 'aspects'. It can be identified and distinguished from other laws through its 'expression'. But in all instances the law is referred back to the grid that gives it its meaning, and which can in turn be changed through the force of law. Moreover, law has its force.

The consideration of the force of law allows Bentham to link the law and the human together. Force leads from the formal description of law to the problematic question of why laws are obeyed. Law relies upon 'motive . . . for enabling it to produce the effects it aims at' and this is why it targets and addresses 'pleasure and pain'. In this way law's operation links a system of governance and the psychology of the human being in a perfectly mechanistic way.

Before examining these themes in detail, let us return to the foundational notion of sovereignty. Sovereignty is defined in relational terms. The sovereign is not 'anything' as such; rather it can be conceived as a relationship between domination and obedience. Power, as 'the power of imperation', can be apportioned or divided up; and by the same token, taken back through 'de-imperation'. The sovereign can, by mandate, give power to other individuals or delegate to institutions. Individuals or institutions can claim a licensed use of power to the extent that they remain subordinate to the sovereign. This is, however, a somewhat rigid spatial model, based on an account of 'divisions' and separations within the sovereign. It is supplemented by a temporal understanding that projects the continuity of the sovereign over time. This temporal extension is carried out by means of the sovereign 'pre-adopting' the mandates of his successor. Why should this be?

> To continue the laws of preceding sovereigns, and the powers of the various magistrates, domestic as well as civil, is . . . a matter of course. To suffer either of those system of institutions to perish, and not to establish anything in their stead, would be to suffer the whole machine of government to drop to pieces. The one course no sovereign was ever yet mad enough, the other none was ever yet industrious enough to pursue.[42]

The sovereign lives on through a kind of entropy. The energy or force necessary to remake government is simply too great or too expensive. The logic of sovereignty is always linked to the continuing force of custom, or to the preservation of structures that maintain the operations of government. The same logic can give us a broader picture of the legal system. Civil and other laws, which owe their appearance to activities in the social world and appear far removed from the commands of the sovereign, must be related to sovereign power. 'Conveyances' and 'covenants' have the validity to the extent that they have been 'adopted by the sovereign' and mandated as laws. Imagine any given contract. The property that changes hands does so only to the extent that sovereign power implicitly validates the contract and will intervene to provide remedies to enforce the deal. This means that the law is an ongoing collaboration between sovereignty and custom. Power appears as something the sovereign has, exercises and divides. How does this relate to the notion of utility?

Bentham's conception of utility and the notion of subjectivity that accompanies it are more deracinated than those of Austin. The subject appears as a form stripped bear—no longer a mystery but something that can be defined, mapped and precisely laid out. The etiology of the subject begins with a principle that can be used to explain all human behaviour: 'Nature has placed mankind under the governance of two sovereign masters, pain and pleasure.'[43] The prior agency—the factor that determines that man is to be defined by capacities for pleasure and pain—'Nature'. The place of God has thus been usurped. Nature plays the role once reserved for divinity. Bentham's work is one possible response to the question posed by Nietzsche's madman: what happens after the death of God? What appears? Bentham's vision is of a social world that does not lack meaning, but whose shape and consistency is articulated by 'natural' or material forces that can themselves be plotted and determined. Indeed, the principle of utility is poised between nature and divinity, between anarchy and determination.

The most pressing question, then, is of the precise constitution of the 'sovereign masters'—of pain and pleasure. Perhaps the metaphor is inappropriate. Bentham himself dispenses with it, but in doing so, he loses an essential insight into his subject matter. Rhetorically, these opening passages of *The Principles of Morals and Legislation* move from a poetic introduction, to a more sober

[42] J Bentham, above n 41, 237.
[43] *Ibid*, 125.

sounding excursus on the principle of utility. Even if this shift in tone is necessary to introduce the more studied discussion of principle, at least the introduction touched upon the essential feature of Betham's vision. The personification of the 'sovereign masters' obscures the sense in which the author has discovered that lying behind the principle of utility are conjunctions of forces. In what sense are pleasure and pain forces? We are first of all introduced to the totality of forces: they determine the very possibility of the subject: 'all we say . . . all we think'[44]—our sense of morality, even causation, can be traced back to the determining potency of contending forces. Let us first note the composition of the principle of utility before turning back to the issue of force.

When Bentham begins to talk about the 'principle of utility' he presents it as the 'foundation of the present work.'[45] This principle allows all actions to be judged 'according to the tendency which it appears to have to augment or diminish the happiness of the party whose interest is in question.' Some preliminary observations are in order. First, the foundation of the principle itself rests on the prior foundation of 'Nature'—or the fact that the human subject, as a piece of nature, seeks pleasure and avoids pain. In other words, the principle of utility is itself an expression of a prior arrangement of forces. Secondly, happiness is a question of the way in which a force is satisfied, or 'moves' along a gradient of intensity from the diminished to the augmented. Thirdly, the operation of forces allows us to speak of the social as a theatre or arena where the same forces pass through both individuals and collectivities. Not just 'private individuals' but also 'every measure of government' is subject to the calculus of pleasure and pain. Indeed, force individuates. We can only talk of people to the extent that we can talk of their individual happiness, and hence, the social appears as the famous calculus: '[a]n action then may be said to be conformable to the principle of utility . . . when the tendency which it has to augment the happiness of the community is greater than any it has to diminish it.'[46]

This theme returns us to the themes of nominalism discussed above.[47] Here, the social is composed of singularities that remain so; they are not dispersed or agglomerated into a whole. It is as if Bentham is thinking in terms of the second law of thermodynamics but this is a question of social dynamics. The individual, like energy, cannot be created or destroyed. It merely changes form. Thus, the social is a vast network of forces, a kind of dumb presence of energies that express themselves through the singularities of individuals. It may be that the development of the argument successfully dodges the question of the constitution of the force or energy by shifting the focus of discussion. Energy can be measured; or it may be that this capacity to be measured gives us a further insight into precisely how we are to understand the energy.

[44] J Bentham, above n 41.
[45] *Ibid.*
[46] *Ibid,* 127.
[47] See chapter 3.

How do we know about the truth or 'value' of force? We know about it, because we are it! Force composes us. Bentham can dispense with proof and argument because the phenomenon is so much part of us that it does not need demonstrating. Its self-evidence is presented first as a matter of logic: 'is [the principle] susceptible of direct proof? It should seem not: for that which is used to prove everything else, cannot itself be proved.'[48] So this logical argument is not conclusive. The truth of the phenomenon is proven by its work upon our bodies, by the 'natural constitution of the human frame.'[49] We are distracted from the principle of utility only by failures of consistency, or an inability to work through false ideas to their underlying substratum. As Bentham, in a Nietzschean spirit, suggests, the 'value'[50] of pleasure and pain can only be known through their effects upon bodies.

Pleasure and pain can be determined by their intensity, duration, certainty or uncertainty, propinquity or remoteness.[51] In keeping with Bentham's nominalism, these are measures of an individual singularity. They become applicable to a group only with the addition of a supplemental term: extent.[52] These terms describe intensity, or the gradation of the degrees of an effect. However, we need to be able to move from this internal description of the movement of energy to a study of its effects on the material of the body. This takes us to the question of the value of a force. Value is a mediation of consciousness and the dumb intensity of force; value is what allows us to talk in terms of a human subject embodied in a material world, where the material is ultimately energy. It is a description of an act or an event, of its tendency or end. We are thus concerned with the 'tendency'[53] of any act that is a reaction to the intensity of a force. Force is therefore always differential, the difference between forces. Thus, 'fecundity', the measure of a tendency of an act, 'is the chance it has of being followed by sensations of the same kind: this is, pleasures, if it be a pleasure: pains, if it be a pain.'[54] In contrast, 'purity' is 'the chance it has of not being followed by sensations of the opposite kind: that is, pains, if it be a pleasure: pleasures if it be a pain.'[55]

There is insufficient space to go into the precise way in which Bentham imagined that such considerations of intensity could be brought together to produce a general reckoning of the tendency of an act in relation to a community. We can also only glance at the way in which Bentham analysed the 'simple or complex' nature of pleasure or pain. What we can note is that Bentham was moving towards a system based on the combination of elements to produce complex states that were built up of simpler states. As with the analysis of intensity or

[48] J Bentham, *Of Laws In General*, above n 41, 128.
[49] *Ibid*.
[50] *Ibid*, 151.
[51] *Ibid*.
[52] *Ibid*, 152.
[53] *Ibid*, 151.
[54] *Ibid*, 151.
[55] *Ibid*, 152.

duration, the analysis of the complexity of pleasure and pain must be referred to the differences that exist in different peoples' capacities to respond to pleasure or pain: the 'quantum' of sensibility is itself produced by other factors or circumstances, which would cover an individual's health, sex, station in life, wealth, age, education, race or lineage, the climate of the place in which they live and the government under which they live.

The law is understandable to the extent that it is an element in a calculation about happiness, or the intensity of forces. It is as if at this point, Bentham and Nietzsche (that most disturbing of spirits) reach out and touch each other. Indeed, this strange encounter is a statement of the problematic of this chapter. At the risk of simplification, it might be suggested that Bentham is the most Nietzschean of thinkers as he discovers the consequences of the death of God. If the world is no more than matter, no more than measures of pleasure and pain, what fictions must we produce to make this reality bearable?

The light on the front of Bentham's locomotive shines into the darkness of the world and it is a chilling place. Nietzsche argued that those who have killed God recreate systems of belief to save them from the absence that they have discovered. It might be said, then, that some form of 'theology' always returns. From this perspective, Bentham's system, the great attempt to catalogue and name, to create a form of universal grammar, is an attempt to refigure theological notions of the completeness and omnipotence of God in 'secular' terms. One could argue, in a slightly different context, that religion returns (and has been returning quite a lot recently) precisely when we realise that there is no God out there, that matter is the only spirit. When our fundaments are seen as fake we turn to fundamentalism. It says a great deal about the English spirit of compromise that the legal philosopher who effectively rediscovered and rewrote the Austin-Bentham tradition for late modernity, HLA Hart, attempted to temper Bentham's extremism and to talk in terms of a world that was not quite as stark and laid bare as that imagined by Bentham.

HART OF DARKNESS

Hart is a latecomer, but he is also a mediator. He comes to jurisprudence after Austin's dark hymn of the social and Bentham's world of industrial energies. Indeed, one might think of Hart as attempting to restore to jurisprudence a kind of balance. This balance is sought in the post-war recovery of an idea of Englishness, English law and of the tradition of jurisprudence. If there is a spirit in Hart's work, it is a spirit of place. It is a mediation of the past, and of what is to come through an acute sense of the present and its intellectual tasks. But, as a latecomer, this spirit of England appears in sharpest form when viewed from elsewhere; indeed, Hart's sensibility is very much that of the last period of Empire, and we shall show that there are ideological links between Hart and the visions of colonial administrators who were trying to save the British Empire.

This diagnosis sits rather uncomfortably with Hart's belief that his project belongs to social science. However, our argument is that Hart's work makes sense only if read in a literary and mythological manner. We will approach these themes by contending, first of all, with Hart's notion of the jurisprudential tradition: his relations to Austin, Bentham, Kelsen and other figures against whom jurisprudence had to be defined.

Like TS Eliot, Hart is concerned with the 'language of the tribe', a language fit for the tasks of English jurisprudence. This is the root of Hart's disagreement with Kelsen. Indeed Hart's celebrated debate with Kelsen is primarily about the spirit of place. Kelsen's 'pure theory' of law could be read as one possible response to European fascism and the need to start again from a de-Nazified present.[56] Kelsen presents the community of law as an empty form, a pure logical abstraction of necessary conditions and relationships. It is precisely this virulent evisceration of content that makes the Kelsenian system a perfect example of the structural conditions necessary for the creation of a new symbolic order. Kelsen writes from the ruins of Europe. His resort to the rigours of reason—to the purity of logical form—is made necessary by the destruction of the world-view and the value consensus to which Hart could make recourse. The first edition of *The Pure Theory* was composed against the chaos of Weimar Germany, and the rise of National Socialism. Against Nazi irrationalism, against blood knowledge and the commands of a Fuhrer who speaks the law of the *volk*, Kelsen wanted to make a claim to a form of law that approximates, as far as possible, logical statements modelled on the natural sciences. He must raise an edifice from the ruins. There can be no appeal to shared conventions, to an innate sense of fair play, or a history lived as the 'triumph' of liberal institutions.

For Kelsen, nineteenth century positivism has failed as a tradition and must be radically rethought. Liberal institutions, at least in the form adopted in the Weimar Republic failed spectacularly. Kelsen interprets this, in jurisprudential terms, as an intellectual failure. Reconstruction must start from a reconceptualisation of the very form of the law. Natural law, although a temptation, remains an ideological error as its conception of the legal 'ought' is too close to a moral imperative. A moral imperative is too subjective and cannot provide the grounding for a strong, objective legal system. Such a foundation can only be located as a 'transcendental' precondition for the very form of the law.

Hart's work, in contrast, could be thought of as a long meditation on the community of the common law. Community is an entity that lives on, that reproduces and perpetuates itself. Hart's acknowledgement of Austin as a predecessor is part of a wider narrative of tradition that could be traced back to Hobbes and his *Leviathan*. It is no wonder that the *Concept of Law*, like *Leviathan*, came after a long and hard war. Both texts aspire to revive and sustain a strong community. Hobbes' 'absolutism' is perhaps echoed in Hart's nostalgia for a settled community with a more or less explicit value consensus.

[56] W Morrison, *Jurisprudence from the Greeks to Post-Modernism* (London, Cavendish, 1997).

Working through this tension is the animus that moves Hart's work. It is necessary to begin with the imperative theory, but this account must itself be refined and supplemented by a broader theory of the social. Underlying the command theory is a mystery that always attaches itself to belonging. It is a 'ground'[57] that lies beneath 'every human society'. Law, or the 'habit of obedience'[58] that allows it to appear, suggests that jurisprudence must explain a power that defines community: subjects must render 'obedience' to a 'sovereign' who is obedient to no-one. Here is the unaccountable excess, the Leviathan.[59] That Hart can tolerate this mystery suggests that he is not inspired by Bentham's need to make the social entirely visible. Hart returns jurisprudence to notions of community and history that are wound up with a sensibility of Englishness. This is the whole point of the celebrated discussion of Rex I and Rex II in *The Concept of Law*. Although this tale is presented in deliberately abstract terms, it is an allegorical re-telling of the problem of the interregnum that confronted Hobbes and Austin: the problem of the break, of the gap, in the legitimately constituted power. Hart uses the interruption symbolically in order to show the weakness of the imperative theory of law. If power operates solely through a habit of obedience, how can the transition be explained? One has to make recourse to concepts such as 'title' and 'right'[60]—ideas that take us beyond a simple notion of obedience. They direct us towards a theory of law as a more complex 'practice' and allow us to speak of the 'acceptance' of a 'rule', according to which the power first embodied by Rex I, is continued by Rex II and is accepted by the community at large.

Why a rule? A rule differs from a habit because it offers a 'critical reflective attitude to certain patterns of behaviour as a common standard.'[61] Let us reflect on this for a moment. The concept of the rule links the sovereign to the community. The sovereign is only accepted to the extent that there is a 'rule' of acceptance, in other words, when something like a 'common standard' keeps the community together. A rule differs from a habit, because habits are not self-examining. Habits return us to the darkness of the ground; we do something because it carries the weight of endless and mindless repetition. A rule, on the other hand, implies (and leads to) reflective reasoning, the questioning of behaviour.

If self reflection is related to rule-orientated individual and group behaviour, it should be possible to generalise the model to provide an understanding of a legal system and an insight into the problem of legitimacy: why is a legal system accepted?

The discussion of legitimacy takes us to the first appearance of the distinction between primary and secondary rules. Rules allow our imaginary community to

[57] HLA Hart, *The Concept of Law* (Oxford, OUP, 1997) 50.

[58] *Ibid*, 51.

[59] Hart may even be describing a bio-power, to the extent that this relationship is as essential 'as backbone is of a man', *ibid*, 50.

[60] *Ibid*, 52–3.

[61] *Ibid*, 57.

have standards of behaviour and to posit master rules that determine which statements of Rex are to count as rules. These master rules make it possible to speak of Rex's right to issue statements considered to be rules. Moreover, if Rex has a right to issue rules, the duty to obey him follows. However, this is not just a habit of obedience. Rex's right takes us beyond habits and towards rules that emerge from their dark ground and can become questioned.

But legitimacy has more elements. Rex's right to rule is legitimate to the extent to which he is himself bound by the rules that he issues. The notion of right also allows us to account for the continuity of power. Right refers both to the authority of the existing ruler, and to his legitimate successor. This gives us a general category, 'the legitimate ruler', that can be inhabited by anyone who can claim the right as defined by this 'general category.'[62]

This general category can account for the persistence of law. It is 'already' law when the monarch ascends to the throne (or however we are to characterise the legislator) and it is 'still'[63] law when the monarch's hearse conveys his body to the tomb. Can this mysterious consistency of the law be explained, as Hobbes suggested, by the idea of the tacit acceptance of the old laws by the new legislator? The 'general category' of right dispels the 'mystery' and presents law to our gaze. Laws owe their being to the continuity of the 'right' to make laws. But note that this is not just a logical category. Hart's reasoning operates by constantly referring the logic to its embodiment in the imaginary community. The legitimacy of any rule presupposes the continuing acceptance of that rule by the community.

The move from this simple example to a theory of complex society means abstracting from this model. Applying it to the English constitution means elaborating the notion of a rule that 'confers powers' on the legislator to make law by following a 'certain procedure.'[64] This demands a wider theory of the reproduction of the social as a whole, but Hart does not move in this direction in a significant way. He does admit however that there is no 'guarantee'[65] of social coherence. There could still be a 'revolution', but this is as likely as a scorer changing the rules of cricket as a new batsman strides out to the crease. Under the English sun—these quiet afternoons enlivened by the sound of leather on wood—history happens elsewhere. Dusk settles over hedges and fields. Dick the ploughboy orders a beer and rolls a cigarette.

In moving from example to actuality, however, there is the risk that the line between habit and rule becomes blurred again. Most people do not have an explicit enough understanding of politics that would confirm the idea of right as common acceptance to be a description of a social reality. At this point a strange image occurs. Hart writes that it is in 'simple societies'[66] where a 'tribe' accepts

[62] *Ibid*, 58.
[63] *Ibid*, 62.
[64] *Ibid*, 77.
[65] *Ibid*, 59.
[66] *Ibid*, 60.

the authority of 'successive chiefs'[67] that this picture of rules and social reproduction is most true. This is a trope that runs through the Imperial view of the native. It posits an original polity to the native institution and acts as a counter vision to the more apparent notion of the white man's burden. The project of Empire consists in bringing to the surface and strengthening this inchoate polity, shaping it through the civilising influence of the common law.

This is precisely why indirect rule was the ideology of Empire, and was giving way to the experiments with re-patriated constitutions at the time of the writing of *The Concept of Law*. Sir David Cameron's vision of the 'good African',[68] who is precisely not a white man but an African rooted in his own context and law, finds his counterpart in this most white of texts, this account of England and its exports. Hart's solution to the methodological difficulties of his edifice is, again, strangely similar to the practices of de-colonialisation. It may be that the majority of people simply passively accept the law. This has to be offset by the active acceptance of the system shown by the professionals who run it. It is necessary to have a well trained governmental elite who will continue the civilising mission.

Thus, *The Concept of Law* can be read as an account of the imposition of a form of law that was always linked to a place and a spirit.[69] It has become a general theory to the extent that the common law was imposed generally, but it remains, in its defining features, a vision of the persistence or consistency of the English common law. This 'general' theory is most properly a theory of the reproduction of the institutions of the common law. One might even suggest that the very example of Rex I and Rex II, the site where the famous distinction between primary and secondary rules is first developed, is a reminiscence of the only point when England was a republic. It is as if Hart needs to account for this interruption, this gap in what is otherwise a more or less coherent monarchical order. Right coheres with the English people and the compromised notion of monarchy that is the condition of the contemporary constitutional settlement. Read in its expanded form, the rule of recognition of the English constitution, the Crown in Parliament, is merely this historical fact in legal, doctrinal form.

But there is another aspect to this history. We have seen that this theory of popular sovereignty is compromised. It becomes an account of how a staff of professionals sustain a tradition in the face of public ignorance or indifference. There are wider features of this position. Just as, economically and emotionally, the Empire 'saved' and perpetuated English hegemony, Hart's theory is an understanding of how the common law, or the commonwealth, sustains itself as a staff of experts united in their cultural attachment to a history and a tradition. *The Concept of Law* is a thinking of a spirit of belonging, a nomadic spirit, but a spirit all the same.

[67] *Ibid*, 60.

[68] Cameron, *The Principles of Native Administration and Their Application* (Lagos, [sn] 1934) 33.

[69] C Stephens, *Shakespeare's Island* (Edinburgh, Polygon, 1994).

To conclude with a misquotation: it is as if, rather than having a jurisprudence, the English have history. For Hart, as we have seen, this is the desire to mend the rupture of the Civil War; to reform and preserve Empire, to return to a history that affirms the continuity of community. The mysticism of belonging underlies the self-proclaimed social scientific bent of the project:

> Here, the intersection of the timeless moment
> Is England and nowhere. Never and always.[70]

It is as if this is the final commentary on *The Concept of Law*. It invokes a spirit, a force of law, a power of sovereignty, an interpellation that creates an order. As such, positivism is an encounter with this intersection as the 'timeless moment' of the law—of a foundational moment that remains strangely separate, and yet part of the order that it founds. For Hart, as for Eliot, this is 'England and nowhere'. It is both an energy manifesting itself in history, as a law making event, and a 'nothing': a command, a pure intensity that creates. Positivism, finally emerges then, as a poetics of power. A nostalgic mechanics of a late, (lost) Empire.

PASSAGES

Full moon on Gower Street. After the roar of the traffic, the street is profoundly quiet; only the occasional taxi or night bus. Even the drunks have gone home. The ghost of John Austin appeared to me on the corner of Store Street. I recognised his melancholic eyes at once. He turned to me and whispered in a voice like the wind through dry leaves: 'nothing is in its right place.'

[70] TS Eliot, *The Four Quartets* (London, Faber and Faber, 1944).

6

Manuscript Found in a Bottle: Notes Towards a Theory of Judgement

POSTMODERNITY SUSPENDED THE megalomaniac attempts to ground moral action on cognition, reason or the law and marks the beginnings of a new ethical awareness. To link again ethics and politics or justice and the law, we need a new conception of the good. But the teleology of the classics has been exhausted, and religious transcendence does not convince. Our world has been disenchanted; it no longer carries meanings, purposes and values, which can found an ethics, as in classical times. Natural laws are the concern of scientists, not of moral philosophers. And while we witness a return to God in the twenty-first century, this is not a sign of a new consensus about values and morality. Religion today leads to disagreement and conflict; faiths present themselves as mutually exclusive and antagonistic. In our deeply historical world, we need an ethical direction and a theory of judgement, which would stand outside legal practice and institutions while being firmly placed within our history and experience. We need a transcendent principle that we can locate in the immanence of our lives. An impossible and urgent task that takes it to an ethics that avoids the pitfalls of neo-Kantian moralism.

Emmanuel Levinas bases ethics on the shifting relationships between self and other.[1] Ethics is my unique encounter with the living other. Levinas argues that western philosophy and ethics share a common attitude towards the world, which reduces the distance between self and other and makes what is different look the same. Classical philosophy promised to reveal the structure of reality by developing universal theories and claiming that the world follows the laws of theoretical necessity. In modernity, self and individual consciousness have become the starting point of knowledge. As a result, what differs from the self-same has turned into a question of knowledge, into an exploration of the conditions under which the self can know the other's existence and understand her mental life. For phenomenology, the ego acquires knowledge by exploring the ways through which my consciousness addresses itself to the outside world. For

[1] E Levinas, *Totality and Infinity*, A Lingis (trans), (Pittsburgh, Duquesne University Press, 1969); *Otherwise than Being or Beyond Essence*, A Lingis (trans), (London, Kluwer, 1991).

Edmund Husserl, its founder, the perceptions of self are the primary material of knowledge. The world discloses itself fully to consciousness; the business of philosophy is to explore the content and actions of (my) consciousness. Heidegger, on the other hand, emphasised the historical and social nature of self. There is no life, that is not life with others. Self does not project the other in its own image but, in discovering itself, it simultaneously recognises the other. But Heidegger makes the relationship between beings and Being the key concern of philosophy and explicitly abandons ethics in favour of a primordial belonging or *ethos*. Self and the other are equal participants in the 'we' through which we share the world. But inevitably all speculation as to the meaning of Being starts from the examination of my own being and returns to ontology's preoccupation with self.

Law and jurisprudence fully share these cognitive and moral attitudes. Cognitively, the law knows the world to the extent that it subjects it to its regulative operations. For modern jurisprudence, the law and the world are potentially co-extensive. The legal system has all the necessary resources to translate non-legal phenomena into law's arcane discourse in order to exercise its regulative function. Legal rules ensure equality before the law and guarantee the freedom of the parties. But this equality is only formal: it necessarily ignores the specific history, motive and need the litigant brings to the law in order to administer the calculation of the rule and the application of the measure. Similarly with legal freedom: it is the freedom to accede to the available repertoire of legal forms and rights, the freedom to be what the law has ordained, accompanied by the threat that opting out is not permitted, that disobedience to a legal norm is disobedience to the rule of law *tout court* and that life outside the legal form ceases. Legal rules and their mentality are strangely amoral; they promise to replace ethical responsibility with the mechanical application of predetermined and morally neutral rules and justice with the administration of justice. But there is more. As we saw above, moral philosophy in its ontological imperialism needs and creates the 'generalised other'.[2] The legal subject is a *persona,* a mask, veil or blindfold put on real people who unlike the abstractions of moral philosophy hurt and suffer. It is doubly important therefore to remove the mask from the face of the person and the blindfold from the eyes of justice. But is there an ethical residue in the law behind the all-concealing veil of formal legality?

The ethics of alterity challenges these ontological and epistemological assumptions.[3] It always starts with the other and challenges the various ways in which the other has been reduced to the same. The other is not the self's alter ego; an extension of the self. Nor is the other the negation of self in a dialectical relation that can be totalized in a future synthesis. Heidegger correctly

[2] See the discussion of the 'generalised other', above chapter 4, p 127 ff.

[3] The discussion of Levinasian ethics in this part has been influenced by Chapter 12, 'The Human Rights of the Other' in C Douzinas, *The End of Human Rights* (Oxford, Hart, 2000).

emphasised the historical and social nature of self. But the other is not similar to self. Self and other are not equal partners in a Heideggerian 'we' in which we share our world, nor is the other the threatening externality and radical absence of Sartrean existentialism which turns self into an object. The other comes first. (S)he is the condition of existence of language, of self and of the law. The other always surprises me, opens a breach in my wall, befalls the ego. The other precedes me and calls upon me: where do you stand? Where are you now rather than who are you. All 'who' questions have ended in the foundational moves of (de)ontology. Being, the Cartesian *cogito*, the Kantian transcendental subject or the phenomenological consciousness start with self and create the other as an *imitatio ego*. In the philosophy of alterity, the other can never be reduced to the self or the different to the same.

The sign of an other is the face. The face is unique. It is neither an empirical entity—the sum total of facial characteristics—nor the representation of something hidden, the soul, self or subjectivity. The face does not represent an absent presence and cannot therefore become a cognitive datum. Nor is the face the surface of a depth, or the image of an essence. The face eludes every category. It brings together speech and glance, saying and seeing, in a unity that escapes the conflict of senses and the arrangement of the organs. Thought lives in speech, speech is (in) the face, saying is always addressed to a face. The other is her face. 'Absolutely present, in his face, the Other—without any metaphor—faces me'.[4] In its uniqueness, the face gets hold of me with an ethical grip, myself beholden to, obligated to, in debt to, the other person, prior to any contracts or agreements about who owes what to whom. In the face-to-face, I am fully, immediately and irrevocably responsible for the other who faces me. A face in suffering issues a command, a decree of specific performance: 'Do not kill me', 'Welcome me', 'Give me Sanctuary', 'Feed me'. The only possible answer to the ethical imperative is 'an immediate respect for the other himself . . . because it does not pass through the neutral element of the universal, and through respect, in the Kantian sense for the law'.[5]

The demand of the other that obliges me is the 'essence' of the ethics of alterity. But this 'essence' is based on the non-essence of the other who cannot be turned into the instance of a concept, the application of a law or the particularisation of a universal ego. 'The other arises in my field of perception with the trappings of absolute poverty, without attributes, the other has no place, no time, no essence, the other is nothing but his or her request and my obligation'.[6] As the face of the other turns on me, (s)he becomes my neighbour, but not the neighbour of the neighbour principle in law. As absolute difference and otherness, my neighbour is at the same time most strange and foreign. The appeal of the other is direct, concrete and personal; it is addressed to me and I

[4] Levinas quoted in J Derrida, *Writing and Difference* (London, Routledge, 1978) 100.

[5] *Ibid*, at 96.

[6] J-F Lyotard, *The Differend*, G Van Den Abbeele (trans), (Manchester, Manchester University Press, 1988) 111.

am the only one who can answer it. The demand does not depend on universal reason or law but on the concrete historical and empirical encounter with the other. It is this situated encounter and unrepeatable unique demand which assigns me to morality and makes me a bound and ethical subject. Our relationship is necessarily non-symmetrical and non-reciprocal because her unique demand is addressed to me and me alone. Equity is not equality but absolute dissymmetry.

The ontology of alterity is based on the absolute proximity of the most alien. When self comes to constitute itself, it faces before the I, I's relationship with the other. Subjectivity is constituted through this opening. All consciousness is intersubjective and all language is given but because the other comes first the nature of (inter)subjectivity is not of two equal parties nor is the other a projection of self. My *principium individuation* is my inescapable call to responsibility, the result of the direct and personal appeal the other makes on me. The other addresses me and not a universal ego or a legal person. To be free is to do what no one else can do in my place. But how can we move from the ethics of responsibility to the law? What is the relevance of a discourse that claims a pre-ontological and pre-rational status and emphasises the uniqueness of the face for a legality that has universalistic pretensions and bases its empire upon the rationality of judgement and the thematisation of people and circumstances?

Ethical responsibility starts with the all-embracing demands of an unknown other. But the law must also introduce the demands and expectations of the third party. 'The other is from the first the brother of all the other men'.[7] The co-existence of 'all the other men' places a limit on my infinite responsibility towards the other. When someone comes to the law, he is already involved in conflict with at least one more person and the judge has to balance the conflicting requests. The judge, seen from the perspective of the litigants, is the third person, whose action removes the dispute from the domain of interpersonal hostility and places it within the confines of the institution. Because the third person is always present in my encounter with the other, the law is implicated in every attempt to act morally. Justice involves 'comparison, coexistence, contemporaneousness, assembling, order, the *visibility* of faces, . . . a co-presence on an equal footing as before a court of justice'.[8]

The law limits our infinite responsibility for the other and introduces the element of calculation, synchronisation and thematisation; it regulates and totalises the demands put before it. The law translates these requests in the universalisable language of rights, legal entitlements and procedural proprieties and synchronises them, makes them appear contemporaneous and comparable. Almost by definition and necessity, the law forgets the difference of the different and the otherness of the other and, in this sense, it cannot escape injustice. To say, therefore, that the law begins as ethics, as the infinite, non-totalisable and

[7] *Otherwise Than Being or Beyond Essence*, above n 1,158.
[8] *Ibid*, at 157.

non-regulated moment of the encounter with another, sounds counterfactual. But the ethics of alterity is unequivocal; the sense of responsibility, the 'internal point of view' that speaks to me and commands me, comes from the proximity of one to another—the fact that we are involved and implicated as we are faced and addressed by the other. In my proximity to the other, within the law or outside of it, I am preoccupied by the absolute asymmetry of the one for the other, and I find myself in an irreplaceable and irreversible relation of substitution.

In a community of equals, I too, am another like the others and, I too, am a legitimate claimant and recipient of the other's care. Community then is double: first, it is an ethical community of unequal hostages to the other and a network of undetermined but immediate ethical relationships of asymmetry where I am responsible and duty bound to respond to the other's demand. But community also implies the commonality of law, the calculation of equality, and the symmetry of rights. It is on this basis of the 'legal as ethical' that we can visualise a politics of law that disturbs the totalising tendency of the legal system. Such politics would allow the other to reappear both as the point of exteriority and transcendence that precludes the closure of ontology, and as the excluded and unrepresentable of political and legal theory.

Here we approach a key contemporary aspect of the paradox or *aporia* of justice: to act justly you must treat the other both as equal and entitled to the symmetrical treatment of norms and as a totally unique person who commands the response of ethical asymmetry. Justice is grounded in the ethical turn to the other; it 'is impossible without the one that renders it finding himself in proximity . . . The judge is not outside the conflict, but the law is in the midst of proximity'.[9] Judges, lawyers and law teachers are always involved and implicated, called upon by the other to respond to the ethical relationship. We must compare and calculate, but we remain responsible, and always return to the surplus of duties over rights. Injustice would be to forget that the law rises on the ground of responsibility for the other and that ethical proximity and asymmetry overflow the equality of rights. The law can never have the last word. Legal relations are just only if they recognise 'the impossibility of passing by he who is proximate'.[10] We cannot define justice in advance, we cannot say 'justice is X or Y', because that would turn the injunction of ethics into an abstract theory and would turn the command 'be just' into an empty judgemental statement. Justice is not about theories and truth; it does not derive from a true representation of just society. If the law calculates, if it thematises people by turning them into legal subjects, ethics is a matter of an indeterminate judgement without criteria and, justice is the bringing together of the limited calculability and determinacy of law with the infinite openness of ethical alterity.

[9] *Otherwise Than Being or Beyond Essence,* above n 1, at 59.
[10] *Ibid.*

THE INDETERMINATE JUDGEMENT

The idea of indeterminate judgement refers us to two seemingly unrelated traditions, Aristotelian practical wisdom and casuistry. In Aristotle, *phronesis* or practical wisdom, becomes a coherent theory of judgement because it is inextricably linked with a clear teleology of persons and actions. The aim of ethics is the achievement of the good life, but similarly every practice, profession or engagement is unified through its 'standards of excellence', which allow us to call an orator, or a politician or a carpenter, good. As we saw in chapter 3, the good life is always situated—it is good for us—and involves an ongoing dialogue and adjustment between our actions, aiming at the standards of excellence of various practices we engage in—and our overall 'life plan', the more or less clear set of ideas, hopes, dreams and expectations that make us believe that our life through its various good and bad episodes is a fulfilled life. Against this background, *phronesis* is the method of deliberation followed by the prudent in order to arrive at judgements that will help achieve the standards of excellence of the various practices as a part of the wider project of establishing the good life.

Practical wisdom is therefore the virtue of praxis. Practical judgements, unlike theoretical statements, do not deal with essences or with necessary and immutable relations; they have a timely and circumstantial character, and they depend on a full and detailed understanding of the factual situation. Aristotle argues that equity, *epieikeia,* corrects the generalisations and uniform applications of legal justice. 'Justice and equity coincide, and both are good, [but] equity is superior'.[11] Justice and the variety of circumstances in which practical judgement is exercised require that the prudent go beyond the application of rules. Aristotle did not take the casuistic route and did not compile lists and classifications of good and bad acts like his medieval followers.[12] But the Aristotelian practical judgement is preoccupied with the specificity of the situation and with the perception, understanding and judging of the singular, as singular and is a major source of inspiration for medieval casuistry.

Casuistry is a method of resolving moral and religious conflicts—a church-based form of moral reasoning.[13] Until at least the seventeenth century, matters such as relations with one's family or neighbours, or with one's one body and soul—as in the correct attitude to suicide; how to behave in public; attitudes to sexuality; to the lending of money at interest and so on—all came within the casuist's scope. Indeed, the Catholic Church, assuming that the world was a *universitas christianorum*, decided that all aspects of conscience came under its

[11] See above p 121.

[12] C Douzinas and R Warrington, *Justice Miscarried* (Edinburgh, Edinburgh University Press, 1995) chapter 3.

[13] See generally AR Jonsen and S Toulmin, *The Abuse of Casuistry* (Berkeley, University of California Press, 1988).

jurisdiction. Christian casuistry, designed to help priests resolve borderline problems in a principled yet sensitive manner, reached its height of refinement and influence around the sixteenth and seventeenth centuries. For a time, it became a widely accepted and respected method for the resolution of disputes and problems faced by the all-encompassing church jurisdiction. Even when casuistry had become predominantly associated with a minority religion, as it did from Elizabethan times in England, it still affected the orthodoxy. Both as something 'other', as a discourse of justice alien to the presumed majority opinion—and even more insidiously—within the very orthodoxy that seemed to reject entirely the basis of casuistry's jurisdiction and method of operation, casuistry triumphed. For a time, even in Protestant England, it was ubiquitous. Casuistry fell out of intellectual favour around 1650, after the violent attacks by religious enemies who claimed that it was the sort of reasoning that could justify anything. Despite something of a recent revival, casuistry became, and is still now, frequently treated as synonymous with another debased tradition—'sophistry'.

Casuistry as a form of moral judgement starts from the position of the unique individual in her natural and social environment and attempts to describe this singularity in morally relevant terms. In the words of casuistry's modern defenders, 'the method of casuistry involved an ordering of cases by paradigm and analogy, appeals to maxims and analysis of circumstances, the qualification of opinions, the accumulation of multiple arguments, and the statement of practical resolutions of particular moral problems in the light of all these considerations.' It is based on general maxims, but these are not 'universal or invariable, since they hold good with certainty only in the typical conditions of the agent and the circumstances of action'.[14]

These maxims were derived from three sources. First, principles came from God either through revelation or reason, which was God's way of allowing human beings to partake in divine wisdom. The obvious starting place, especially for Puritan casuistry, was the Bible.[15] Secondly, the casuists relied on the opinions of the learned who had, in the past, written about moral problems broadly conceived, and whose opinions, like those of common law judges, had come to be recognised as authoritative. Since at least the eleventh century, the Catholic church had been wedded to the importance of 'authority', and the casuists used it extensively.[16] Bishops, priests, doctors, saints, recluses, learned men of religion of all sorts had written, some of them in exhaustive quantities, on the detailed results that the confessors and advisers should reach in coming to conclusions in particular cases. Although mostly couched in terms of hypotheticals, the discussions were usually based on actual cases that had occurred.

[14] See generally AR Jonsen and S Toulmin, *The Abuse of Casuistry*, *ibid*, at 256–7.

[15] DR Bellhouse 'Probability in the Sixteenth and Seventeenth Centuries: An Analysis of Puritan Casuistry' (1988) 56 *International Statistical Review* 63, 66.

[16] W Ullman, *The Growth of Papal Government in the Middle Ages* (London, Methuen, 1962) 360–1.

The endless works of casuistry were intended as a sort of handbook for those involved in day to day 'adjudication' over matters religious and moral (if indeed such a distinction was a valid one in *societas christiana*).

But the most important source for the determination of moral disputes was 'conscience'. Conscience, like equity's conception of the term, was not merely individual thoughts or reactions to moral dilemmas and conflicts. The irreducibly personal acts of conscience 'weave norms and circumstances and opinions together into a strand of will and understanding called a judgment of right action.'[17] Cases of conscience act 'simultaneously as demonstrations of the principle that each human action is unique and as models of decision-making process to be imitated by all men with similar cases of conscience'.[18] Conscience depended on individual circumstances—the who, what, when, where and how of the rhetoricians—and was always the final arbiter. But its judgement was intimately linked with the wisdom of past practices and the open-ended principles. The locus of this link is the 'case', which brings together the various public and private aspects of the moral dilemma; the concrete persons with their unique histories, the time and place of the action and the wider considerations involved. Casuistry follows the rhetorical topics and organises its problems as narratives. This allows as many aspects of the situation as possible to come to bear on its narrative closure which is also the moral answer.

It is evident that one discipline has taken the injunctions of casuistry seriously for centuries: the common law. However, common law reasoning has only very rarely acknowledged its close cousin. Both casuistry and the common law treated the specific facts of any case with great respect; each claimed that its decisions were based on principles; each was directly concerned with adjudications over 'consciences', though by the end of the middle ages the scope of each jurisdiction's conscience applications had been separated. Especially in the jurisdiction of the court of equity, conscience is paramount. As the Court of Appeal once put it: for a claim of conscience to be pleaded successfully 'it must be shown to have an ancestry founded in history and in the practice and precedent of the courts administering equity jurisdiction'.[19] Conscience is both principle and individual mental comprehension of the possibility of right action. Finally, and above all, the common law, like casuistry, has the inherent potential to consider sensitively the specifics of the person before it. The common law's frequent failure to take this possibility seriously has been a main factor of its moral failings.

The growth of statutory interventions and positivism, the introduction of doctrinalism and the decline of casuistry as a church art, undermined the casuistic method in law. The treasure chest of common law decisions is full to

[17] J Keenan and T Shannon (eds), *The Context of Casuistry* (Washington DC, Georgetown University Press, 1995), xii.

[18] CW Slights, *The Casuistical Tradition in Shakespeare, Donne, Herbert and Milton* (Princeton, Princeton University Press, 1998) 297.

[19] *Re Diplock* [1948] Ch 465.

the brim with cases where the uniqueness of the other person has been disregarded—and we will examine some later in this chapter. In theory, however, the common law has never rejected the working procedures of the case method. Its particularity is to be found in the dialectical relationship between the general principles to be derived from common law, custom and statute, and the specific facts involved in any particular dispute. Past decisions are sources of general but open-ended principle, precedents for future cases, and careful, often lengthy examination of all 'relevant' surrounding circumstances which, in the best judgements, are woven into complete and aesthetically constructed narratives. In recognising the uniqueness of each case, the common law retains the potential for an ethical application of principles and the development of a notion of justice which is aware of the requirements of the individual before the court and of the contingency of decision-making.

This analysis can be of great importance for the revitalisation of justice in law. We need to develop a new secular form of casuistic reasoning that will draw from the repressed traditions of case reasoning. The Aristotelian *phronesis* insists on the importance of situation and context but is predicated upon a teleology that does not exist and cannot be recreated. The judge may be the person closest to the classical and casuistical model of the *phronimos* in modernity, but in the absence of a shared universe of value we must envision new ways of giving the other her due and of returning law to justice. The morality of legal duty and right produces inevitable and inescapable conflicts and injustices that the legal institution can address only if it returns to the initial intuition of ethics: practical judgement only works in the context of the good (life). But this universal can no longer be the consensual virtue of the *polis* of classical teleology, nor the abstract duty to follow divine or state law. At the end of modernity, the good can only be defined according to the needs and demands of the other, the person in need, and the self-defining autonomous person whose request asks for the re-awakening of the sensitivity to singularity inherent in the sense of justice. The demand that the other is to be heard as a full person, in other words the demand for ethics, introduces certain minimum communicative and moral requirements for legal procedure as to the type of hearing to be given to the person before the law and the nature of the interpretation and application of the relevant legal rules.[20] The sense of justice returns the law to the other and the

[20] Narrative theory can be of great use in this moral envisioning of legal judgement. Jackson has argued that both the interpretation of the law and the construction of the facts in the judicial syllogism take narrative form: *Law, Fact and Narrative Coherence* (Liverpool, Deborah Charles Publications, 1988). Jackson, in his semiotic ultra-positivism is uninterested in the ethical aspects of narrativity, or indeed in the political significance of the assumption of roles of narrator/narratee. P Ricoeur, *Oneself As Another* (Chicago, Chicago University Press, 1992) p 88–168 and S Benhabib, *Situating the Self* (Cambridge, Polity, 1992) 121–30 analyse the ethical importance of the narrative construction of life stories. The political imperative of postmodernism is to keep the 'tales in motion and circulation, keep interchanging narrators, narratees and narrated, keep making the judge defendant and the defendant judge': C Douzinas and R Warrington with S McVeigh,

good. But we should repeat and conclude: law's inescapable commitment to the rule means that injustice is the inescapable condition of all law.

Justice cannot be represented or be turned into a normative sentence. But although we cannot say what justice is we can attempt to say what injustice would be. The first thing to emphasise is that while legal justice asks the judge to sit in judgment 'justice is impossible without the one that renders it finding himself in proximity . . . The judge is not outside the conflict, but the law is in the midst of proximity'.[21] The judge is always involved and implicated, called upon to respond to the ethical relationship when he judges. Justice is not a mere legality regulating the subjects or the subsumption of particular cases under general rules. He who judges must compare and calculate, but he remains responsible and always returns to the surplus of his duties over his rights. Injustice would be to forget that the law rises on the ground of responsibility for the other and that ethical proximity and asymmetry overflow the equality of rights. The law can never be the last word. Legal relations of equivalence, comparison and attribution are just only if they recognise 'the impossibility of passing by he who is proximate'.[22]

This is another instance of the sense of justice, which again takes the form of an *aporia*: to be just you must both be free *and* follow a rule or a prescription. A just and responsible decision must both conserve and destroy—or suspend—the law enough to reinvent it and re-justify it in each case. Each case is different and requires a unique interpretation that no rule can guarantee absolutely. But at the same time there is no just decision if the judge does not refer to law or rule, if he suspends his decision before the undecidable, or leaves aside all rules. This is the reason that we cannot say that a judgment is just. A decision may be recognised as lawful, in accordance with legal rules and conventions, but it cannot be declared just because justice is the dislocation of the said of the law by the—unrepresentable—saying of ethics.

> For a decision to be just and responsible, it must, in its proper moment if there is one, be both regulated and without regulation: it must conserve the law and also destroy it or suspend it enough to have to reinvent it in each case, re-justify it, at least reinvent it in the reaffirmation and the new and free confirmation of its principle.[23]

Justice seeks the particular at the moment when the universal runs the risk to of turning its opposite, and as such, it has the characteristics of a double bind. The action of justice requires an incessant movement between the general rule and the specific case that has no resting place and finds no point of equilibrium.

Postmodern Jurisprudence (London, Routledge, 1991) at 110. An ethically aware theory of legal judgement must combine the narrative nature of law with the recognition that a 'just' decision responds to the demands of the other as put before the law in the story (s)he constructs.

[21] E Levinas, *Otherwise than Being or Beyond Essence*, above n 1, 159.

[22] *Ibid.*

[23] J Derrida, 'The Force of Law: The "Mystical Foundation of Authority"' (1990) 11 *Cardozo Law Review*, 961.

There is a dislocation, a delay or deferral, between the ever-present time of the law and the always-to-come temporality of ethics

We can conclude that justice has the characteristics of a promissory statement. A promise states in the present moment something to be performed in the future. Being just always lies in the future, it is a promise made to the future, a pledge to look into the event and the uniqueness of each situation and to respond to the absolute unrepeatability of the face that will place a demand on me. This promise, like all promises, does not have a present time—a time when you can say there it is, justice is this or that. Suspended between the law and the good in-the-face-of-the-other, justice is always still to come or always already performed. But as the ethical exposure to the other is inevitably and necessarily reduced to the simultaneity of the text, the law and the judge are unavoidably implicated in violence. There is violence in law; the violence of turning the other to an instance of interpretation but also the physical violence that follows every verdict and judgment. Critical jurisprudence has to keep disrupting the law in the name of justice and to keep reminding the law of its inescapable violence. The law is necessarily committed to the form of universality and abstract equality; but it must also respect the requests of the contingent, incarnate and concrete other—it must pass through the ethics of alterity in order to respond to its own embededness in ethics. In this unceasing movement between the most general and calculating and the most concrete and incalculable, or between the legality of form and the ethics of respons(ibility) to the concrete person—law answers the primordial sense of another justice.

THE MOMENTARY PRINCIPLE OF JUSTICE

After the 'hermeneutic turn' in jurisprudence represented by Ronald Dworkin's jursiprudence of rights and the wide popularity of the school of 'law and literature' crude positivism is no longer fashionable. The hermeneutic approaches emphasise practical reasoning and the principled and interpretative nature of legal decision-making. In so doing, practitioners of hermeneutics open legal judgments to considerations and materials, including moral philosophy, not immediately available or ascertainable from within the strict confines of legal rules. The aim, however, is still only to present legal *interpretation* as more creative, or more flexible, or as value orientated. It addresses exclusively the constative part of the legal sentence and judges its justice according to the 'rightness' of the expanded conception of what it is to interpret. The field from which the 'right answer' is to emerge has been considerably and admirably extended; but it is still from within this past field of law-worked-by-principle and its interpretation that the sentence will act upon the other. The translation from theory (the right answer according to the legal facts and principles) to ethics (the demand for and performance of just action) remains unquestioned and unperformed. Our analysis does not deny the interpretative nature of legal judgement, but questions the automatic identification of its ethical and just character with the 'correct' interpretation of the law. Law's claim to represent reality and to impose judgements and order in its name may still be a kind of dogmatism even though reality now appears larger or more nuanced, open-ended and principled.

The operation of the judgement can be compared with the formal structure of performative speech acts. The performative says and does; saying what it does by doing what it says. If a speaker says 'I thee wed', 'the meeting is declared open', 'war is declared', the statement initiates an act or a set of actions in the world. Similarly, every judgement is implicated with force; the force of the interpretation which turns the singular and unique into an instance of the norm, subsumes a particular to the universal and punishes the body of the condemned. The 'rightness' of the judgement depends on the institutional felicity of the interpretation of law and, in hermeneutical jurisprudence, on its accord with some moral standard. But the justice of a statement can only be judged according to the effects it has in the world. Its action is neither the continuation of the legal interpretation nor its opposite. In many key respects *logos* and *kratos,* discourse and force are separated by a gulf.

But the time of justice differs from the time of interpretation. Interpretation turns to the past or measures up to the future as they inhabit the ever-present. Interpretation's time is synchronic. The time of action—violence or justice—on the other hand is diachronic. It addresses the other here and now in each here and now, and answers or denies the call. This is the pure ethical time, the time of what Levinas calls 'il y a'—it is there, it is happening now.

Let us examine the two conceptions of time in a case involving an application for political asylum. The case of *R v The Secretary of State for the Home Department, ex parte Sivakumaran*[24] involved a number of Tamil refugees fleeing an offensive by the Sinhalese government and the Indian army against the Tamil areas of Sri Lanka. Their asylum applications had been denied by the Home Office and the House of Lords was asked to determine the circumstances when a 'well-founded fear of persecution for reasons of race, religion, nationality, membership of a particular social group or political opinion' exists—the necessary precondition under international and British law for establishing an asylum claim. The Court of Appeal had held that the test for finding a 'well-founded fear' should be largely subjective. It would be satisfied by showing that the refugee had (a) actual fear and (b) good reason for this fear. Unless an applicant's fear could be dismissed as 'paranoid', 'fear is clearly an entirely subjective state and should be judged accordingly'.[25]

The House of Lords reversed this ruling. According to the Lords, a genuine fear of persecution could not suffice. The fears should have an 'objective basis' which could be 'objectively determined'.[26] Justified fear should be based on

[24] [1988] 1 All ER 193 HL.
[25] *Ibid,* at 195.
[26] [1988] 1 All ER 193 HL, at 196.

'true', 'objective facts' which, as such, could be ascertained by an objective observer like the Home Secretary or the immigration officers. The authorities were entitled to decide not only 'on the basis of the facts known to the applicant, or believed by him to be true' but also on 'unknown facts which would help assess whether 'subjective fear was objectively justified'.[27] The Home Secretary had taken into account various reports from relevant sources (the refugee unit of the Home Office, press articles, information supplied by the Foreign Office) and had concluded that while army activities 'amounted to civil war' and 'occurred principally in areas inhabited by Tamils', they did not 'constitute evidence of persecution of Tamils as such . . . nor any group of Tamils'.[28] He was therefore justified in dismissing the fear of persecution and rejecting the asylum application, because on the basis of the 'objective' facts known to him the applicants had been or was likely to be subjected to persecution.

In the Court of Appeal, the Master of the Rolls illustrated the 'subjective' test by means of an allegory.

> A bank cashier confronted with a masked man who points a revolver at him and demands the contents of the till could without doubt claim to have experienced a 'well-founded fear'. His fears would have been no less well-founded if, one minute later, it emerged that the revolver was a plastic replica or a water pistol.[29]

The House of Lords, however, dismissed the analogy in summary fashion. An 'objective observer' of the robbery would accept the cashier's fear as well-founded only until he discovered the fact that the firearm was fake. Before that he would not have been an 'objective' observer in any case. While he was still defrauded he was in exactly the same state as the cashier, possibly in fear but certainly not seeing the truth. The objective observer must reserve judgement until such time as all relevant facts are in. According to the Lords, immigration officers and judges should also act as objective observers. From that position the refugees' fears were not 'of instant personal danger arising out of an immediate predicament' and the official response should be determined after 'examining the actual state of affairs in [the refugees'] country'.[30]

We can draw a parallel here between the time of fear and pain and the time of justice. When fear, pain or justice are dealt with as 'real' entities that can be verified or falsified according to objective criteria their time or the time of the response to them is the time of constancy and omnitemporality of descriptions,

[27] *Ibid*, at 202.

[28] *Ibid*, at 199.

[29] (1987) 3 WLR 1053. As is well known, Hart uses the gunman analogy repeatedly to distinguish the meaning of 'being obliged' from that of 'having an obligation': HLA Hart, *The Concept of Law* (Oxford, Clarendon, 1961). Only the latter is supposed to be the correct response to normative, specifically, legal commands. Lord Donaldson, in accepting that the fear is necessarily an individual and unshareable feeling and in responding to it is, in this instance, following the principle of justice of the ethics of alterity. But this principle is momentary. It is neither a generaliseable rule nor does it derive from the consistent and coherent action of a prudent judge.

[30] [1988] 1 All ER 193, at 196, 197.

theories and institutions. Truth is atemporal and theory is all-seeing. Fear and pain on the other hand are individual feelings experienced as temporal responses to stimuli. In treating the time of fear as non-instant and non-immediate the House of Lords is violating the time of ethics. To remind ourselves of the Biblical story—God who knows that Ishmael will in the future shed innocent blood—still gives him water because he is dying of thirst and therefore suffering injustice now. 'I judge each for what he is now and not for what he will become,' God tells the protesting Angel.

Violence or justice can only happen at the moment of their occurrence. They are the performative aspects of the legal judgement. Nothing that happened earlier—a reading of the law or a commitment to principle—and nothing that anticipates the future—a promise or a vision of what should happen—can account fully or preempt the uniqueness of the response. And, as in the robbery analogy, the response of the person obligated can only be instant and immediate. We can now understand why, for Derrida, the instant of the just decision is a madness and has an urgency that obstructs knowledge. Justice, like the robber and the fear he created, cannot wait for all relevant facts. Even if the addressee of justice had all the information and all the time in the world 'the moment of decision, as such, always remains a finite moment of urgency and precipitation . . . since it always marks the interruption of the juridico—or ethico—or politico-cognitive deliberation that precedes it'.[31]

Derrida in his last published text has cryptically argued that to be responsible and within reason would be to create 'maxims of transaction for deciding between two just as rational and universal but contradictory exigencies of reason as well as its enlightenment.'[32] The tension between the urgency of the call to justice, the responsibility of ethics, and the omnitemporality of law, the discipline of reason, reminds us that there is an imperceptible fall from interpretation to action, that an invisible line both separates and joins the legal sentence as the right answer of the legal problem and the (forcible or just) sentence of the legal verdict. This trait conjoins and separates the constative from the performative. But at the same time as the space and time of action, and of the encounter with the other, the trace is where the interpretative part of the judgement is brought before the law of its performance. This trace is justice, perhaps a justice that dwells in juridical discourse but is always also a justice to come. A judgement is just if it follows and creates its momentary principle. The paradox of a 'momentary principle' best paraphrases just action which, qua action, resists and denies all paraphrase. The trace is a *principle* in so far as it answers the call of the suffering other, who is one among many, in a community of ethical sensibility which, like Kant's *sensus communis*, acts as the regulative principle always still to come; but it is only a *momentary* and transient

[31] *Ibid*, at 967.

[32] J Derrida, *Rogues*, Pascale-Anne Brault and Michael Naas (trans), (Stanford, Stanford University Press, 2005) 158.

principle, because the encounter with the other is always concrete and unrepeatable.

A just judgement is the momentary and principled response to the other's concrete generality. This is the law of justice, of 'whose subject we can never say, 'there it is', it is here or there. It is neither natural nor institutional; one can never attain to her, and she never arrives on the grounds of an original and proper taking place'.[33] This momentary principle of justice, inscribed at the heart of the judgement but always before the law is what turns force into justice and force that does not heed its call into violence. We can conclude that the justice of a judgement is inscribed and suspended in the space between the statement of the law (what exists and is right legally) and the invocation of the ethical demand (what I ought to do to the other following my absolute responsibility). Two types of reason—rationality and reasonableness—meet and clash in this space and at this time. The rationality of law which subjects everything to reason and 'gives itself reason, to do so, so as to protect or keep itself, so as to keep within reason.'[34] But here too appears another reason, the reasonable, a 'rationality that takes account of the incalculable so as to give an account of it, there where this appears impossible. So as to account for or reckon with it, that is to say, with the event of what or who comes.'[35] It is the space where the other brought before the law is acted upon, where justice is done or violence is inflicted. This oxymoronic maxim, the momentary principle of justice, constitutes and regulates the just judgement, both as legal and as ethical, with the law and for the other, and . . .

PASSAGES

After the conference, I couldn't get to sleep because I was thinking about Professor Outis. Years ago, I had worked with him at the University of Deal when the department was full of Marxists. I remember him as a stooped figure, a man in exile, always talking about his home. A long time ago he'd written a well received book. I think it was published in New York in the early eighties. It was called *The Phenomenology of Forgetting*. He'd done nothing since. One day in June, Outis drove to a quiet beach in a secluded cove. He calmly undressed and walked into the sea. They identified his clothes from a copy of the *Inferno* that he had left in his jacket pocket, full of cryptic notes. His body was never found. Rolled gently in the currents, it must have drifted through the shipping lanes to merge with the ocean. The last voyage to Ithaca.

[33] Above n 23, at 983.
[34] Above n 32, at 159.
[35] *Ibid.*

Part 3

Philosophical Differences

7

The Colour of Law: Identity, Recognition, Rights

THE VOLUMINOUS LITERATURE of rights pays scant attention to the role that rights play in building individual selves. Legal philosophers discuss classifications of rights, the internal consistency of rights discourse, the social effects of rights or the goods that rights guarantee. But on the subjective side, the operative assumption is that rights express, uphold and guarantee pre-existing characteristics, their task typically being to promote free will. The characteristics, elements and traits of human personality exist prior to rights and other public institutions, which are treated as tools intended to allow the public expression of pre-formed and complete selves. These assumptions are part of liberal theory's impoverished view of the subject as a closed and monological entity and of the social bond as an atomocentric collection of individuals whose relations to each other are external, superficial and interest-driven.

The shortcomings of the liberal theory of rights have been attacked from many perspectives, particularly by American critical legal scholars. Indeed critical theory has great difficulties in reconciling its occasionally scathing critique of rights with radical lawyering, which uses rights in order to protect the underprivileged and oppressed. This conflict has been particularly in evidence in the writings of critical race theorists and exemplified in Patricia Williams' statement that rights are 'a symbol too deeply enmeshed in the psyche of the oppressed to lose without trauma and much resistance'.[1] In seeing rights as 'symbols' with important psychological effects, Williams invites us to reconsider the liberal approach to rights as external to the self and to examine the ways in which rights are 'enmeshed' in the psyche. Following Williams' invitation, we will examine here the constitutive role of rights in building human identity. Our project aims to develop the insights of Hegel's theory of recognition in the business of creating the self.

Descartes and Kant had presented consciousness as a solitary entity confronting the outside world. But for Hegel, the self is not a simple, stable entity

[1] P Williams, *The Alchemy of Race and Rights* (Cambridge, Mass, Harvard University Press, 1991) 165.

which, once formed, goes into the world. Self is created in relations with others and the community. The subject is always inter-subjective. Moral conflicts, personal disputes and social antagonisms are expressions of a struggle for recognition which is necessary both for the creation of the individual and his socialisation. My identity is constructed through the recognition of my characteristics, attributes and traits by others, both other persons and the social and legal institutions which, following Lacan, we may call the Big Other. Lack of recognition or misrecognition undermines the sense of identity, by projecting a false, inferior or defective image of self. Acknowledging the vital contribution others make to the constitution of self reconciles us with or, in the case of non-recognition, alienates us from the world. But recognition of my identity by others also makes me aware of my uniqueness and helps my individuation.

Hegel's starting point is that the ego as self-consciousness is a creature of desire. Desire reveals a fundamental lack in the subject, an emptiness that must be filled through the overcoming of external objects. Desire makes me realise that I am missing something to be complete, and makes me aware of my difference from the object, the not-I. Behind all types of desire a deep dialectic is at work: human life depends for survival on the external world and, as a result, part of the self is always outside itself and the otherness of the object is already launched in self. Philosophy aims to integrate all aspects of existence, to overcome alienation and to unite man and world, freedom and social determination. Hegel believes that history moves towards a 'total integrity',[2] in which the opposition between self and other will have been overcome and the external world, which determines us, will no longer be alien or hostile.

Hegel presents the way in which self is created as a continuous struggle to overcome the foreignness of the other. The unmediated self suffers from the delusion of self-sufficiency and treats the other as inferior. The first reaction of the desiring self when faced with the other is to seek immediate satisfaction and heal the split between subject and object by negating the object. The desire for food, for example, negates the otherness of the foodstuff by eating it. But this satisfaction of desire does not differentiate humans from animals. Desire is not addressed towards an object, but towards another human consciousness. Next, the self accepts that he depends on the other but keeps the relation external. In this type of relationship, the other's desire and recognition is forced—subjugation, domination or marginalisation. Desire becomes narcissistic and the other becomes the foil in a quest for non-reciprocated prestige, typically in the relationship between master and slaves.

Mutual recognition is the third step, which completes and overtakes the first two. Now the other is accepted both in her identity and her difference from self, and as a result, self realises that he is dependent upon the other. The other's recognition and desire allows self to see himself reflected in another and to create a nexus of links and dependencies which affect both selves. Recognition

[2] C Taylor, *Hegel* (Cambridge, Cambridge University Press, 1977) 148–50.

works if it is mutual. I must be recognised by someone I recognise as worthy. I must reciprocally know myself in another. I can only become a certain type of person, if I recognise in the other the characteristics of that type—which are then reflected back onto me in her desire. I cannot change myself, therefore, without changing the other and changes in the other who stands in recognition of me, change me too. A typical example of such a relationship is that between lovers. Each sees himself through the eyes of his lover and understands his partner through the same ideas and emotions that he uses to reflect on his own motives, desires and actions.

Liberal jurisprudence, in its attempt to glorify the individual, denies our dependence on the world, artificially erases the traces of otherness and imagines self as identical with itself. The illusion of self-identity is evident in a number of ways. In law, the idea that self stands at the centre of the world, fully in control of himself, clear about his motives and in possession of his rights which allow him to enter instrumental only relations with others is prevalent. The delusion of self-identity is a palliative only for the painful but inescapable realisation that we depend on the other and are determined by the outside world. Full self-consciousness is the 'unity of oneself in one's other-being' and is achieved by seeing oneself in the other and accepting self as the 'identity of identity and non-identity'.[3] The self-conscious subject, created through the other's desire, retains the separation from the other as one part of his identity and recognises himself both in the other and in his difference from her. In this sense, self-consciousness both negates the split between self and other, and preserves it. As a result, the self can never be self-identical: he is an amalgam of self and otherness, of sameness and difference.

Identity is therefore dynamic, always on the move. It is an ongoing dialogue with others which keeps changing my image for others and re-drawing my self-image. Significant others, such as parents, close relatives, intimate partners and friends, are the primary interlocutors. But the dialogical construction of identity through the (mis)recognition of others extends to further interlocutors—from acquaintances and colleagues all the way to strangers in the street, who fleetingly but crucially become collaborators or victims in our struggle for recognition. But while recognition takes the form of a conversation, this is a 'distorted' dialogue. When aspects of my self-image are not recognised by others, the conversation turns into a violent conflict, typically in hate speech and crime. Furthermore, our recognition by others is mediated by the Big Other, the order of legal and social institutions. Our exchanges with the law usually take the form of law's monologue in which aspects of self are recognised or not. Our ability to answer back or ask for greater or different recognition is restricted. But legal rights and other institutions remain important weapons in our struggle for recognition—bargaining chips in the negotiation for identity.

[3] G Hegel, *The Phenomenology of Spirit,* AV Miller (trans), (Oxford, Oxford University Press, 1977) 140.

LAW, RECOGNITION AND LEGAL PERSONALITY

Love, legal recognition and solidarity are three ways of constituting identity. But they are not mutually exclusive. Each is associated with different historical and institutional stages. But love with family; legal recognition with early capitalism, and solidarity with the welfare state they are also overlapping layers of the self.

First, love. Its primary terrain is the family. In a loving relationship, the lover partly negates his independence but gains a richer and more nuanced self. The lover identifies himself through the characteristics and idiosyncracies of his loved one, finds the other in himself and finds in his lover both himself and the other. Each sees himself through the eyes of the lover and understands his partner through the same ideas and emotions that he uses to reflect on his own motives and desires. Similarly, family members are in a state of mutual dependency and affection and recognise each other as a concrete person, as father or daughter, with particular needs and unique desires. Power plays a part in these relations, but the metaphor of conversation emphasises the centrality of the other presence in the constitution of self. This combination of autonomy and community can be sustained, however, only between the members of small and closely-knit units.

Legal recognition could not be more different. It is the effect of the operation of a legal system, which enforces equally the universalisable interests of all. Legal personality expresses the ability of self to remove himself from all particularities such as family, personal history, social and cultural background, and to become abstract, indeterminate. Legal recognition is a type of recognition based on the minimum commonality of people and not on the differences and individual characteristics which make them unique individuals. Legal recognition places the individual 'in the form of universality, that I am apprehended as a universal person, in respect of which all humans are identical. A human being counts simply because he is human and not because he is Jew, Catholic, Protestant German, Italian, etc.'[4] The personality of legal rights is 'thin', an empty vessel, since it negates the contingencies of existence such as race, sexuality, colour or religion and emphasises an individualistic concept of self. The will of the legal person is negative: it negates what makes a person real but it also negates others by excluding them from his areas of entitlement.

Legal personality comes to the fore when private rights become the basic building block of modern law. The law expresses and realises personal freedom, the great achievement of modernity, and rights—the subjective element of law—bring persons together in exchanges, sales and other deals which externalise their freedom.

[4] *Ibid*, 209.

But how do legal rights help in this process of recognition? The examples of property and contract can help us here. The possession and enjoyment of property enables the abstract personality to acquire specific characteristics, to objectify itself.

> The self as abstract will claims to be essential reality, but the existence of external things, that is, objects, and our dependence on external reality contradicts this. The self, therefore, needs to appropriate external objects—it must own property. The self becomes particularised and concrete, rather than abstract, through ownership. Potentiality becomes actuality.[5]

Property is a necessary moment in the struggle for recognition because the desire for objects is one aspect of the desire for others. When I take possession of an object, I externalise myself by placing my will in that object and so in the world. My will stops being abstract; it takes determinate existence. But simple possession is contingent, transient, always threatened. Without recognition by others, possession cannot become actual and offer satisfaction. This is what property rights achieve. Others recognise my rights in my possession on condition that I recognise their property too. My property is secure only through the operation of law. Property therefore leads to a form of interpersonal recognition in which others recognise me by respecting the existence of my will in the object. In Hegel's terms, property helps constitute subjectivity as intersubjectivity through the mediation of objectivity.

Respect for the rights of others and the recognition of their abstract humanity which underlines property becomes concrete in contract. The exchange of offer and acceptance allows the two wills to come together and create a common will which leads to the passing of the object. Recognition now moves from the universal humanity of abstract right to the concrete embodiments of will—the exchanged objects of the contractual relationship. The possession and enjoyment of property identifies subject and object for another subject, while alienation, the third element, actualises the free will of the abstract person and turns her into a concrete individual through the recognition of another already recognised as subject. Property is a pre-condition of the recognition of others. The right to property is what leads to the right to have other rights and thus be recognised as a (legal) person. Lack of assets not only leads to poverty and material hardship but also excludes people from universality and the recognition it bestows.

Contract is, therefore, the minimum recognition offered by legal relations. The property contract symbolises the birth of the subject. In conveyancing, the contractors not only exchange objects but they also recognise each other as separate, free and as possessors of rights and duties—in and through the contract they constitute one another as subjects. We desire objects not for their own sake but as means to the desire of and for other persons. Subjectivity is therefore

[5] *Ibid*, 34.

constructed symbolically and the property contract has a little bit of magic. The contractors get their object of desire but on top they receive something more than they bargained for: they become recognised, they achieve their true desire of the other.[6]

Still, however, this more concrete recognition of conveyancing remains rudimentary and defective. The convergence of wills is contingent and transient. What is recognised is not the other as unique individual but as owner externalised in his property. It is as if people exist in their property. Private rights lead to the external convergence of people based on self-interest. Similarly with the contract; once it has been signed and the exchange completed, the contractors return to their previous stage of non-recognition and their fleeting and superficial reciprocity disappears. From a subjective perspective, private rights have very little to do with principle and everything to do with the utilitarian calculations of unrelated and often opposed personalities. From an objective perspective, rights present the self in things, which become the attributes of personality. Their greatest achievement is organising relations amongst strangers—in facilitating respect for their dignity, the universal attribute of humanity. The legal mentality teaches us to respect others, as much as ourselves, as right-holders whose legitimate claims will be honoured. But this is also their greatest limitation from the perspective of identity. They keep the two selves separate and the relationship superficial—a surface event of no lasting consequence.

From a Hegelian perspective, therefore, the imperative of rights is to be a person and to respect others as persons. The interpersonal relation of right recognises self and other for what unites them with all others, their abstract humanity. It is a recognition of what is universal in every particular. By upholding rights, the law gives the person dignity and by upholding contracts makes that dignity actual in the world. Legal recognition has three components. Rights presuppose a universalistic legal system under which people extend respect to one another because they are legal subjects aware of the laws that create and protect rights. Secondly, the recognition of the other as legal person is the effect of the fact that he enjoys free will, moral autonomy and responsibility and possesses legal rights. This type of recognition is typically called respect (f)or human dignity. Finally, legal recognition leads to self-respect. Self-respect is the outcome of the realisation that I too am capable of moral action and that, like others, I am an end in myself. Human dignity, self-respect and respect for others are synonymous with the ability to make moral decisions and to raise legal claims. 'Indeed respect for persons . . . may simply be respect for their rights, or that there cannot be the one without the other. And what is called 'human dignity' may simply be the recognisable capacity to assert claims.'[7] Having

[6] J Shroeder, *The Vestal and the Fasces* (Berkeley, University of California Press, 1998).

[7] J Feinberg, *Rights, Justice and the Value of Liberty* (Princeton, Princeton University Press, 1980) 151.

rights is nothing more than the symbolic expression that one is equal in his freedom with everyone else or, what amounts to the same thing, that one is a legal subject.[8] If according to Bob Dylan, to be outside the law you must be honest, according to Hegel, to be in the law—to be a subject—you must have rights.

THE FAILINGS OF LEGAL RECOGNITION

The dialectic between self-image, the recognition of others and social and legal acknowledgment leads to the endless proliferation of rights. Right-claims are the result of inadequate or defective recognition. New rights are created when the struggle for recognition fails, when the self-image of an individual or group mismatches the identity claims the current state of the law allows them to project. A typical case of deficient recognition is that between masters and slaves.

In Hegel's story, when self desired a thing, it did so in order to make another self recognise his right to that thing and his superiority. But as a multiplicity of desires desired to be so recognised, their action turned into a war of all against all. For the universal struggle for recognition to stop, Hegel assumed that one of the combatants was prepared to fight to the end, to place his freedom and recognition higher than survival and risk his life, at which point, the other who values survival more than freedom accepts his superiority and surrenders. He who risks his life for prestige becomes the master, the other, the slave. The slave recognises the master but the master does not reciprocate—he treats him as non-person, an object. This is the typically deficient process of recognition because it is unequal: one party recognises the other but this is not reciprocated. It is this type of non-recognition that legal rights negate.

Legal recognition has nothing in common with the inequality of slavery. The function of property rights and contract is precisely to establish the minimum element of universality necessary for the full and mutual recognition of identity. But legal recognition suffers from a different deficiency: the legal person is far too abstract and the law offers an insufficient acknowledgement of concrete humanity. The inadequate respect generated by law motivates the criminal and, crime, incredibly, facilitates the move from abstract right to morality and eventually to the ethical state. Let us examine the respective positions of the two protagonists, the criminal and the victim.

A thief may be stealing to meet unfulfilled material needs. But in the game of recognition, crime represents a much bigger stake. The criminal brings forth those parts of his personality not yet recognised by the legal order. The criminal

[8] From a naturalist perspective, Jacques Maritain comes to a similar conclusion: 'The dignity of the human person? The expression means nothing if it does not signify that, by virtue of natural law, the human person has the rights to be respected, is the subject of rights, possesses rights': *The Rights of Man and Natural Law*, D Anson (trans), (New York, Charles Scribner's Sons, 1951) 65.

may be offended, for example, by the abstraction of the legal rule and the disinterested uniformity in its application. To paraphrase Anatol France, the law in its majesty punishes equally both rich and poor for stealing bread and sleeping under bridges. Insult may also be the result of the promise of formal equality followed by the lack of the material conditions necessary for the realisation of rights. The essence of criminality is therefore the criminal's demand to be recognised and respected as a concrete and unique individual. On the side of the victim, legal rights have two kinds of concentric effects: the theft negates the owner's entitlement to his property but it also negates the wider recognition offered by the law. Victim and thief make two different claims: the damage or loss affects the property-owner partly in his external attributes and partly in his dignity. The thief's desire for recognition, on the other hand, makes him negate legality altogether. But the violence of the conflict teaches the parties important moral lessons, which help the law move forward. Law's abstraction and formalism is a type of disrespect that calls for greater sensitivity to social context and to individual need and desire. Another type of disrespect stems from law's privileging of formal procedure over the material conditions of life and calls for a move towards greater substantive equality. At the same time, the criminal's attack on legal relations and on the recognition they support alerts people to their dependence on community and its institutions, makes them desire the universal as universal. Crime reveals that right is not just external and subjective but a necessary precondition of community—that it must become universal and objective.

Law's formalism becomes the ontological motive for its negation by the criminal, and one would expect that, in turn, crime would contribute to the dialectical overcoming of formal legalism. But Hegel did not take this step. The most complete type of recognition that Hegel discusses is honour. Honour results from membership of a corporation, guild, estate or profession. These mediating institutions 'treat the individual in all his particularity not as a mere particular, but as a universal.'[9] Honour is bestowed not for what one is, as in antiquity or in the family, but for what one does. Through the honour of one's estate, the abstract legal person becomes somebody, acquires determinate social status. But the reverse is also true: a person without honour is derided, scorned, humiliated by others and, as a result, his own self-image suffers. In the recognition of honour, people pursue their self-interest to the extent that it is consistent with that of others. Legal relations are overtaken by mutual recognition, in which individuals understand themselves as fully dependent on one another and at the same time as unique. Self finds herself in the other and finds the other in the self.

This is the recognition of (self) esteem. It supplements the respect that legal personality gives to all people on account of their autonomy and morality with the feeling that they have a concrete, unique and unrepeatable identity

[9] G Hegel, *Vorlesung uber die Philosophe des Rechts* (Frankfurt, Suhrkamp, 1983) 205.

recognised by others who honour and value their specificity. In this combination of respect and esteem, ethical existence unites the universal (the state and its law) and the particular (the citizen of legal recognition and honour). But this coming together of universal and particular in what Hegel calls the 'concrete universal' takes place only in the limited environment of the guilds and professions, typically, in England, in the Inns of Court. For the vast majority of people who did not enjoy the recognition of professional or corporate membership when Hegel wrote, the recognition deficit of legal relations cannot be overcome.

Poverty, finally, can help us understand the inadequacy of legal recognition. Hegel argued that the inequality necessary for capitalist production leads inevitably to extreme poverty and social conflict. A society of riches has obligations to provide for the people inescapably reduced to slave-labour and unemployment. What concerns us here, however, is Hegel's analysis of the lack of recognition that the poor suffer. Lack of assets in the midst of a society based on the right to property makes the poor feel 'excluded and shunned, scorned, by everyone . . . Self-consciousness appears to be driven to the extreme point where it no longer has any rights, and where freedom no longer has any determinate existence . . . Because the individual's freedom has no determinate existence, the recognition of universal freedom disappears.'[10]

This formulation is of great importance. The abstract right to property, the potential to hold property, does not offer adequate recognition if it cannot be realised. For a second time, Hegel justifies theft: 'Life, as a totality of ends, has a right in opposition to abstract right. If for example, life can be preserved by stealing a loaf, this certainly constitutes an infringement of someone's property, but it would be wrong to regard such an action as common theft.'[11] The abstract right must become concrete, the potential actual. Poverty leads to lack of recognition and destroys respect. But the harm inflicted is even greater. The poor recognise themselves as free, but their material deprivation negates their self-respect. They feel torn between the universality of personhood and the contingency of exclusion that they experience. 'The poor man feels as if he were related to an arbitrary will, to human contingency, and in the last analysis what makes him indignant is that he is put into this state of division through sheer arbitrariness.'[12] The universal and the particular have been severed. The poor person is placed in the position of a radical particularity whose existence is challenged and excluded by the universal. The typical harm of defective recognition is to de-link someone's self-image and the image that social institutions or others project upon him.

[10] *Ibid*, 194–5.
[11] *Ibid*, paragraph 127.
[12] *Ibid*, 194–5.

HUMAN RIGHTS AND RECOGNITION

These are the harms that the law both commits and tries to heal through human rights. Indeed we can see the whole human rights movement as a continuing effort to negate the inadequacies of legal recognition. Civil and political rights, the first generation of human rights, lead to a very similar type of recognition to that of property rights. The right to the freedom and security of the person, the rights to fair trial, political participation and free speech are expressions of the universal dignity bestowed to a person on account of their humanity. In this sense, all legal rights are human rights since their basic action is precisely to extend abstract recognition and respect to all. The main and quite substantial contribution of the modern legal system is to extend this type of recognition from private right and inter-subjective morality to the public domain.[13]

But the recognition implied in civil and political rights goes further than the respect and self-respect of ordinary legal rights. Community is both the background and the effect of recognitions. New rights create new ways of being in common and push the boundaries of community. The main consequence of the early declarations of natural and human rights was to reduce *domination*, the non-recognition typical in the master-slave relationship. People given the civil and political rights of citizenship were recognised, as equal not only in formal legal relations, but also as regards political power. Political rights, in particular, express the mutual recognition of citizens as citizens—they recognise the constitutive role of recognition itself. Participation is the prime form of political rights, and in this sense, all rights can be seen as political rights—as an extension of the logic of participation to areas of activity not hitherto public.[14] But self-determination was initially restricted—as to subject—to white male property owners and—as to scope—to public political life. The political history of the last two centuries is marked by the struggles to extend the recognition of citizenship to excluded groups, from poor men to women, to various minorities and non-nationals.

Formal political equality, like property rights, has been accompanied by *oppression*, the denial of self-development, which takes various forms such as economic exploitation, social marginalisation, cultural worthlessness and violence.[15] Here the law suffers from two defects: first, formalism—the lack of concern for the material circumstances that allow the realisation of rights (the defect revealed in poverty). Second, abstraction—the recognition of a non-

[13] All positive legal systems, all codes and statutes, create rights and depend for their operation on the existence of legal persons—owners of such rights.

[14] The psychoanalytical approach accepts the subject-forming role of the other and of rights but is much more sceptical about the contribution of rights to the creation and expansion of community. See C Douzinas, *The End of Human Rights* (Oxford, Hart, 2000) chapters 11 and 12.

[15] IM Young, *Justice and the Politics of Difference* (Princeton, Princeton University Press, 1990) 56.

substantial, a thin personality (the defect attacked in crime and redressed through honour). Both are instances of defective recognition, of a public image that seriously mis-matches people's self-image. Domination calls for greater participation, oppression for substantive equality. Taken together, they aim to combat the inadequacies of legal recognition. Self-determination requires the expansion of democratic decision-making from politics to other areas of social life. Self-development requires the expansion of the principle of equality from the formality of law to an ever-increasing number of substantive areas of social life, such as the work-place, domestic life, sexuality, the environment, etc. Recognition now moves from the formal and universal to the concrete and specific, to the characteristics that make people unique.

We can pursue this analysis in relation to the history of human rights. The struggles for political rights and for the introduction of the universal franchise were aimed at removing the non-recognition between master and slave from public life and at extending citizenship rights to groups such as the poor, women or ethnic minorities. Similarly, the right to self-governance, which characterised the decolonisation process of the 50s and 60s, and prefaced the main human rights documents of the period,[16] extended collective political recognition from the excluded groups of the metropolis to whole nations and ethnicities in the developing world. In other cases, citizenship rights were expanded to new areas. Workers' rights extended the principle of participation to the shop floor and to some aspects of industrial management. Consumers' rights enlarged the decision-making bodies in education, health and other public utilities. Each extension enlarges either the number of people entitled to decide issues of public concern or the issues open to the logic of public deliberation and decision.

Citizenship is the local expression of universality. Political rights emerged out of the destruction of traditional communities and the undermining of the pre-modern body politic, and these rights, in turn, accelerated the process. Recognition has moved from the relations of love, care and inequality, which characterised the pre-modern world, to legal recognition and the construction of identities through rights. If citizenship is the essence of universality, if community participation turns the abstract legal person into a socially recognised self, its essence is negative. It negates the closing down of the political space around some unique value or good and 'sustains . . . the groundlessness and the dislocation of power constitutive of democratic practice.'[17] But as Marx insisted, political community both upholds and denies the universality of rights, since rights support and are supported in turn by the inequalities of economy and culture. Secondly, citizenship is a limited universality which is exhausted

[16] 'All people have the right of self-determination. By virtue of that right they freely determine their political status and freely pursue their economic, social and cultural development.' This is the first article of both the Civil and Political Rights and the Economic, Social and Cultural rights Covenants, adopted by the United Nations in 1966.

[17] J Bernstein, 'Rights, Revolution and Community' in P Osborne (ed), *Socialism and the Limits of Liberalism* (London, Verso, 1991) 113.

within the confines of the nation-state and excludes the non-citizens, the foreigners, enemies without and within.

Using Young's terminology, we can argue that the negative universality of political rights addresses the problem of domination but not of oppression. Oppression denies people's ability to decide what is the best life-plan for them and deprives them of the necessary means to carry it out. It does not allow its victims to be recognised as concrete and unique selves, it prevents the fulfilment of their aspirations and capacities.[18] Economic exploitation of the metropolitan poor through unemployment, breadline wages, poor health and casualisation, or of the developing world through unequal trade and crippling debt, undermines and eventually destroys the possibility of self-development. When daily survival is the order of the day, all aspirations for social improvement or cultural expression are extinguished. The oppressed cannot enjoy, or even aspire to, the complete life that allows personalities to flourish and be recognised in their complex integrity.

THE PARADOX OF IDENTITY AND RIGHTS

Can legal recognition become the full recognition of concrete identity? The great achievement of legal rights was precisely to abstract all predicates and create the person without determination. As species existence, the 'man' of the rights of man appears without differentiation or distinction in his nakedness and simplicity, united with all others in an empty nature deprived of substantive characteristics. The universal 'man' of the Declarations and Conventions is an unencumbered man, human, all too human. As species existence all men are equal, because they share equally soul and reason, the *differentia specifica* of humans. But this equality, the most radical element of the classical Declarations, had limited value for non-proper men (that is men of no property), even less for women, and was denied altogether to those defined as non-humans (slaves, colonials and foreigners).

The contemporary concept of human rights has moved a long way. Social and economic rights, a few rights for gays and lesbians, some for women and children, for minorities and indigenous people promise to fill the abstract legal person somehow and to construct a kind of strong recognition. But can we have a consistent concept of (human) right that transcends this minimum state of recognition that legal rights give? To answer this question we must analytically distinguish between the struggles for the adoption of new rights and individual claims for recognition. Let us start with group rights.

Using the terminology of semiotics, one can argue that the 'man' of the rights of man or, the 'human' of human rights, functions as a floating signifier. As a *signifier*, it is just a word, a discursive element that is not automatically or necessarily linked to any particular signified or meaning. On the contrary, the

[18] See generally, A Gewirth, *Self-Fulfilment* (Princeton, Princeton University Press, 1998).

word 'human' is empty of all meaning and can be attached to an infinite number of signifieds or concepts. As a result, it cannot be fully and finally pinned down to any particular conception, because it transcends and overdetermines them all.[19] But the 'humanity' of human rights is not just an empty signifier; it carries an enormous symbolic capital, a surplus of value and dignity endowed by the Revolutions and the Declarations and augmented by every new struggle for the recognition and protection of human rights. This symbolic excess turns the 'human' into a *floating* signifier, into something that combatants in political, social and legal struggles want to co-opt to their cause, and explains its importance for political campaigns.

To have human rights, which in modernity is synonymous with being human, you must claim them. This claim attaches a demand for social recognition or legal protection to the floating signifier. A new right is recognised, if it succeeds in fixing a—temporary or partial—determination on the word 'human', if it manages to arrest its flight. This process is carried out in political, ideological and institutional struggles. Typically, diverse groups, campaigns and individuals fight in a number of different political cultural and legal arenas such as public protest, lobbying or test-cases, to have an existing right extended or a new type of right accepted. The creative potential of language and of rhetoric allows the original rights of 'man' to break up and proliferate into the rights of workers, women, gays, refugees etc.

A new claim succeeds when the claimants assert both their similarity and difference with groups already admitted to the dignity of humanity. First, similarity; the new group claims that it shares the abstract characteristics of human nature, that it is a valid sub-group of humanity which should enjoy dignity and equality of treatment. Equality, despite the assertions of Declarations and Constitutions is not given or obvious. It is a political construct, as Hegel and Marx argued, typically expressed through the law, as Kant saw. In this sense, equality before the law acquires its concrete meaning: it has nothing 'natural' about it. If anything, the main claim of the liberal-democratic tradition is that it can transcend social differences and accidents of birth and construct equality *contra* nature. Right-claims have, therefore, two aspects: an appeal to the universal but undetermined character of human nature. Secondly, the assertion that the similarity between the claimants and human nature *tout court* admits those making the right-claim to the surplus value of the floating signifier and grounds their claim to be treated on an equal footing with those already admitted.

Second, difference. The shared dignity of legal personality and the community of citizenship are inadequate recognitions of concrete identity. I am a legal person and citizen but, more importantly, I am a man or woman, straight or gay, black or white, English, African or Greek, Tory, Labour or anarchist, married or divorced, a teacher, miner or poet, an immigrant, refugee or staunch

[19] For a use of the psychoanalytical concept of 'overdetermination' in political theory see E Laclau and C Mouffe, *Hegemony and Socialist Strategy* (London, Verso, 1985).

patriot, a Northerner or Southerner, a drinker, raver or teetotaller. But claims to difference and the recognition of plural cultural identities are not happy companions of liberalism. As Amy Gutmann put it:

> one reasonable reaction to questions about how to recognise the distinct cultural identities of members of a pluralistic society is that the very aim of representing or respecting differences in public institutions is misguided . . . an important strand in contemporary liberalism . . . suggests that our lack of identification with institutions that serve public purposes, the impersonality of public institutions is the price that citizens should be willing to pay for treating us all as equal, regardless of our particular ethnic, religious, racial or sexual identities.[20]

The law, as Hegel argued, is drawn to the same and the universal and is ill-equipped to accommodate difference. This is the reason why the subjects of human rights have no female gender, and sexual orientation is not recognised as an unlawful ground of discrimination in human rights instruments. Difference remains a contested ground in liberal codes of human rights; social, economic and cultural rights are commonly ring-fenced with statements that they are inferior to civil and political rights, non-justiciable, mere aspirations rather than hard rights. Human rights-claims, therefore, involve a paradoxical dialectic between an impossible demand for universal equality, initially identified with the characteristics of western man and, an equally unrealisable claim to absolute difference. Because the nature of western, white, affluent man cannot subsume under its universal aspirations the characteristics and desires of workers, women, racial or ethnic groups etc., the claims to specific workers', women's or ethnic rights arises. When these claims succeed, universality becomes a horizon continuously receding before the expansion of an indefinite chain of particular demands based on the particularity of the group.[21] But this success is always provisional and reversible, as the logic of law tends to prioritise the universal over the general and the same over the different.

The argument for women's rights, for example, involves two apparently antagonistic claims: both that 'women are like men' and that 'women are different from men'. Women have been invisible to human rights for too long, because the feminine was seen as an inferior state that did not deserve the full dignity accorded to humanity. But the admission of women to the status of humanity (the action of similarity) without responding to the demands of difference is equally problematic. It assumes that simply extending the rights of the representatives of humanity (white well-off males) to women exhausts their claim. But as the feminism of difference has cogently argued, the universality of rights necessarily neglects the specific needs and experiences of women.[22] The

[20] A Gutmann, 'Introduction' in A Gutmann (ed), *Multiculturalism* (Princeton, Princeton University Press, 1994) 4.

[21] E Laclau, *Emancipation(s)* (London, Verso, 1996), chapter 2.

[22] L Irigaray, *Thinking the Difference*, K Montin (trans), (New York, Routledge, 1994); *An Ethics of Sexual Difference*, C Burke and G Gill (trans), (London, Athlone 1993); *I Love to You*, A Martin (trans), (New York, Routledge 1996).

concerns and claims of women cannot be subsumed under the universal entitlements of human nature, precisely because the feminine is the difference from equalising humanity. Domestic and international law have had great problems in accepting, for example, the special nature of domestic rape or of rape and sexual abuse during war. The non-criminalisation of marital rape was the result of non-admission of women to the status of the universal. As a result, the law treated women as inferior to men, as their property, which could be subjected to brutal abuse with impunity. The non-enumeration of rape in war among the crimes against humanity was, on the contrary a, result of the non-recognition of the difference of women. The standard provisions of criminal law protecting universal bodily integrity from assaults are considered adequate protections from sexual violence. The special traumatic effect of sexual abuse is discounted and sexual violence equalised with general violence, undermining the magnitude of the offence steeped in male power and female degradation.

In the struggle for rights, the rhetorical ruses of similarity and difference can be used to promote the most contradictory objectives. A claim to difference without similarity can establish the uniqueness of a particular group and justify its demands for special treatment, but it can also rationalise its social or economic inferiority. Aristotle wrote that 'some men are free by nature and some are slaves . . . From their birth some are marked out for subjection and others for rule.'[23] A Greek or Roman slave was seen as an *animale vocale*, a worker in the nineteenth century was treated as a 'cog in the machine' or as disposable merchandise, a wife until relatively recently was the husband's chattel. In all these cases, empirical difference established and justified domination. More generally, the appearance of linguistic, racial, gender and other difference has been used in most cases to create hierarchies and legitimise power imbalances.

The question, therefore, is not why but when, how, and in relation to which attributes are 'women (not) like men'? Most human rights struggles adopt this form of timely, historical and specific comparison and contestation. Their aim is to re-define the dominant way of understanding the relations amongst classes, groups and individuals and, to this aim, rhetorical tactics and discursive reasons are one of their main weapons. The cultural aim of anti-slavery, workers' and women's struggles was to re-articulate the relations between the free—the property owners or men (usually the three predicates coincided in the same part)—and the slaves, the workers or women. The old hegemonical position claimed that the first groups related to the second on the basis of natural differences, that inequalities were the logical and necessary outcome of dissimilarities. The rebels and protesters, on the other hand, construed the relationship not as one of difference but of inequality, of an immoral denial of similarities and illegitimate domination—a case of turning differences into hierarchies.

The assertion of difference is what gives the self identity, and makes it a rich, complicated 'thick' personality. The differentiated characteristic, whether

[23] Aristotle, *Politics,* H Rakham (trans), (Cambridge, Mass, Loeb, 1990) I, 6.

gender, ethnicity or sexuality, is put forward as a valid partial predication of universality, as one way of mediation between the universal and the particular. Womens rights claim certain entitlements for all women, race relations law tries to prevent discrimination against members of ethnic minorities. The distance between abstract human nature and the concrete characteristics of the group justifies their demand to differential treatment, which respects one aspect of their identity. If equivalence and equality result from political and legal action against abstract nature, the claim to difference reintroduces the particularity of concrete nature, situated, localised and context-dependent.

Here we reach the crux of the matter: once we move from group claims to the individual struggle for recognition, to the continuous conversation with others and with the social institutions that construct our identity, the law will always fall short of a full recognition of identity. It may recognise aspects of my sexuality, ethnicity and family standing by upholding certain rights. But the politics of difference will still remain wedded to the generality of certain positions, to that of being woman or gay rather than this woman or that gay. The law can only deal with universalities and generalities. A concrete identity, on the other hand, is constructed through the contingent and highly mutable combination of many positions. It is the outcome of a highly specific group of characteristics, only some of which are generalisable and shared with others. In relation to these, human rights extend the recognition of honour by turning the relevant group (women or gays) into subjects of right. Human rights and wrongs operate and proliferate in the gap between the universal and the generalisable.

But most elements of identity remain immersed in personal history and background, with its defining moments, turns and traumas, with its combination of, for example, gay sexuality, support for Arsenal and for the Tories. This combination is tested and recognised or not daily, in an infinite number of encounters with others, as what is singularly myself: a creature of shared dignity and rights ensconced in citizenship and symbolised by the right to vote, but also of total idiosyncrasy and absolute difference, exemplified by the uniqueness and unrepeatable epiphany of my face. This is a second crucial space, that between the general and the singular. Here the universalising logic of the law always fails the uniqueness of the other.

The reference to the face and the other introduces us to that aspect of identity which defies the dialectic of the universal and particular, or of the same and the different. For Hegel, the honour bestowed by corporation membership introduces the individual to the ethical state. But in postmodernity, these associations, memberships and belongings have proliferated immensely but are unable to create identity on their own. The struggle for recognition and the politics of identity are about creating self as a unique individual. The main elements of my identity, the building blocks of what I consider the 'real me', refer to a huge variety of positions, beliefs and traits which have very little relationship with the shared dignity of legal rights and cannot be captured by the difference-promoting extensions of human rights. My identity is the shifting articulation of all these disparate elements or 'subject positions' which combine in various ways, occasionally and transiently under the direction of one particular dominant element, but other times without any particular hierarchy. Concrete identities are constructed in psychological, social and political contexts—they are, in psychoanalytical terms, the outcome of a situated desire of the other. In this sense, claims for differentiation are initially constructed outside the equalising logic of the law.

Negotiating the potential or real conflicts of these positions with others is a main part of the individual politics of identity. In following my football team to an away game, for example, membership of the tribe of Arsenal supporters becomes the dominant characteristic. But when my fellow supporters start goading a player for his race or sexuality, which happens also to be my race or, if their behaviour offends my ideological allegiances, then my two commitments come into conflict. In these cases, my loyalty to Arsenal (or to the Tories) becomes strained, (if, say, my party publicly and vociferously attacks my sexuality). I may try to forget the conflict by either rationalising the behaviour of my fellows or by accepting that somehow my race or sexuality is problematic and by replacing self-respect with shame.

In all cases, my identity is being constantly (re)created through the recognition of others who are involved in an actual or silent conversation with me. Any relevant rights, created by discrimination or hate speech law, will become important in negotiating my response to others and my own self-image. But often these conversations fail. As Charles Taylor puts it, 'what has come about with the modern age is not the need for recognition but the conditions in which the attempt to be recognised can fail.'[24] This failure may be the result of the withholding of recognition by our closest and most intimate fellows. But in most cases, it is the result of inevitable and avoidable misrecognitions by legal institutions and rights.

DESIRE, (MIS)RECOGNITIONS AND RIGHTS

Human rights struggles are symbolic and political: their immediate battleground is the meaning of words, such as 'difference' and 'equality' or 'similarity' and 'freedom', but, if successful, they have ontological consequences—they radically change the constitution of the legal subject and affect people's lives. Rights formalise and stabilise identities. The law uses the technical category of the legal subject and its repertory of remedies, procedures and rights to mediate between the abstract and indeterminate concepts of human nature and right, and the concrete people who claim its protection. The legal validation of a contested category of rights, like women's rights, acts as the partial recognition of a particular type of identity linked to the relevant rights. Conversely, a person

[24] C Taylor, *Hegel*, above n 2, 35.

recognised as the subject of women's rights is acknowledged as a person of a particular identity, the bearer of certain attributes and the beneficiary of certain activities, and finally, as the carrier of the dignity of abstract humanity. An individual is a human being, a citizen, a woman, a worker etc to the extent that she is recognised as the legal subject of the respective rights, and her legal identity is constructed out of her cluster of rights. But she is also much more than that.

The abstract concept of human nature, which underpinned the classical Declarations, has been replaced in postmodern societies by the proliferating claims to new and specialist rights. Desire, the motor behind the struggle for recognition, has replaced human nature as the ground concept and has become the empty and floating signifier, which can be attached either to the logic of power and the state or to the logic of justice and openness. We moderns know only what we can make; the legalisation of desire means that as postmoderns we can now 'make' ourselves by investing desire with legal significance. We are entitled to become legally what we believe we are, to turn our self-image into our publicly recognised identity. The common complaint about the excessive legalisation of the world is precisely the inevitable outcome of this endless legalisation of desire. Desire became the formal expression of the subject's relationship with others and the polity and was given, initially limited, legal recognition, when self-development and fulfillment became a matter for law in the 1950s and 1960s. After that the multiplication of right-holders, the proliferation of claims and the endless mutation of the objects of right was a matter of time, of letting language, politics and desire do their work. Rights have become recognitions of a mobile desire, which turns a growing number of aspects of my identity into enforceable legal claims. As Arthur Jacobson puts it, for Hegel, the human species is under 'the erotic claim . . . to fill the universe with every legal relation imaginable'.[25] This drive has become the major force of human rights. The greater my agglomeration of rights, the fuller the recognition of my identity by others. But at the same time, this type of recognition is forced, based not on the reciprocity of belonging to a family, corporation, group or community but on the alienating and coercive logic of the law. Legal form, whatever the content, has not changed its character—so forcefully described by Hegel. 'To describe an individual as a 'legal person' is an expression of contempt', he declares.[26] This inevitable misrecognition follows the legal person of human rights.

But human rights do not just confirm or enforce certain universal personality traits. Their continuous extension to new groups and novel areas of activity indicates their deeply agonistic character. Their recognition goes to the heart of existence, addresses the fundamental other-appreciation and self-esteem of the individual, beyond respect, and touches the foundations of identity. We are doomed or blessed to strive endlessly for concrete recognition of our unique

[25] A Jacobson, 'Hegel's Legal *Plenum*' in D Cornell, M Rosenfeld and D Carlson (eds), *Hegel and Legal Theory* (New York, Routledge, 1991) 114.

[26] G Hegel, *Phenomenology of Spirit*, above n 3, 480.

identity. But the avoidable misrecognitions, the myriad instances of mismatch between the self-image of an individual or group and the identity that the law and rights allow them to project, make law a necessary but inadequate and defective partner in the struggle for identity. A complete identity cannot be based on the universal characteristics of law, but on the continuous struggle for the other's unique desire and concrete recognition. Human rights, like desire, are a battlefield with ethical dimensions. Social conflict may be occasionally destructive of the social bond, but it is also one step in the development of political and ethical forms of community. But the desire for the other, remains a step ahead of law. It keeps seeking greater formal recognition but, as soon as the claim for legal form has been granted, its achievement undermines the desire for the other. Human rights create selves in this intricate but paradoxical intertwining with identity and desire.

THE COLOUR OF LAW: RACE RELATIONS AND LEGAL (MIS)RECOGNITION

Recognition is a vital necessity for the formation of self and defective recognition is a crucial evil.[27] Lack of recognition and the misrecognition of individuals or groups demeans and degrades them. The damage misrecognition inflicts on people is to project an image of self that does not match their own self-image. Misrecognition places people in an inferior position and, as a form of oppression, becomes the basis for wider maltreatment. The misrecognised person or group often internalise their distorted external image and descend to self-loathing and shame.

The history of race relations is the history of our modernity. Race is a thoroughly modern concept, and racism and xenophobia are intricately linked with the creation of the nation-state in early modernity. Legal responses to race and racism indicate the way in which the institutions of modernity constructed difference and otherness as racial. In examining the colour and race of law, we can understand the ways in which the law defined the real and symbolic injuries of race. Race relations are instances of non-recognition and misrecognition of the different and the other. As we argued, recognition passes through the mutual acknowledgment of the other. The other is not an object, but a subject, and this recognition allows the self to understand herself as a subject too. The structure of recognition involves, therefore, two moments. Its mutuality allows the self to understand herself as free, independent, with dignity and self-respect. But secondly, recognition reveals the self as related: the self interacts with and depends on others and gains important insights through this relatedness. Being for another is part of being oneself. This ideal structure of recognition fails in the various expressions of racism.

[27] C Taylor, *Hegel*, above n 2, 35.

Slavery and racial or ethnic exclusion, such as apartheid, are two forms of non-recognition. Slavery is total non-recognition. The other is turned into an object, the opposite of the subject, literally a thing or *res*. As thing, the objectified slave does not enjoy the basic characteristics of personhood, independence, freedom and respect. Modernity rejects objectification. The abstract equality of modern humanism prohibits the reification of people and helps abolish slavery. After the abolition of slavery, the question of race becomes internal to the structure of recognition. The total lack of recognition now mutates into misrecognition.

The first form of misrecognition places the other into a position of direct inferiority. The racially different is seen as a second class person, she does not enjoy the dignity and respect that universalistic liberal law recognises in all persons. This type of misrecognition characterises the euphemestic 'separate but equal' doctrine of American constitutional law and all forms of apartheid and racial exclusion. Racial difference becomes the basis for the denial of formal equality. A two-tier legal and social system is created, under which entitlements, amenities, protections and remedies are differentiated according to which side of a real or symbolic frontier people find themselves. This frontier is often real. This was the case in the South African townships, in the segregated facilities of the American south and, more recently, in the detention camps for asylum-seekers and suspected terrorists, in the security wall of the Middle East and in the policing of 'Fortress Europe'. The ghetto, the camp, the border, create two distinct legal orders. The first applies to the racially 'superior' and meets the minimum characteristics of legality. It controls the border and ensures that movement between its two sides is strictly regulated. The second order is an instrument of policing. It keeps the 'inferior' within the boundaries of the ghetto, it maintains rudimentary legal relations amongst them and regulates the limited transactions with the other side. The inhabitants of the ghetto are structurally oppressed, their position similar to that of a nation under occupation. Indeed the removal or relaxation of the (real or symbolic) frontier is often seen as an act of liberation not dissimilar to the removal of an external conqueror.

This dual legal system is the law of colour. The law turns colour and race into determinants of personhood, entitlement and status. It is not so much that the law discriminates but that it creates two laws and places people under separate jurisdictions according to their colour and race. What type of recognition does the legal system give here? The law recognises difference—indeed it raises it into its cornerstone. Difference is emphasised, it becomes central to the recognition and treatment that the law accords and is construed normatively as distance from normality, as lack of completeness. A surface characteristic, colour, is turned into the outward expression of a deeper inferiority and as the essence of personality. One aspect of appearance is picked up and becomes the defining property of character, ability and belonging. Colour overwhelms individual traits, qualities and attributes—all those elements that constitute concrete identities are set aside as insignificant. People are not just of colour, colour is the only quality that counts in their dealings with the law.

In the camp, the ghetto and the border, difference become absolute and normative. Similarities are written out of the law, they disappear against the background of colour. Recognition based on colour emphasises difference from what has been defined as the norm, the standard, the rule—and is a continuous reminder of inferiority, lack, absence and deprivation. People are accorded inferior legal status and treatment not for what they do—the defining characteristic of the rule of law—but for how they look.

A similar operation is encountered in extreme racial or homophobic hate speech. As critical race theorists have argued, verbal racial attacks intend to provoke the victim to question her identity and to acknowledge herself as inferior to the attacker.[28] In hate speech, one characteristic of the person, her colour, race or sexual orientation, is picked, presented as determining the person's overall value, and denigrated. Racist or sexist speech emphasises one particular trait of the person and denies her integrity. Furthermore, by devaluing an element or characteristic which is central to the identity of a group, it aims to withhold recognition and respect from the whole group and from each of its members, without concern for the individual's other capacities and desires. The terrain of the racist is identity and his weapons are, first, the withdrawal of moral recognition and legal equality and, secondly, the withholding of esteem from the whole group. The first denies the recognition of dignity and equal respect, the second aims at undermining esteem and respect amongst members of the group and at destroying the positive evaluation of its shared character and history.

A similar analysis helps explain why critical race theorists have distanced themselves from the critique of rights associated with American critical legal movement.[29] Racist oppression and domination denies the minimum legal recognition of a liberal legal system, something taken for granted by the successful members of the legal academy. For the historically oppressed person of colour, having rights and scrupulously following legal procedures offers much more than the actual contents of these rights; it offers the respect of others and the self-respect that legal recognition ensures but which has been systematically withheld. Being admitted to right-holding is a symbolic admission to the dignity of humanity and a very real introduction to the legal recognition of (formal) equality. This is the indispensable precondition of critique. Kant must be in place before we move to Hegel or Marx.

While the border, the ghetto and dual law have been accommodated by liberal law, they offend formal equality. After the abolition of apartheid and the symbolic defeat of genocidal and white supremacist ideologies, the injuries and humiliations of racism, and those the legal system permits and tries to heal, are more nuanced. This is the stage at which the legal system adopts more or less

[28] M Matsuda, C Lawrence III, R Delgado and K Crenshaw (eds), *Words that Wound: Critical Race Theory, Assaultive Speech and the First Amendment* (Boulder, Westview Press, 1993).

[29] P Williams, *The Alchemy of Race and Rights* (Cambridge, Mass, Harvard University Press, 1991) 165. Duncan Kennedy, 'The Critique of Rights in Critical Legal Studies' in W Brown and J Halley (eds), *Left Legalism/Left Critique* (Durham, Duke University Press, 2002) 178–228.

extensive provisions against racial discrimination. Preferring people on the basis of colour becomes illegal, benefits are to be given according to abilities and qualifications, decision-making procedures are to exclude racial considerations from their purview. The idea of the rule of law enters race relations; the person of the anti-discrimination provisions has no race, colour or ethnicity. The social processes for selection and conferral of benefits become 'colour blind', racially neutral. In contrast to the earlier stages, colour, in theory at least, disappears. The law sees all in the same colour, white or grey, but certainly not black.

Let us remind ourselves here of one type of defective legal recognition, using the example of fraudulent property transactions. The legal protection of property rights supports an abstract but universal type of recognition, while a contract of sale creates a temporary and contingent common will between the two parties which is exhausted by the exchange of object and consideration. A contractual relationship therefore involves both the universal recognition of right and respect owed to everyone as legal person, and the particular recognition between the parties created through their dealings. But when an impostor frustrates the contract through misrepresentations which make the victim pass on property without proper consideration, the culprit uses the law parasitically. By entering into the transaction in order to perpetrate his trickery, he acknowledges the other as an autonomous legal person, but withholds the specific recognition instituted by the transaction. The victim is shown respect as a person and is offered a semblance of right as part of the deception. The impostor, on the other hand, while accepting the respect of universality, asserts his absolute difference from the other by negating the common and particular will to perform the contractual obligations they have entered into.

We can draw an analogy between this type of defective recognition and that offered by 'colour blind' legal measures. People of colour receive the recognition of formal equality, the protections of 'equality of opportunity'. But this is often a fraud. The law both recognises and negates the difference of race. It recognises it when it claims that universal personhood should not be negated on the basis of a determinate characteristic like race. But while it recognises the universal, the law negates the particular. It does not acknowledge or confront the effects of persistent, tolerated and cumulative racism, which places minorities in a position of structural disadvantage. The effects of racism are negated, similarities are absolutised and the putative sameness of all deprives the harms inflicted by racism of recognition and legal significance.

But this undermines the right to dignity and denies the esteem the law claims to uphold. The non-acknowledgment of difference undermines the social recognition that persons of colour receive, and marginalises them. Formal equality rights remain sheer potentialities, they cannot be realised in the absence of the recognition of the whole self. A kind of splitting occurs undermining the sense of unity and the uniqueness of self. While in principle legal recognition negotiates and unites the universal and particular aspects of identity, a colour blind legal system disassociates the two. The black person's right to non-discrimination secures her position in the realm of the universal with its rights, dignity and respect. Non-discrimination is a public declaration of equality and, to that extent, the universal but formal recognition of personhood is bestowed.

But the lack of recognition of race, colour or ethnicity means that the universal and the particular cannot be united in a singularity. They remain separate, confronting each other and undermining both respect and esteem. The law treats as contingent and insignificant a part of self which, for the victim of racism, is central and defining. It is as if the self is viewed from two deeply antagonistic perspectives, one internal, the other external. From the position of the subject, the universal and the particular are united in the feeling of freedom and self-esteem with its central racial element, but from the external perspective these two aspects of self are hopelessly divided. A dislocation separates the person's own sense of self and the image others have of it. She finds herself emptied; what is most determinate in her has no recognition, and what is the least determinate—abstract freedom and respect—cannot be fully actualised in the world. As far as the majority is concerned, the lack of esteem for the differentiating characteristic helps undermine the universal formal respect.

The quest in such situations is for integration of the two parts of existence. The well-documented experience of black people—emphasised by the Algerian French writer Franz Fanon—who often see themselves from two separate perspectives, their own and that of those around them, deprives them of even their basic dignity and liberties.

Fanon argues that to distinguish between 'white' and 'black' is to posit a divide, a separation that serves to partition and demarcate experience. To be black within a world ordered by racism is to have a sense of one's being divided into a world that one shares with one's fellows, and a world from which one is excluded: the world of the white racist. This splitting of the world places the black subject in a dilemma. Not only is his or her being divided but, s/he is prevented from belonging in either category. The black must appear non-black to find his or her place in the white world; or, rather, the black must appear as 'more than white' to be accepted. For a black to 'become' white, it is necessary that some original lack or fault in black being is repaired. However, the 'assimilated' black is never quite accepted, never quite 'one of us'. Not only can the black never quite be assimilated, but the very act of assimilation implicitly or explicitly acknowledges that one's fellows are not 'good enough'; that there is some profound lack of being in the culture into which one was born:

> The black man has no ontological resistance in the eyes of the white man. Overnight the Negro has been given two frames of reference within which he has had to place himself. His metaphysics or, less pretentiously, his customs and the sources on which they were based are wiped out because they were in conflict within a civilisation that he did not know that imposed itself on him.[30]

[30] P Tuitt, *Race and Resistance* (London, Cavendish, 2004) 29.

To be black, is to belong nowhere; or, as Tuitt stresses, the world of racial domination is characterised by a failure or 'disjunction' where what was familiar is made strange and disconnected. This kind of ontological disjunction has pervaded the legal response to race and colour.

Slavery and apartheid misrecognise the similarities between people and deny formal equality. The misrecognition of colour-blind laws, overlaid on centuries of racism, extends formal equality but forgets difference. It forgets the long history of oppression and domination active in culture and law, in which races and minorities have been defined as inferior. Difference is acknowledged by being denied as a relevant criterion. Colour is recognised by being erased, whitened out, not only irrelevant but also offensive to mention. The segregated person is full of colour, it is just colour. The person of anti-discrimination laws, on the other hand, is colourless, empty of hue and style. In its different ways, the law perpetrates the injury it is supposed to cure.

8

Letter to a Wound: Marxism, Justice and the Social Order

INTRODUCTION: SOMEONE HAS BEEN TELLING LIES ABOUT KARL MARX

WITH THE FALL of the Berlin Wall in 1989, Marxism entered into what appeared to be a period of terminal crisis. The crisis was political and theoretical. Marxism has been built on the premise that the validity of its theory depends on its verification in political practice. Marxist theory makes two fundamental claims. First, that Marxism describes social reality accurately and, secondly, that the inevitable triumph of socialism would confirm that Marxism correctly explains history and society. The link between theory and reality is provided by political practice, which will facilitate and expedite what Marxism has explained. The revolution is the moment in which a class, through an act of political and rational will, grasps the underlying meaning of history that Marxism has revealed, becomes history's conscious subject and transforms society into a rational order. In so doing, it reclaims a realm of freedom from the realm of necessity and creates a new world in the interests of all rather than those of the privileged few.[1]

The claim of correspondence, actual and eventual, between theory and the world, placed Marxism within nineteenth-century positivism. Positivism in the social sciences is committed to an analysis of causation that allows the prediction of patterns and the control of social phenomena. If the laws of history and society's movement become transparent, then conscious action may be taken to manage and control them. Marx himself argued that his object of analysis, the capitalist mode of production, 'might be determined with the precision of natural science.'[2] Marxism can thus be placed within a specifically modern scientistic idiom that models itself on the natural sciences and bases the will to know on a technical interest in production, leading to the control of production in the interests of all members of society.

[1] K Marx, *Capital*, volume 3 (London, Lawrence and Wishart, 1972) 820.

[2] Cited in B Smart, *Foucault, Marxism and Critique* (London, Routledge and Kegan Paul, 1983) 11.

But political reality did not follow the predictions of theory. The collapse of the communist states, which followed the various tragedies of 'existing socialism', became the starting point of Marxism's theoretical crisis. An outward sign was the immense proliferation of theoretical output in the 1970s, 80s and 90s. Whenever theory multiplies, it is the surest sign that something has gone badly wrong. Political, cultural, legal, or institutional practices are informed by theoretical understandings. But the production of theory takes off dramatically when the relevant practice enters into crisis. Its underlying assumptions become explicit and 'denaturalised', they cease to be the taken-for-granted parameters of debate and become contested. Theory, in other words, tends to become self-conscious when we are no longer sure what we are doing. Typically, at such moments of crisis, two strategies open: theory may try to supply a 'correct' interpretation of the doctrine that has gone wrong in practice and offer a new rationale for it, or it may attempt to substitute a new theory for the old and inadequate one, in order to 'suggest that an entirely different way of behaving is now on the historical agenda.'[3] Marxism's many new theories may be seen as responses to the crisis of Marxism and are closely related to the effort to re-theorise power, politics, and the state. They also respond to a parallel crisis in legal practice and theory.

However this crisis should not lead to the rejection of Marxism. Hitherto people have formed many incorrect ideas about Marxist theory. Now is the time for a re-appraisal of Marx. Understanding the relevance of Marx's inquiries to our present situation means stripping away the clichés and misrepresentations of his work: rediscovering a mode of thinking that allows an engagement with legal, economic and social relationships from a position of critical immanence. It can be neither a question of fetishising existing economic relationships and reading backwards into a 'truth' of the human subject, nor of grand, totalising gestures that announce the immanent demise of capitalism.

This chapter is an attempt to engage with a heretical or reinvented Marxist legal theory that can articulate the complex relations and differences between law and economy—providing a place for the subject and politics. It is aimed against a form of law and economics that presents economics as a benign operator distributing wealth and resources in a way that maximises utility. Marxism explains how capitalist economic relations lead to the alienation, exploitation and domination that determine the forms of modern social structures. But the chapter is also aimed against a crude Marxism that insists that the economy determines politics, law, morality and all other aspects of social life. We will sail between the Scylla of law and economics, and the Charybidis of reductionist Marxism, plotting a course towards a new discovery of Marxist thought.

Our argument begins with a short history of Marxist theory, particularly its attempts to relate law and ideology to the wider economic organisation of soci-

[3] T Eagleton, 'Roland Barthes and After' in L Appignanesi (ed), *The Legacy of French Theory* (London, ICA, 1985) 11.

ety. It examines the problems and impasses of Marxism. We then move on to examine two specifically jurisprudential areas: human rights and the theory of the legal person. In Marx's writings on human rights, the relationship between law and economics is complex, nuanced and open to revision and re-assessment. We will argue that the idea that Marxist politics must opt exclusively for a 'class' politics that ignores the specificity of individual struggles must be rejected. A Marxist model that reduces everything to the economy cannot understand how various institutional 'spaces' combine and create the forms or 'supports' that give rise to subjectivity. Our return to the theory of subjectivity is not a reinvention of humanism, but an attempt to account both for the interiority of the subject and for its location in the material world.

THE EPISTEMOLOGICAL FOUNDATIONS OF CLASSICAL MARXISM

Classical Marxism claimed to have unveiled the underlying meaning of history by identifying the laws of evolution of human society. Against the metaphysical and historicist conceptions of his time, Marx had the 'brilliant insight'[4] to trace historical change in the dialectical relationship between the main dimensions of reproduction of human societies.

In all stages of human evolution, societies reproduce themselves materially by putting available technologies to work on existing resources. The continuous development of the forces of production ensures an ever increasing control over nature and, in capitalism, overcoming material scarcity becomes a possibility. But technical activity takes place within an institutional framework (the relations of production), which regulate the distribution of rewards, obligations, rights, and power. People are grouped in classes according to their position in the relations of production that place them in asymmetrical positions of domination-exploitation. Within this framework, ideologies arise, through which people perceive their position in society and organise their lived experiences. Ideologies are also the site of political forms of integration and the crystallisation of social antagonisms that further buttress or undermine institutional frameworks.

Each stage in the historical evolution exhibits a specific combination of forces and relations of production. Marx identified a number of such stages (or modes of production) of which the present, capitalism, is the penultimate leading to socialism and communism. Social change, the transition from one stage to the next, results from the increasing tension between the incessantly developing forces of production and outmoded relations of production that hinder their development. This tension is reflectively appropriated and then translated into political activity by social forces whose interests are suppressed by the existing institutional framework. In contemporary capitalism, for example, science and technology have reached a stage at which their further development is limited by

[4] J Habermas, *Theory and Practice* (London, Heinemann, 1979) 168–9.

capitalist relations of production with their commitment to private appropriation and profit. The role of the working class as the historical agent of change is given by its position as the exploited and dominated class in the relations of production. But its success depends on political struggle.

Marx's theory has three levels: It describes the laws of evolution of human history and of the operation of capitalism. Secondly, it is a devastating critique of capitalist domination and exploitation and, finally, it is a political manifesto and a call to revolutionary consciousness. In theory, social change comes about through the dialectical interplay between technical and political activity. But in his major theoretical work, *Capital*, Marx did not emphasise political and practical activity. While ideology and domination are central concepts in his political writings, Marx did not give them the epistemological and philosophical attention that labour and the economy received. Technical and instrumental activity was given primacy over politics.

This emphasis explains Marxism's claim to scientific status. If certain laws exist in the economy and can be described, explained and utilised, its methodology is similar to that of the natural sciences. The iron logic of these laws constitutes a rational substratum in history and opens up the theoretical possibility and political necessity that the present stage in the historical evolution will be transcended. 'The past development of the productive forces makes socialism possible and their future development makes socialism necessary.'[5]

Advanced capitalism, however, negated the main tenets of the classical model. The prediction that large sections of society would become impoverished, would join the working class and prepare for the final showdown with the capitalists, precipitated by economic crises, was not realised. The working class did not unify around the communist parties and the social structure was not simplified around the two antagonistic poles. Class was split and fractured, and political movements became fragmented. Law, ideology and culture seemed to resist the primacy placed on the economy. Rather than being an instrument of class oppression, the welfare state helped improve the lives of working people. The claim that Marxist theory has a privileged insight into political practice started coming unstuck.

Marxism produced various responses. Initially, the primacy of the laws of the economy was re-affirmed. If these laws no longer described observable experiences, they were raised to metaphysical guarantees: reality would eventually coincide with them. Alternatively, the unity of the class became a future horizon. According to this approach, classes and individuals are constituted at the level of the economy, which endows them with objective interests. People either recognise their interest and translate it into political and ideological commitment or they mistake it and opt for a 'false consciousness', that is to say misleading appearances instead of the underlying essence.

[5] GA Cohen, *Karl Marx's Theory of History: A Defense* (Oxford, Oxford University Press, 2000) 206.

In this approach, the concrete—people's motives, ideas and actions—is reduced to the abstract. 'History, society and social agents have an essence which operates as the principle of their unification. And as this essence is not immediately visible, it is necessary to distinguish between a surface or appearance of society and an underlying reality to which the ultimate sense of any concrete presence must necessarily be referred.'[6] The increasing gap between theory and reality determined the role of politics. Left-wing parties and their intellectuals claimed to have an insight into the historical mission and objective interests of the class. If the ontological status of the class is inscribed in the relations of production, the party's role is epistemological and didactic: it understands the laws of history and teaches them to the class. Politics equals the representation of the objective interests of the class and ideology equals their revelation. The combination of the two opens the road for what can be called a 'progressive substitutionism': the party substitutes for the class, the leadership for the party and, finally, the cult of personality replaces leadership altogether.

ATTACHING CAUSES TO EFFECTS

Marxist political and legal theory has been built around the famous base-superstructure metaphor, which in its classical version states that:

> In the social production of their existence, men inevitably enter into definite relations of production appropriate to a given stage in the development of their material forces of production. The totality of these relations of production constitutes the economic structure of society, the real foundation, on which arises a legal and political superstructure and to which correspond definite forms of social consciousness. The mode of production of material life conditions the general process of social and political life. It is not the consciousness of men that determines their existence, but their social existence that determines their consciousness.[7]

The crucial formulation in this passage is that the 'mode of production' determines the political, legal, spiritual (ideological) aspects of life and the social consciousness of an era; its culture. Society is seen as a building whose floors stand on the foundation of the economy. But how does the economy influence or "determine" the other levels? The question of determination became the hallmark of Marxism. According to Stuart Hall, '[w]hen we leave the terrain of 'determinations,' we desert, not just this or that stage in Marx's thought, but his whole problematic.'[8]

[6] E Laclau and C Mouffe, *Hegemony and Socialist Strategy: Towards a Radical Democratic Politics* (London, Verso, 1985) 21.
[7] K Marx, 'Preface', *A Contribution to the Critique of Political Economy* (London, Lawrence and Wishart, 1971) 20–1.
[8] S Hall, 'Rethinking the Base-and-Superstructure Metaphor' in J Bloomfield (ed), *Class, Hegemony and Party* (London, Lawrence and Wishart, 1977) 52.

A first interpretation of the metaphor follows the model of a mechanical, cause-effect relationship. The cause (economy) is external to its effects (superstructural levels). The levels are external to each other and their link moves one way from bottom to top and, as result, the effects of the whole on its parts are lost. The economy determines, in a billiard-ball model, the form and content of politics and law; the effects of politics and law on the economy, however, are seen as minimal. This model has been rejected but it retains a certain attraction because of its longevity and its affinity with legal positivism (with its belief that the law determines the other levels of society and economy). Indeed the importance politicians and social scientists place on the economy is evidence of Marxism's influence.

In a second version, expressive causality—deriving from Leibniz and Hegel—society and history form an organic totality. The various levels, law, ideology and culture, are sites in which the essential contradictions that unfold in the economy are played out. This theory of expressive causality presupposes that society can be reduced 'to an inner essence, of which the elements of the whole are then no more than phenomenal forms of expression, the inner principle of the essence being present at each point in the whole.'[9] The inner essence totalises the social and is expressed in all its phenomenal forms. The fundamental contradiction between forces and relations of production is expressed in the irreconcilable conflict between workers and capitalists. The two classes are constituted in the economy but their struggle is reproduced throughout the social structure.

The most rigorous critique of mechanical and expressive causality has been put forward by the French Marxist philosopher Louis Althusser.[10] Althusser proposes a third conception of 'structural' causality. In this approach, the economy, politics, law, and ideology are levels of one common structure, the mode of production. The cause is the structure, not as an essence or hidden law, but as a cause immanent in its effects. Each level has its own specificity, history, and conditions of existence, it is 'relatively autonomous' from the others and helps reproduce the overall structure.

Indeed, the mode of production is nothing more than the complex set of relationships among the various levels, and causality consists in the articulation of the practices and effects among them. The economy remains the determinant level in every society 'in the last instance'. It decides, in other words, which level of the structure (politics or law or the economy itself) will become dominant. Structural causality acknowledges the specificity and effectiveness of the various levels and their contribution to the reproduction of the whole and has become the starting point for a number of analyses of the capitalist state, politics and law.

[9] L Althusser and E Balibar, *Reading Capital* (London, New Left Books, 1972) 186.

[10] L Althusser, *For Marx* (London, Allen Lane, 1965); *Lenin and Philosophy and Other Essays* (London, New Left Books, 1971); *Reading Capital*, above n 9.

The structuralist conception of determination could rally in its support a series of letters written by Engels between 1890 and 1895, which attempted to redress the economism of Marxism. Engels wrote:

> The economic situation is the basis . . . but the various elements of the superstructure . . . also exercise their influence upon the course of the historical struggles and in many cases determine their form in particular. There is an endless interaction of all these elements in which. . . the economic moment is finally bound to assert itself.[11]

> In a modern state, law must not only correspond to the general economic condition and be its expression, but must also be an internally coherent expression, which does not, owing to internal conflicts, contradict itself. And in order to achieve this, the faithful reflection of economic conditions suffers increasingly.[12]

The 'relative autonomy' of the superstructure, and of law in particular, became the focus of theoretical work in the 1970s and 80s and the hallmark of western Marxism. But if the economy determines 'in the last instance' then at that instance at least—however one interprets the expression—the economic base still determines in the 'final analysis', and the problems of determination and autonomy that Marxism faces are not resolved. Relative autonomy seems to give a linguistic rather than a theoretical answer, and the causal relationship between the economy and the superstructure remains mechanical. If one prefers a theoretical approach that emphasises the autonomy of the various instances, then, according to Hall's law, the theory would not qualify as Marxist, and liberal legal theory, sociology, and politics would have no great quarrel with it. Relative autonomy merely points towards a desired type of analysis that retains the 'connectedness' between the economy and the other levels, while avoiding the pitfalls of determinism. However, we will argue later in this chapter that it is possible to re-read this model. In place of structural causation, we will suggest that the social can be seen as a totality of differences. This will allow us to retain a critical angle on law and society, and not to produce an anodyne or merely descriptive model of social, legal and economic relations. We want to retain the sense, after all, that Marxism provides a guide to social action. Before we engage with this re-reading, though, we need to ask some further questions about the location of this thinking of the social structure within Marxist thought more generally.

Similar problems beset the Marxist theory of the relationship between thought and reality. Marx and Engels set out their ideas on this relationship, in *The German Ideology*. These ideas were later further developed, though never set out at length. In the first part of *The German Ideology* they argued that all thoughts were a response to material factors, and all forms of ideas were tied to material production:

[11] K Marx and F Engels, *Selected Correspondence* (Moscow, Progress Publishers, 1975) 394–5.
[12] *Ibid*, at 399.

> [M]en, developing their material production and their material intercourse, alter, along with this their actual world, also their thinking and the products of their thinking. It is not consciousness that determines life, but life that determines consciousness. For the first manner of approach the starting point is consciousness taken as the living individual; for the second manner of approach, which, conforms to real life, it is the real living individuals themselves, and consciousness is considered solely as their consciousness.[13]

This analysis seems problematic. 'Life' is not just there, waiting to determine 'consciousnesses' as they appear. Material 'life' and 'consciousness' are not meaningfully separable: they are each the result of the other in a complex process of interactions that makes determinism highly suspect. If we take a similar dualism of 'legal thought' and 'social thought,' we are faced with a situation where again it will be very difficult to draw boundaries between the two, let alone give determining priority to one or the other. Our legal theories are likely to be fashioned by our more general responses to society. But we very much doubt whether any rigorous, detached, neutral theory of our fundamental beliefs about society is possible. Our legal theory, no matter how much we dress it up in would-be scientific clothes is likely to be a more or less organised response to what our passions and emotions suggest. And however precise we try to be about our legal reasoning, it seems very unlikely that we can rigorously answer the question of why we take one particular view of the world rather than another.

Marxism remains committed to the creation of a society without exploitation and domination, but its grand theory appears problematic. Specific analyses relating to law and jurisprudence may have a greater relevance for our effort to rescue the political kernel of the struggle for justice.

START AGAIN: MARX ON THE RIGHTS OF MAN

We have to start again and re-situate our quest towards the political economy of (legal) ideology and personality or subjectivity. Marx wrote on legal subjects incidentally and usually in relation to questions of politics. One area of law about which Marx wrote repeatedly, because it brings together his various concerns, is that of natural (today human) rights. To understand Marx's approach to human rights, we must place it within the wider perspective of his thought. His early writings were an attempt to radicalise the Hegelian dialectic, to 'turn it on its head', by accepting the dialectical method but rejecting its idealist assumptions about reason's incarnation in history. In his later political writings, Marx became more interested in the potential of political and economic rights.

[13] K Marx and Frederick Engels, 'The German Ideology', *Collected Works*, volume 5 (London, Lawrence and Wishart, 1976) 19, 37.

A good starting point is Marx's commentary on the French Declaration of the Rights of Man and Citizen, in the essay *On the Jewish Question*.[14] Marx, following Hegel, argued that the bourgeois revolution split the stratified and static feudal society into a political part, which concentrated on the state, and a predominantly economic one, civil society. The split was repeated in the realm of rights. The rights of man (or human rights) correspond to and uphold the selfish interests of the private person, the bourgeois, while the rights of the citizen (or political rights) are unclear and idealistic. Marx based the distinction between man and citizen or society and state on his insight that the French revolution, despite appearances, had not completed the historical process. The revolution was bourgeois and political and would be superseded by another revolution that would be universal and social. While, in theory, the capitalist state and human rights claim to serve the good of all, in reality they promote the narrow class interests of the capitalists and defend their dominance over civil society.

How can we account for this? Marx gives an exemplary presentation of the dialectical method with its paradoxes, twists and turns. In feudal society, political power, economic wealth and social status coincided in the same person. Feudal lords, of which the crown was—at least in theory—the most powerful—composed the dominant political and economic class. However, the political predominance of capitalists could be ensured precisely through the apparent loss of direct political power. The main innovation of the revolution and its rights was to remove politics from society, and bring an end to the automatic identification of the economically dominant class with political leadership. Politics became confined into the separate domain of the state; property and religion, on the other hand—which guaranteed class dominance—were turned into social institutions belonging to the private sphere, and protected from state intervention through the operation of rights. This separation and 'demotion' to the private realm made property more effective and safeguarded its continued dominance better than the medieval fusion of public and private power. In this dialectical formulation, the main aim of human rights was to remove politics from society and depoliticise the economy. The separation presents the state as (politically) dominant, while capitalist society is where real (economic) power lies. The bourgeois abandonment of the direct political power that characterised feudal lords and kings was the precondition for the ascendancy of bourgeois society and its capitalist principles.

The rights of man were the dominant ideology of the revolution. Article 1 of the French Declaration states that 'all men are born free and equal in liberty and rights'. But while these rights are proclaimed in the name of abstract universal 'man', they promote, in practice, the interests of a very concrete person, the selfish and possessive individual of capitalism. From this perspective, Marx's

[14] K Marx, 'On the Jewish Question' in *Early Texts*, D McLellan (trans), (Oxford, Blackwell, 1971) 85–114.

critique of human rights was total and constant. Rights idealise and support an inhuman social order; underpinned by the abstract man of the declarations, they help turn real people into abstract ciphers. For a contemporary theory of human rights, Marx's work suggests that the subject of human rights appears without history or tradition, gender or sexuality, colour or ethnicity. Those characteristics that make us human are sacrificed on the altar of the abstract man lacking history and context. But at the same time, this abstract man stands in for what is all too human: the white, heterosexual, male bourgeois. As a result, the emancipation of the unreal man subjects real people to a very concrete rule: 'the rights of man as distinct from the rights of the citizen are nothing but the rights of the member of bourgeois society, i.e. egotistic man, man separated from other man and the community.'[15]

When Marx turned to specific rights he was equally critical. They proclaim a negative freedom based on a society of isolated monads who see each other as threats. The right to ownership is nothing more than the protection of the means of production. This type of property, which is very different from property or personal goods, separates people from the tools of their labour and divides them into capitalists and wage labouring slaves. Freedom of opinion and expression is the spiritual equivalent of private property—a position which seems highly plausible to us in the era of Murdoch, Turner and Gates. For Marx, formal equality promotes real inequality and undermines close human relationships: 'Right by its very nature can consist only in the application of an equal standard; but unequal individuals (and they would not be different individuals if they were not unequal) are measurable only by an equal point of view, are taken from one definite side only . . . One worker is married, another not; one has more children than another and so on and so forth . . . To avoid all these defects, right instead of being equal would have to be unequal.'[16] Anticipating the knee-jerk reaction of governments to security concerns, Marx considered the right to security as the only real right. It constructs artificial links between (fearful) individuals and the state and promotes the ultimate social value—law and order and the principle of policing—the 'supreme concept of bourgeois society, the insurance for [bourgeois] egoism'[17]—which is entrusted with keeping social peace and public order in a highly conflictual society.

In this bourgeois hall of mirrors, human rights support selfishness, while politics and the state replace religion and the church and become a terrestrial quasi-heaven in which social divisions are temporarily forgotten and the citizens participate equally in popular sovereignty.

[15] K Marx, 'On the Jewish Question', *ibid*, 102.

[16] K Marx, 'Critique of the Gotha Programme' in *Selected Writings*, D McLellan (ed), (Oxford, Oxford University Press, 1977) 569.

[17] K Marx, *Early Texts*, above n 14, 104; See also W Benjamin, 'Critique of Violence' in *Reflections*, P Demetz (ed), (New York, Schocken Books, 1978).

> [Man] lives in the political community, where he regards himself as a communal being, and in civil society, where he acts simply as a private individual, treats other men as means, degrades himself to the role of a mere means, and becomes the plaything of alien powers. The political state, in relation to civil society, is just as spiritual as is heaven in relation to earth . . . In the state . . . where he is regarded as a species being, man is the imaginary member of an imaginary sovereignty, divested of his real, individual life, and infused with an unreal universality.[18]

People live a double life: a daily life of strife and conflict during the working week and a second, which like a metaphorical Sabbath, is devoted to political activity in pursuit of the 'common good'. In reality, a clear hierarchy subordinates the political rights of the ethereal citizen to the concrete interests of the capitalist presented as natural rights. Equality and liberty are ideological fictions, which belong to the state and sustain a society of exploitation, oppression and individualism.

Marx was critical of the rights of the citizen too because they cannot deliver what they promise in capitalist societies: 'Political emancipation is of course a great progress. Although it is not the final from of human emancipation in general, it is nevertheless the final form of human emancipation inside the present world order.'[19] Unlike human rights, political rights do not belong to 'an isolated monad withdrawn into himself . . . without regard for other men.' Rights create a political community, in which man 'counts as species being', is 'valued as a communal being' and 'a moral person.'[20] But while political rights prefigure the future community of communism, their operation in capitalism helps obscure the nature of the social order.

Attacking natural lawyers, Marx argued that rights are not natural or inalienable but historical creations of state and law. Their emergence and operation, however, was quite complex. The separation of the state from society and the creation of the political realm was the creation of the developing capitalist economy. The modern state was created in order to serve the needs of the economy; its greatest success was to turn the preconditions of capitalism into legally recognised rights and to consecrate them as natural and eternal, thus guaranteeing the survival of its creator. Human rights are therefore real and effective, but they achieve much more than is apparent: 'Insofar as legal form is construed as the protection of natural right, the structural and historical conditions of civil society are suppressed.'[21] For Marx, a real revolution would be social, not just political, and would abolish the rights of property and religion, which perpetuate social inequality and class domination. Commenting on the Revolution of 1848, Marx spoke of a very different right, which would represent the spirit of such a revolution: 'The right to work is, in the bourgeois sense, nonsense, a

[18] *Ibid,* 94.
[19] *Ibid,* 95.
[20] *Ibid,* 93, 94, 95.
[21] J Bernstein, 'Right, Revolution and Community: Marx's "On the Jewish Question"' in P Osborne (ed), *Socialism and the Limits of Liberalism* (London, Verso, 1991) 109.

wretched, pious wish. But behind the right to work stands power over capital. The appropriation of the means of production, their subjection to the associated working class. That is the abolition of wage labour, capital and the mutual relationship.'[22]

The proletarian revolution will realise the aspirations of human rights by negating both their moralistic form and idealistic content, exemplified by the abstract and isolated man. The combined negation of content and form, in communism, will give fundamental rights their true meaning and will introduce real freedom and equality for a new socialised man. Freedom will stop being negative and defensive—a boundary and limit separating self from other—and will become a positive power of each in union with others. Equality will no longer mean the abstract comparison of private individuals but catholic and full participation in a strong community. Property will cease being the obstructive portion of wealth to each to the exclusion of all others, and will become common. Real freedom and equality look to the concrete person in community, abandon the various formal definitions of justice and social distribution, and inscribe on their banners the principle 'from each according to his ability, to each according to his needs.' The French Revolution, on the contrary, consecrated the right to hold property and to practice religion and, in this way, the capitalist pre-conditions of exploitation and oppression were ideologically reversed in the discourse of rights, and were fraudulently presented as freedoms.

The real rights of the citizen belong to the spirit of the future revolution and will be fully realised only when 'the actual individual man takes the abstract citizen back into himself and, as an individual man in his empirical life, in his individual work and individual relationships becomes a species-being; man must recognise his own forces as social forces, organise them and thus no longer separate himself from this social power in the form of political power.'[23] This realisation of rights in association with others will reconcile universality and human singularity and, as a result, state law, the effect and defender of the earlier gap between the two, will become obsolete and wither away. In communism, human qualities, aptitudes and interests will not be described as rights; they will be the attributes of individual existence, accepted and celebrated as integral elements of each person. Although rights can be seen as invented by capitalism, it can only realise them in an exclusively negative form. But when their real preconditions come into being in socialism, they are no longer of use and disappear. It looks as if human rights have little positive role in Marxism.

Undoubtedly many problems plague Marx's analysis, some contingent on the historical constraints of his period, others more structural and basic. The most important issue is the relative devaluation of moral, legal and political institutions and the excessive privileging of the economic 'base'. But Marx was also the

[22] K Marx, 'The Class Struggle in France: 1848 to 1850' quoted in JL Ferry and A Renaut, *From the Rights of Man to the Republican Idea*, F Philip (trans), (Chicago, University of Chicago Press, 1992) 88.

[23] K Marx, *Early Texts*, above n 14, 108.

first critic of human rights who insisted on their historical character against the assertions of the natural rights ideologues. After Marx's critique, it became clear that while human rights were presented as eternal, they are the creations of modernity; while they passed for natural creations, they are social and legal constructs; while they were presented as absolute, they are the limited and limiting instruments of law; while they were thought of as above politics, they are the product of the politics of their time; finally, while they were asserted as rational, they are the outcome of the reason of capital and not of the public reason of society. All these reversals between phenomena and reality meant that, for Marx, human rights were the prime example of ideology of their time.

But whatever his criticisms of historical rights, Marx forcefully expressed sentiments not dissimilar to those of radical natural law, and based his attacks on capitalism on the principles of dignity and equality, which only socialism could realise. In his critique of Hegel's *Philosophy of Right*, Marx was unequivocal: 'The critique of religion ended with the doctrine that man is the highest being for man, and thus with the categorical imperative to overthrow all relations in which man is a degraded, enslaved, abandoned, or despised being.'[24] Marx sided with those who, despite the declarations, were neither free nor equal. He may have despaired of the idealism and unreality of human rights but not with their aim. As Ernst Bloch put it, 'precisely with respect to the humiliated and degraded, Marxism inherits some of this wealth of natural law . . . Socialism can raise the flag of the ancient fundamental rights which has fallen elsewhere.'[25] We could argue that Marx was critical of human rights because they were not human enough and their rights were not equally shared. His exalted belief in the scientific character of his theory often derailed his moral vision, but Marx cannot be faulted for lack of passionate commitment to the end of human dignity and social well-being.[26]

Marx was also right in pointing out the dissymmetry between the universal 'man' of rights and the concrete capitalist whose image fills the frame of the abstraction. Contemporary feminist or critical race theories follow this path of critique of ideology: the 'man' of human rights is literally a western white middle-class man who, under the claims of non-discrimination and abstract equality, has stamped his image on law and human rights, and has become the measure of all things and people. But Marx neglected the possibility that the groundlessness of the discourse of rights and the non-determination of the concept of man—admittedly more asserted than real in the eighteenth century—would install indeterminacy at the heart of human identity—and undecidability in politics—and thus create the conditions of future self-realisation. Concrete people can be recognised and realised if they are allowed to shape their

[24] K Marx, *Critique of Hegel's Philosophy of Right*, Introduction in *Early Texts*, above n 14, 123.

[25] E Bloch, *Natural Law and Human Dignity*, D Schmidt (trans), (Cambridge, Mass, MIT Press, 1988) 188.

[26] C Douzinas and R Warrington, 'Domination, Exploitation and Suffering: Marxism and the Opening of Closed Systems of Thought' (1986) 4 *Journal of the American Bar Foundation* 801.

identities freely outside the diktats of state, law or party. In this sense, the critique of the false abstraction of human nature finds its horizon not in true abstraction but in the proliferation of local and partial contents that will fill the empty 'man' with a multitude of many colours, shapes and characteristics.

It is in this context that we now turn to one of the more sophisticated parts of neo-Marxism, the theory of ideology. The role of ideology in the construction of the subject has been a mainstay of Marxism. Initially, ideology was approached as the 'false consciousness' of the objective interests that people as members of a class had. The shortcomings of this approach soon became evident and a large part of recent Marxist political and legal theory has been trying to develop a more complex and nuanced understanding of ideology that would explain how individuals, rather than classes or groups, understand their position in the world. The importance of this for law is obvious, as the legal institution with its rights, duties and claims contributes greatly to the construction and identification of (legal) subjectivity.

MARXISM AND THE PROBLEM OF THE SUBJECT: FURTHER NOTES TOWARDS AN INVESTIGATION

What remains of Marxism? So far, we have argued that Marxism can be understood as an ethics of justice. Justice has to be understood as an engagement in particular social struggles. To elaborate this position, we will now suggest that Marxism can still provide a compelling theory of the subject as engaged with, and defined through, a social eristics.[27] We will see that this issue comes sharply into focus for Marxism with the question of legal subjectivity: how law defines us, and how we can resist the law. Our initial focus will be on perhaps the most celebrated (at least in the western academy) of Marxist legal scholars: Evgeny Pashukanis. It will be suggested that although Pashukanis did open the question of the legal subject, he also limited the way in which the subject could be perceived. In finding a way forward, we will turn to the work of Louis Althusser. Althusser is central because he can be read as attempting to move out of Pashukanis' impasse by employing psychoanalytic theory to understand the work of ideology and subjectivity. For us, it is a question of re-reading Althusser, and through this diversion, re-createing a Marxist theory of political subjectivity.

Pashukanis attempted to provide Marxism with a theory of the legal subject. It would seem that the subject is the 'atom', the point at which Marxist inquiry discovers the very foundations of legal matter. The very notion of subjectivity is

[27] Ultimately, this would have to be connected with an ontology of labour that includes an understanding of aesthetic labour. Thus, a Marxist ontology of the human subject would have to take into account the dandy and the *flanneur*, who engage in acts of self-creation, as much as it does the rural or the urban proletariat. To suggest, in shorthand, what this might mean: Baudelaire and Trotsky; Wilde and Lenin.

tied up with the form of private property. This legal form is seen as reaching its most developed state with the triumph of bourgeois capitalism. Capitalism presupposes a market where goods can be freely alienated. One can see here how this question of property, the nature of the subject and a particular historical moment are brought together. The legal subject is not derived, as natural law theorists might think, from a human essence. Pashukanis' analysis works in the opposite direction. Law is what allows us to speak of a general human essence. There is a radical extension of this thesis. Legal subjectivity is a kind of booby prize. It is received by the subject at the moment when the world is lost, when capitalism becomes the dominant form of social organisation.

What replaces any inquiry into human essence is a study of the relationship between law and economics. However, Pashukanis shows that he is unable to develop this analysis of legal subjectivity. Indeed, he returns to a reductionism with which we are already familiar:

> . . . your jurisprudence is but the will of your class made into law for all (Marx, 1884).
>
> But, though it is this signature of a society, you cannot know a society by looking at its law. For that gives undue importance to the law, in that it assumes that law can be an object of study unconstituted by any theory. For us, however, law is an object of study only in so far as it is constituted by Marxist theory.[28]

There is no room for a nuanced understanding of the subject emerging from this framework. In particular, as important as Pashukanis' criticisms of a certain natural law theory might be, to condemn the law from the beginning as an element of alienated consciousness is a strategic mistake. There is also a crude reductivism operating behind Pashukanis' argument. Law is part of a social structure that is ultimately reducible to its economic organisation according to the famous metaphor of the base and superstructure. Critical jurisprudence starts precisely with this critique of Marxism. But we cannot simply 'throw out' Pashukanis' work. We must develop his idea that the subject is derived from within a social field; a complex of relationships.[29] This theory of the subject is impoverished if economy is privileged, but the theory must retain some notion of the economic as an element in the structuring of the social field.

We can develop this line of thinking by examining Althusser's notion of the social as a 'fractured' totality of relationships that are ultimately dedicated to their own reproduction. What does this mean?

The main aim of Althusser's text, *Reading Capital*, is to examine the reproduction of society. We encountered these ideas above. Capitalism is a social formation that must reproduce the conditions of its own production.[30] That is to say that both the productive forces, and the relations of production, must renew themselves. This is a global operation that laces together the various sectors of economy and society. Ideology is located within this general reproduction of the

[28] E Pashukanis, *Law and Marxism* (London, Ink Links, 1978) 8.

[29] Pashukanis is clearly drawing on Marx's own notions of subjectivity here.

[30] L Althusser, *Essays on Ideology* (London, Verso, 1984) 1.

social. The theory of ideology accounts for the means by which the skills and beliefs, the idea and the practices, that are necessary to work, manage and coordinate production, are themselves reproduced. As such, the reproduction of these relationships also accounts for the power hierarchies and the struggles that characterise social order.

Despite the sophistication of Althusser's analysis, this model of the relationship between economy and society remains rooted in an economic determinism. However, we can look more closely at Althusser's characterisation of the relationship between the 'instances' of the ideological superstructure, the 'politico-legal',[31] and the economic base. Although it is possible to trace conjunctions between these instances, Althusser also shows that there are disjunctures.[32] Whereas Pashukanis suggests a more or less simple homology between juristic form and economic form, we now have a structure of 'difference'. No simple argument that insists on the correspondence between economic base and legal superstructure can be made.[33] There are of course still problems with Althusser's analysis, especially when he insists upon 'economic determinisim in the last instance'. This model appears to retain its grounding reference to the economic instance as the most central structuring moment. However, towards the end of his life, Althusser modified his understanding of the social structure. He suggested that 'the last instance never comes.' What sense can we make of this?

Arguably, Althusser's gnostic comment allows us to re-read the model of social structure that *Reading Capital* provides. If there is no final determination by economy, then the social totality appears as totality of differences with no ultimate grounding instance. We have insufficient space to develop this in detail in this chapter, but we do want to focus on one particular issue.

[31] *Ibid*, 8.

[32] To build this argument, we would need to interrogate Althusser's celebrated notion of the economy as the 'structure in dominance', and the equally problematic concept of 'overdetermination' (188). Lying behind these terms is the 'structure of production'. These terms impose a form of thinking that is founded on notions of totality and coherence. However, they also gesture beyond these suppositions, indicating the path that a different approach might take. It may be possible to appropriate Althusser's notion of 'structural determination', to conceptualise the way in which a whole and its elements relate, without reducing the whole to a unity that is the expression of its elements. There are many risks; in particular the insistence on the notion of 'economic determination in the last instance'. Economic determinism in the last instance recuperates the notion of a totality with an essence, even though this essence may be 'deferred'—either in the sense that the 'final instance never comes'—or—in the sense that the notion of relationship is predicated on the idea that the truth of the law, or any other 'social structure', lies elsewhere, not of itself, but explicable by reference to an 'economic reality'. Overdetermination, or the 'structure in dominance', are ultimately part of the metaphysical mechanisms criticised in the opening chapters of this book.

[33] Furthermore, we need to stress that it is not as if the economic sits outside this structure. It is inseparable from the structure. The base-superstructure metaphor is simply too crude. What we need to understand is the complexity of a system where, even if the determining factor could be posited, it is within the system itself. But, we need to push this model further still. Precisely because it is a totality of effects, a combination of combinations, it cannot be understood or grasped in any single phenomenon.

What might this mean for a theory of subjectivity? Or, more precisely, a theory of subjectivity rooted in the social conceived of as a structure of difference? We would part company with Hall at this stage, as we feel that there is a way of holding together Marx, subjectivity and the notion of the social as a totality of differences. The first conclusion that we can draw from a theory of the social as difference is that we no longer fetishise the economy as that which determines the social structure. If we are concerned with an economic influence on subjectivity, we could say that it cannot be a question of reading directly from social relations to economic relations. In other words, the analytic of 'class' needs to be suspended or bracketed. We could suggest that the relationship that an individual has to the work that he or she undertakes is a factor in determining what that person thinks, but that it is not the only or the determining factor. Furthermore, any account of subjectivity that does not relate, at some point, to a person or a group's relationship to the means of production is necessarily impoverished, and runs the risk of simply fetishising another 'instance' which is then seen as the overall determinant.

There is another problem. If Marxism is seen as the theory of an organised class who set their face against their own exploitation, how does our re-reading relate to this essential aspect of the Marxist tradition? Our heretical Marxism would resist any sense of organisations or parties dedicated to a single cause. We would see the noble continuation of the Marxist legacy as existing in those events or moments when individuals or groups take part in specific actions that are aimed at protesting their oppression, or altering the social or economic conditions that have resulted in their impoverishment. This is a Marxism without a party; but with a plurality of causes. If the task of Marxism is thus to make a series of interventions, then what is required is a 'user's manual'; a guide to the politically possible. Once again, this means that we have to appropriate the theory of ideology. We need to account for the operations of the social.

The Marxist tradition understands the state as an instrument of the ruling class. Although Althusser's general theory takes this position as a starting point, it can be read as developing into a much broader account of the nature of ideology. The tools at the state's disposal include the Repressive and the Ideological State Apparatuses (RSAs and ISAs). Repressive State Apparatuses include: 'the Government, the Administration, the Army, the Police, the Court [and] the Prisons'.[34] These institutions do not all operate through physical repression (even though this may be true in the last instance). 'Administration', for instance, works through bureaucratic structures that regulate and distribute resources.

Ideological State Apparatuses must be distinguished from RSAs. Their operation is much more diffuse. Indeed, ideology takes us along way from state power, directly repressive or otherwise. The ideological state apparatuses vary enormously in their functions and include religions, education, the family, legal,

[34] L Althusser, *Essays on Ideology*, above n 30, 17.

political, trade union, communications and cultural institutions.[35] The plurality of the ISAs distinguishes them from the more fixed and located repressive institutions and extends their influence into the private realm. Indeed, we would prefer to refer to these structures as ideological apparatuses because the reference to the state is not useful. For Althusser, however, is it imperative to 'anchor' ideology. For instance, despite their plurality, ISAs are organised 'beneath the ruling ideology.'[36] Althusser has to make this point, because if he does not maintain an ultimate class determinant for ideology his theory becomes effectively a system of different apparatuses that have no ultimate, grounding reference. So, to protect this model from becoming one of difference without determination, ideology has to be geared towards reproduction in the interests of the dominant class. Ideology and economy are quilted together by this thread.

Althusser's argument twists and turns as it attempts to provide an economic basis for ideology. As Althusser himself explains, it could be that ideology as 'something' in itself 'disappears'; it can have no history, no 'substance'. Ideology is a 'dream' that can only be understood as a form of 'residue'[37] of the day's events in the mind of the dreamer. Because it is always driven by something 'external' to it—economy—ideology is never at home for itself; it is always elsewhere. A strange idea. So strange that Althusser must immediately move away from this non-object that is both something, in that it has effects that can be observed, and a nothing: a dream. Can we suggest a different reading?

If ideology is, by its nature, resistant to a reductionism, it must, in its 'nature' take us towards a phenomenon that both exists 'elsewhere' (the unconscious), but which nevertheless connects and expresses itself through the social; or, more precisely, a social that is itself conflictual and riven with tensions. This embedding describes the political unconscious; an 'idea' coherent with Deleuze and Guattari's insistence that desire is the social. We could say that ideology necessarily relates subjectivity to its inherently social expression (rather than that of the atomised bourgeois subject). If we re-align Althusser's theory of ideology around this point, it becomes an intriguing account of the constitution of subjectivity through the social. Ideology 'represents' something in an 'imaginary form';[38] more precisely, 'the imaginary relationship of individuals to their real conditions of existence.'[39] Ideology is not the 'false consciousness' of a class, the mistaken understandings of their real interests. On the contrary, ideology comes about through the practices of individuals. It is the lens through which they understand their lived experience.

To put this position somewhat differently: it cannot simply be that 'Priests' or 'Despots'[40] forged the earliest ideological form, religion, in order that they

[35] *Ibid*, 17.
[36] *Ibid*, 20.
[37] *Ibid*, 33.
[38] *Ibid*, 36.
[39] *Ibid*, 36.
[40] *Ibid*, 37.

could represent the world in such a way as to perpetuate their own power. The problem with these interpretations is that ideology reflects in an imaginary form, a 'real' world.[41] There is a more accurate way of conceptualising ideology. Instead of the notion that ideology is a veil that separates the real from the unreal, it becomes the very 'point' or a 'hinge' that connects the subject to the real world. Ideology is thus a way of describing the mechanism through which the subject is inserted into a given material reality. In its most extended form, this is a theory of the subject as 'made' by material circumstance. Thus 'subjective' states are not to be seen as 'essences', 'ideas', or 'spiritual substances', but as the very complexes that attach the subject to an external world. The private, inner world of the dream, of the separate self, disappears. Consciousness—freely formed, and belief, are thus the points when the subject is the least free, when the subject is 'inscribed into material practices.'[42]

Law is central to ideology. Indeed, Althusser writes that the 'category of the subject is the constitutive category of all ideology.'[43] It is perhaps this part of Althusser's account of ideology that is most useful. Although his approach has been criticised,[44] it is perhaps the least flawed aspect of the account of the differentiated social totality. The law is of central importance as it provides the mechanism through which the subject is called or 'interpellated' into the ideological structure. This universal function or calling is perhaps not so much associated with 'bourgeois ideology'[45] but legal ideology in general. Law and legal ideology open the space that allows a subject of any sort to be recognised. How does that happen? Literally through law's call:

> I shall suggest . . . that ideology 'acts' or 'functions' in such a way that it 'recruits' subjects among individuals . . . by that very precise operation which I have called interpellation or hailing, and which can be imagined along the lines of the most commonplace everyday police (or other) hailing: 'Hey, you there.'[46]

As soon as the subject turns round and sees that she is called by a policeman, she is caught; interpellated as a subject of ideology. She accepts the terms by which she is called; she accepts that the policeman, the law, has the power to call

[41] *Ibid*, 38.

[42] *Ibid*, 42.

[43] *Ibid*, 45.

[44] Judith Butler complicates the scene. The success of the word of law that radically changes us by turning us into subjects relies on a certain anticipatory attachment on our part, a readiness to be compelled. We are already in relation to the voice before we respond, through an original acceptance of guilt, a desire to be reprimanded in order to gain purchase on identity, an original guilt upon which God, conscience and the law feed. Subjectivity is achieved through the guilty embrace of the word of law, guilt guarantees law's intervention and, through it, the subject's false and provisional identity. We feel guilty before the law calls upon us, and in answering its call, we finally identify, with a degree of satisfaction, with the fear and guilt of transgression that always determined our actions. J Butler, 'Conscience Doth Make Subjects of us All' in *The Psychic Life of Power* (Stanford, Stanford University Press, 1997).

[45] L Althusser, *Essays on Ideology*, above n 30, 44.

[46] *Ibid*, 48.

her to account and, in doing so, to give her identity and responds: 'here I am officer'. Identities are created when the individual recognises herself as the subject to whom the call is addressed. This recognition of self through the call of the Other, the law in this case, symbolises the way in which we become conscious of ourselves as having a particular identity. To be a thinking, speaking being, is to be already thinking and speaking an ideology. The example is dramatic; it illustrates the way in which ideology always addresses itself to the individual. It is as if we are always 'already' interpellated by ideology. Marxism opens up to psychoanalysis in an attempt to hold on to the material reality of economic and social subjection, while acknowledging that identities are individual and can be called to being by a number of different and antagonistic institutions and practices. But if we become subjects by being called to account this way, to have an identity is to try to mould together (and often fail) a number of different calls, to integrate different 'subject positions' into a single subject.

However, is it simply the case that the individual accepts the law's hailing of them? Let us look at the law's operation in the street, when a policeman calls, stops somebody to search, ask questions or make an arrest. This is literally the moment of 'interpellation'. In these rather 'peripheral' aspects of police powers Althusser's conception of subject-creation through law's calling comes alive. In a series of cases, the courts have held that we are not obliged to answer questions to people in authority if we have not been properly arrested and cautioned. When the police call out, 'Hey you', and proceed to ask questions about our movements or identity, we are under no legal obligation to respond. Indeed, we can see that these questions run through one of the central cases in this area: 'a person is prima facie entitled to personal freedom [and] should know why for the time being his personal freedom is being interfered with . . . No one, I think, would approve of a situation in which when the person arrested asked for the reason, the policeman replied "that has nothing to do with you: come along with me . . .'.[47]

At common law, it was always necessary for the person making the arrest to make it clear that the person under arrest is under compulsion. This can happen through either physical restraint or orally, by making clear to the arrestee that he is not free to go. The common law, and its later statutory form, the Police and Criminal Evidence Act 1984, thus create arrest as a symbolic moment, a liminal zone where one moves from free subject to detainee. It is the point at which the state bears down on the individual. The question of arrest and the violence associated with it then becomes crucial. The issue is how this violence is to be encoded; whether it is to be interpreted as legitimate state power, or as the individual's resistance to a power that has 'overstepped the law'.

In law, we are entitled to resist unlawful unrest or police questioning not based on clear legal power, such as the police power to interrogate the detainee after a lawful arrest. In one celebrated case, a police constable had attempted to

[47] See *Christie v Leachinsky* [1947] AC 573.

question a juvenile by taking hold of his arm; the juvenile had resisted and assaulted the constable.[48] The conviction for assaulting a police officer in the execution of his duty was quashed by the Divisional Court. The narrow line that separates legitimate resistance from assault on a police officer suggests the fraught nature of the ideological struggle over the meaning of the event of arrest. Precisely what is at stake here is the point at which the 'imaginary' relation to the real will be created. In a later case, the constable had not actually seized the suspect.[49] As this was only a *de minimis* interference with the suspect's liberty, it did not take the constable out of the course of his duty.

These cases show a struggle over the precise terms of arrest and of the ideological constitution of the subject it symbolises. But once we move from the environs of the High Court to the street and from the law-reports to police actions the picture is quite different. A great number of stops, searches and questionings in the street do not follow any particular form and are not recorded. Furthermore, very few cases involving street incidents reach the courts and are examined for their legal niceties. This is an area of the law that gets litigated very rarely and as a result some of the key authorities are still common law cases despite the many recent statutory interventions and the radically changed nature of policing the streets. More importantly, the overwhelming number of people stopped, questioned or arrested obscures the fact that under the law they may be entitled to refuse to answer or to follow the police to the station or help them with their enquiries. Most people believe that the police have the power to stop, search and ask questions without any formalities, and obey unquestioningly. They turn around at the 'Hey you' and accept that their identity and personality is at the command of law and its ideology. The law has created the ideological conditions for seeing ourselves as free but these support a material reality of lack of autonomy.

Here we find the nub of the Althusserian claim. Interpellation is a complex phenomenon. The 'Hey you' and the turning towards the policeman may be seen as an experience of violence, an 'acoustic' violence that carries within it the amassed power and ideological legitimacy of the institution of law. It is an allegory for the way we come to identity through an ideological misrecognition: law and other ideological institutions ascribe identity to us ('You the law's subject'), but it is imaginary when it suggests that our subjection to law/ideology gives us freedom ('You the law's subjects are free and have rights'). There is always the possibility of telling the policeman 'Officer, you have no power to call me or to question me'—or perhaps a more risky strategy, 'Fuck you Copper.'[50] We may refuse unlawful questioning, we may flee or even assault the policeman to resist an unlawful arrest, the law says, but we rarely do. We could challenge the law, we could try to create a different identity from the authorised recognition and

[48] See *Kenlin v Gardiner* [1967] 2 WLR 129.
[49] See *Donnelly v Jackman* [1970] 1 WLR 562.
[50] See *Collins v Wilcock* (1984) 79 Cr App R 229.

self-recognition that institutions give to us and in so doing become different from who we are, change ourselves and the world. But it happens rarely, if at all. Hearing the word of law (literally juris-diction) brings us to identity (we accept our position as subjects subjected to the law) albeit a false one (we are free to resist). We can generalise from the scene of stop and questioning, or arrest in the street, to the multiple legal transactions, dealings, forms and practices that make us who we are. Our identity is based on a mis-recognition because we experience ourselves as something we are not. It is not so much that we have legal and human rights and obligations. More likely it is these rights, procedures and duties with the ideology they promote and the practices, habits and patterns they impose upon us that make us who we are.

CONCLUSION: MARX; OUR CONTEMPORARY

In this chapter we have tried to argue that Marxism is paradigmatic for one of the key theses of this book. The critical tradition cannot be expelled from conventional or bourgeois jurisprudence. In our understanding, Marxism has always taken its essential meaning from an ethical position: the struggle against oppression. There are at least two aspects to this approach. Firstly, we can thus speak of a Marxist approach to justice as substantive justice. Marxism carries the conscience of modernity. It is impossible to exorcise or exhaust the Marxist presence in modern thought, because it constantly raises this most difficult of questions. This question remains current because it provokes further issues. Why should the law protect those interests that preserve their own private profits at the expense of others? Why should law protect those technological advances that could potentially destroy the drudgery, pain and boredom of daily lives?[51]

Secondly, if Marxism is an ethics, it can, for us, be seen as a guide to practical action. One of the most pressing issues in this respect is a theoretical knowledge of the structure of the social: a sense of constraints and possibilities. One area, and perhaps the most important, is the question of the ideological structure of subjectivity. We have tried to suggest that one of the most relevant

[51] For clarification, though, the present approach to these matters is not concerned with the 'contents' of consciousness. It is not an attempt to provide an empirical study of an individual's thinking or feeling. Its brief is to provide a sense of how this consciousness might be determined by institutional factors; by the meta-discourses that structure our worlds. It is precisely this 'meta' sense that has preoccupied the other discussions of this issue in the present work. For instance, critical race theory has opposed a political sense of a 'black' self with the implicit and explicit racism of the law. Psychoanalysis has sought to provide a language that can articulate this sense of interiority: what it means to 'be' a person, to have a particular form of consciousness. We can sense that these forms of critical thought would take issue with a crude form of economism. At best this would see one's consciousness as proletarian or bourgeois as relating to a means of production; a question of whether one had to sell one's labour to survive. Surely, there is more to a structural account of consciousness, to a sense of self, than merely this referent?

to critical jurisprudence is that provided by the intersection of psychoanalysis and Marxism. It is from this perspective that we offer our interpretation of Althusser's general theory of ideology. It suggests that subjectivity is always already embedded in social eristics. We are our struggles. As if reading backwards from this point, we have tried to show how Althusser's text *Reading Capital* can be seen as providing a theory of the social order as a structure of differences; or, most precisely, ideological differences, that, if associated with a theory of subjectivity, reveal the social space as fractured by conflicts over values and identities. Thus, the common law should not appear monolithic and incapable of change. Rather, it is open to intervention: it is itself structured by ideological conflict over its key terms. We believe in a practice of interruption. If one is so minded, one can use the resources offered by the law in strategic ways. Thus, the law of arrest could be viewed as the point at which the power of the state manifests itself in the most direct way on the individual. At the same time, we can appreciate how the law itself offers nodes of resistance, or at least qualifications to the power of arrest. This is not to suggest that the law somehow ultimately achieves a balance of different social interests. However, as far as a strategy of intervention or resistance is concerned, such questions of ultimate resolution are of no practical importance.

The only relevant question to ask of the law is: what can I do with it?

PASSAGES

During the colonel's dictatorship in Greece between 1967 and 1974, the military regime offered an image of omnipotence. Based on what was presented as an all-powerful army and on a kitsch ideology of Christian orthodoxy, family values and classical glories, it sailed through 7 years with the tolerance of the silent majority. In July 1974 Cyprus was invaded by the Turkish army which occupied some 40% of the island and expelled 200,000 Greek-Cypriots. The Greek dictatorship which had precipitated the Turkish invasion through its actions had to react. After all, its claim to authority was based on the need for the security of the Greek 'vital space'. A general mobilisation of all males to the age of 50 was ordered, and people turned up in great numbers at conscription centres and barracks throughout Greece. I turned up at one of those with friends, fearful of the dictatorship and of the predicted war with Turkey. For the first few hours, people spoke in hushed voices, speculating, trying to get information about what was happening, worrying about loved ones. But soon we realised that the army had no uniforms or arms to give to the mobilised multitude. In many cases, the officers had disappeared and there was no-one who could give orders and prepare the conscripts. Anxiety soon turned into boredom, people started playing football and backgammon on boards marked on the sand. Eventually the hushed conversations became shouts and swearwords and laughter. We had come face to face with Power and had found that its secret was that it had no secret, that its power was something assumed, something that we had accepted and even desired. It was not so much that the Emperor was naked but that there was no Emperor. At that point the dictatorship collapsed and in a few days was replaced by a democratic government.

Part 4

Critical Jurisprudence

9

News from Nowhere: Anxiety, Critical Legal Studies and Critical 'Tradition(s)'

> But what is closer to me than myself? Assuredly, I labour here and I labour within myself; I have become to myself a land of trouble and inordinate sweat. (St Augustine, *Confessions*)

INTRODUCTION

CAN WE BEGIN to speak of a tradition of Critical Legal Studies (CLS)? A radical intellectual and political tendency becomes a movement or a school of thought when it can claim a history and a community or a tradition and an identity. For Critical Legal Studies (CLS), this history is doubly problematic. One problem is that American CLS, for many the acme of critical thought, represents only a starting point. We should not make the mistake of limiting the reach of CLS by constantly referring it to the 'American' moment in legal critique. But there is a more profound difficulty. History is what CLS has been rebelling against. Is it correct to impose a tradition on a body of thought that has set its face against tradition? Can these tensions be negotiated? Can the authenticity of CLS be found in a realisation of its own profoundly historical and iterative nature?

We will suggest that the defining feature of CLS as a critical form of thought is an anxiety towards its own constitution. In American CLS, the repeated announcements of its own death have marked this unique anxiety. Most other jurisprudential schools have a more or less explicit concern with their continuation, with the updating of their foundational truths for new times. We will relate this critical anxiety to a broader concern. The movement of CLS away from its American beginnings is also a transformation of CLS from a restricted to a general jurisprudence. We will trace this development from the concerns of the American founding fathers, through their metamorphosis in postmodern thinking and feminism, to British and European CLS and into the most recent manifestation of Australian Critical Legal Studies or Oz Crit and South African CLS. These later manifestations of CLS are increasingly engaging with the peculiarities of their own material histories. Whilst grappling with their own authenticity, they display a radical openness that feeds on law's lack of completion, and welcome a justice still to come. Anxiety becomes the way in which critical thought constitutes itself around the need to start again, to think afresh, to disturb its own axioms.

To tell the history of critique is therefore an exercise both in political history and in the history of ideas. This history has been told repeatedly in the United States. Under the pressure of the academic star system, a greater number of long and learned articles have been written about the history of critical theory than those actually practising critique. For various reasons this obsession with the history of CLS has not emerged in Europe and we do not want to start it here. This chapter is more of a genealogy than a history. It reads the past from the concerns and crises of the present. We are concerned with the beginnings, theories and lines of flight that have led to the present. What contingencies, what destinies and bad luck have combined to bring us to where we are?

BEGINNINGS: THE MIGHTY DEAD

CLS did not leap fully formed into the world, like Monkey from his egg. Its beginnings can be found in the radicalisation and redefinition of a prior critical tradition. The European trajectory traces the beginnings of CLS to Marxist theories of law. The Americans return to the Realist adventure in legal theory,[1] and see it as a break with the past, an opening of new paths. We have discussed the unique and central contribution of Marxism. Here we want to trace the American roots of CLS, and start with two key figures in American Realism, Felix Cohen and Roscoe Pound.

For Cohen and Pound, the common law is to be judged from the perspective of a 'now' that is trying to understand its place in history. Pound's starting point is a nuanced approach to the supposed central achievement of nineteenth century jurisprudence, the separation of law and morals. The narrowness of this approach, although not without its benefits, has made for the 'abdication of all juristic function in improving the law.'[2] Reflecting the dominant *laissez faire* model of economics, law became a way of assuring freedom from restraint for capitalist economic activities. Law showed no interest in regulating the more rapacious and socially harmful activities of big business.

Pound identified judicial activism as a central theme, a concern which positivistic jurisprudence failed to address. Pound argued that all positivistic 'schools' failed to realise the value of relationship and reciprocity, a failure that can be traced to the influence of Kant's 'metaphysical jurisprudence' with its emphasis on formal freedom and the individual will. However, it can also be

[1] N Duxbury, *Patterns of American Jurisprudence* (Oxford, Clarendon, 1995).

[2] R Pound, 'The End of Law as Developed in Juristic Thought' (1917) *Harvard Law Review* 201–25 at 203.

found in Bentham's utilitarianism and in the controlling ideas behind Roman law (at least as recovered and made influential by the school of historical jurisprudence). These schools and philosophers failed to identify the true genius of the common law. Whether one looks at the law of fiduciary obligations, of landlord and tenant, or of the Constitution, one finds that the law does not operate with the controlling concepts of individualism, but with mutual obligations, rights and duties created by legal relationships.[3]

This account of the law prefigures certain crucial themes and strategies. Before engaging with these concerns, let us have a brief look at the work of Felix Cohen. Cohen's assertion that '[t]he good life is the final and indispensable standard of legal criticism'[4] is particularly resonant. Although the good life remains unknowable, it is necessary to affirm a moral vision. This affirmation is itself an 'ethical' obligation.[5] Its success can be judged by the extent to which it can 'bring light to the foundations of our thinking.'[6] The moral affirmation allows the development of a 'critical attitude' which can weigh up the claims powerful social interests make on the law.

Ethics as evaluation and criticism cannot be squared with a blind adherence to rules or a fetishising of logic as the sole guide for judicial reasoning. Although a decision 'necessarily'[7] contains the material that allows the rule to be correctly posited, Cohen argues that a legal decision can be read in a variety of ways. Ultimately, a rule 'derived' from the facts is a product of the interpreter's 'choice.'[8] Thus, in a striking metaphor, 'logic provides the springboard but it does not guarantee the success of any particular dive.'[9] Alternatively, the decision can be thought of as a 'dough' that can be worked into the desired shape. The success of the 'dive', the shape of the 'dough', will be determined by the ethical vision that is brought to bear on the case. This approach rejects the possibility of a final 'right' answer. There can be no definitive answers to the ethical questions life throws to law. Should a rich and a poor woman accused of theft be treated in the same way, when the former does it for the excitement of the act while the latter to feed her children? Should a rich plaintiff be treated

[3] *Ibid,* at 217. Pound's argument can, of course, be criticised. Even if one accepts that the common law is relational, this does not prevent it being one sided or exploitative. It could be said, however, that this is implicitly acknowledged when Pound calls these reciprocal relations 'feudal.' In other words, this term would acknowledge that these are power relationships. Power may cohere in law, but not in any simplistic manner: law contains ideas that can be used to oppose manifestations of power.

[4] F Cohen, 'The Ethical Basis of Legal Criticism' (1931) 41 *Yale Law Journal*, 201.

[5] Any account of the good life is thus linked to a kind of modesty in thought. Here, strangely, is a kind of Nietzschean thesis. Cohen is drawing on the French jurist MP Tourtoulon: 'the first step towards wisdom is the knowledge that we are ignorant of nearly all the functions of our laws, or of the evil or the good which they may bring us'—*Les Principes Philosophiques de l'Histoire du Droit* (1908) translated in (1922) 13 *Modern Legal Philosophy Series*, 24. The inability to calculate means that any individual decision must suspend its question of good and evil.

[6] F Cohen, 'The Ethical Basis of Legal Criticism', above n 4, 207.

[7] *Ibid*, 216.

[8] *Ibid*, 216.

[9] *Ibid*, 216.

in the same way as a poor plaintiff? The law must admit that it uses ethical criteria in resolving such questions.

So, although the liberal economic doctrines of the nineteenth century have distorted the law, the genius of the common law can still be recovered. The common law contains within itself resources that can be uncovered and utilised by those who define themselves differently and approach law with a set of political challenges and radical projects. This re-awakening of the law operates at both the doctrinal and the philosophical levels. The most important and pressing matter is to keep asking the question; to separate and demarcate a present from a past and to make an urgent demand. Thus, in their different ways, Pound and Cohen can be seen as forerunners of a kind of thought—an approach to law that will name itself Critical Legal Studies. Their intellectual proclivities can be positioned retrospectively as part of the genealogy that will extend and divert the work of Legal Realism in new directions.

IN AMERICA WHEN THE SUN GOES DOWN: CRITICAL LEGAL STUDIES

The work of Duncan Kennedy offers a useful insight into the strengths and weaknesses of American CLS. This section will consider Kennedy's work as an exemplification of a form of thinking that founds itself on the insights of the Realists like Cohen and Pound. Carried forward is both a sense of the historical construction of the tradition, and the political or ethical choices that are open to the common law judge. CLS can thus be seen as founded on a return to history and as a new start, but how does Kennedy relate his work to the legal tradition; how does he resolve the tension between tradition and critique?

We will begin with the celebrated essay, *The Structure of Blackstone's Commentaries*. The essay is as much a statement of a new kind of thinking as it is a commentary on a commentary. Although a long way from contemporary liberal legal theory, Blackstone was important for American lawyers in the young Republic. He provided a model for the dissemination of professional knowledge and a foundational fiction for American law. Blackstone's presentation of the common law as a challenge to arbitrary royal power gave an important reference point for the law-obsessed American polity. Moreover, his legal and political theory offers a defence of liberalism different from those of Hobbes and Locke. It rests upon a notion of method defined by the rule of law[10] and the rights of persons. *The Commentaries* take into account the perennial problem of the conflict of rights and proposes a process of legal argument which, unlike the work of Blackstone's contemporaries, had a pronounced role for the judiciary.[11]

[10] D Kennedy, 'The Structure of Blackstone's Commentaries' (1979) 28 *The Buffalo Law Review* 209–321 at 214.

[11] In distinction to Hobbes and Locke, who imagined the state as making for the preservation of civil order, Blackstone developed a clear institutional picture of the state as a protector and enforcer

Kennedy reads Blackstone differently. There may be the venerated Blackstone; the philosopher of the common law's genius, but there is another way of reading *The Commentaries*. This alternative approach is prompted by a set of political questions; what does Blackstone's thought conceal? What social structures and political ideologies underlie the text of *The Commentaries*?

This attitude informs the celebrated idea of the 'fundamental contradiction'. In its most pithy formulation, the contradiction expresses the troubled nature of social life: 'relations with others are both necessary and incompatible with our freedom.'[12] The contradiction itself has a history, we are told, which both obscures it and allows it to appear. Obfuscation is the result of the mediation of the contradiction by structures of thought. Legal thinking itself, with its rhetoric of checks and balances, is an attempt to deny, or at least to minimise the disruptive effects of that which it cannot face. The denial may appear as a functionalism or a formalism but the system cannot silence the rumblings that are heard from within. Other techniques used to underpin the orderliness of law and deny its darkness are practices of categorisation, disciplinary and doctrinal thematisation and schematic thinking. These are ways of imposing discipline on the diversities of the legal materials. They satisfy a rage for order and interface with 'modes' of reasoning. If only the correct categories could be defined and maintained, if only legal reasoning could be clarified and performed correctly, the wonderful design of the law would reveal itself; its innate rationality would shine forth.

The dominant form of liberal legal scholarship can be approached from the perspective of the fundamental contradiction. Legal scholarship has been marked by debates over the correct classification of legal phenomena. For those within the debates it might appear that scholarship was a process of gradual clarification and refutation of error. This slow, incremental sifting would one day arrive at the best possible realisation of the shape, the form and the function of the law. If one remembers the contradiction, however, it would appear that this endeavour is doomed to failure. The very fact that something needs to be explained, suggests that something is not quite right, that law's house is not in

of rights (364). Consider the following example taken from Book Three of the *Commentaries*. The defence of the right to property exemplifies the 'private law paradigm' (365). It is asserted that rights to property are acquired by occupancy. Once acquired, rights can be transferred by a variety of legal devices. If the owner suffers a wrong, and the property is taken from them or control lost, the wrongdoer may be guilty of breaking a law that is founded both by law and nature: by nature in that the property has been acquired through some act of freewill, by law in that social order would collapse unless natural rights were protected. The judge's authority thus rests on the legitimacy of a law that can protect rights. Kennedy argues that this position remains blind to an important concern. Imagine a poor farmer who begins to farm part of his lord's estate. This could be thought of as a 'conflict of rights', but only if one were able to expand the sense of rights beyond that of the liberal paradigm. Kennedy's point is that Blackstone's presentation of the law makes it seem as if the private law paradigm can resolve the problem; in the widest of senses it makes this theory of the state provide a definitive answer for the problem of how we are to live with others, and how the distribution of property is to be achieved.

[12] *Ibid*, 1774.

order. The contradiction reflects deep-seated conflicts in the organisation of social life that are reflected in legal scholarship. Irresolvable tensions exist between liberalism with its suspicion, if not hatred, of an interventionist state and, communitarianism with its belief in collective ownership and a more active state. Locked in a struggle that cannot be solved, both positions circle around the same trauma. The altruist's attack on liberalism succeeds to the extent that it prevents the generation of concepts and rules that justify political order. Liberal criticisms of the collectivist tradition, on the other hand, show that fundamental problems about human nature and perception have not been adequately resolved and remain damaging.[13]

The fundamental claim of 'the contradiction' is thus ontological and sociological. Its articulation takes us towards political philosophy. In the realm of ideas, the contradiction veers between the so-called Hobbesian 'problem of order' (how can there be an obligation of obedience once freedom has become the principle of social organisation?) and the Marxian class struggle or its reformulation in the conflict between individualism and communitarianism. The contradiction is a condition of thought, and a condition of being. No stepping outside the contradiction is possible. By the same token, there can be no 'balancing'[14] of the rival interests and claims in a way beloved of legal reasoning and realism.

Although the fundamental contradiction is the condition of our social being, this does not mean that informed action is not possible. The best way of describing Kennedy's approach to this practical and theoretical question is to understand this phase of CLS as a 'critical phenomenology'. We will examine an paradigmatic instance. A strategy of American legal scholarship is to place the author in the position of a Supreme Court Justice who examines the lacunae, inconsistencies and contradictions of a particular doctrine and, from his Appellate position, suggests ways of straightening out the law. Kennedy in his *Freedom and Constraint in Adjudication* adopts the strategy. He is an interventionist judge who has to decide a politically hard case.

The hypothetical case involves a bus company that has applied to a federal court to obtain an injunction against striking drivers who have staged a sit in protesting against the company's employment of non-unionised labour. Can Kennedy the judge refuse the injunction? His personal politics and his ethical position make him sympathetic to the union members. He is aware, though, that the law is bent against unions in a case such as this. Cohen's image of the law as 'dough' appears in Justice Kennedy's first encounter with the problem. The law appears as a kind of substance that must be worked and shaped in such a way that the workers' case can be successful. The essay presents the interpreting legal consciousness as informed by a tension between the tradition and its own sense of justice.

[13] *Ibid*, 1774.
[14] *Ibid*, 1775.

The use of a phenomenology can help explain the movement of the judicial consciousness as it involves itself with the case. The ideological position of the judge is a question of his own engagement with the law: an individual's prejudices will determine the restraints and possibilities that they find in the law. In one sense, this is a meta-theory of judicial consciousness; its other use is to show a 'progressive' interpretation of the law. No doubt another article could describe the movement of a different political consciousness in its manipulation of the law. When we ask about the way these primary choices are made and our deep premises adopted, the answer is simple: through authentic action justified by an existential choice.

This phenomenology of judgement begins with a conflict between 'the law' and 'my existentialist decision' about 'how I want it to come out.' The existentialist position presents the world and law as what resists desire:

> Resistance or opposition is the characteristic of the law when I anticipate it as a constraint on how I want to come out . . . .I am suggesting that one of the ways in which we experience law . . . is as a medium in which one pursues a project, rather than as something that tells us what we have to do.'[15]

This approach takes Cohen's insight much further. Like Cohen, the 'ethical', or here more properly the political, is a 'project'—something to work towards; a passage that takes the interpreter through the law.[16] In this approach, rules are not inductively derived from cases, they are 'verbal formulae'[17] that drift in and out of consciousness, or become illuminated in different ways when a project presents itself. What needs to be plotted is the sense of freedom and constraint. It is peculiar that this piece does not dwell to any great extent on alienation, but shows how, even in the conditions of alienation, the law can be pushed towards an end that realises what? This is a question of 'the ethics of conflict.'[18]

Let us follow the phenomenology of judgement further. The judge faces a conflict between his internal sense of the case, and the way it will be perceived by others. Interpretation is always marked by a kind of self-reflexive and projective interpretation of itself interpreting. The institutional position of the judge is one element in this process. How would a refusal of the injunction be perceived, if there was an appeal? How would it aid the workers' cause? Indeed, how would it influence the future career of the judge himself? Refusing the injunction might end up being counter-productive. But there is another possibility. The legal issue itself could be framed in different terms. If the legal problem is whether the workers can legitimately obstruct the means of production, then it would be hard to resist the injunction.

[15] D Kennedy, 'Freedom and Constraint in Adjudication: A Critical Phenomenology' (1986) 36 *Journal of Legal Education* 526.

[16] *Ibid*, 548.

[17] *Ibid*, 530.

[18] *Ibid*, 527.

But the case could be recast as a 'First Amendment' prior restraint problem.[19] Granting the injunction would be an illegitimate interference with the rights of free speech of those protesting. Effectively, this would show that the operation of industry should be limited in the interests of a more compelling constitutional guarantee. Recasting the issue in this light shows a further dialectical movement of the interpreting consciousness. Does obstruction count as free speech? The task becomes different. The judge now has to show that a sit-in can be considered a freedom of speech issue. The law constrains the available argument to the extent that prior decisions and policies have limited the room for manoeuvre of the individual interpreter. How an individual judge wants to decide a present case and influence the future development of the law has a bearing on what these boundaries mean; as will the willingness of the judge to compromise short and long term objectives.

Viewed from the position of a more conventional jurisprudence this exercise is unacceptable. The judge's job is to apply the rules without prejudice. The point, of course, is to show that this is not a realistic model. Although interpretation is constrained in some ways, it is also open to the personal desires of the judge. More precisely, this essay shows that the 'grey area'[20] of rules can be manipulated and influence the way in which the dispute is perceived, and hence resolved.

But Kennedy warns us not to underestimate the anxious weight of the tradition. Accepting the court and judge-centred work of American academics, he hails the generations of judges who have contributed to the 'collective wisdom' of the common law.[21] Indeed, the influence of the judges is so pervasive that their voice appears as your own. In this sense, a problem that was initially defined as a contrast between internal and external perspectives must be redefined. The tradition is already present to the extent that you can talk at all. If the individual can make these feelings present to consciousness, she may be able to distance herself from the tradition—but this is not a reliable strategy. Hope lies in the fact that the tradition is itself a multiplicity of voices, some of which have been silenced, suppressed, forgotten.

Kennedy's work thus represents something of a continuation of the Realist concern with the tradition and its reinvention. What is perhaps distinctive about his contribution is the creative endeavour to articulate his own position. Part of this enterprise is also an anxious and impatient attempt to locate himself in the tradition. Our own location in history forces a confrontation with the 'fundamental contradiction'. We must make ethical and political choices from within this profound dilemma, this anxious moment of reflection and imagination. But we are still left with the question whether this contradiction represents a wider social and political conflict, or whether it is a localised anxiety of American rad-

[19] *Ibid*, 524.
[20] *Ibid*, 523.
[21] *Ibid*, 550.

ical lawyers who receive less recognition from the world than they feel they deserve.

Thus, CLS appears as a 'movement' in search of its own identity. In the dialogue with Peter Gabel, for instance, the trouble with CLS is seen as an obligation to define itself and have a 'slogan'. These marks of identification are limitations, even betrayals of essential insights. CLS should perhaps not define itself at all; it should not even have an institutional history. But this can also be understood as a sign of the defining individualism of American CLS and its pervasive 'anxiety of influence'. The authentic is such because it is not trapped or restricted by the past. This pervasive 'anxiety of influence' is marked by the extent to which the movement must acknowledge its antecedents, but not become trapped or restricted by the past. Critique demands that one always starts again. Perhaps, this is the 'question' that 'killed American Critical Legal Studies'. But this approach is linked with a more fundamental dilemma. How can we create a 'critical' body of thought that is not compromised by its own position and its links with wider movements for social justice? Being 'in and against' the tradition is a good start, but thought must not settle into a series of rehearsed questions and fall into the inauthenticity that it sets itself against. We will attempt to trace this anxiety through feminist critical legal studies as both a continuation and interruption of CLS.

CAR WHEELS ON A GRAVEL ROAD: FEMINISM AND AUTHENTICITY IN AMERICA

Feminism as critical legal thought redoubles the dilemma of the critic. We have seen how critique has to define itself against the tradition. But the feminist critic must define herself against both the established tradition, and a critical tradition that is as inhospitable as the mainstream. Feminist critical legal thought thus sheds a particularly acute light on the torn being of the critical legal thinker. Feminist thought is animated by a need to work this problem through: to remain authentic to a gendered position, and to create an intellectual home (whilst at the same time finding home most un-homely). It is as if feminism poses the questions that haunt this form of thought: Who am I? Where do I belong?

We can understand this dilemma if we consider the vortex created by the critique of essentialist feminism by a more problematic and troubled thinking of gender. Essentialist feminism was attractive and original. Its initial impetus was to present the central social and intellectual conflict as between an authentic oppositional community and a corrupt 'mainstream': a female 'us' and a male 'them'. The trope of authenticity was reworked around gender. Feminists were as critical of the blindness of the CLS to the gendered nature of law's power as they were of the liberal legal system. Law's objectivity, its norms and categories, were shown to be male standards which effectively enshrine female oppression and render it invisible because it does not conform with the male construction of social reality. At the centre of this web of oppression, the state ensures that 'the rule of law-neutral, abstract, elevated, pervasive, institutionalises the power of men over women'.[22]

Critique was also directed at a form of equally lazy and self-regarding 'male' writing, which was unable to see that gender functioned as a key term in the construction of power relations and subjectivity. One option was a form of 'separatism' that created an intellectual community of feminist critics aligned to CLS on its own terms. At the same time, there was a sense that this critical exile led to the creation of a feminist ghetto. The point was not to withdraw but to recreate the critical 'universal' so that it did not continue to operate in such a way that was blind to gendered oppression. These were profound issues of institutional, intellectual and emotional solidarity. From this perspective, a crude oppositionalism of 'male' and 'female' was too weak a foundation for a body of thought that should be able to define, or redefine, a gendered ontology.

Different feminist thinkers have approached this issue with varied inflections. We will concentrate on the work of Drucilla Cornell, who embodies the dilemmas of this approach. Cornell's theory of the law and state is an explicit critique of gender essentialism and in particular of the work of Catherine MacKinnon. Cornell sees a danger in returning to fixed definitions of female nature, which define women solely as mothers or carers. This is not necessarily negative, 'if both are understood to figure the desire for intimacy',[23] and public life is defined differently. Indeed, at the heart of Cornell's project is an affirmation of 'equivalent rights' which would not assimilate women to men's standards but would effectively enfranchise female realities.[24] Rights would cover issues such as virginity, motherhood, and various strictures that prevent the penalisation of celibacy. These rights would move away from merely attaching criminal sanctions to crimes against women, and would resemble the great enlightenment claims made for the rights of man. Cornell is re-imagining the notion of community. If there is a starting point, it concerns what is shared, the intimate space as the invitation to live differently.

This, in turn, leads to a rethinking of the terms of CLS. Cornell reworks the celebrated critical legal theory of indeterminacy. Her notion of recollective imagination is rooted in the refusal of the ideal schema or the totalising account. One's life is always one's own. It 'is' to the extent that it is immersed in one's unique personal experiences. In its original development, the thesis stated that legal norms and rules are without foundation and their linguistic openness and inescapable conflict means that no universally acceptable 'right answers' exist.

[22] C MacKinnon, *Towards a Feminist Jurisprudence* (Cambridge, Mass and London, Harvard University Press, 1989) 238.

[23] D Cornell, *Between Women and Generations* (London, Palgrave Macmillan, 2002).

[24] It is here that Cornell's work acknowledges a debt to Irigaray. Irigaray's argument is a demand for a legal statement of female identity. This 'right' would make for the 'legal codification' of virginity, Luce Irigaray, *Je Tu, Nous* (New York, Routledge, 1993) 86—a right to motherhood and the enshrining of the obligations of 'mothers-children' in civil law (88).

For Cornell, this thesis must be understood in a more precise way. The argument is not that claims to identity or to the foundations of knowledge are illusory. Rather, the thesis must be re-formulated to argue that the questions one can ask of an institution do not emerge from a transcendental or external viewpoint but come from within our own context. But no theory can render up the truth of context, because no given reality can find its truth in an account of its totality. Something in the real resists reduction to the ideal, and a key aspect of this something is it future-directedness, its orientation towards what is yet to be achieved, rather than what has already been realised. The real is fissured by—and addresses—its 'incomplete possibility.'[25]

Cornell thus returns to the question of an unrefined and authentic 'life', re-articulating the existential thematic that runs through Critical Legal Studies. CLS is re-figured and forced to start again with a new agenda for critical thought. At the same time, there is an anxiety of belonging that expresses itself through a critique of the mainstream, and urges the creation of a new intellectual community. This body of ideas would be both a continuation of, and a break with, CLS. The phenomenology of judgement that dominated the first wave of CLS becomes re-configured around a much broader economy and a more plural encapsulation of the critical task, which now looks towards the gendered body. The location of bodies in their personal and impersonal histories comes to the fore and links critical thought with psychoanalysis, aesthetics and queer theory. British Legal Critique carries forward this same anxiety, and continues to rethink its essential terms.

'BRIT CRIT' OR THE CRITICAL LEGAL CONFERENCE[26]

A longer chapter would attempt to articulate more thoroughly the links between American CLS and the Critical Legal Conference (CLC) or Brit Crit.[27] Given the

[25] D Cornell, *ibid*, 26.

[26] There is a problem with 'Brit' Crit. Many of the scholars associated with this position are not British. Although some may have become British through long association with British bad habits, others are resolutely non-British, or even anti-British. A promising area of study may attempt to define the bizarre heteroglot nature of this grouping. For example, as at the date of writing, one may be able, if indeed, one accepted these terms of nationality as useful or relevant, to identify Americans, Afro-Americans, Asian-Americans, Latino/as, Irish, Asians, Canadians, Afro-Caribbeans, South Africans, Slovenians, Scots, Greeks, Finns, English, Australians, French, Indians, Pakistanis and Sri Lankans. 'British' ultimately signifies no more than a bastardy, a mixing together: brown beer, curry, dark summers and rain.

[27] T Murphy, 'Britcrits: Subversion and Submission, Past, Present and Future' (1999) 10 *Law and Critique* 237. It would be possible to depict the various positions as organised around certain central ideas: there are alignments around versions of feminism, groups of scholars who borrow explicitly from Marxism or Critical Theory, a defined tendency to queer studies, and other groupings who lean towards continental philosophy and psychoanalysis. There are also people working with semiotics, social and political theory and post-colonialism. These tendencies should not be seen as an exhaustive description, nor as mutually exclusive. Perhaps they represent a nexus, a grid across which the movement both coheres and falls apart. It is a movement in as much as certain people

demands of this chapter, we will characterise this relationship as one of dis/continuity. The diverse forms of British critical scholarship show no interest in returning to the gamesmanship of 'names' or to many of the positions that define American CLS. Brit Crit can be read as a continuation of a certain disturbance within jurisprudence and a concern with the pervasive anxiety of influence. The Brits have to define themselves against a jurisprudential orthodoxy, and also against the American critical legal tradition[28] and have to determine a sense of intellectual coherence within the 'movement' itself.

The differences between American CLS and the British CLC are quite pronounced, although not always acknowledged. CLS was a political movement with little politics. Its main intellectual activity was the critique of judicial institutions and reasoning, while the politics of the movement were largely exhausted in the intrigue of the academy and the endless search for media exposure. European scholars found the pre-occupation of leading members of the American CLS with the internal (in)coherence of judicial reasoning a little bizarre. CLC, on the other hand, is an intellectual movement with lots of politics. The annual CLC started in 1984 and has taken place without interruption ever since. In all these years of operation no officers or posts, chairmen or secretaries, committees or delegates were created. The conference was and remains just that: a conference and an umbrella name. CLC is 'a community always to come'.

Over the years, these conferences introduced themes, schools of thought and movements unknown or dismissed by legal scholarship. Western Marxism, postmodernism and deconstruction were the main theoretical influences of the early conferences but soon the new radicalism of race, gender, queer and postcolonial theory were introduced to the legal academy through the CLC. Indeed these conferences were the only academic venues in which such themes were discussed for many years before they became respectable and entered, albeit marginally, mainstream academia. Twenty years after the first CLC conference, radical theory has slowly but steadily seeped down to all levels of legal scholarship and has led to a renaissance in legal study. Indeed whatever their shortcomings and problems, Brit Crits have reintroduced legal scholarship where it always belonged, at the heart of the academy.

might identify themselves with the loose title, without then going on to define membership or a set of clear objectives.

[28] To some extent the present chapter compresses the genealogy of British work. There was a first wave that was primarily Marxist in its orientation and contemporary with the work discussed above. It did produce some vital texts. The British Critical Legal Conference first met in 1984. Although not by any means exclusively Marxist, there was a sense in which Marxism was perhaps the most important source of reference. There is a sizeable literature generated by scholars directly or indirectly connected to the conference; and also more latterly produced. See B Fine, *Democracy and the Rule of Law* (London, Pluto Press, 1984) and A Norrie, *Crime, Reason, History* (London, Weidenfeld and Nicolson, 1993). See also the Pluto series *Dangerous Supplements*.

What are the peculiar anxieties of Brit Crits? From the beginning, CLC recognised its roots in a feeling of 'dissatisfaction'[29] with the many injustices perpetrated by law, and with the orthodox legal tradition that either explained away or ignored law's failures. This explicit combination of political and theoretical agendas meant that British CLC never had the coherence of American CLS. An accurate description of the diversity of CLC stated that '. . . the movement consists of a plurality of approaches and strategies to get at the power in the law.'[30]

Some of the early Brit Crit writings were attempts to find a common thematic. Alan Hunt, for example, wrote that 'there is a general agreement around the necessity of an hermeneutic approach, broadly conceived, which insists upon the social/cultural construction of social life . . . The positions adopted by individuals within the critical camp will continue to be influenced by the positions which they espouse on the general philosophical issues but there is no barrier to a fruitful exchange . . .'.[31]

Hunt's use of hermeneutics as an umbrella term is appropriate. Hermeneutics studies the transmission of messages, the dissemination of information and the construction of meaning. It describes the essential 'perplexity'[32] about law that runs through critical scholarship. Brit Crit is not just an attempt to 'show law in its worst positive light' but to suspend law's claims and subject them to the inquiring gaze. The hermeneutic approach does not follow the 'trashing' American method, but attempts to offer an intellectual agenda organised around the theme of 'law's (in)justice'. It might indeed be possible to define Brit Crit around such a loose hermeneutic idea, but its constitutional anxiety is not dispelled. Critical work, by definition, must maintain a sceptical distance from the justification of the system by its apologists.

The political direction of CLC has led to a question of priorities. Should critique engage with particular areas of law and legal issues or should it attempt to produce a general theory? Alan Thomson has drawn a pertinent distinction between the 'trashing' and 'structuralist' aspects of CLC.[33] Whereas the former is content to show the inconsistencies and contradictions in liberal legal theory, the latter seeks to identify the 'deep structures of power', creating links with wider social theory and developing its own language. This is another expression of the divide between an intellectual movement that addresses exclusively professional legal concerns (what we have called throughout this book 'restricted jurisprudence') and a political movement that operates in the intellectual interstices of institutional practices including law ('general jurisprudence').

To some extent, this tension was resolved by a Marxism that could provide a link between specific struggles and interventions and a total theory of class

[29] A Hunt and P Fitzpatrick (eds), *Critical Legal Studies* (Oxford, Blackwell, 1990) 5.
[30] P Ireland and I Grigg-Spall (eds), *The Critical Lawyers Handbook* (London, Pluto, 1992) 2.
[31] A Hunt and P Fitzpatrick, *Critical Legal Studies*, above n 29, 194.
[32] *Ibid*, 11.
[33] 'Critical Legal Education in Britain' in *Critical Legal Studies*, above n 29, 194.

power. Marxism provided a palliative to Brit Crit's anxiety, offering a central, unifying insight.[34] It promised an account of the fragmentation of society into 'its economic and juridical forms of appearance' by reference to 'definite social relations of production.'[35]

However, CLC's anxiety was not ultimately salved by Marxism.[36] Indeed, a general mistrust of the models of classical social and critical thought came to mark critical legal writing. Feminism was a major force in the development of new forms of critique. It tended towards a reluctance to employ meta-theories, preferring to use the term 'patriarchy' descriptively rather than as indicator of a fixed entity[37] or indeed, to concern itself with particular constructions of femininity.[38] Coupled with psychoanalysis, work began to focus on the role of language in constructing both subjects and social spaces. An analysis in terms of class was seen to lack precision, and could not map the complex conjugations between linguistic meaning and power relations.

With the advent of postmodernism, this type of critique reached its apotheosis. The anxiety of critique renewed itself in a desire to start again—to re-think the terms of critique—to reinvent around a 'new' problematic. Postmodernism in critical legal studies represents a return to the continental tradition. Instead of Sartrean existentialism, or Frankfurt School Marxism, however, the main philosophical tendencies are represented by the names of Nietzsche, Freud, Foucault, Derrida, Lacan and Levinas. As much as these names are important points of orientation or horizons of thought, no grand systematising urge appears in the critical work influenced by them. If anything, these bodies of

[34] But, the nature of CLC meant that not all subscribed to Marxism. This can be seen in the writings of one of the most mercurial of scholars, Angus McDonald. McDonald's leanings are towards Anarchism and Situationism (see 'The New Beauty of a Sum of Possibilities' in (1997) *Law and Critique* 141–59 and experimentation in general, see (2001) 23 *Liverpool Law Review* 221. See also McDonald's work on sovereignty, in particular 'Dicey Dissected: Dominant, Dormant, Displaced' in S Millas and N Whitty (eds), *Feminist Perspectives on Public Law* (London, Cavendish, 1999), 107–28.

[35] S Piciotto and B Fine 'Marxist Critiques of Law' in I Grigg-Spall and P Ireland (eds), *The Critical Lawyers Handbook*, above n 30, 18.

[36] This is not to present Marxism as a fallen form of criticism. Even from within legal theory that presents itself as explicitly Marxist, there was an attempt to redefine a theory of power. For instance, in *Democracy and the Rule of Law* Fine argues that: 'Marxists argue that everywhere and always power is an expression of social relations between people: the form and the content of power change with time and place, but not its human foundations. People always remain the real subjects of power . . . The task of theoretical criticism is to reveal the human relations which lie hidden beneath the fetish of a power abstracted from people, as a first step towards the practical task of making it possible for people to take control of power rather than for power to determine the fate of people.' (Fine, 192). Fine's redefinition of Marx, his movement away from the 'vulgar' opposition between base and superstructure and the economic determinism it makes for, moves this theoretical paradigm on a pace. The transformative dynamic of Marxism must remain, but in what could be described as a spectral or ghostly sense.

[37] A Bottomley, 'Feminism; Paradoxes of the Double Bind' in P Ireland and I Grigg-Spall (eds), *The Critical Lawyers Handbook*, above n 30, 27.

[38] See M Drakopoulou, 'Women's Resolutions of Lawes Reconsidered: Epistemic Shifts and the Emergence of the Feminist Legal Discourse' (2000) 11 *Law and Critique* 47.

thought are used as different perspectives on social being and existence[39] and their very real differences are not obscured in a futile attempt to create an unproblematic unity.[40]

Perhaps this manifests, in a different way, a critical anxiety: an awareness that legal philosophy has not been rigorous enough. One of the great announcements that initiated the postmodern project was the announcement of the death of a kind of jurisprudence: there was no longer a need to answer the great question 'what is law?' Not only had the traditional debate stagnated into a 'jaded pedagogy of theory'[41] or become bogged down into a kind of armed peace between various warring jurisprudential factions, but, and more importantly, these great questions represented the end point of a particular mode of enquiry. The most pressing concern was now the issue of how law is lived in particular situations, and the focus for critical thinking became the troubled connections between the lived world and the forms of the law.

Study shifts from a classical analytic scrutiny of the logic of legal structures—or the abstract categories of legal reasoning—to law's involvement with sexed and gendered bodies; to people of race—with memories and histories different from those licensed by the doctrines of case law and conventional legal philosophy. The political demand is to return to the 'truths' of lived experience, to the emotions and the senses as they are taken up and are disciplined by law. Responding to this demand, critical legal scholarship has increasingly looked to a much broader sense of how the subject is constituted as a product of power. Power is seen as 'relational' and exercised in a diversity of social, economic and sexual relationships. This approach moves away from the Marxist location of

[39] See chapter 1.

[40] Nor should 'postmodernism' be seen as a shared point of reference. Indeed, if anything, there is a tendency amongst CLC scholars to resist the very idea of 'names' or schools, to confound the very idea of Critical Legal Studies, and to affirm the freedom of a thinking that determines its own rigour. This tendency manifests itself in different ways. For instance, in the work of Wolcher, there is a pronounced eclecticism that borrows from Eastern thinking, as well as Wittgenstein and the continental philosophical tradition. Risking distortion of a body of thought whose engagement with issues of representation, suffering and justice is complex and developing, Wolcher's approach can perhaps be suggested in his juxtaposition of a ninth-century Chinese Zen riddle with Immanuel Levinas' thinking of the face. Wolcher is mobilising non-western thought to suggest how a different perspective on justice may be possible. (L Wolcher, 'Ethics, Justice and Suffering in the Thought of Levinas: The Problem of Passage' (2003) 14 *Law and Critique* 93). It is precisely this need to experiment, to look behind the certainties of both conventional and critical thought, that links Wolcher's work with that of Minkinnen. However, Minkinnen frames his central question in a different way to Wolcher. He has argued that the very idea of Critical Legal Studies is somewhat imprecise. If there was such a thing, then it could only be understood if a philosophy of law had first been elaborated. This philosophy would have to return to the very question of 'correct knowledge', a criteria that itself sees a conjunction of philosophy and law, or a 'juridisation of metaphysics' (P Minkkinen, *Thinking Without Desire* (Oxford, Hart, 1999) 6). At the heart of the endeavour, though, is a form of pre-philosophical 'desire to see' or an endless desire for a truth that 'remains non appropriable'. A philosophy of law must engage with this contradiction. For both Minkinnen and Wolcher, jurisprudence is inseparable from an engagement with the thinking of thinking itself: a task that cannot be delimited or reduced.

[41] P Goodrich, *Languages of Law* (London, Weidenfield and Nicholson, 1990) 1.

power in class. The various discourses that create knowledge of the social world effectively organise, define and deploy power.[42]

Postmodern feminism[43] and Queer Theory intensified this analysis, privileging the body and discourses of sexuality as key areas where power defines people as objects of knowledge to be studied, classified and disciplined. For feminists, patriarchy is the principal 'organising framework;'[44] for Queer Theorists, the 'genital order'[45] of heterosexuality.[46] Integral to both these approaches is the argument that power cannot simply be escaped or opposed. It is impossible to find the 'outside' of power because it inheres in every form of knowledge. Contestations of power are, however, possible. Every application of power invites subversions and oppositions.[47] From this perspective, any mode of analysis which returns to sovereignty and a concept of power that 'belongs' to some person and institution, or is codified and controlled by constitutional

[42] These themes could be followed through the work of those critics whose work is orientated towards autopoesis. See, in particular, the work of M King (with C Piper), *How the Law Thinks about Children* (Aldershot, Arena, 1995). See also A Philippopoulos-Mihalopoulos, 'The Silence of the Sirens: Environmental Risk and the Precautionary Principle' (1999) 10 *Law and Critique* 175. Philippopoulos-Mihalopoulos also draws on sources other than autopoesis, see 'Mapping Utopias: A Voyage to Placelessness' (2001) 12 *Law and Critique* 135, also 'The Suspension of Suspension', (2003) 15 *Law and Literature*. Another scholar whose work borrows from both autopoetic and other traditions is Emilios Christodoulidis, see below, fn 70.

[43] The term postmodern feminism obscures as much as it reveals. In general, see (1998–2003) *Feminist Perspectives on Law*, a book series edited by Anne Bottomley and Sally Sheldon dealing with feminist perspectives on subjects in the law curriculum. Another productive way of establishing a sense of the conjunction between feminism and varieties of postmodern or post-structuralist thought, would be to examine particular critical engagements. Thus, the work of Sally Sheldon in medical law would be one site; see S Sheldon, *Beyond Control: Medical Power and Abortion Law* (London, Pluto, 1998). See also "Who is the Mother to Make the Judgment?': Constructions of Woman in UK Abortion Law' (1993) 1 *Feminist Legal Studies* 3, reprinted in H Barnett (ed), *A Sourcebook on Feminist Jurisprudence* (London, Cavendish, 1997).

[44] L Moran, *The Homosexual(ity) of Law* (London, Routledge, 1996) 11.

[45] *Ibid,* 167. Moran's work is built on the essential insight that law operates through a classification of our pleasures, a process that can perhaps be glimpsed most clearly through those categories that are considered pathological. This can be understood as an investigation of the categorising of values to create the legal and the illegal, the normal and the abnormal. Once categories are created they can in turn be described in moral terms, and entire ways of being criminalised and hence in need of punishment, medicalisation, cure or rehabilitation. Law has a lexicon that it can use to define the behaviour it observes and give it meaning. Rather than being invisible to the law, acts considered to be homosexual have a vast body of description. This is not to say that crimes such as buggery and sodomy have always had the same meaning. What are important are the taxonomies, the techniques and practices that allow 'crimes' to be given a meaning.

[46] Queer Theory provides a critique of identity; and thus the bald statement in the text above is completely inadequate. The very term 'queer' has to be understood as suggesting the disturbance, rather than the settling of notions of foundational identity. See M Davies, 'Taking the Inside Out: Sex and Gender in the Legal Subject' in N Naffine and and JO Owens (eds), *Sexing the Subject of Law* (London, Sweet and Maxwell, 1997) 26–46. See also, L Moran, D Monk and S Beresford (eds), *Legal Queeries: Lesbian, Gay and Transgender Legal Studies* (London, Cassell, 1998) 24.

[47] See D Cooper, *Power in Struggle* (Buckingham, OU Press, 1995). As Cooper points out, there are many forms of feminism that draw on Foucault's work; it is necessary to acknowledge this diversity. It would include V Bell, *Interrogating Incest: Feminism, Foucault and the Law* (London and New York, Routledge, 1993); see also I Diamond and L Quinby, *Feminism and Foucault: Reflections on Resistance* (Boston, Northeastern University Press, 1988) and L McNay, *Foucault and Feminism* (Cambridge, Polity Press, 1992).

arrangements, misses both the sites where power is exercised in everyday life and the sites for its subversion.

The end of jurisprudence means that we are in the position of starting again; the tradition is alive with possibilities; it can no longer be a question of carrying forwards the old certainties, but of reading anew and reading differently: from the book to the text. We have already encountered this kind of claim in the American work considered above. Its construction, largely through existentialist thought, however, obscures its own thinking of its task, and of its wider relationship to the jurisprudential and philosophical traditions. In the words of Hirvonen[48] the world is now in fragments, but we must acknowledge this as 'a great gift.'[49] If the 'grand' narratives are dead, how can critical thought continue?

Two strategies can be seen as running through the postmodern position. A return to history and a demand for a revived ethics. The historical turn places emphasis on the history of English law but not as the parochial study of an 'insular jurisdiction.' It is a profoundly European philosophy that allows the examination of the condition of England. If anything the turn to English history is also a turn to the world. The demand for ethics rises from the melancholy observation that justice has miscarried in the common law. But this cannot be the ethics of neo-Kantian philosophies of right or of utilitarian policy-makers. The exhaustion of the moral resources of modernity, acutely witnessed in law, creates the most pressing intellectual and political obligation: to imagine a new type of natural law for which justice is both a part and always still to come. Uniting both the historical and the ethical approaches is an orientation towards the close reading of legal texts and legal history. This reading traces the omissions, repressions and distortions, the signs of power and the symptoms of the traumas created by the institution. Working between the texts themselves, and the effects of these texts in the 'real world', critical theory explores the textual and institutional organisation of the law.

Arguably, the anxieties of Brit Crit towards its constitution were approached through a return to history; or, rather an attempt to reclaim history from a critical perspective. In this sense, postmodernism is ironically marked by a return to the past as a way of creating a place for itself. For Peter Goodrich, the present may be determined by the past, but present structures, institutions and ideologies cannot claim any greater legitimacy from this fact. Of central importance are the excluded, whose trace remains in the archives and the records and can be picked up today. To understand possibilities that were not realised, potentialities that did not become actual, one has to return.

Goodrich's reading of Abraham Fraunce, a scholar of the late fifteenth century, conjures up the possibility of returning to an approach rejected from the syllabus of the Inns of Court. Its institutional location makes it a critical

[48] A Hirvonen, 'After the Law' in A Hirvonen (ed), *Polycentricity* (London, Pluto Press, 1998).
[49] *Ibid*, 193.

resource within the common law. Fraunce's radical Aristotelianism sought to return the law to its 'customary roots' in the face of a forgetting by lawyers who had severed its connection with any sense of its history, of law's time and place. This localism was not an isolated nationalism, but an attempt to re-situate the common law within the 'common law of Europe', a call for the study of both English writers and those major European figures such as Ramus, Hotman, Cujas and Bude.

Fraunce's rediscovery can be linked to another aspect of the common law. Goodrich revels in the double meaning of the 'post': in chronological terms, it announces the sense of the end time, of being 'late' in relation to modernism. But the 'post' also carries the sense of the delivery of messages, of sending and receiving epistles and texts. These two meanings come together when one considers the postal rule in contract law: an offer is binding once it has entered the post. Although a product of classical nineteenth century contract doctrine, the rule offers a paradigmatic instance of law's operation. Law's subjects are bound by texts that they haven't read. More generally, the institution pre-exists the subject, who can only enter into the discourses that it allows by accepting its priority.[50] The individual is always late when it comes to the law. Taking the place of any direct communication between parties, the postal rule suggest that the law is the necessary intermediary. Its language is the 'relay' that allows messages to circulate and be understood.

If we can only speak because the law allows us to do so, does this not suggest the triumph of tradition over any possibility of critique? This would be a misreading of the possibilities that history offers. We can imagine the tradition as a river in which the debris of the past are borne along by different currents; or we can think of the past as a conversation in which many voices are drowned out. But the sensitive ear can choose to listen to different tones, murmurings and whisperings. This is how the central insight that wo/man's being is historical should be understood:

> Whether logocentric or Christocentric, historiography remains an act of fiction, of imaginative and rhetorical creation. That does not make history unreal. But it undermines the effort to transfer truth and meaning from the text or the author to the authority of history and the tradition.[51]

History as the predetermined working out of a pattern, or as something to which we have access through a central narrative, must be rejected. We are forced to create our own histories out of the materials that become available, always with an eye and an ear to the fact that what appears to be the dominant or licensed view is only so because other voices have been erased; but nothing is completely forgotten. Only from this perspective can our historical sense be

[50] Goodrich, above n 41, 150.

[51] C Douzinas, R Warrington and S McVeigh, *Postmodern Jurisprudence* (London, Routledge, 1993) 46.

actively engaged. We are always grappling with a dilemma, with a specific task that appears historically located. But we cannot rely on the principles, the values, the essences that characterise historicism and reduce the different to the same. Otherwise, we risk remaining within the interpretations authorised by the tradition and resolving every conflict according to the terms that authority allows. The encounter with the strange should be preserved. The forgotten and the repressed are the sources of authentic thought, and the unhomeliness of home.

These currents of scholarship are marked by the tensions that we have been describing above. As has been pointed out, the question of the possibility of a Critical Legal Studies is a question of the institutions in which it takes place, the lines of filiation and alliance between scholars. Brit Crit raises the question of the possibility of authentic thought and action, of the moment when the tradition is defied in the name of the present—in the name of the personal. There is a risk that this thematic could turn into a restricted mode of examination; there is always the problem that the search for what is personally authentic has the effect of denying other equally compelling values—particularly those of community and belonging—and of becoming solipsistic. In their different ways, these modes of scholarship open up the question of the legal tradition itself. To what extent can it be read as offering alternative resources, as inviting its own re-invention?

This latest manifestation of Brit Crit repeats the critical question: how can the law be opened to those currents of thought that it resists; or, how can the law be made different from its present forms? At the same time, there is the sense of the difficulty of making the different tendencies of thought cohere, of finding any sense of a meaningful shared identity. However, perhaps it is not a question of leaving behind the anguish of thought; if anything, it is about intensifying it still further. One can hope to understand the nature of the tradition—of transmission and reception—and move towards a more informed sense of what this can offer.

OZ CRIT OR *MABO* AND THE ANXIETY OF INFLUENCE

Australian Critical Legal Studies—or Oz Crit—can be seen as perhaps the latest manifestation of the spirit of Critical Legal Studies. As a way of understanding what is at stake in Oz Crit, it is worth elaborating one of the themes that has flowed through this chapter. The concern with the anxiety of influence is, in part, a mark of the problem of translation. Thus, with Oz Crit, we return to one of the founding scenes of postmodern CLS: the borrowings of continental thought by Anglo–American jurisprudence.[52] But, as we look at the work of the

[52] See also P Minkkinen, *Thinking Without Desire*, above n 40 *supra* on the situation of the Finnish critic.

Oz Crits, we will see what it means to be reading such texts at the end of the European tradition at such a meridian, with such an intense, desert light.

The impulse of CLS is to start again; its dilemma, as we have seen, is just how to make this new beginning. Of course, this is to separate itself from what has gone before, and to argue that the interruption in the tradition demands a new problematic:

> If you start with the assumption that the central case of law looks like British law seen through the eyes of the reasonable man, it is hardly surprising that the theoretical reduction of the central case reflects the characteristics of British law from this perspective, and not of Aboriginal law, or Islamic law, or the law of the Hopi Indians.[53]

We might suggest, then, that Oz Crit endeavours to create a jurisprudence fit for the peculiarities of its own history. Or, rather, to re-orientate jurisprudence around the critical question: what do these texts of the law mean for us now? In part, this means turning away from the white, Anglo-American tradition. The line that divides Oz Crit from both the critical and mainstream traditions is thus a question of its own being and location; how can an authentic Australian voice create itself. Oz Crit thus presents itself as an engagement with the law in Australia; an understanding inseparable from the nation's colonial and post-colonial position. The reference to Aboriginal law in the quotation above is telling. Perhaps the key issue around which Oz Crit composes and decomposes itself is this very question of the rights of the Aborigines; but this must be understood in the broadest of senses as a question of origin and identity.

If one accepts this as the problematic of Australian CLS, one can immediately sense its identity and difference within the critical traditions that we have been examining. When Manderson writes that '[l]aw is a cultural medium of expressive form',[54] he is articulating one of the fundamental insights of Oz Crit: law has to be understood as profoundly rooted in a time and a space; defined in a sharp light—like that described in the outback poems of Les Murray. Whereas American CLS never particularly engaged with the problematic of race, Oz Crit is founded on this very issue. Whereas Brit Crit introduced a turn towards history and interpretation, Oz Crit concretised it through an application to the problem of a young nation. Oz Crit thus repeats the central gesture of CLS, but differently. It demands that we start again.

How to think history, how to think the invention of a nation? The various myths of Australian nationhood tend to stress—in different ways—the escape from old Europe to a land of freedom, equality and personal liberty. Undercutting these myths is the sense that the land was stolen from the original inhabitants of the continent. We cannot go into these themes in any great detail, but we can see how they play into one of the most important decisions of an Australian court in recent times: the landmark ruling on Aboriginal land rights,

[53] M Davies, *Delimiting the Law* (Pluto, London, 1996) 27.
[54] D Manderson, *Songs Without Words* (Berkeley, University of California Press, 2000) 201.

Mabo v State of Queensland No 2.[55] It is worth considering the outlines of this case (it might even offer a paradigm of Australian history).

Before the arrival of the Europeans, the lands in question in Mabo (three islands constituting the Murray Islands: Mer, Dauar and Waier) were already occupied by the Meriam people. In 1879, they were annexed to the colony of Queensland, although a few years later, the islands were reserved by proclamation for the 'native inhabitants'; and some years later still—in 1912—the islands were permanently reserved, being placed in trust in 1939. The action against Queensland was for a declaration that the Meriam people had good title to the land, and that they had never been 'Crown lands'. On the screen of *Mabo*, the history of Australia plays itself out. The case reveals the conflict between the coming of modern European law and the laws of the aboriginal peoples, between the pre-modern and the modern, between conflicting versions of the common law. Ultimately, it is about a nation's very constitution.

Mabo can be read as a legal exemplification of the anxiety of influence. If the court itself exhibits an anxiety in defining the Australian essence of Australian law, critical commentators on the case have suffered from a critical anxiety: what way of writing or thinking can provide sufficient purchase on the anxiety that animates the spirits stirred by *Mabo*? We should begin by looking at the reasoning in the case itself.

One of the central themes in *Mabo* was a question of the authority of the court. This is bound up with the concept of Australian law and its relationship to the indigenous laws and customs it supplanted. The court had to affirm its own authority to develop the law of Australia and to deal with the problem of native title from the perspective of a nation that considers itself to be a modern democracy. At the same time, the court is a product of its history. It cannot simply depart from the common law if its jurisprudence is out of step with contemporary political reality: 'Australian law is not only the historical successor of, but is an organic development from, the law of England. Although our law is the prisoner of its history, it is not now bound by decisions of courts in the hierarchy of an Empire then concerned with the development of its colonies.'[56]

Australian law is both enabled by the English common law tradition and more than English common law. Thus, it can develop 'independently' of the authorities of the English courts, and it is 'free' of the control of the 'Imperial' Centre. As critics have pointed out, this legal fantasy is part of a broader fantasy of the Australian nation as being the same, but different, from its European roots. At an interpretative level, this fantasy determines the way in which the court will resolve its own anxiety of influence. Legal principles can be updated, but not to the extent that they 'fracture' the 'skeleton of principles.'

The argument focuses on the principle of '*terra nullius*'. As a principle of the common law, recognised by 'the European family of nations', *terra nullius*

[55] (1992) 175 CLR 1.

[56] S Dorshett and S McVeigh, 'Just So: The Law which Governs Australia is Australian Law' (2002) 13 *Law and Critique* 288, 289.

founded the sovereignty of the Crown over uninhabited territories. In other words, *terra nullius* has the pedigree of recognition from other European legal traditions. *Terra nullius* is perhaps the reason why critical thinking is based on the profound need to start again, to keep re-opening the past. For *terra nullius* expresses the law's immanent power to take over and order a place seen as 'desert uninhabited' country.

As a legal fiction the doctrine was not particularly disturbed by the fact that territory was, in reality, occupied. The use of the fiction was based on the presumption that as it was unoccupied, the law of England became that of the newly inhabited territory. Indeed, as a settled colony, Australia itself is based on this wiping clean of what went before, the radical imposition of the common law. If the Australians are a people defined by the common law, it would appear that the court in *Mabo* has pulled off an incredible coup. The common law tradition has been appropriated, and, to some extent, re-defined. If one wants to see *Mabo* as a 'triumph of the common law'[57] then perhaps its greatest success is this fragile resolution of the anxiety of influence by the successful identification of a people with a law: the common law is thus no longer merely 'English'—it is re-imagined as authentically Australian; an historical inheritance, admittedly, but one that must be radically re-shaped to successfully resolve Australian problems.

The critical task in the face of this judgement is to create a politics of memory. Clearly, the imposition of the law rests on the claim that those living in the territory were without law. Moreover, as far as the common law was concerned, this same doctrine brought the indigenous peoples into being. Critical work, then, demands a return to history, to a questioning of the inheritance. As Dorshett and McVeigh write, 'The settlement of Australia has been conducted . . . as the transmission of an inheritance: an affiliation and an attachment to the order of law and of people and places.'[58] In *Mabo*, the people who are to be one under the law are included into a common law history, are given an 'origin' synonymous with the arrival of the common law.[59]

Once again, the critic must urge that this beginning must be disturbed. Thus, for Fitzpatrick, it is necessary to be sceptical of both the common law's claim to an origin in time immemorial, and to any constructions of history that place Australia safely and unproblematically into the fold of a common law that can

[57] R Bartlett, '*Mabo*: Another Triumph for the Common Law' (1993) 15 *Sydney Law Review* 178.

[58] S Dorshett and S McVeigh, 'Just So: "The Law which Governs Australia is Australian Law"', above n 56.

[59] One of the key themes that emerges from the case is the issue of justiciability. Whether or not territory had been acquired was not justiciable; however, the courts do have the jurisdiction to determine 'the consequences of acquisition under municipal law.' The court's conclusions were somewhat double handed. Native title was affirmed, even though it did not fit within the categories of possession at common law. Indeed, the precise terms on which native land was to be held could only be resolved by reference to the laws and customs of indigenous peoples. However, the final conclusion, that the Meriam people could claim good title to the land, was qualified. Such native title was subject to the power of the Parliament of Queensland. Moreover, the courts did not have the jurisdiction to challenge the issue of the Crown's acquisition of territory.

adapt to history and a foreign clime. After all, this grounds the claim that the common law is able to resolve the issue of native title by 'draw . . . [ing] into itself'[60] those social relations that it can order, determine and articulate in the best possible way. Behind this claim, is a far more difficult and subtle operation. *Mabo* effectively denies the reality of the indigenous claim, at the same time as acknowledging it. This decision thus reveals an insight into the law as such. We 'are all native now'[61] to the extent that we are subjects of legal interpellation.

For the critic, then, it is necessary to approach the construction of Australia that is linked to *Mabo*. In part, this critical move is based on an acknowledgement of Aboriginal rights; or more precisely, a troubled thinking of how the past and the present can be reconciled. Perhaps it is already too late. For some, Australia appears as no more than a source of despair; its inability to sustain a culture of critique within its Universities, a symbol of its descent into the mundane and the barbarous.[62] The difficulty is the creation of a way of thinking, an analytical language, equal to the challenges posed by Australian politics. Some scholars have turned back to their Aboriginal heritage, and dream of a once and future law that is not that of European sovereignty; a form of law that connects with memory, and a belonging to the land.[63] Others have looked to the insights of the continental tradition, carrying the texts of old Europe to the new continent. For Motha, the issue must be thought of as a problem of ontology, of the being of community. Offering Aboriginal rights cannot be seen as a 'palliative' to the 'exclusions'[64] that founded the colonial nation. This would replace one sovereignty with another. The problem cannot be addressed until a new ontology of singularity opens the sovereign univocity: 'I am a singular being among a multiplicity of other singular beings.'[65] It may be that it is necessary to oppose sovereignty to achieve any viable sense of pluralistic community.[66]

[60] P Fitzpatrick, 'No Higher Duty: *Mabo* and the Failure of Legal Foundation' (2002) 13 *Law and Critique* 239.

[61] *Ibid*, 252.

[62] I Duncanson, 'Writing and Praxis: Law, History and the Postcolonial' (2002) 7 *Law Text and Culture* 1.

[63] For instance, see I Watson, 'Buried Alive' (2002) 13 *Law and Critique* 253.

[64] S Motha, 'The Sovereign Event in a Nation's Law' (2002) 13 *Law and Critique* 232 at 236.

[65] *Ibid*, 236.

[66] Given the urgent need to work through the construction of the nation, it is not surprising that Oz Crit has turned to psychoanalysis. Again, there is a double imperative: to engage with cosmopolitan theory, and to show its application to a specific reality. It is to these ends that scholars such as MacNeil, Duncanson and Gribich (to name only three) have engaged in different ways with the theory of the phantasm. What runs through these different bodies of work, is the concern with Freud's description of the child's *fort/da* game in *Beyond the Pleasure Principle*. It is as if this metaphor describes, at conscious and unconscious levels, the position of the white Australian subject. Cast out from Europe, and troubled by what a 'return' could mean; destined to play out a game of escape and return around the trauma that was the foundation of a settlor society. But, it is not just the constitution of their own subject positions that attracts these scholars to psychoanalysis. Duncanson has used Lacanian theory to investigate the constructions of identities in the discourses around refugees and the Australian 'homeland'. The discourse of the 'ordinary Australian' stresses a certain set of values that link together heterosexuality, the family, work and the defence of the nation's border against refuges, asylum seekers and other 'interlopers' ('Telling the Refugee Story' (2003) 14 *Law and Critique* 29, at 39). Running through these values is the idea of a nation

A somewhat different emphasis can be found in the work of Kerruish.[67] Addressing the ten year process, announced in 1991, and intended to engage with the structural disadvantages suffered by Aboriginals in Australian society, Kerruish writes that 'reconciliation as a policy . . . [is] something which cannot be embraced and cannot be spoken against.'[68] The endeavour is to use a dialectical thinking that can create a form of political metaphysics able to address contemporary political realities from a philosophical position; or, rather, an uneasy, anxious questioning mode of enquiry that is aware of its own problematic constitution. Reconciliation in these terms may ultimately be phrased in the terms of Hegel's phenomenology; it has to be thought from the position of the subject's *dasein* or historical location; a subject whose thought is rooted in a finitude.

However, this must connect with another theme, another rupture. Any thinking of an institution is finite and articulated in its own terms. Thus, any claim to Aboriginal title or law has to be made through the medium of the common law of the colonist. It appears unlikely, especially in the wake of the *Mabo* decision and the law's retreat from a notion of native title, that the ongoing violence of the original imposition of settler's law can move towards reconciliation. Tentatively, Kerruish suggests that: 'reconciliation is conceivable as a form of sublation. That is, as the thinking through of a contradiction; indeed of a particular *hard* contradiction, such as those between finite and infinite, or necessity and freedom.'[69] This hesitancy is necessary. It is the index of a reading that uncomfortably locates itself in legal theory but reaches towards a broader theory of the political world where terms like rights and property must be located, and their constructions contested.

that can provide belonging; and the law figures as one of the main supports of this fantasy of wholeness and purity. In psychoanalytic terms, fantasy provides the very source of identity. To build the description, the law figures as one important way to structure fantasy. The key question for the institution of the law is how to make itself constitute a symbolic order that will sustain the subject. It is necessary that the symbolic order be organised and articulated in such a way that the subject can find itself reflected in social institutions and thus gain a viable sense of social being. But, this is not just a question of the constitution of a nation. For MacNeil, the broader discourse of rights can be understood from the perspective of a legal fantasy. As with other scholars', though, there is a feel for the corporeality of those subjects that are destined to be subjects of law and rights. It is the body itself that is essential to the hold of the law: indeed, rights can be thought of as an elaboration of the zones of the body: 'metonymised eyes, ears and mouth reappear, in metamorphosed form, as the right to freedom of speech, belief and thought; hands and feet, as the right to freedom of movement': 'Law's Corpus Delioti: The Fantasmatic Body of Rights Discourse' (1998) *Law and Critique*, 48.

[67] V Kerruish, *Jurisprudence as Ideology* (London, Routledge, 1994).

[68] V Kerruish, 'Reconciliation, Property and Rights' in E Christodoulidis and S Veitch (eds), *Lethe's Law* (Oxford, Hart, 2001) 191 at 194.

[69] *Ibid*, 199.

THE WORLD MADE NEW: SOUTH AFRICAN CRITICAL LEGAL STUDIES

Critical Legal Studies continues to re-invent itself. Although the anxiety of influence is a theme in Critical Legal Studies, it would unbalance our account of this impossible movement if we let this chapter conclude with an image of the past determining the present. The importance of South African Critical Legal Studies is that it affirms the creative, poetic urge that was always the greatest strength of critical thought. In these most difficult times, South African scholars have accepted the challenge of creating a thinking equal to the problems that we face. It could thus be suggested, that South African CLS takes as its theme the im/possibility of the new South Africa, as a nation defined by law.

So, how can we reclaim the present? This question is, as for all critical scholars, an issue of both an intellectual genealogy, and a practical orientation towards the tasks of thought. The great distinction between South African work and American, European and Australian scholarship is the immediacy of the South African situation. For all the injustices and violence of law in its European or American setting, scholars from these jurisdictions have not had to deal with an apartheid order that was so systematic and all pervasive or a war of liberation. This is not to suggest, however, that the work of American and European writers has not been important to the framing of South African critical problematics. The present is a holding to account of a legacy of European thought in the light of a political situation.

The Truth and Reconciliation Commission can be seen as providing South African CLS with its definitional focus. Law is called to perform a difficult task: to mark the transformation from apartheid to democracy. The Commission is a prism that diverts and focuses the critical gaze. In looking at South African scholarship, we will try and show how the urge to begin again, to re-define the critical endeavour, engages with the dilemmas of the Commission and the broader process of truth and reconciliation that involves law in the remaking of a political community.[70]

Van Marle's work carries the imprimatur of South African critical scholarship.[71] Her use of literary and artistic texts and works as a source of jurisprudence attest, in part, to a sense of the exhaustion of what passed as apartheid legal philosophy. In place of conventional legal philosophy, is a regard to a particular kind of literary production. This is not just that of South Africans, for the European novel, and in particular Milan Kundera, provide Van Marle with the focus of her work: a question of time; the time of judgement, and the need, in political terms, to address the new times; to be up to the challenges that they

[70] The links between these different expressions of Critical Legal Studies can be seen in the relevance of the work of Emilios Christodoulidis to South African Scholarship. See 'Law's Immemorial' in E Christodoulidis and S Veitch (eds), *Lethe's Law* (Oxford, Hart, 2001).

[71] K Van Marle, 'Law's Time, Particularity and Slowness' (2003) 19 *South African Journal of Human Rights* 239.

present. Kundera's narrator draws attention to a certain 'slowness'; the ecstatic slowness of the speeding driver, who is focused upon the moment, effectively cut off from the past and the future in this intense concentration on the task in hand. How can this slowness be understood as an approach to the political question of law's place or law's regard? The critic shares the experience of the speeding driver; the challenge is how to create a jurisprudence of slowness within wild, historical movement. In this sense, Van Marle's work is rooted in recent history, but attempts to determine a view, a moment from which events make sense. Unlike Stephen Dedalus, history is not the nightmare from which we must awake, but the process which we must slow down and understand.

Law's speed is seen in these temporal terms. Law must force a conclusion; it must resolve a particular conflict through the imposition of general rules. Indeed, law must always be ready to move on to the next case, to create and sustain its 'seamless web', its knitting together of the social world. In this sense, the particular moment is always to be subsumed in the general. It is impossible to escape these features of legal judgement; there is a necessary violence to law. Moreover, there was a need for resolution in the Truth and Reconciliation process; a need to bring to account the violence that apartheid had occasioned. Slowness urges a reconsideration, a holding together of events or opinions that will not be, or should not be resolved by a decision, or perhaps even a Commission, no matter how well intentioned. Law's present is always that of the need to establish, to distinguish, to create sure foundations. The present can only be redeemed by affirming a time that is not one of resolution; rather, a holding open of many versions of events, of differently inflected truths. These truths are present in a collective memory. Since the past is irretrievable, collective memory is a retrospective imagination of what the past was. It can be imagined as a plurality of voices, a community of differences. Van Marle hears these voices in the depositions made to the Commission:

> She is sitting behind a microphone, dressed in her beret or kopdoek and her Sundaybest. Everybody recognises her. Truth has become Woman. Her voice distorted behind her rough hand, her undermined Man as the source of truth. *And yet nobody knows her.*[72]

She, the truth, sits behind the microphone: she addresses us from a long way off. A great deal could be said about the conjunction between the voice, truth and memory, but we will take as our essential problematic that of Van Marle's: how is it possible to talk about TRC now, from our present? This is a generational question. It clearly raises issues somewhat different from the need to respond to the TRC in the moments of its operation. Any discourse about the TRC is problematic, as it can never respond to the pain of those who spoke before the Commission. Van Marle's work prompts us to see that the essential question is how it is possible to talk about the TRC, how a notion of 'public

[72] A Krog, *Country of My Skull* (London, Jonathan Cape, 1999) cited in Van Marle.

discourse' or 'public life'[73] can configure itself; how an approach to the law might become possible:

> If a court procedure, for example, follows the suggested approach of slowness, of accepting the possibility of multiple truths, the disruption of chronological time and the idea of justice as the limit of the law and institutionalised legal procedures, then the justification that is provided, the reasons given for a decision might be richer, more reflexive and more reflective of the open and democratic society that we strive for . . .

This conclusion points at the need for an ethics of law. Its register brings together a notion of deconstruction, 'the idea of justice as the limit of law', the necessity for a recognition of plural truths and a call for a different practice of judicial reasoning. Recent judgements of the South African courts give the impression that the judiciary have orientated themselves to a new democratic polity. In keeping with the spirit of this work, though, it is not a question of seeking closure, but an intensification of the problematic itself. In turning to Van der Walt, it is possible to see this intensification, this struggle with the difficult questions.

Johan Van der Walt's work provides a thinking of the new beginning. The thinker is a poet, a maker; putting materials together materials like a *bricoleur*; a new composition; the world anew. This returns, in part, to Kennedy's indeterminacy thesis, but it is only one of its reference points. The poetic, or even the philosophical poetical—is a need to posit the general account, to provide foundations, but is not outside of the processes it observes; rather it stands in 'reciprocal' relationship to it.[74] It is no more prior to the law or to politics than these terms are independent of the philosophical. This reciprocal constitution of these different discourses attests to our own situation or 'state', which, in a certain philosophical vocabulary is the way in which our intellectual engagement with the moment is in part determined by an inheritance; a set of concepts and ways of thinking. Rather than separate out any of these strands of thinking, or 'moments', we perhaps need to appreciate their historical location; a history that is not necessarily one of a working through of a spirit or a determining logic, but an arrival at a particular conjugation that is enabled by its past, but cannot be thought of as some ideal embodiment. This demands a new approach. It cannot be understood on the basis of sociology, or a history of South African law and politics; which is not to say that it does not make use of these modes of thought. Perhaps, then, it is ultimately a poetics because it is concerned with a style of thought, a way of recomposing differently so that something new can appear.

What appears? This is the central question of community. We can focus this concern most sharply if we return to the question of style, of a way of saying. Certain discourses have always sought to speak for the community. Law, in this

[73] K Van Marle, 'The Literary Imagination, Recollective Imagination and Justice' (2000) 15 *SAPL* 137.

[74] See P Lacoue-Labarthe and J-L Nancy, *Retreating the Political* (London, Routledge, 1997).

sense, has always been an account of the community under law through its articulation of sovereignty. Of course, law, or jurisprudential reflections on sovereignty, are not the exclusive articulations of community. One could equally find it in modernist sociology, where the consensual or conflictual underpinnings of human community provide an orientation to study. Likewise, political discourse seeks to talk of community in terms of power and authority. Hobbes' Leviathan, rethought in different ways in the liberal tradition; Rousseau's or Mandela's notions of the people; the notion of *ujamaa* in Nyerere, the different African traditions, are all variations on this essential theme. Again, risking generality, and banality, a poetics would follow a certain line or a disturbance within these fields. Once again, this is not to say that poetics opposes either law, politics, or other discourses of the social. It is to suggest that it takes a different inflection, a different way of saying: but it also says something different. Community cannot be thought on the basis of the inclusion into a collectivity that is then spoken for by party, president or spirit. Poetics would seek to delink the movement from community to sovereignty, or, at least to see what gets left out, what is lost, in an easy movement between the two. It would prefer to speak in terms of a sharing, a relationship of specifics that cannot be turned into a generality.

What is at stake here is the mutation of a certain Heideggarian discourse; it is as if Heidegger is being re-thought to privilege the idea of being together (*mitsein*) as the primordial human condition. But there are many difficulties in this approach. Being in the World as a structure is already a given an original and indivisible whole: it 'always comes first.'[75] If one accepts that Heidegger represents only a beginning, then this way of thinking does not have to lead to a grand theory of the unveiling of being; a philosophical discourse that creates itself as an ambitious and exclusive monument to a way of speaking the truth. The task is how to interrupt this discourse without losing its essential and important insight: the notion of our being in a world that makes sense for us. If, as Heidegger tells us, this returns to Being in the World[76] then it must also return to the idea of being together, and to what is shared in community as the form of being in the world. Such an orientation would lead us to the idea of care. Care is always a kind of disposition to the world, to projects in the world. Care, and hence a notion of truth that relates to it, indicates the way in which life is always thrown up ahead of itself, enabling projection. But, might this projection be related to a truth that does not seek an essential revelation, or to a return to a truth of being as that which is unveiled or revealed? Truth might be 'something' that must be shared amongst us, 'something' ongoing.

It is precisely this thematics that Van der Walt's work suggests. Community becomes an 'event'; it does not posit a substance, a new sovereignty, a way of

[75] M Heidegger, *Being and Time*, J Macquarrie and E Robinson (trans), (Oxford, Blackwell, 1962). See part one, division one of the introduction.

[76] *Ibid*, at 261.

gathering together the 'being' of the new South Africa. As an event it is a telling, a sublime marker: to undo three centuries of oppression and violence in two years; to save the law from the filth into which it had fallen.

There are at least two separate but related aspects of this account; they could be described as an idea of non totalisable 'we' and a future directedness. Risking schematism, we shall develop these two themes in such a way as to appreciate their specificity, and their relationship. The 'we' that is to be addressed here is the 'we' of a *nomos*, and hence a law, yet not a 'we' that can be spoken for by the law. Perhaps, then, there is a *nomos* that may coordinate with the law, but is not identical to the law. This difficult relationship can be put in less normative terms by thinking of a certain temporality, which is not necessarily historical time:

> The time or timing of reconciliation can therefore not be thought in terms of presence. Nor can it be thought in terms of a future not yet present, a future that will become present . . . it must be conceived in terms of the non time or negative time between present and future . . . It occurs as the time or timing that holds past present and future in play.[77]

A time of being together, a time of a pure sovereignty that could found the law, is not available. We must understand the Commission's task as one of radical incompletion; a paradoxical openness and irresolution that must nevertheless provide a mark, a foundation, and a boundary between what was, and what can come to be. In words stolen from Jean-Luc Nancy, it is what happens when we risk saying 'we are inaugurating history' instead of simply saying 'this has been history';[78] anticipating the way that we will speak of this problem, we could say that the paradoxical task could be understood in a poetic register: to redeem time from time in time; or rather, in a more political mode; to represent a break in a history.

CODA: AUTHENTICITY, ITERABILITY AND CRITIQUE

CLS began as a profoundly historical way of thinking about the Anglo-American legal tradition. We can reflect on this position, and generalise our reflections into a description of the distinctive qualities of critical legal thought.

Critical thought locates itself within the tradition. But, the tradition cannot become a dead weight of the past. Critical legal thought is perhaps, then, rooted in this opposition of an authenticity, a time of epiphany or *satori* where the pattern can be glimpsed, to time empty of vision; time as the dull repetition of the same.

We can identify, and possibly speak more 'properly' of Critical legal thought as a 'deconstructive moment'. Most precisely, our argument is that Critical legal

[77] J Van der Walt, *Law as Sacrifice* (London, Birkbeck Law Press, 2005).

[78] J-L Nancy, 'Finite History' in *The Birth To Presence* (Stanford, Stanford University Press, 1993) 144.

thought is 'structured' by iterability. Iterability describes a sign or a mark that is both unique, and capable of repetition. We can elaborate this notion of iterability by thinking of law and criticism as modes of iteration; and re-appropriating critical anxiety from this perspective. Let us re-examine the relationship between tradition and authenticity. The two moments are not opposites, but mutually constituting. In the same way that the unique moment is temporal and capable of repetition, history is open to contingency: it is not so much a repetition of the same, as it is a fabric constantly torn and repaired. Indeed, anxiety is the profound realisation of the contingency of history: things do not always turn out the same, nothing can be predicted: history could always be different. American CLS's announcement of its death, rather than being an instance of authentic anxiety, is a seeking of refuge in an event that can be presented as terminal and definitive: an end time that pronounces the final judgement. One needs to affirm iteration: history will always turn out differently; the moment of critique must re-appear and carry on re-appearing. Remaining authentic means sustaining the anxiety of a thought that juggles the relationship of contingency and history. Any announcement of a terminal point betrays the insight of iteration as temporality.

Thinking in this way will allow us to recover the critical energies of a deconstructive critical legal thought that is rooted in the recovery of history as a past that is yet to come. This returns us to history as contingency, as that which is lived, material and structured by surprises. Critical legal thought must be understood as something that could repeat itself. In its most developed sense it is a recovery of the impulse of CLS, and its elaboration in different contexts.

The reader encounters the tradition. In taking up the text, one feels a great weight: the accumulated opinions, texts and commentaries that make up jurisprudence. This is the original moment, where one is either crushed by despair, or takes on the tradition and attempts to redefine it in one's own terms. History arrives at the doorstep of the 'now'. One's own history becomes involved. For critical legal thought, this is a question of a starting point; are you crushed by the past, or, are you strong enough? Can you summon the strength to start anew, anew, anew.

PASSAGES

In New York, I take a taxi down town with Badmeadow to his Apartment. We talked about family; sons and daughters of; absent friends and other filiations. When we got there, Critch Lee had already arrived with a bottle of cooking brandy. We talked into the night: 'perhaps our friends tell us that we owe them nothing. They remind us of the nothing we are, and provoke us to do something about it before we become nothing again.' After they went to bed, I watched the lights of the city; the great cathedral of loneliness. Before I left, I placed a copy of *The Inferno* on Badmeadow's desk: a gift.

10

White Law, Black Power: Racism, Resistance and Critical Jurisprudence

When a judge tries a case he must remember that he is himself on trial (Philo, quoted in the Lawrence Inquiry (6:47)).

IN ITS AMERICAN beginnings, Critical Race Theory (CRT) can be understood as a response to the failures of anti-discrimination law to achieve any real sense of social improvement for the black community. In a more extended sense, CRT provokes a critical thinking that is not limited to a historical time and place, but confronts law's complicity in the violent perpetuation of a racially defined economic and social order. This chapter attempts to negotiate between these two approaches, and to show that CRT is now potentially an international movement. One can indeed move beyond the American context; a specifically British critical race theory has been developing in the last ten years and critical scholarship in other jurisdictions has been engaged with law and race. Most CRT scholars adopt a careful, incremental approach and avoid the pitfalls of universalist or globalising thought. However, the attempt to link American and British scholarship should not be troubling since CRT is characterised by another equally strong element: its orientation[1] to history, and the different ways in which it is lived and experienced.

Critical Race Theory is an expanding and diverse field. It embraces the history of many different peoples in their encounters with western law and now includes work by Latinos/as, as well as Asian Americans.[2] We cannot possibly

[1] Critical Race Theory in the US has always presented itself as a movement, organised around conferences, journals and institutions. Although it is perhaps too soon to speak of a movement in Britain or Europe, the recent interest in the Critical Legal Conference shown by African-American scholars suggests an interesting development. For a consideration of the beginnings of a British critical race theory, see P Goodrich and L Mills, 'The Law of White Spaces: Race, Culture and Legal Education' (2001) 51 *Journal of Legal Education* 15.

[2] The relationship between CRT and recent work on Islamic law and identity is yet to be traced. For elaborations of the problematic of Islamic law, British identity and the war on terror, see Q Mirza, 'Islamic Feminism, Possibilities and Limitations' in J Strawson (ed), *Law after Ground Zero* (Sydney, London and Portland, Glasshouse Press, 2002); see also 'Islamic Feminism and the Exemplary Past' in J Richardson and R Sandland (eds), *Feminist Perspectives in Law and Theory*

cover the diversity of approaches within the limits of this chapter. Instead, we will trace the response of African-American scholars to American law, and attempt to make connections with the experiences of racism in post-war Britain. The focus will be on those citizens who came to Britain from Jamaica, Africa and the Caribbean.

GREAT AMERICAN SATAN: RACISM, LAW AND HISTORY

History is the key to unlocking the intersection of race and law. For instance, when Derrick Bell, one of the foremost American critical scholars, wrote that the 'black people's struggle' is 'as old as this nation', he was stressing the centrality of race and the struggles against racism for any concept of nationhood. Indeed, it would appear that the perpetuation allowed the foundation of American Constitutional government.[3] From the drafting of the constitution in 1787 to the Hayes-Tilden Compromise of 1877, the right to property was repeatedly raised above black freedom. If any lesson can be drawn from these documents, it is that 'blacks seem uniquely burdened with the obligation to repeat history, whether or not they learned its lessons.'[4] From the end of the Civil War until the present, a pattern can be traced which shows that black advances in civic status were effectively crushed by white backlashes. Persistent and deep-rooted racism meant that black rights were always compromised by other economic or social interests. The experience of the 'first reconstruction'—the time from the end of the Civil War to 1877[5]—was repeated in the fate of the civil rights movement. In both cases, formal equality was stated in law, but economic and social dispossession remained.

Perhaps this is precisely the problem with the use of the law as a means of fighting oppression. The litigation engaged in by the National Association for the Advancement of Coloured People (NAACP), can be accused of becoming too fixated with symbolic advances. At root, the problem of discrimination rests on the inequitable distribution of social and economic power. Legal rules only 'reflect and uphold' the ways in which these distributions are preserved.[6] A central insight of CRT is that litigation will not alter racism's ingrained structures. The main hope for the future rests with the struggle: 'We must realise, as our slave forebears did, that the struggle for freedom is, at bottom a manifestation

(London, Cavendish, 2000). John Strawson's work is also important. See 'Revisiting Islamic Law: Marginal Notes from Colonial History' (2003) 12 *Griffith Law Review* 362; also 'Islamic Law and the English Press' in J Strawson (ed), *Law after Ground Zero* (London, Glasshouse Press, 2002) 205–14. On the intersection between common law and Islamic law, see Eve Darian Smith and Peter Fitzpatrick (eds), *Laws of the Postcolonial* (Ann Arbor, University of Michigan Press, 1999), 109–26.

[3] D Bell, *Race, Racism and American Law* (New York, Little, Brown and Company, 1992) 6.

[4] *Ibid*, 7.

[5] K Crenshaw et al (eds), *Critical Race Theory* (New York, New Press, 1995) 939.

[6] *Ibid*, 18.

of our humanity which survives and grows stronger through resistance to oppression.'[7] These claims fed into the scholarship of 'racial realism.' Just as the legal realists had shown that law was not a formal system of rules and principles, racial realism sought to uncover the racism that lay behind claims to neutrality and to reveal the political and ideological substratum of the law.

Bell has shown how critical race theory builds on these insights. Consider the Supreme Court case of *University of California Regents v Bakke*.[8] The court had to decide on the legality of an affirmative action programme that would allow black candidates to enter the University of California's medical school. Employing a very narrow definition of equality that ignored the social and economic causes of disadvantage, the court held that no white students could be refused entrance in preference to black candidates: 'Bakke serves as an example of how formalists can use abstract concepts, such as equality, to mask choices and value judgements.'[9]

So, can the law ever understand racial discrimination? If we accept the definition of discrimination as 'positional', it is extremely difficult. Positional discrimination describes the existence of structured disadvantages in education, work, access to justice, housing and health care, and the associated 'withering' of one's self-image that accompanies such marginalisation and exploitation. The law tends to be blind to such a reality. Litigating on a civil liberties issue, for example, the desegregation of schools, tends to re-create this problem. It atomises and individualises discrimination into a series of disputes, and avoids the more structured sense in which discrimination results from an inter-relation of disadvantage. Notions of causation and fault may be central to law's conception of discrimination, but their effect is to remove any sense of collective responsibility for acts of discrimination. Would it be possible for the law to move to an appreciation of the 'positional' nature of discrimination? Such a shift would challenge not only the legal construction of responsibility as individual fault, but would also risk antagonising a majority who are reluctant or unwilling to perceive their own complicity in discrimination. Given this problematic reality, anti-discrimination law has attempted to find ways of breaking out of its 'formal'[10] restraints, whilst trying to display an adherence to the form of the law.

The development of anti-discrimination law is itself marked by the triumphs and reverses of legal strategies to combat racism. The history of anti-discrimination law can be divided three broad phases. Central to the first is *Brown v Board of Education*.[11] Current understandings of civil liberties law read this case as both a major victory of early litigation, and a problematic high water mark. Although the Supreme Court ordered an end to segregation in state

[7] *Ibid.*
[8] *University of California Regents* v *Bakke* 438 US 265 (1978).
[9] K Crenshaw et al (eds), *Critical Race Theory*, above n 5, 304.
[10] *Ibid*, 30.
[11] *Brown v Board of Education* 349 US 294 (1955).

schools, the impact of the decision is questionable. *Brown* was met with resistance from school boards, and a *de facto* re-segregation by wealthy white families who moved away from desegregated schools. All the evidence points to the fact that the case did not effectively end black disadvantage in education.

The second phase also saw some successful litigation. One of the landmark cases was *Griggs v Duke Power Co*,[12] a Supreme Court decision under the Civil Rights Act of 1964. The defendant had applied a condition to his employees under which a candidate for promotion should have a high school education. Although this requirement was not directly discriminatory, it had a disproportionate effect on black employees, who were not able to comply with the condition. In holding that this was not acceptable, the court effectively pressured employers into adopting affirmative action programmes. Similar substantive advances were made in the area of education.

But these advances were reversed in the period after 1974. This retreat was seen as a direct result of the success of the earlier phase of anti-discrimination law. The official line was that the problem had now been solved, and vigorous affirmative action was not required; indeed any further measures would violate the equality provision of the Fourteenth Amendment of the Constitution (under which the early affirmative action cases had been decided). *Washington v Davis*[13] can be seen as the stalling of anti-discrimination litigation. Like *Griggs*, it concerned a work related test, this time in a police training programme. The failure rate of black candidates was 25% higher than that of whites. The court held that unless it could be directly evidenced, or shown clearly by inference, that the test was intended to produce results that tended to disadvantage a certain racial group, the rate of failure was not in itself sufficient to establish a case.[14] In the field of school desegregation, the court began to favour local autonomy and to limit affirmative action programmes. It was argued that local autonomy was more suitable for the protection of 'racial homogeneity.' If we reflect on this history of litigation, it would appear that the assumptions of the 'racial realists' are borne out. American law seems unable to move beyond its fundamental tensions. Scholars have sought answers to this impasse in the very constitution of race consciousness in America.

RACISM AND IDEOLOGY

A central difficulty in critical race theory is the meaning of the word race itself. Indeed, perhaps the word should appear under erasure to suggest that it is necessary, problematic and contested. We can receive an understanding of these problems if we approach the changing sense of the term in the Anglo-American

[12] *Griggs v Duke Power* 401 US 424 (1971).
[13] *Washington v Davis* 426 US 229 (1976).
[14] K Crenshaw et al (eds), *Critical Race Theory*, above n 5, 44.

post-war scholarship.[15] It is clear that the terms 'race' and 'racism' have been redefined over time. Any global definition cannot do justice to the sense in which these terms are overdetermined by their particular history.

It is important to note that American CRT writings show a preference for a notion of race as ideology. This is not a rejection of the lived reality of race, but a more subtle account of the interactions between lived reality and a politics of representation.[16] The ideology of 'race consciousness'[17] is bound up with black subordination and the perpetuation of 'the white hierarchy.' The frequent failure of anti-discrimination law to achieve substantive change could thus be attributed to the 'white' perception that 'they' would thus lose out to black interests. Race in other words, unites whites across boundaries of class or gender.[18] Ideology, in this sense, operates to create a 'hegemony' of interests. For

[15] See R Miles, *Racism* (London, Routledge, 1989) 41–53, 66–8. The modern history of the terms race and racism can be traced to the revulsion towards the Nazi Holocaust. Miles shows how the modern problematic of race began with Magnus Hirschfeld's 1938 book translated into English as *Racism* that, without defining the term, associated it with nineteenth century ideas about the dominance of one race over another and offered a refutation of this thesis. Four UNESCO reports, published between 1950 and 1967, discredited the scientific arguments that race determined human aptitudes, as well as offering a definition of racism as 'antisocial beliefs and acts that are based on the fallacy that discriminatory inter-group relations are justifiable on biological grounds.' A set of arguments can also be traced through the post war scholarship (Miles, 351). J Huxley and AC Haddon, *We Europeans: A Survey of Racial Problems* (London, Jonathan Cape, 1935) was a critique of the notion of race as a scientific category, but still maintained that it was possible to construct categories which distinguished 'ethnic groups rather than races.' J Barzun, *Race, A study of A Modern Superstition* (London, Methuen, 1938)came to similar conclusions. Barzun used the term 'racialism' rather than racism to describe a kind of pseudo scientific thinking about race. R Benedict's *Race and Racism* (London, Routledge, 1942) preferred a definition of race as 'hereditary' and affirmed the possibility of the scientific study of race, and a tripartite distinction of races: Caucasian, Mongoloid and Negroid (Miles, 347). For Benedict, racism was the erroneous privileging of one race above another. Racism was defined differently in A Montague's *Mans' Most Dangerous Myth: The Fallacy of Race* (New York, Columbia University Press, 1942) as an 'ideology' rather than a scientific category. However, a key text in the African–American struggle, K Ture and CV Hamilton, *Black Power and the Politics of Liberation* (New York, Vintage Books, 1992) showed the importance of a different perspective on the question of race. It became necessary to appropriate an idea of race as a means for 'Black people [to] redefine themselves' (236), to determine a workable idea of community, of black institutions and a proper representation of black interests in the face of white America. Race, then, is redefined by a notion of black power: 'Racism is not merely exclusion on the basis of race but exclusion for the purpose of subjugating or maintaining subjugation' (239).

[16] There seems to be very little reference, for instance, in the work of CRT scholars to the texts of the Marxist sociologist OC Cox. Although Cox plays down the role of race in *Caste, Class and Race* (New York, Monthly Review Press, 1970), his work could perhaps be re-appropriated as a broader ideological theory that traces the complex relationship of race to other economic and political factors. For instance, at least in a British context, Robert Miles' *Racism After Race Relations* (London, Routledge, 1993) suggests that Cox's work could be part of a broader articulation of Marxism and deconstruction (Miles, 35). Racism needs to be studied from the perspective of 'the political economy of labour migration' (Miles, 35).

[17] K Crenshaw et al (eds), *Critical Race Theory*, above n 5, 112.

[18] Critical Race Theory develops a theory of law that is intrinsically linked to the ideology of race. In developing this approach, it was necessary to re-think some of the earlier work on the subject done by CLS scholars, as race was simply not a central category. The work of Gabel and Kennedy takes as its starting point the notion that law is an ideological distortion of the world. Ideas/practices of law have to be examined to see how they interface with wider social, economic

example, it is interesting that the trade unions, which were primarily composed of immigrant white workers, excluded black workers as a means of displaying their compatibility with the mainstream of American society.[19] The removal of the more obvious aspects of discrimination does not mean that this hegemony has been broken and that discrimination will disappear. For instance, civil liberties advances are effectively qualified by the common perception that black failure to adapt to the supposed 'norms' of hard work and discipline has to be 'made up' by positive discrimination programmes and affirmative action. Further demands for 'special treatment' show the continued failure of the black community to match up to social standards, and also reveals the partisan and one-sided nature of anti-discrimination law.

Understanding this failure of anti-discrimination law means wrestling with the legacy of the civil rights movement. In the ideology of the civil rights movement, racism is seen as a product of prejudice,[20] an inability to perceive a common humanity because of the distortions of stereotypes and ignorance. Discrimination can be countered, and the false distortions of race overcome, when people are seen for what they are, 'individuals free from racial group identifications.' This end can be achieved through the judicial and legislative deployment of neutral principles of equality. Of course, there are variations and different emphases within integrationist approaches, but, in its most 'extreme' form, race disappears completely in the truly integrated society. Culturally, this ideology has had immense impact. It allowed advances to be made because it won the support of white liberals. All appeals to common humanity have great force, as the human rights movement has realised.

However, there are problems with this account. For a start, there is a difficulty with the linearity of the 'we shall overcome narrative'—the epic tale that starts with slavery and ends with the proper integration of the Negro into American society. Linked to this narrative is a peculiar ideology: an 'evolutionary' narrative of almost inevitable progress. The centrality of the integrationist approach has led to the marginalisation and misrepresentation of a different tradition linked to the names of Malcolm X, the Black Panthers and to militancy. This alternative position can be referred to as the 'black nationalist critique.' In its most crude form, it insists that black people will never be accepted, and that secession, separatism and resistance are preferable to integration. The militant demand for a separate black homeland should be understood as a 'symbol . . . that race consciousness constitutes African–Americans as a distinct social community in much the same way that national self identity operates to establish the

and political concerns. The basic CLS understanding was that legal reform could never transform a social order, because the law is already implicated in the power structures that the reformers are attempting to change. In the face of this challenge, CLS scholarship made use of a technique called 'trashing' (110) that was meant to reveal the problems that lay under the surface of the law, and could be shown to compromise its claims to universality and objectivity.

[19] K Crenshaw et al (eds), *Critical Race Theory*, above n 5, 114.

[20] *Ibid*, 129.

terms of recognition and identity in a 'regular' nation.'[21] As Bell puts it: 'America . . . is a white country which means that flourishing black institutions of any kind are unnatural, suspect and not to be encouraged.'[22] These approaches see identity as dynamic and inter-subjective, created differently in different social groups. Such approaches are the forerunners of contemporary concerns with difference and with perspectives that resist the dominant versions of universality.[23]

Contemporary critical race theory in the United States is not necessarily politically militant, but it is building on the legacy of black critiques of civil rights to produce a sophisticated understanding of the reality of racism. As it is impossible to review the entire range of writings, the following will engage with a representative piece by Anthony Farley. Farley is reflecting on his own experiences of being discriminated against by presenting a story of a school trip 'on a spring day of my eighth grade year, 1976.'[24] It is a homely scene, set on a 'bus chartered for a class trip to Washington DC'. There is a sense of community, of belonging. Indeed, the bus is taking the children to the nation's capital. The author is describing a 'schoolmate' combing her 'long, brown hair', someone 'tall and cool and pretty.' She knows that her schoolmates are watching her. She then turns and addressing the group, asks whose comb she has been using; 'one of our classmates answered in a mirthful voice: "Its Farley's comb."' The author records his response: 'I, Farley, was the only black person on this otherwise all-white school trip to the nation's capital.' As the bus breaks into laughter, 'The girl with the long brown hair turned crimson and began to cry in loud, long sobs. The sobs quickly turned into the sounds of retching which were accompanied by shudders running through her hunched form. She may have vomited.' While 'her personal trauma unfolded, accompanied by squeals of laughter . . . I said nothing'.

The image of vomiting[25] presents an extreme bodily reaction as a metaphor for the social attitude of whites to blacks. They have to be removed, vomited out of the social body. Setting the scene on a bus also connects it with the quintessential civil rights image of the 'segregated bus of the 1950's.'[26] The point is that racism remains in different but no less powerful forms. Most importantly, though, the act of recording and writing about this experience manifests a kind of thought, a way of appropriating experience; a means, ultimately, of finding in the body a site of resistance. A tension is created between the silence of the character in the story and the fact that he is now writing the story, giving a voice to his previous silence. The character 'Farley' becomes an object for the author Farley as part of the definition of self with which this story is concerned. He

[21] *Ibid*, 137.
[22] D Bell, *Race, Racism and American Law*, above n 3, 48.
[23] See chapter 7.
[24] A Farley, 'The Black Body as Fetish Object' (1997) *Oregon Law Review* 480.
[25] See also A Farley, 'Thirteen Stories' (1999) *Tuoro Law Review* 2.
[26] A Farley, 'The Black Body as Fetish Object', above n 24, 492.

draws the conclusion: '[a]ll of us experienced our connection through the colorline as a physical sensation, not as an abstract idea.'[27] Racism is reality. What unites the children on the bus is a complicity in the 'microaggressions' of racism. This is experienced at the level of the body, its reactions of nausea, shame and self-loathing. Community is organised around the ridicule and exclusion of the 'other.' Race is understood as a 'sadomasochistic form of pleasure.'[28]

The description of racism as 'ideology made flesh' suggests that whiteness and blackness are constructed. 'Whiteness' has to be 'created' in the same way that the social world as a whole is constructed. The creation of whiteness is predicated on the fetishisation of the black body. The white body is experienced as pleasure and the black body is denigrated as loathsome and ugly. Farley argues that the extent of the 'colorline' can be further studied in the masochistic attitude of blacks towards their own bodies. This cannot be resolved by passing laws: 'Civil rights will not create the raceless society. We reify the colorline even as we attempt to draft statutes to eliminate it from our lives—this is because we continue to preserve the notion of race.'[29] In accepting your body as defined through race, there is an act of identification, of self creation, that could have been otherwise. To become aware that you are a 'fetish object' is to become a 'subject': '[w]e are condemned, not to slavery, but to freedom.'[30] Sartrean echoes in this statement indicate a thinking that, to summarise brutally, connects the personal and the political.

CRITICAL RACE THEORY AND BRITISH RACISM[31]

British legal scholarship lacks the institutional solidarity of the American movement. This gives the British work a tentative and rather eclectic feeling as it pulls themes from sociology, cultural theory, politics and history into a jurisprudential orbit. Nevertheless, some attempt will be made to sketch some controlling themes and concerns.

One central theme that emerges from the scholarship is a linking of race to political economy. Industrial and capitalist production depended upon an initial

[27] A Farley, 'The Black Body as Fetish Object', above n 24, at 480.

[28] *Ibid,* at 461.

[29] *Ibid,* at 528.

[30] *Ibid,* at 530.

[31] In British scholarship, the problem of race has always been most concretely linked to questions of modernity, empire, migration and uneven development. See R Blackburn, *The Making of Colonial Slavery and the Overthrow of Colonial Slavery* (London, Verso, 1988). The Marxist strand in British thinking can be crudely divided into two groups. The earlier group, which would also include Williams, is perhaps best represented by John Solomos' early work. See 'Varieties of Marxist Conceptions of "Race", Class and State' in J Rex and D Mason (eds), *Theories of Race and Ethnic Relations* (Cambridge, Cambridge University Press, 1986). Later work drawing on Marx, but less reductivist, is represented by Stuart Hall and those such as Paul Gilroy, drawing on the legacy of CLR James.

accumulation of wealth.[32] The racist component of capitalism was first expressed in slavery, which facilitated the economic development of the West[33] and was retained in subtle and less covert forms after the abolition of slavery. Slavery, however, was only the first phase of an ongoing process. The decline of slavery resulted, in part, from a realisation that it was no longer an efficient means of exploiting black labour.[34] Racism becomes intimately linked with the global division of labour and periods of expansion and contraction in world markets. In periods of expansion, migrant labour is imported to supplement the insufficient supply of labour within the nation state. In times of contraction, tensions develop between the guest workers and the indigenous populations over jobs and resources. For instance, the effects of the 1980's economic 'restructuring' hit 'black people particularly hard because of their market position' as 'the deindustrialization of Britain affected above all those who had come here to do unskilled and semiskilled labouring jobs.'[35] The legacy of empire in the area or race relations is complex. The theoretical challenge is to 'address the complex syncreticisms which have been a feature of the junction between race and class in contemporary Britain.'[36] The aim of critical race theory is to theorise law's involvement in this structure.

In critical jurisprudential terms, race can be understood as a historical and political problem.[37] Law represents a totality of shared habits, conventions and traditions; law and its institutions are seen as embodying the spirit of the nation

[32] The following account is based on R Miles and A Phizacklea, *White Mans' Country* (London, Pluto Press, 1984) and E Williams, *Capitalism and Slavery* (London, Deutsch, 1964).

[33] Robert Miles, in *Race after Race Relations*, makes the point that this process does not happen in the way described by Marx. If one considers the Caribbean, one does not find a class of property owners, and a class who have to sell their labour power. Rather, labour is provided by slaves and indentured workers. Thus, '[w]hat distinguishes the establishment of agricultural commodity production in the Caribbean, and in several other parts of the world, was the *absence* of proletarianisation' (33). This is not an argument that Marx must be rejected, but rather, that his insights must be rethought to become relevant.

[34] This description is drawn from *White Mans Country*. C Holmes, *John Bulls Other Island* (London, Macmillan, 1998) draws attention to the effect of the end of post-war prosperity in the period 1961–2 and the effect it had on immigration policy; in particular the need for unskilled labour (262).

[35] L Lustgarten, in B Hepple and EM Szyszczak (eds), *Discrimination: the Limits of the Law* (London, Mansell, 1992) 459.

[36] P Gilroy, *There Aint No Black in the Union Jack* (London, Routledge, 1991) 17.

[37] See P Fitzpatrick, 'Racism and the Innocence of Law' in P Fitzpatrick and A Hunt (eds), *Critical Legal Studies* (London, Blackwell, 1987). One development of Marxism would understand racism as alien to capitalism's ideology of universal rights; another approach would see a 'symbiotic' relationship where migrant workers provide 'cheap labour.' Fitzpatrick's point is not that Marxism must be rejected, but that questioning race can also lead to a different understanding of Marxism. This appears coherent with the work of cultural theorists such as Paul Gilroy. More importantly, Fitzpatrick is concerned with a dynamic of liberalism that both links race to law, and then denies that racism is a central problem. Understanding the reach of this problem demands a work of historical and philosophical acumen that can trace the inter-relations between liberalism, enlightenment reason and a colonial project. In terms of this chapter, Fitzpatrick's statement that 'liberal capitalism [both] opposes and is maintained by racism' (121) offers a particularly accurate and pithy summary of a central tension that runs in different ways through British and American law.

or at least as representing a nation's historical and cultural achievements.[38] Post-war immigration provides a particular challenge to this construction of the present and the past. As Gilroy writes, the contemporary perception of the problem was not so much 'the volume of black settlement but rather its character and effects, specifically the threat to legal institutions.'[39] Immigration was perceived as a threat to English constitutional values, and, the threat, in its most paranoid form, was seen to place the destiny of the west at stake.[40] This perception of immigration as threat, rather than as an opportunity to create a different history—a different institutional response—represents the failure of English law when faced with racism.

This is part of a broader cultural and political failure that reveals a blindness to the wider problem. The industrialisation of the first world at the expense of the third has produced a developed core, and an underdeveloped and exploited periphery.[41] The political will to deal with the redistribution of resources that would help repair this situation does not exist; but the dislocations wrought by the process continue to cause social and economic effects. It is from this perspective that British immigration and race relations law must be considered.

An over-riding concern in immigration law is the distinction between 'colonial periphery' and 'imperial centre.'[42] In the post-war period, despite differences in political ideology, a broad consensus emerged amongst the political elites about the need to stem and control immigration. A useful starting point is the 1962 Commonwealth Immigrants Act, passed in the context of reducing immigration through issuing employment vouchers.[43] The organising concept

[38] See P Fitzpatrick, *The Mythology of Modern Law* (London, Routledge, 1992). The nation is defined in terms of race; the colonised people are everything that the English are not. Whilst sustaining this division, the constitution of Englishness is largely left unexamined. In the wider colonial worldview, although there are differences between, say, the English and the French, they are still united by a 'something' that allows them to be posited as the colonisers and the natives as the colonised. Race, is therefore in some senses empty. It can be filled with the contents of Englishness and Frenchness yet still opposed to the otherness of the savage. Moreover, it raises a standard against which the 'new' nations can be judged, but against which they must always fall short. The native can only be civilised to a certain extent, they can never quite be 'one of us'.

[39] P Gilroy, *There Aint No Black in the Union Jack*, above n 36, 86.

[40] For instance, following Enoch Powell's 'rivers of blood speech' in 1968, race was presented in the terms of the disastrous encounter of two different civilisations.

[41] In the sense developed by Etienne Balibar: 'the (shifting) distinction between the core and the periphery of the world economy corresponds also to the geographical and politico-cultural distribution of strategies of exploitation' in I Wallerstein and E Balibar, *Race, Nation, Class* (London, Verso, 1991) 177.

[42] K Paul, *Whitewashing Britain: Race and Citizenship in the Postwar Era* (Ithaca, Cornell University Press, 1997) 184. Paul's account on the legal construction of citizenship is a useful supplement to the histories of immigration in C Holmes, *John Bull's Other Island* (London, Macmillan, 1998), Z Layton-Henry, *The Politics of Immigration: Immigration, 'Race' and 'Race' Relations in Post-War Britain* (Oxford, Blackwell, 1992).

[43] SS Juss in *Immigration, Nationality and Citizenship* (London, Mansell, 1993) argues that the 1962 Act ended what had been an 'open door policy' to Commonwealth citizens. It was a knee jerk response rather than a reasoned consideration of factors such as housing, education and health that could have given some indication of the country's capacity to accommodate immigration: 'the result was the enactment of an exclusion policy rather than an immigration policy so called.' (4) Although

of the Act was that of 'belonging', defined as having a link with Britain either through birth or the possession of a British passport. At a symbolic level, the Act signified the withdrawal from Empire and the Commonwealth and created the 'blueprint' for a regime of racial control.[44] Whilst the government was concerned about the social problems that resulted from coloured immigrants settling in Britain, they were less concerned about white immigrants from the 'old dominions.'[45] This distinction was made through acts of overt discrimination between coloured and white immigrants:

> Operating the 1962 Act [in this way] reinforced the differentiation of communities of Britishness: the imperial, familial community consisting of white-skinned Britons was privileged and protected from the letter of immigration law, while the political community of Britishness consisting of black-skinned Britains was subjected to increasingly tight regulation.[46]

The defeat of the Conservative government in 1964 did not produce any change in the law by the incumbent Labour administration. The second Commonwealth Immigrnts Act, the 1968 Act, attempted to create an even tighter legal definition of British nationality. At one point, the Home Secretary proposed to increase the powers of immigration officers and effectively redefine immigrant British subjects as aliens[47] (although these proposals did not move beyond the White Paper). Debates in the press and in Parliament contributed to the impression that both settled coloured peoples and immigrants were suspect communities whose presence was problematic and troublesome for the majority. Given this background, it is no wonder that the later Race Relations Act in 1965 was also severely compromised. The 1965 Act will be considered in more depth presently, but it would not be going too far to suggest that the Act perpetuated the idea of hierarchised 'communities' of Britishness.[48] This weighting

this 'ad hoc' feature of the Act is important to note, it is worth stressing the racist attitudes that also fed into the legislation; attitudes that were the legacy of empire. C Holmes writes that: 'pre-existing hostility towards Blacks and those from the Indian sub continent . . . can hardly be ignored' (*John Bull's Other Island* (London, Macmillan, 1998) 262).

[44] As J Solomos points out in *Race and Racism in Britain* (London, Macmillan, 1993), this reflects a set of concerns developed slightly earlier, as the Labour and Conservative Governments of 1945–51 attempted to implement policy for stemming the flow of black migrant workers coming to Britain: 'It was during this time that the terms of the political debate about "coloured" immigration were established, leading to a close association between race and immigration in both policy debates and in popular political and media discourses.' (57).

[45] K Paul, *Whitewashing Britain*, above n 42, 173.

[46] *Ibid*, 173. J Solomos, *Race and Racism in Britain*, above n 44, 61, quotes William Deedes, Minister without portfolio, who wrote that: 'The Bill's real purpose was to restrict the influx of coloured immigrants. We were reluctant to say as much openly. So the restrictions were applied to coloured and white citizens in all Commonwealth countries—though everybody recognised that immigration from Canada, Australia and New Zealand was no part of the problem.'

[47] K Paul, *Whitewashing Britain*, above n 42, above 175. For a broader perspective on this process, see R Miles, *Race and Racism*. Miles points out that the notions of alien and foreigner are predicated on the entire history of the nation state, 80–104.

[48] K Paul, *Whitewashing Britain*, above n 42, above 176. For a more radical account of the thinking behind the Act, which sees the state as acting on behalf of capitalist interests, see A Sivandan, *A Different Hunger* (London, Pluto Press, 1982).

towards separate and not particularly equal spheres undercut any official commitment to ideas and practices of neutrality or integration. In its most extreme form the discourse of the National Front can be seen as the logical extension, rather than any great departure from, the official government discourse on the need to police race.

The colonial background of the legislation is also starkly apparent in the background to the 1968 Commonwealth Immigrants Act. Prior to the Act, Commonwealth citizens who had a parent or grandparent 'born, adopted, registered, or naturalised' in the UK had an automatic right of entrance. A large group of Kenyan citizens of Asian descent were facing discrimination in Kenya and sought to enter the UK. The law was changed to restrict their right of entrance. Later, in 1972 similar treatment was meted upon the 'Ugandan Asians', albeit under a different legislative regime. The European Commission of Human Rights found that this amounted to 'inhuman and degrading treatment.'[49] The reason for allowing this group to enter the UK was thus not associated with any enlightened immigration policy, but with the impact of the Commission's ruling.[50]

A racist logic works itself through into the Immigration Act 1971. Largely informed by the 'separate spheres' concept of nationality, it gave legislative form to overtly discriminatory practices that had long been in operation by dividing British subjects into 'patrials' and 'nonpatrials', nonpatrials being so deprived of rights of settlement and work as to be 'virtually aliens.'[51] The practical upshot of this definition also meant that patrials were almost completely white. Despite the language of the 1976 Act, and the developing case law, immigration law remained racist in the most crude of senses. Reflecting continuing public concerns with the 'swamping' of the nation, the British Nationality Act 1981 provides a further attempt to classify and control. Nationality was divided into British citizenship, British Dependent Territories citizenship and British Overseas citizenship. These classifications and the hierarchy of rights they reflected were predicated on notions of descent, themselves dependent on a notion of Britishness that excluded any broader notion of belonging to the Commonwealth.[52]

[49] K Paul, *Whitewashing Britain*, above n 42, 182.

[50] *Ibid*, 182. S Juss, *Immigration, Nationality and Citizenship* (London, Mansell, 1993) also describes this later Act as marking another watershed. After 1968, government controls increasingly targeted secondary immigration. For example, the 1962 Act had retained the right of a child to join his/her parent in the UK. The 1968 Act limited this provision by stating that both parents had to be resident in the UK before the right could be exercised.

[51] S Juss, *Immigration, Nationality and Citizenship*, above n 50 181. P Fryer, *Staying Power* (London, Pluto Press, 1984) states that this Act, when it came into effect in 1973, 'virtually ended all primary immigration'. As well as increasing the power of immigration officers and the police to detain immigrants, it came into force in a context of increasing violence against black communities.

[52] There is a problem with research into recent history. The thirty year rule over the release of official papers means that the following discussion is not up to date.

THE RACE RELATIONS ACTS

The 1965 Race Relations Act was expanded by the 1968 Act, redefined by the 1976 Act and redefined again in 2000. The Acts themselves are largely compromised, and leave racism largely intact.

The 1965 Race Relations Act was passed by a Labour Government with a small majority and was profoundly affected by political compromises made to achieve the parliamentary support on the eve of a General Election.[53] It was a limited measure, creating a criminal offence of incitement to racial hatred and an overseeing body, the Race Relations Board, which lacked basic powers to call for witnesses and documents. The emphasis was on conciliation; only if conciliation failed could the Board refer the case to the Attorney General who had a discretion to determine whether litigation was necessary or not.[54]

Political exigencies combined with wider ideological failures to severely limit the Act's effectiveness. The 1965 Act was explicitly linked to the problem of a coloured immigrant population that had to be controlled both at the point of entry and in their ongoing settlement and 'integration'.[55] We can examine the claims made by apologists for the Act by looking at the following extract written by Anthony Lester, one of the major champions of the bill:

> Our law has two faces. One face confronts the stranger at the gate, grudgingly and suspiciously; the other is turned benevolently towards the newcomer and his descendants within the gate, guaranteeing the treatment of members of ethnic minorities as individuals on their merits, rather than discriminatory treatment on the basis of racial stereotypes, prejudices and assumptions. With one face, the law embodies and reinforces racial inequality; with the other it expresses and urges racial equality. The positive impact of race equality law continues to be diminished by the negative impact of unfair and discriminatory immigration and asylum laws.[56]

Our law has two faces, without being two-faced. This passage accepts the necessary linkage between immigration and anti-discrimination law, but, projects the tension into an image of balance, and potential resolution. To resolve the problem, we need only identify the 'negative' elements and work to expunge them. However, we have seen that the legal response was so thoroughly bound up with political priorities as to be inextricable from them. The racism of immigration law feeds into and sustains the failures of anti-discrimination law. It would be harder, from this perspective, to blame the Act's failure on external elements, those 'Maoists' and 'other militant tendencies, brought together

[53] C McCrudden, DJ Smith, C Brown, *Racial Justice at Work* (London, Policy Studies Institute, 1991) 9.

[54] *Ibid*, 9.

[55] R Miles and A Phizacklea, *White Man's Country* (Pluto Press, London, 1987) 57.

[56] A Lester, 'Politics of the Race Relations Act 1976' in M Anwar, P Roach, R Sondhi (eds), *From Legislation to Integration: Race Relations in Britain* (London, Macmillan, 2000) 29.

under the tattered banner of "Black Power." '[57] Instead of the tired rhetoric of law's balance, what is needed is an understanding of law's wider implication in sustaining a postcolonial order. One might have to search much deeper than a limited criticism of the common law that 'had at best been neutral, at worst [given] preference to property and contract rights over the right to equality of treatment.'[58] Policy makers had missed the opportunity to link anti-discrimination legislation with poor social conditions, exclusion and policy failures in housing, education and welfare. Thus, the 1965 Act did not apply to the areas of education and housing. The Act conceived of the problem as one of 'biologically discrete populations'[59] whose interactions with the white majority had to be protected by the law.

An overview of more recent legislation displays an ongoing inability to understand the nature of racism. The 1968 Act extended the provisions of the 1965 Act. It made discrimination in housing and employment subject to civil remedies. Discrimination was defined as less favourable treatment on the grounds of colour, race, ethnic or national origins. The Race Relation Board's conciliatory role remained, but the Board was now empowered to litigate cases in the county court.[60] Alongside the Board, a new body was created. The Community Relations Commission was to sponsor 'harmonious community relations.'[61] But the 1968 Act was as flawed as its predecessor. It was orientated towards individual forms of behaviour and failed to generate resources needed to implement effective programmes.

The 1976 Act widened the scope of anti-discrimination law still further.[62] The statutory definition of discrimination specified that a higher proportion of the

[57] A Lester, 'Politics of the Race Relations Act 1976', *ibid*, 27.

[58] *Ibid*, 29.

[59] P Fryar, *Staying Power*, above n 51, 58.

[60] C McCrudden, DJ Smith, C Brown, *Racial Justice At Work*, above n 53, 10. There was a slightly different procedure for employment discrimination cases which stressed that they should be resolved by the employment/ Union bodies. Only if a relevant body did not exist, or a case was appealed, would the Board become involved.

[61] *Ibid*, 12, quoting Race Relations Act 1968, section 25.

[62] Problems with the Act do not end with the definition of discrimination. There are other critical approaches to both the failures of the Act itself, and the case law that develops around it. As L Lustgarten argues (*Legal Control of Racial Discrimination* (London, Macmillan, 1980)), no matter how the Race Relations Act is assessed, one is compelled to acknowledge that it has been largely ineffective. Thus, a consideration of incidents of successful prosecution after the Act became law shows that in 1982, 30 out of 200 cases heard in Employment Tribunals were successful. This is lower than the 25% success rate in unfair dismissal cases. (Information from the CRE consultative document *The Race Relations Act* (1983). If one looks at evidence for changes in employers' attitudes, one finds patterns of 'ignorance and inaction'—See A Young and J Connelly, *Policy and Practice in the Multi Racial City* (PSI 1981). J Solomos in *Race and Racism in Britain* (London, Macmillan, 1993), argues that '[a]lmost all the academic research that has been done on the effectiveness of the 1976 Act has pointed to three ways in which policies have proved to be ineffective. First, the machinery set up to implement the Act has not functioned effectively. Second, the policies have not produced the intended results. Third, the policies have failed to meet the expectations of the black communities'. See also R Jenkins and J Solomos (eds), *Racism and Equal Opportunity Policies in the 1980s* (Cambridge, Cambridge University Press, 1989). Another glaring omission was the exclusion of the police from the provisions of the Act.

group experiencing discrimination must be unable to comply with the condition than the population at large. As there was no guide to this proportion, the court has to use its discretion; a discretion that also applied to the question of whether the condition was justified. Given that 'tribunals and courts tend to be norm reflecting' and not likely to encourage interpretations that disturb or challenge norms, these terms were always going to be limited by the courts inherent conservatism.[63] An Act that presented, at least potentially, a challenge to ingrained practices was profoundly compromised by its reliance on mechanisms that would, either directly or indirectly, allow old modes of thinking to perpetuate themselves.[64]

This problem can be traced to the Act's definition of indirect discrimination. Indirect discrimination went some way towards acknowledging the social reality of racism's operation. Acts of discrimination are often not obvious and direct, but have a more sophisticated and covert nature. The kind of indirect discrimination covered by the Act is the imposition of a condition that, on the face of it, is colour blind, but in application occasions discrimination. Take for instance, the situation that led to litigation in *Mandla v Lee*. A Sikh boy was unable to conform with a school rule that forbade non-regulation clothing. Clearly no direct discrimination had taken place: the boy had not been refused entrance to the school because he was a Sikh. However, a condition had been applied which would have made it impossible for Sikhs to comply because wearing a turban is an expression of their ethnic identity. Thus, the statutory test concerns the imposition of a condition with which significantly fewer people in the discriminated group could comply.

As commentators have suggested, this concept of indirect discrimination falls far short of any meaningful idea of institutional discrimination.[65] As we shall see, *The Lawrence Inquiry* stressed the institutional nature of racism as:

> [t]he collective failure of an organisation to provide an appropriate and professional service to people because of their colour, culture or ethnic origin. It can be seen or detected in processes, attitude and behaviour which amount to discrimination through unwitting prejudice, ignorance, thoughtlessness and racist stereotyping which disadvantage minority ethnic people.[66]

[63] Fitzpatrick's study of tribunal decisions (above n 37) quotes Lustgarten's *Legal Control of Racial Discrimination*: 'in every case in which there was a split tribunal decision against the complainant, the non specialist wingman joined the chairman to make the majority.'

[64] This is a variation on Fitzpatrick's radical critique of the Act (above n 62). Precisely because the liberal order must both rely upon and combat racism, the Act must both draw attention to racism, and then limit its own ability to effectively combat discrimination. Consider the Commission for Racial Equality. It is given investigative powers and can issue non discrimination notices; this power is then limited, in that notices can only be issued for particular acts. This is then further limited by judicial interpretation of the CRE's statutory powers.

[65] B Hepple, 'Have Twenty Five Years of Race Relations Acts in Britain Been a Failure?' in B Hepple and EM Szyszczak (eds), *Discrimination: The Limits of the Law* (London, Mansell, 1992) 25.

[66] *The Lawrence Inquiry*, Cm 4662-I (London, HMSO, 1999) 6:34.

This definition is far more useful than that provided by the 1976 Act.[67] It draws attention to the informal networks, the unofficial but influential social interactions where a culture's racism coheres. The concept of discrimination in the 1976 Act was limited because the condition that allegations of discrimination were based on had to constitute an absolute bar. A 'preferred profile' would not constitute a condition for the purposes of the Act. Thus, the reality of prejudice operating at a shop floor or informal level would not necessarily be prohibited by the Act. Arguably, the Act should have covered any practice that had a 'significant adverse impact' on levels of employment amongst ethnic minorities. Institutional racism thrives in an environment where unreflective and conservative thinking persists.[68] Weaknesses in the definition of key terms meant that it was difficult to combat this thinking.

The failures of the 1976 Act can be seen in the murder of the black teenager Stephen Lawrence. The subsequent inquiry into the failure to obtain a prosecution revealed the continuing nature of British racism.

THE LAWRENCE INQUIRY

The first investigation into the murder investigations, the *Kent Report*, found no evidence that racism had significantly contributed to the failures to make arrests. Admittedly, the *Kent Report* addressed complaints against individual officers, and did not have a remit to research wider issues—but this in turn reflects the nature of the problem: an inability to conceptualise racism, and an underestimation of its persistence.

[67] Within the sociological literature, there is a critique of the legal construction of race in English law. There is a claim that the legal definition of race should be adopted in social science, as opposed to the analytical categories used to date (M Banton, 'The Race Relations Problematic' (1991) 42 *British Journal of Sociology* 115). The virtue of the legal definition of race is that it is based on an everyday understanding of the term, as is evidenced by the House of Lords judgment in *Mandla v Lee*. There are a number of problems here. Firstly, as the history of the litigation shows, the Court of Appeal was content to employ a narrow definition of the term ethnic as a means of limiting the effectiveness of the 1976 Act. This was based on an everyday understanding. That the House of Lords preferred a broader, but equally everyday meaning shows that the definition of the term is not fixed, and that everyday semantics cannot be relied upon; neither can the common sense of the judiciary. Furthermore, as R Miles argues above n 33, if one allows everyday meanings to assume dominance, it is difficult to challenge the power relations that cohere in language. The legal definition assumes that everyone 'belongs' to a 'race' (6), and that these relations must be regulated by the state; this 'orders social relations in such a way that they are structured and reproduced' as racialised (6) (Drawing here on C Guillaum, *Racism, Sexism, Power and Ideology* (London, Routledge, 1995)). To extend Miles' analysis would to be to contend with a law that can be used creatively. There seem to be two theoretical problems involved here. One is the question of hybridity and identity developed by H Bhaba in *The Location of Culture* (London, Routledge, 1994); another is the problematisation of the forms of racist and antiracist thought as articulated by P-A Taguieff, *La Force du Prejuge, Essai Sur Le Racisme et Ses Doubles* (Paris, Editions la Decouverte, 1988). How would this feed into post-Lawrence law?

[68] *The Lawrence Inquiry*, above n 66.

Lord Scarman's Report into the Brixton Disorder in 1981 had rejected the allegation that British institutions were systematically involved in racial discrimination. *The Lawrence Inquiry* picked up on this explanation of the problem as one of 'unwitting' racism.[69] Thus, the Metropolitan Police were not racist; apparent prejudice at an operational level was to be explained by 'errors of judgement . . . lack of imagination and flexibility.'[70] At the level of everyday policing, 'occasional' racism could be explained as the 'immaturity' of certain officers. In Lord Scarman's Report, however, there is an acknowledgement that the problem is wider and more structural. It appears as an explanation as to why individual officers, who are not racist, may become so. Because of racial stereotyping, officers facing a rising tide of 'street crime' may 'lapse into unthinking assumptions.'[71] It is not as if Lord Scarman is dismissive of racism. Where unwitting racism has been proved, it warrants remedy. Racism is the cause of social tension that cannot be allowed to fester and destroy good order. However, the legacy of the Scarman report is an understanding of racism that distracts attention from its invasive, systematic or institutional nature, and tends to see it as either unconscious or the unwitting acts of individuals.

The limitations of Lord Scarman's definition of racism were apparent to *The Lawrence Inquiry*. Both the Police Complaints Authority (PCA) and the police had failed to understand the problem of discrimination because it was limited to the acts of a few 'rotten apples', who 'let the side down.'[72] Equally at fault was the practice of following the 'traditional way of doing things'. The over-arching aspect of this ideology is the reluctance to come to terms with the need to police a multi-racial society. For a police force that is attached to a notion of unarmed and consensual policing, such a refusal to move with the times is profoundly damaging.

The Lawrence Inquiry also found that the culture of policing does not encourage a critical self-understanding that would make prejudice easier to identify and to challenge. Evidence from officers in the Black Police Association (BPA) drew attention to a powerful 'occupational culture'[73] which was shaping or influencing black officers' own views about race and crime from the perspective of 'white experience, white beliefs and white values'. This was self-perpetuating, as white officers tended only to meet black people in 'confrontational' situations that supported assumptions and stereotypes about black criminality and lawlessness. As the Lawrence Inquiry was told, it 'may be' that these attitudes are prevalent throughout British society. Such a concern was obviously outside the Inquiry's terms of reference, although some tentative suggestions were made about wider attitudes. As institutional racism it is expressed not only in the failures of the Lawrence murder investigation, but also in the

[69] *Ibid*, 6:7.
[70] *Ibid*, 6:8.
[71] *Ibid*, 6:10.
[72] *Ibid*, 6:14.
[73] *Ibid*, 6:28.

disparity in the numbers of black people stopped and searched,[74] the under-reporting of 'racial incidents'[75] and the inability of the police to take the issue seriously at the level of training.[76]

The law might begin to understand racism through a concept of 'institutional' discrimination.[77] Interestingly, the report itself refers back to a text by two black American activists, Stokely Carmichael and Charles V Hamilton, to develop this definition. Racism must be seen as operating within the most 'respected forces' and as a combination of both 'active' and 'pervasive' racist attitudes; underlying these is a belief in black inferiority. This does need supplementing by assumptions about black lawlessness that have their own particular history. For instance, one account of black history in Britain quotes a Metropolitan Police Commissioner as saying: 'in the Jamaicans, you have people who are constitutionally disorderly . . . It's simply in their makeup. They are constitutionally disposed to be anti authority.'[78]

Also important is the perception of mugging as a 'race' crime. Although official Home Office investigations into race relations tended to stress the role of a difficult minority amongst a fairly respectable majority, the panic over mugging in the later 1970s led to a series of violent confrontations between the police and black youths. Still the subject of complex and fierce debate in criminology and policy circles, it is difficult within the space of this chapter to account for these explosions of violence. One fact is salient. Official accounts tended to play down the political motivations of the rioters. In the wake of the Notting Hill riots of 1976, a new set of stereotypes was created. The image of the 'black mob' entered into the public imagination: 'violence made the link between blackness and disorder more complex and profound.'[79] This in turn perhaps led to a new escalation in the tensions that had produced rioting in the first place. The police strategy of containment and aggressive use of powers of search and arrest led to further riots in the 1980s.

After *The Lawrence Inquiry* these attitudes are no longer acceptable. In the words of Sir John Woodcock, the Chief Inspector of Constabulary, the Inquiry reveals a wider 'cultural failure.'[80] Thus in its recommendation for tacking English racism, there is a need for, in the words of the Reverend David Wise, a 'radical transformation' involving not only the police but all levels of society. The Inquiry becomes the point at which a previously radical critique enters into official discourse. Again, with reference to the words of Sir John, the police

[74] *The Lawrence Inquiry*, 6:45.

[75] *Ibid*, 6:45.

[76] A Her Majesty's Inspectorate of Constabulary Report: *Winning the Race*, showed that before 1998, 'not a single officer' had received training in racism awareness.

[77] *The Lawrence Inquiry*, above n 66, 6:22.

[78] P Fryer, *Aspects of British Black History* (London, Index Books, 1993) 37.

[79] P Gilroy, *There Aint No Black in the Union Jack*, above n 36, 99.

[80] *The Lawrence Inquiry*, above n 66, 6:61.

remain a nineteenth-century institution, a 'mechanism set up to protect the affluent from what the Victorians described as the dangerous classes.'[81]

TOWARDS A CRITICAL JURISPRUDENCE OF RACE

Is there a distinctive mark to 'British' critical race theory? In attempting to answer this important question, two preliminary themes must be addressed. Critical Race Theory, to date, has theorised the experience of race in America. Given the orientation of CRT to history, any scholar working within this tradition must produce a 'local', or non American, account of specific historical experiences. Thus, to the extent that we can talk of British CRT, it must engage with the experience of race and discrimination in Britain. The problem is that of determining a precise sense of context. As we have seen from the discussion above, the post-war history of race relations is inseparable from a broader history of the British Empire and its aftermath. It might appear, then, that CRT is one of the tasks of a broader post colonial jurisprudence. Whilst this might suggest a general sense of orientation, it leaves the precise frame of British CRT to be determined. In this final section of the chapter, we will look at the work of scholars who are producing a critical jurisprudence of race, and examine the suppositions and trajectories of their arguments.

A critical jurisprudence of race understands that racism itself is a complex phenomenon; interpreting this phenomenon demands a subtle and nuanced approach that resists easy conclusions:

> Racism is not a unitary event based on psychological aberration nor some ahistorical antipathy to blacks which is the cultural legacy of empire and which continues to saturate the consciousness of all white Britons . . . It must be understood as a process. Bringing blacks into history outside of the categories of problem and victim, and establishing the historical category of racism in opposition to the idea that it is an eternal or natural phenomenon, depends on a capacity to comprehend political, ideological and economic change.[82]

This approach resists the reductionism of a certain Marxism or a form of Weberian sociology that would like to relate all phenomena directly to economic relationships.[83] In the most extreme form of these arguments, race becomes a term that merely masks the truth of more fundamental economic relationships of subordination and dominance. Although an important aspect in accounting for the shape of any particular society, economic relationships cannot be seen as overdetermining and primary. As far as legal analysis is concerned, the conjunction between racism and law must not make a similar mistake. It has to be sensitive to economic factors, without seeing them as an

[81] *Ibid.*
[82] P Gilroy, *There Aint No Black in the Union Jack*, above n 36, 26.
[83] *Ibid,* 21.

interpretative key to social relations. Legal analysis must accord law its autonomy, and inscribe the law in broader social practices.

Peter Fitzpatrick's notion of the 'innocence of law' provides just such a way of understanding the law's relationship with racism. Law's innocence is founded on the liberal claim that it is 'incompatible with racism.'[84] How is this claim substantiated? As law is autonomous and separate from social life, it can provide general, normative structures that organise and restrain particular interests. Such a perspective would be blind to those experiences where law has failed to provide remedies, or, indeed, failed to perceive that problems exist in the first place. Precisely because it is separate from the life it is meant to order, law cannot be seen as 'complicitous'[85] with the failings of the social world; alternatively, any instances of failure can be seen as 'exceptional', thus 'affirming the great virtue of the norm'.[86] If we are critical of this model, then how can we conceptualise the relationship between racism and law?

The relationship between racism and law is inherently complex: '[l]aw could . . . be seen as contradictory, as integrally opposed to and supportive of racism'; indeed, law assumes its 'identity' by 'taking elements of racism into itself and shaping them in its own terms.'[87] This is not to argue that the law cannot be used to combat and oppose racism; it does suggest, however, that in so doing, the law allows racism to take different social forms. Consider, for example, the Race Relations legislation that we have studied above. The formal legal regime that applies to racial discrimination at work operates through the creation of employee rights that correlate with employer's duties. Disputes between employer and employee are to be resolved by a neutral tribunal; questions of relevance in relation to evidence submitted in a case are in turn regulated by legal rules. As we have seen, the law itself was based on tests for direct and indirect discrimination. Undoubtedly, this law allowed litigation against employers who had discriminated against employees. At the same time, however, practices of discrimination adapt themselves to the law, or, become made invisible to the gaze of the law. One particular example of this phenomenon would be the willingness of tribunals, in the sample studied by Fitzpatrick, to accept employer's evidence on what counts as a 'trivial' incident.[88] Whilst an act of discrimination may remain such from the perspective of the victim, for the tribunal it is not worthy of remedy, as it is merely part of the everyday oppressions and inequalities of the social world.

The peculiar way in which law takes elements of racism into itself can be seen at a different and more general level in the following extracts from speeches made by Enoch Powell in November 1971 and September 1968:

[84] P Fitzpatrick, 'Racism and the Innocence of Law' in P Fitzpatrick and A Hunt (eds), *Critical Legal Studies* (Oxford, Blackwell, 1987) 119.
[85] *Ibid*, 121.
[86] *Ibid*.
[87] *Ibid*, 122.
[88] *Ibid*, 127.

> Of the great multitudes, numbering already two millions, of West Indians and Asians in England, it is no more true to say that England is their country than it would be to say that the West Indies, or Pakistan or India are our country.
>
> The West Indian or Asian does not, by being born in England become an Englishman. In law he becomes a United Kingdom citizen by birth; in fact he is a West Indian or an Asian still . . . With the lapse of a generation or so we shall at least have succeeded—to the benefit of nobody—in reproducing in 'England's green and pleasant land' the haunting tragedy of the United States.[89]

Here again 'racism marks the constitutive boundaries of law'.[90] In the first extract, the notion of nationality is used to create bounded and defined identities that are separate and formally equal: just as a British person can make no claim to being a Pakistani, so too a Pakistani cannot make a claim to being British. Law is made synonymous with this national identity, and hence, in Powell's rhetoric, with a racist position, in that it allows a separation between groups of people defined by race and nationality. Furthermore, this equation allows Powell to present immigration as a legal problem. The presence of foreigners within Britain is an anomaly, a matter of the failure of the policing of boundaries. This argument is taken further in the second extract. Law now draws a racial boundary in granting at least a limited form of citizenship to the immigrant. The argument becomes one of the correct legal boundaries of citizenship. For Powell, the law no longer corresponds with the truth of nationality: indeed, law is not racist enough! It is as if Powell's position appreciates that law can never be neutral; it must defend the idea of Englishness and of racial purity.

Powell's argument about the nature of the law must be separated from his objectionable politics. It is an advance on the liberal position, because it denies that law can be separated from a social world in which it is embedded. Furthermore, Powell's invocation of a mythical Englishness, of a sense of attachment to a country, points to the profound sense in which law is linked with belonging and identity.[91] Powell appreciates that law operates in ideological terms. To counter his argument, the discussion of race and racism must move onto this territory. We need an account of racism that operates at a 'depth level'.

Peter Fitzpatrick's work has emphasised the conjunction between race and the human sciences. This genealogy of racism counters the argument that race is a biological given. Returning to the approach of American CRT, this genealogy of racism stresses that race is a product of ideology. But ideology cannot simply be understood as misrecognition or ignorance. It must be seen as an account of social being. The study of ideology is one element in a wider study of social consciousness. It is only if we track racism in this way, to the very constitution of 'ourselves', that we can appreciate its dynamic.

[89] R Miles and A Phizacklea, *White Man's Country*, above n 55, 2–3.

[90] P Fitzpatrick, 'Racism and the Innocence of Law', above n 87, 122.

[91] C Stephes, '"*Fiat Justitia*" Narratives of Englishness in Lord Dennings Constitutional Jurisprudence', unpublished PhD manuscript, University of London.

The pioneering work of Patricia Tuitt moves in this direction. It describes both the political and the psychic constitution of racism. It can be read as an articulation of the insights of the psychoanalyst Frantz Fanon within a critical, jurisprudential context. We will see how Fanon's account of racism relates to Hegel's dialectical philosophy of social being, but for the moment we can examine how Tuitt uses Fanon's work to found a critical jurisprudence of race. For Fanon, racism is a 'dislocation'[92] of being, a separation that fractures 'humanity' into white and black. The terms 'black' and 'white' refer to a logic of colonialism or racism that effectively destroys being. As such, 'white' and 'black' are abstract terms in an ontological argument: 'not only must the black man be black; he must be black in relation to the white man.'[93] However, these terms must be connected back to their material contexts and to lived experience. Fanon's arguments about racism are rooted in a phenomenology for which language expresses being 'for the other' (*pour autrui*)—for an experience of being in a world that is inherently social and shared with others. These are the others that the ego or the consciousness encounters. The encounter, though, is not always between equals:

> Look, a nigger.

An encounter on the streets of colonial Dhakar, of Marseilles, London: 'look, a nigger'—an everyday insult—but one that represents the basic form of discrimination: the reduction of another being to the status of 'an object in the midst of other objects.'[94] The form that this experience takes is itself founded on a phenomenological truth: one experiences one's being through the recognition of others. If others withdraw that recognition, then one ceases to exist as another subject, another source of consciousness, and one sinks back into the world of nature or worse. As Tuitt stresses, racism is experienced as a destruction, a dismembering of the body:

> . . . the corporeal scheme crumbled, its place taken by a racial epidermal schema . . .

The body provides the reasoning self with coordinates.[95] To be conscious, is to be conscious of one's body as something different from, but located within, a

[92] P Tuitt, *Race, Law, Resistance* (London, Glasshouse, 2004) *ix*. Tuitt links Fanon's theory of consciousness with Marx's theory of alienation. This allows an understanding of the way in which law has been complicated in various economic forms of organisation that are explicitly or implicitly racist. It also suggests interesting parallels between the phenomenology of consciousness and an account of labour. In alienation, life, or the realisation of itself as such, becomes experienced as a means to an end; a kind of reversal. Alienation is not just the loss of the self—but the loss of a relationship between the self and others. To lose one's sense of species being is to lose connectivity: 'the essence connects one to the other' (75). One's sense of self can be expressed both through concretisation in labour and the realisation that labour links to others. This is the co-existence of self and other as different sides of the same phenomenon of consciousness. In particular economic circumstances, if one is an alienated worker, lost in oneself, one views the other as such; in other words, the way in which the social appears is one of fear and loathing of the self and the other that one encounters.

[93] F Fanon, *Black Skin, White Masks* (London, Pluto, 1986) 110.

[94] *Ibid*, 109.

[95] M Merleau-Ponty, *The Phenomenology of Perception* (London, Routledge, 1989).

world of things. The coherence of the body allows consciousness to become conscious of the world in which one lives. A consciousness coming up against discrimination literally falls apart. If, in the eyes of the other, one is an object to be pointed at, feared and despised, how can one have a sense of oneself at all? For instance, in the most extreme and organised form of racism, the slave is little better than a thing (*res*); a chattel. In Roman law, for instance, a slave, as something that can be owned, is defined by 'rightlessness.'[96] By being a thing, a slave is not capable of having rights. More recent forms of racial ordering such as apartheid or colonialism may move from slavery to wage labour, but they operate with a similar logic. The black is a worker, a labourer in a production process: a subhuman to be controlled and used in the most profitable manner. Discourses of assimilation or reform carry a related sense of the black as something not quite human, to be 'brought up to' the level of the white man. Across these very different historical forms of discrimination, then, is a similar denigration of the being of the non-white.

Thus, to distinguish between 'white' and 'black' is to posit a divide, a separation that serves to partition and demarcate experience. However, Fanon's analysis suggests that the situation is more complex still. Fanon makes use of this dialectic of recognition.[97] The struggle for recognition, is the struggle against non being:

> The dialectic that brings necessity into the foundation of my freedom drives me out of myself. It shatters my unreflected position. Still, in terms of consciousness, black consciousness is immanent in its own eyes. I am not a potentiality of something, I am wholly what I am. . . . My Negro consciousness does not hold itself out as a lack. It is. It is its own follower.[98]

The phenomenology of consciousness thus suggests how resistance to racism emerges from racism itself. The experience of being an object of discrimination, has the potential to turn the object back into a subject. This is because the subject is grounded in a more radical and open 'freedom'. Fanon's explanation of this process is interesting. It is an awareness of a 'Negro consciousness' or a 'black consciousness'. This is an interpellation, a coming to oneself through oneself. It is not imposed, but available within the consciousness, if consciousness is sufficiently provoked. This is not a 'potentiality': it is simply what one is. In Fanon's reading, the conclusion is the same: consciousness is not 'lack'; desire is not founded on absence. Desire is political.

[96] WW Buckland, *The Roman Law of Slavery* (Cambridge, Cambridge University Press, 1908) 37.

[97] As we will see, for Hegel, man is human only to the extent that he is able to impose himself against another man in order to win recognition of himself. You 'are' to the extent that you are recognised as such. As soon as 'I' go beyond my sense of my immediate being, I come up against the being of the other person. A 'circuit' or a 'movement' takes places between the self and the other. To the extent that an individual is not recognised by another, there is a kind of social death, a non-being.

[98] WW Buckland, *The Roman Law of Slavery*, above n 96, 35.

Where does this leave us? For Tuitt, it leads to a focus on certain doctrinal subjects: the construction in both European and national law of the refugee, and the way in which tort law can be used to address racial harms. Whilst these doctrinal engagements are timely and necessary, the use of Fanon's work arguably allows a broader focus and provides a foundation for a critical jurisprudence of race that would bring together the insights of phenomenology and political and social theory:

Where the focus of analysis must lie, is in accounting for the way in which the articulation of race can become a basis for 'social action.'[99] This very privileging of action reflects the old Marxist stress on praxis, but it is an orientation that does not shirk the difficult task of explaining how 'meanings' can be constructed through understandings that include class, but are not completely explained by class. Moreover, it reflects the way in which, in the 1980s, race began to become a concrete way in which various black communities organised themselves and began to articulate their grievances.[100]

We can elaborate Gilroy's insights. The concern with social action moves away from the connection of racism with victimhood, and shifts the focus towards the way in which black communities have used the law to define themselves. As a variation on Fitzpatrick's argument, this might suggest a way in which the constitutive boundaries of law are again being redrawn as law is used differently. There may, in other words, be a resource within the study of race and law in Britain that moves away from the somewhat melancholic conclusions of some of the American scholars who tend to the view the field as marked by the failure of the civil liberties struggle. But, this is not to suggest that racism has disappeared from British social and political life. Our concern with phenomenology suggests that racism is always a tendency of consciousness that can be encouraged or resisted through political means. In this sense, perhaps a 'popular' front is required. This would operate at both intellectual and practical levels. At the level of theory, it would be to correlate the insights of CRT with work in studies of ideology, social consciousness and psychoanalysis; at the level of practice, it would mean intervention in those areas where immigrants, refugees or anyone perceived as 'not one of us' are threatened or denied basic hospitality and humanity.

[99] P Gilroy, *There Aint No Black in the Union Jack*, above n 36, 27.
[100] *Ibid*.

11

'At the Stroke of Midnight . . .': Postcolonial Jurisprudence

> It was the task of civilisation to . . . establish courts of law, to inculcate in the natives a sense of individual responsibility, of liberty, and of justice, and to teach their rulers how to apply these principles . . . I am confident that the verdict of history will award high praise to the efforts and the achievements of Great Britain in the discharge of these great responsibilities . . . I am a profound believer in the British Empire and its mission in Africa (Lugard 1965, 5).

'*A Luta Continua*'

INTRODUCTION: EVERY DOG HAS HIS DAY

POST COLONIAL JURISPRUDENCE TRACES a legal trajectory that moves from colonialism to the achievement of independence by former subject territories. It is a jurisprudence of new beginnings, but it also examines the legacy of the past. Postcolonial jurisprudence addresses the following dilemma: the imposition of a legal order defines empire and colonialism; the foundation of an independent legal order marks the birth of the newly independent nation. How can law serve both these masters?

In this chapter, we will work through these themes with primary reference to the European Empires and their aftermath in Africa. Firstly, we will describe a specifically legal understanding of the postcolonial and focus on the creation of the colonial legal order. We will then turn to examine the tensions and problems that resulted from the achievement of independence by former colonial territories through either revolution or constitutional settlement. We will draw on the examples of two nations whose experience of the colonial and the post colonial can be contrasted: Nigeria and Mozambique. Indeed, the achievement of independence by these two nations marks the opening and closing of the period that saw the end of European Empire in Africa. Both newly sovereign nations faced an epic task: how was the law to be made to correspond with a newly independent people? How could customary and national laws be used to create an idea of nationhood?

The use of customary law in the creation of colonial legal orders was a practice of colonialism. As Mahmood Mamdani has argued, rather than exclude the native, the law included the colonial subject into institutions that guaranteed their subordinate status.[1] After the end of empire, it was necessary to re-define indigenous law and to articulate its relationship to the law of the new state.

We can hazard certain generalisations. Legal systems were 'de-racialised'; customary law was not abolished, but access was made available to 'modern' justice. Some nations, such as Tanzania, aimed at a unified court structure, and a codification of customary law that ignored tribal boundaries. Others, such as Mozambique, attempted to push forward with broader, political reforms of the legal system. Legal, social and economic reforms brought new governments into conflict with existing interests, in particular those who wished to see the preservation of customary courts and laws. These difficulties were exacerbated by what could be described as a problem of ethnicities. Colonial territories were composed of different ethnic groupings yoked together by violence. If the foundation of the new nation was synonymous with the preservation of national boundaries, then the law had to navigate the tensions that existed between national and ethnic identities.[2] Tensions frozen out in Empire returned to haunt the new nations.

Would the newly independent nation be able to bring together a diverse collections of ethnic groupings into a unified nation? How can we understand the moment of independence; can there be a negotiation between a colonial past, and a post colonial future? This chapter will endeavour to elucidate these questions of law, identity and politics.

A BACKWARD GLANCE OVER THE TRADITION

The Postcolonial

We need a working definition of the postcolonial. The term carries a bewildering set of meanings. Its primary meaning is perhaps historical, as it describes a period defined by the formal end of western colonial relationships with dependent and subject territories. But this periodisation is not as straightforward as it sounds. The postcolonial remains an epoch in which the developing world is exploited by the developed world. However, we can still insist on a difference between European colonialism prior to 1945, and the contemporary world order.[3] The postcolonial is not only bound up in arguments about history. The

[1] M Mamdani, *Citizen and Subject* (Princeton, Princeton University Press, 1996).

[2] This theme is present in traditional legal scholarship, but needs to be studied more explicitly. For instance, see AN Allott, *Essays in African Law* (London, Butterworths, 1960) 2: 'Every country has . . . altered, and some countries have revolutionised, the systems of courts which they inherited at independence. Mostly these alterations have implied the suppression of the traditional native courts or their integration into the national judicial system'.

[3] See A Gearey, *Law and Globalization* (Boulder, Rowan and Littlefield, 2005).

idea of the postcolonial has associations with poststructuralism. The emphasis here is on the way in which a historical period is represented and comes to have a presence in thought. Poststructuralism and postcolonialism are indeed related intellectual tendencies. Poststructuralism sought to problematise hegemonic ways of thinking in the humanities and the social sciences. Similarly, the postcolonial is the theorisation of a time of transition. It is concerned with the qualification of hegemonic ideas and the creation of ways of thinking that challenge the intellectual impositions that were part of the colonial period. As far as the study of postcolonial *legality* is concerned, the postcolonial remains in communication with these currents of thought, but focuses on the specificity of the legal instance. The postcolonial is the mark of the latecomer, who takes a backward glance at the western legal tradition.[4]

Although it is possible to draw attention to general patterns, the 'post' of postcolonialism should not be seen as an attempt to homogenise the different histories of nations that emerged in the retreat of the western powers from Empire. Although British colonialism in Africa—the focus in this chapter—had certain factors in common with that of other European powers, it also had its distinctive features. British colonialism was itself complex and diverse. One cannot simply separate the colonial experience in Africa from the wider dynamic. For instance, we will see that indirect rule was first developed in India. However, if one is concerned with the experience of indirect rule in Africa, distinctions have to be drawn. Policy in Kenya, for example, was very different from Tanganyika or Uganda. Furthermore, when we move to the postcolonial period, we have to engage with the different experiences of those nations that gained independence. There is undoubtedly a certain risk of reductionism in using a general term that elides the different experiences of, for example, Nigeria and Ghana, in becoming independent nations. So, while trying to discern patterns and continuities, it is also necessary to be sensitive to the diverse and heterogeneous methods of colonialism and the particular histories of postcolonial nations.[5]

How, then, can we describe postcolonial jurisprudence? If the classical jurisprudential project was to provide an over-arching definition of law as thought and practised, how does any latecomer to the field understand its operation in colonial territories? The most obvious link between classical and postcolonial jurisprudence is that they are both concerned with the construction

[4] In the terms of cultural studies, it could describe artistic production that is non Western, and could thus, for example, replace the idea of 'Commonwealth Literatures'. See P Mongia, *Contemporary Postcolonial Theory* (London, Arnold, 1996) 72.

[5] We need to deal with another preliminary issue. Does the 'post' of postcolonialism carry the associated risk that postmodernity is heralded in cultures for which it may be inappropriate? The difficulty here is perhaps not so much the postmodern *per se*, but theorisations of the postmodern that declare the end of history. What is perhaps more important is to see the postcolonial as sharing one possible sense with theorisations of the postmodern. We are concerned with a break; a problematic separation between the past and the present; or rather, a moment of rupture that declares a new order or a new beginning, but which is compromised by the enduring presence of the past.

of a theoretical perspective on law. The constitution of this perspective, though, is radically different.

Postcolonial jurisprudence emerges out of the independence struggles of nations extracting themselves from Empire. As a result, its main task is to help fashion a new law and to grapple with the intersection of European and indigenous traditions. This would lead to a theorisation of legal 'hybridity'[6] in general, but in this chapter, we will concentrate on an outline for a more general historical location of the problem of postcolonial law.

This leads back, once again, to an understanding of history as that which is both lived by individuals and influenced by 'forces' that are general and anonymous. An acute historical sense marks postcolonial legal theory. Indeed the common orientation of the various types of postcolonial jurisprudence is their rigorous engagement with history and genealogy.

This historical sensitivity calls for an engagement with the intellectual premises of colonial jurisprudence. A central concept of western jurisprudence is that of 'primitive' law. Primitive law represents a crude beginning that must be superseded. This is a view of history that takes as its central reference point the birth of the modern western state. The 'gift' of law to the 'savage' becomes one of the central justifications of the colonial project and becomes synonymous with the modern nation.

The Savage Economy of Jurisprudence

Peter Fitzpatrick's work has shown that the distinction between the savage and the civilised is central to the line of legal thinking running from Thomas Hobbes to Herbert Hart. It is as if English jurisprudence fixes disorder 'outside of law—in the eruptions and disruptions of untamed nature or barely contained human passion against which an ordering law is intrinsically set.'[7] This is part of a wider intellectual operation: the creation of a western, European identity[8] in opposition to the figure of the pre-modern savage who inhabits an undifferentiated natural world and has beliefs that are mythological, unscientific and fantastic. Cast out from the world of culture, the savage as an object of nature is destined to become something upon which reason will act, civilise and reform. Above all, the savage will be made subject to reason's sovereign power. It is not difficult to see how these philosophical presuppositions fed into the ideologies informing the establishment and perpetuation of both slavery and the colonial project.

[6] H Bhaba, *The Location of Culture* (London, Routledge, 1994).

[7] P Fitzpatrick, *The Mythology of Modern Law* (London, Routledge, 1992) 81. See also E Darian Smith and P Fitzpatrick (eds), *Laws of the Postcolonial* (Michigan, University of Michigan Press, 1999).

[8] P Fitzpatrick, *The Mythology of Modern Law*, above n 7, 65.

These foundational ideas of the western Enlightenment are themselves refined and adapted over time in the incremental development of the sciences of man. Studying the forms of definition, classification and periodisation that were used in these disciplines, one can trace a slow movement towards modes of understanding that stress ideas of progress and development. In anthropology and racial science, the intellectual project of constructing classifications that sought to establish identity through the negation of difference was developed with increasing sophistication.[9] Fortified by a sense of progress and the need to civilise the 'savage', the colonial powers increasingly expressed their identity through the denigration of those who they perceived to be 'unlike' themselves and could thus be subjected to a civilising process.[10] Scientists such as Robert Knox or Herbert Spencer drew on Charles Darwin to create accounts of the superiority of the white race. These attitudes are reflected in the words and work of the colonial administrators. Fitzjames Stephens, for example, wrote that English law 'is in fact the sum and substance of what we have to teach them. It is so to speak the gospel of the English, and it is a compulsory gospel which admits of no dissent and no disobedience.'[11]

We can trace this opposition of law and savagery to one of the major foundations of contemporary jurisprudence. Thomas Hobbes' proclamation of the Leviathan, the mortal god who will preserve the order of the community, can be seen as a definitional moment. Hobbes' vision of the chaotic state of nature, where man turns against his brother in a 'war of all against all' is directly informed by the structuring separation of savage nature from organised and regulated culture. Law is grounded in the covenant that founds the power of the Leviathan. Leviathan is the supreme sovereign, the line of separation, the bulwark that protects from a return to anarchy. Only when law guarantees social peace can the commonwealth come together. Although written much later than *Leviathan*, John Austin's *The Province of Jurisprudence Determined* takes shape in the same mythological space. Austin's definition of law as the command of the sovereign to which political inferiors owe habitual obedience is itself determined by Hobbes' *Leviathan*. Underlying Austin's jurisprudence are

[9] *Ibid*, 93.

[10] *Ibid*, 70.

[11] *Ibid*, 107. The background of empire and imperialism is central to this trope. To make use of Pakenham's terms, (developed with reference to Africa, but applicable here: T Pakenham, *The Scramble for Africa* (London, Weidenfeld and Nicolson, 1991) the issue is that of visible and invisible empire. The visible empire is founded and sustained through overt acts of violence. It is founded on the annihilation of anything that resists the *Pax Britannica*. Law is signified through a kind of martial justice that prepares the way for, and then polices, trade and economic exploitation. Invisible Empire, on the other hand, also makes use of the law as a way of setting up and sustaining an economic order. It operates, however, more subtly, through creating a legal and social order that includes and interfaces with native social structures. Perhaps invisible and visible empire are only a difference of degree, a more or less explicit violence that operates alongside economic exploitation. Invisible empire may be more effective, as it operates through a powerful thematics of normalisation. Imperialist legal relations enter the social world covertly under the guise of everyday routines, which can only be glimpsed partially in the alienated and reified relations that they leave as their trace. Visible empire relies on acts of force that are easier to resist.

the same assumptions about the desirability of law as a protection from the disorder of savage nature. Society could not possibly cohere without this line of demarcation. Consider the following example of the necessity of law in Austin's text. A 'solitary savage' could not be a 'social man', because he would not appreciate the necessity for communal living, and hence government: 'The savage mind is "unfurnished" with certain notions essential for society.'[12]

Although these concerns reached their apogee in the nineteenth century, we can discover a further development of this same mythology in Hart's *Concept of Law*. Hart's thesis tries to describe the most basic social functions that underlie any notion of law. Unless law has a minimum moral content 'men, as they are, would have no reason of obeying voluntarily any rules.' It is in justifying this particular minimal content of law that Hart employs a theory of human nature drawn from Hobbes.[13] Here again is the vision of savage society as unregulated and, anarchic; awaiting the coming of rational legal order. A stereotypical and racist understanding of indigenous law can easily emerge from this understanding of the 'primitive'. Modern law is, of course, marked by its flexibility. It can be distinguished from the primitive by a 'rule of recognition' that allows the system of rules to be changed by identifying a criterion that both marks rules and allows them to be changed. Primitive law is inflexible, rigid and impossible to change.

This genealogy of jurisprudence must be linked with the history of Empire. We need to move from the world of texts and ideas to examine the tensions occasioned by the coming of European law to Africa.

COLONISATION AND THE LAW

Following recent scholarship, it is possible to suggest a broadly tripartite typology of Empire.[14] Although this is somewhat simplistic, it does allow both generalisation about the law and, the observance of cultural specificity. Colonial history begins with the first attempts by European powers to exploit the resources and manpower of Africa, a period running from the sixteenth through to the eighteenth century. The second phase roughly corresponds with the nineteenth century, where direct appropriation was replaced by regimes of treaties

[12] P Fitzpatrick, *The Mythology of Modern Law*, above n 7, 79. Most interestingly, Austin makes a link between this savage state of nature and the unruly and restless poor, who do not appreciate the need for the law.

[13] Here is a fairly abysmal list of traits that are said to be characteristic of the human. The 'minimum purpose' of the law is survival. Men are marked by a human vulnerability that makes the prohibition of killing perhaps the most necessary link between law and morality. The 'approximate equality' of men makes necessary a mutual 'forbearance and compromise' which is again basic to both normative systems. It is, moreover, the need to improve these restraints that necessitates the move to formal systems of law. What also determines the human is a limited altruism; man is neither angel nor devil, but somewhere between, and it is this problematic quality that again makes for rules that restrain the more aggressive aspects of human character.

[14] K Mann and R Roberts, *Law in Colonial Africa* (London, James Currey, 1991).

and trading agreements. The third phase is that of the more formal colonial rule of the later 1900s. This latter phase could be seen as concluded, or redefined, by the withdrawal from Empire and the independence of the new sovereign states. Cutting across this typology are the different developments of law and colonialism that reflect the various traditions and experiments in government of the colonial powers. For instance, if one compares the British and the French colonial or dominion territories in Africa, one finds that law was used very differently.[15]

Let us return to the first phase. Within this period, European traders and settlers arrived on the West African coast. Research suggests that the relative weakness of the Europeans meant that they had to defer to existing indigenous structures of dispute resolution in matters of trade, although the increasing interactions between the various communities led to an intermingling of indigenous and European ideas and forms of law. For instance, attention has been drawn to conflicts between local customs and those of the Portuguese in claiming title over goods lost in the grounding of ships. The trading treaties drawn up at this time show a similar tension between the desire to maximise profits and the need to placate the indigenous people. Legal conflicts also arose between the rival jurisdictions that claimed authority over the employees of the various companies. The tensions produced by the presence of European trading concerns also impacted upon the traditional systems of legal regulation between Africans. Disputes arose over trading privileges and the distribution of the proceeds of the trade in slaves and other commodities.

The nineteenth century saw a shift in the legal relationships between Africans and Europeans. Driving these changes were factors such as the industrial revolution, the ideological mission to civilise and the consequences of the abolition of slavery in 1807. There was also a greater European penetration into the interior of the continent. Legal relationships in the areas around the coast became increasingly Europeanised. Local customs and legal practices were eclipsed as commercial transactions were regulated by contract and property relationships rather than by traditional forms. Consider the Nile Delta and the Gold Coast. British trading companies extended their jurisdiction over areas where previously they had been content to see 'native' authority prevail. The Courts of Equity that developed did take some account of local customary laws, but reached their decisions primarily based on what a panel of white men thought was correct.

[15] For an earlier account of the differences between the British and French colonial experiences, see WR Crocker, *On Governing Colonies: Being an Outline of the Real Issues and a Comparison of the British, French and Belgian Approach to Them* (London, G Allen and Unwin Ltd, 1947). More recent studies would include: J Kent, *The Internationalization of Colonialism: Britain, France, and Black Africa, 1939–1956* (Oxford, Clarendon, 1992) and P Gifford and WR Louis (eds), *France and Britain in Africa: Imperial Rivalry and Colonial Rule* (New Haven, CT and London, Yale University Press, 1971). For an engagement with the aftermath of colonialism, see WH Morris-Jones and G Fischer (eds), *Decolonisation and After: the British and French Experience* (London, Cass, 1980) and AI Asiwaju, *West African Transformations: Comparative Impact of French and British Colonialism* (Ikeja, Lagos State, Nigeria, Malthouse Press, 2001).

This period also saw the formalisation of colonial rule. The French possessions, the Four Communes (St Louis, Goree, Dakar and Rufisque) and the British Crown Colonies (Freetown, the Gambia, The Gold Coast and Lagos) were subjected to new bureaucracies and court structures. However, it is important to note the important differences between the British and French approaches to colonial administration. In the British Crown Colonies the common law of England was meant to apply although the lack of resources and training meant that the courts operated somewhat differently than was desired. In the late 1900s, the colonial courts were reorganised. The jurisdiction of the local customary courts was revised. On the Gold Coast, a path of appeal was created from customary courts to the British courts, whereas in both Freetown and Lagos, African courts were not officially recognised. The major difference between the operation of the courts in the Crown Colonies and the Four Communes was an issue of access: Africans could use the British courts, whilst the French courts were reserved for French citizens.

The nineteenth century was marked by the 'Scramble for Africa' by the nations of Europe. This was an intensification of the processes of colonialism, triggered by a growing commercial and political rivalry that brought home to the western European powers the vital necessity of securing the only remaining fields for industrial enterprise and expansion. The French and the British created vast empires. The law that Empire brought with it was suited to the demands of a territorially extended power. Whereas the French conquest through arms from 1850 to the 1890s produced subject peoples that did not enjoy the privileges of the Four Communes, the British preference for establishing protectorates rather than conquered subjects led to a certain countenancing of local customs and laws. For the French, the tension between policies that gave powers to local administrators and those which centralised administration were resolved with the publication in 1903 of a legal code that created a system that pertained to French citizens and a separate one that applied to colonial subjects.

There is obviously more to an understanding of colonial law than this historical sketch suggests. We will turn our attention to the principles that underlay colonial legality. However, we can only suggest in our following arguments the subtle way in which colonial law refined itself as it developed. In Anglophone Africa, the development of colonial law built on experiences in India. In India, the British had inherited a diverse body of customary laws drawing on Hindu and Moslem traditions. The former was not as well developed and organised as the latter, but both were based on sacred texts and had a written tradition. Legal policy for India was founded on the principle of applying English law to the English, and Indian law to Indians. The period from 1823–35 was one of procedural and criminal re-organisation, influenced in part by Bentham. The Law Commissions of 1833, 1853 and 1861 laid down the foundations of a universal and codified law. However, the form of Indian law was largely left in place. The colonial administration recognised that:

> The problem for the British was primarily to find a system of law which would avoid emphasising to India the fact that it was passing under the dominion of a power professing an alien faith.[16]

The response to this problem was the development of indirect rule. Consider Warren Hastings' letter of 1772 to the directors of the East India Company:

> It would be a grievance to deprive the people of the protection of their own laws, but it would be a wanton tyranny to require the obedience to others of which they are wholly ignorant—and of which they have no possible means of acquiring a knowledge.[17]

Indirect rule developed slowly and incrementally. Even in India there was a distinction between the Princely States where the British Resident supervised indigenous rulers, and other areas where direct rule applied. Different approaches were also adopted in other part of the empire. Indirect rule perhaps reached its most sophisticated development in the protectorate of Northern Nigeria through Sir Frederick Lugard's administration. And after 1914, indirect rule became the preferred model throughout the areas of Africa that the British controlled.

Indirect rule was a solution to the problem of governing a vast empire with scarce manpower and increasingly tight fiscal controls over the available resources. Indirect rule proposed an equal—but different—set of duties and responsibilities for the native and the British courts. For instance, Lugard made use of the power of the Muslim Emirs in the North of Nigeria to regulate affairs between the subject population and the demands of the colonial state. He also promoted Islamic judges to staff native courts. If there was a territory where the indigenous forms of authority and dispute resolution were not sufficiently hierarchical, Native Authorities were created or imposed; one such case was that of Igboland in the east of Nigeria. The Igbo had been a tribe where authority was vested in village councils, a relatively democratic forum. The imposed Native Authorities thus lacked the legitimacy that they might have enjoyed elsewhere. In general, though, the native courts had to be authentic and to be based on the traditions of the people over whom they had authority. 'Each clan' had to be able to bring cases before the tribunal. It was recommended that authority was best created and sustained through operations at the village level. The procedures and operations of native courts could be rooted in perceived tribal traditions, but their operation had to be impartial.

Behind indirect rule lay the force of imperial law. Native law was nothing without its imperial supplement. The native rulers were not independent.[18] Government reserved the right to control the central mechanisms of power: law making, levying taxation, control of the armed forces and the key powers over

[16] Lord Haily, *An African Survey* (Oxford, OUP, 1943) 263.
[17] *Ibid.*
[18] D Cameron, *The Principles of Native Administration and Their Application* (Lagos, 1934) 33.

land distribution. However, in the name of the efficient functioning of the system, the fact that all authority rested on the force of imperial law had to be concealed. Indeed, native administrations were encouraged not to present their decisions as if they emanated from the Government, but to utilise the power they had to frame their own rules. The native administrations were not supposed to be seen to 'lean'[19] on the government as this avoided the 'odium' that might be associated with an unpopular measure. If the natives appreciated that their own chiefs and headsmen issued orders' colonial power effectively disappeared.

We can perhaps see the later phase of the British Empire as an attempt to extend the principles of indirect rule even further. If it was inevitable that former colonial territories would claim their independence, then indirect rule had to become a way of inculcating a legal culture in the most 'forward' natives. Indeed, indirect rule became a means of preserving good order in the transfer of power from Westminster to those 'nations' that could show that they were ready for responsibility. As Sir David Cameron pointed out, indirect rule 'is designed to adapt for the purposes of local government the tribal institutions which the native peoples have evolved for themselves, so that the latter may develop in a constitutional manner from their own past[.]' Indirect administration was thus, in this later period, a method of creating individual responsibility[20] and a civic culture that valued justice and the rule of law. In Cameron's words, we 'must graft our higher civilization upon the soundly rooted native stock.' It was vital not to 'destroy the African atmosphere, the African mind.'[21] We could call this the ideology of the good African. The good African realises that his fate is attached to his land and his people, and cannot be achieved through merely adopting European manners and styles of government. The discourse of the good African is connected to the supplemental character of native administration. Given its backwardness and primitiveness, a 'true African civilization' must be 'stimulated' by the British. A people only become such when they are completely identified with the law.

ENTERING THE POSTCOLONIAL: THE EXAMPLE OF NIGERIA

The transition from dependent territory to sovereign state marks the beginning of the postcolonial. However, this apparent moment of new beginnings conceals a colonial inheritance that was to influence the law and politics of the independent nations. This is precisely the problem with the granting of independence

[19] *Ibid*, 46.
[20] *Ibid*, 15.
[21] *Ibid*, 8.

constitutions to former dependent or colonial territories. Although the constitution symbolises a new beginning, it also marks a point of continuity.[22]

Can a constitutional structure allow a nation to come into being? Nigeria, a concept of British administrators, was founded on tactics of divide and rule. An independence constitution had to unify and create a people who were not yet properly 'Nigerian'. We will read these tensions in a tract by the celebrated lawyer and patriot, Obafemi Awolowo. Awolowo begins with a ghost; a shade summoned from the past to face a nation that has 'skeletons in the cupboard:'[23]

> To-day, if Mungo Park[24] came back to life and visited Nigeria, he would say a word or two of prayer for those countrymen of his who have been administering the country.[25]

The shade of Mungo Park knows that the old order does not have much time left. We have reached the 'turning point.'[26] However, can the British continue in their claim to Nigeria? Can the past maintain its hold on the present?[27] Awolowo's text makes the necessary move from what Nigeria was, to what it might become:

> When Britain decided to annex the territories that now constitute Nigeria, her motives were to advance her economic interests, to gain strategic military positions, and to enhance her political prestige. In order to secure these things it was imperative that the people, after having been subjugated, should be pacified. Order and law must be maintained. Commerce does not flourish in a turbulent country, nor can military posts be

[22] We can study this process with reference to Nigeria. Nigerian scholars have dubbed the period up to 1946 as that of 'complete subordination' (BO Nwabueze, *A Constitutional History of Nigeria* (London, Hurst and Co, 1983) 36). Governmental power over Nigeria rested in the hands of the governor; the country had been split into two protectorates in the north and the south, and over this vast territory the Governor was both 'sole executive and legislature' (*ibid,* 36). Lagos was treated somewhat differently, but, by 1914 had been amalgamated with the southern and northern protectorates to form one unit: the Colony and Protectorate of Nigeria. However, this early constitutional structure attempted to incorporate Nigerian interests in decision making. The 1922 constitution created a legislative council, with a jurisdiction over the south of the country and Lagos. For the first time, the governor's legislative powers were qualified by a requirement that he act on the 'advice and consent' (*ibid,* 37) of the council, although there was no real sense in which executive or governmental power had been taken out of the hands of the British administrators. The two constitutions of 1946 and 1951 made further changes. The 1946 constitution saw the establishing of a Nigerian legislative council whose jurisdiction covered the entire country; regional assemblies determined the membership of the council. The essential function of this arrangement was not to 'associate the natives of Nigeria in the conduct of their country's government but to enable the British officials to avail themselves of local opinion' (*ibid,* 44). Certain advances were made by the 1951 constitution, including elected majorities in the central and regional legislatures, and the devolution of limited legislative powers to the latter bodies. These were moves towards 'internal self government' (*ibid,* 52).

[23] O Awolowo, *Path To Nigerian Freedom* (London, Faber and Faber, 1957) 20.

[24] Mungo Park (1771–1806) was one of the first European explorers to travel into West Africa. Park drowned whilst leading a British government mission to chart the course of the River Niger.

[25] *Ibid,* 17.

[26] *Ibid.*

[27] On the riddle of the nation, see P Fitzpatrick, *Modernism and the Grounds of Law* (Cambridge, Cambridge University Press, 2001).

maintained in a state of efficiency where the inhabitants are not amenable to orderly government.[28]

'Nigeria' is a country that will be brought into being by the law, but a law that has not, as yet, been stated. When Awolowo wrote in 1957, one could not talk of Nigeria as an independent nation. It was still either a convenient division of land, a line drawn on a map by Sir Charles Goldie—an administrative organisation to better enable the exploitation of its resources—or, a collection of diverse peoples whose only common language was English. At the same time, Awolowo is invoking constitutional values and linking them to his imagination of Nigeria as a nation defined by its constitution. The goal is 'the United States of Nigeria'; a 'federal unity.'[29]

However, Awolowo also had profound misgivings about the fissiparous tendencies of the different ethnic groups that composed the body politic. The federal constitution would have to allow the representation of all groups and local autonomy. If these issues were not resolved, Nigeria would fall victim to 'tribalism' and 'clannishness'. Indeed, events were to show that the nation's federal structure was distorted by the power of the regional assemblies that represented local and ethnic interests. Moreover, the structure of the republic was such that the populous north could always dominate the other states that composed the federation. This tendency was enshrined in the first-past-the-post system of elections that had been inherited from British politics.[30]

Despite the attempts made in the Independence Constitution to hold the nation together, Nigerian unity began to unravel. The regions themselves reflected the groupings of ethnic majorities.[31] In the north, the Hausa/Fulani were the dominant grouping; the western region was controlled by the Yoruba and the East by the Igbo. This could be called 'indigenous colonialism'[32] as the minority ethnic groups within the three regions were forced to attach themselves to the majority groupings. Regionalism vied with a set of claims that the minorities were best protected by the creation of a nation in which ethnic identities were to be resolved in a broader sense of belonging. Majority groups claimed the right to 'lead' the country or made threats of secession.

These tensions, exacerbated by the British administration,[33] were suspended and deferred in the moment of independence, but revisited themselves upon the

[28] O Awolowo, *Path to Nigerian Freedom*, above n 23, 58. On the writing of nation, see H Bhaba, *The Location of Culture* (New York, Routledge, 1994). See also A Mbembe, *On the Postcolony* (California, University of California Press, 2001).

[29] O Awolowo, *Path to Nigerian Freedom*, above n 23, 55.

[30] E Osaghae, *Crippled Giant: Nigeria since Independence* (London, Hurst and Co, 1998) 36.

[31] K Saro-Wiwa, *Genocide in Nigeria: the Ogoni Tragedy* (Lagos, Saros International, 1992) 20.

[32] *Ibid.*

[33] The political problems inherited by the independent state have their roots in the colonial order. Colonialism fostered strong central institutions rather than participatory democracy. Nigerian scholars have dubbed the period up to 1946 as that of 'complete subordination.' Governmental power over Nigeria rested in the hands of the governor; the country had been split into two protectorates in the north and the south, and over this vast territory, the Governor was both 'sole executive and legislature' (BO Nwabueze, *A Constitutional History of Nigeria*, above n 22, 36.

young nation. Within six years of independence, the Prime Minister, Sir Abubakar Tafawa Balewa, was killed in a military coup[34] that was led by the Igbo against Yoruba and Hausa/Fulani factions. Violence bred violence, as the leader of the coup, Major-General Aguiyi-Ironsi, was in turn murdered in a second revolt led by Hausa/Fulani generals. In the wake of violence came renewed calls for the break up of the federation; moves opposed by ethnic minority groupings. As a response to these tensions, General Ojukwu announced, in May 1967, the independence of the state of Biafra, an Igbo nation. Civil war broke out later that year.

We have not got the space in this chapter to trace the post-war history of Nigeria, but the fundamental constitutional weakness is evidenced by the succession of military coups.[35] As Nigeria is at present under civilian rule, the problems of holding together the 'imagined community' of the nation have taken a different form.[36] A juristic response can be seen in the contemporary writings of Nigerian legal scholars. In particular, the work of Von Savigny and the historical school of jurisprudence is seen as offering an account of the conjunction of nation and law; an understanding of law as 'an aspect of the total common life of the nation, not something made by the nation as a matter of choice or convention, but, like its manners and language, bound up with its existence.'[37]

This position allows criticism of both the colonial legacy and the period of dictatorship. In the colonial period, the recognition of native law and custom was an acknowledged source of law, but this was not a valid expression of national being as the guiding spirit was 'imperialism.'[38] It is only with the catalogue of fundamental human rights in the Constitution of 1960 that any movement of Nigerian law towards the protection of the rights of citizens could be identified. The Independence Constitution thus coordinates fundamental rights with an independent nation. This could only be given any real sense if the

[34] *Ibid*, 26.

[35] After the civil war, military government continued until 1979, and oversaw the re-unification and reconstruction of the country (E Oshagae, *Crippled Giant: Nigeria Since Independence*, above n 30, 68–77). However, tensions remained, as it was widely perceived that resource distribution was inequitably organised along ethnic lines. The return to civilian government after the foundation of the Second Republic in 1979 did not entirely resolve these problems. Indeed, one of the reasons given by the military for their coup in 1983 was the corruption and incompetence of the federal government (*ibid*, 155). The coup led by General Buhari brought the end of the Second Republic, and a second coup in 1985 ousted Buhari and brought General Babangida to power. In 1992, the creation of an Interim National Government signalled the tortuous restoration to civil rule. This was interrupted by General Abacha's military coup of 1993.

[36] One example would be the ongoing agitation for the imposition of Shari'a law in the north of the country. The Shari'a appears to provide an alternative constitution, a text over which the politics of belonging in Nigeria are playing themselves out. Moreover, the concerns over Shari'a law suggest that the need to develop a coherent postcolonial identity returns to the issue of the law as the structure that allows a nation to cohere.

[37] TO Elias, *Groundwork of Nigerian Law* (London, Routledge & Kegan Paul, 1954) 16. See also TO Elias, *Towards a Common Law in Nigeria* (Lagos, University of Lagos, 1972) 254–73 and TO Elias and MI Jegede (eds), *Nigerian Essays in Jurisprudence* (Lagos, MIJ Publishers, 1993).

[38] K Eso, *Thoughts on Law and Jurisprudence* (Lagos, MIJ Publishers, 1990), at 261.

Nigerian courts sought to protect those rights against the executive and legislative arms of the state. In the landmark decision of *Olawoyin v Commissioner of Police*,[39] the Supreme Court declared that as the legislation was obscure, the court itself must 'assum[e] the role of legislator, since we are dealing with a case which the legislature can hardly be supposed to have considered.'[40] If the courts have the jurisdiction to create law, then they can express the fundamental spirit of the people.

The grounding idea is that law 'benefits the people generally.'[41] Here is a radical claim that reflects both a theory of history and a faith in a notion of a Nigerian people. What problems must this law face? Nigerian jurisprudence is clearly making use of the democratic potential of the courts to uphold the Constitution, but the argument goes much further than this. There are indications that the law enshrines a substantive notion of justice: *State v Gwonto* is the most striking expression of this theme:

> The picture of law and its technical rules triumphant and justice prostrate may no doubt have its admirers. But the spirit of justice does not reside in forms and formalities, nor in technicalities, nor is the triumph of the administration of justice to be found in successfully picking one's way between pitfalls of technicalities.[42]

The precise sense in which an appeal to a substantive justice at common law can be coordinated with a broader concept of nation building remains vague. One particularly pressing issue is the relationship between national legal orders and the international jurisdiction of the African Union. The sense that both the civil libertarian bent of the common law and the impact of international human rights provide a way forward points towards the ongoing transformation of the discourse of law in Nigeria. If there is a positive legacy of the common law and the rule of law tradition, it might be found in these efforts to define a just polity; to invent Nigeria as a stable, constitutional nation in the face of the colonial legacy of military dictatorship.

THE END OF THE PORTUGUESE EMPIRE: REVOLUTION IN MOZAMBIQUE

The relatively peaceful, if problematic, achievement of Nigerian independence can be contrasted with the revolution that gained independence for Mozambique from the Portuguese Empire.

The Portuguese Empire in Africa can be contrasted with that of other European powers by the nature of its commitment to its African territories[43] in

[39] *Olawoyin v Commissioner of Police* [1961] 1 All NLR 203.
[40] Eso, above n 38, at 275.
[41] *Ibid*, at 18.
[42] *State v Gwonto* [1983] Nigerian Monthly Law Reports 142, at 160.
[43] Portugal's African territories were: Portuguese Guinea, Angola and Mozambique.

the period after the Second World War. Indeed, when other western nations were either negotiating independence, or accepting that it was necessary, the Portuguese intensified their colonising activities. Both political and economic factors lay behind this policy. The revised constitution of 1951 renamed former colonies 'overseas provinces' of a Greater Portugal. The military government made the Empire a central aspect of its ruling ideology. Economically, the position of the metropolitan power was shifting slowly away from the reliance on the colonies as a source for cheap raw materials and as a market for products, but there was also still ongoing emigration.[44]

Although this late and continuing engagement is a distinguishing factor of Portuguese colonialism, its empire can be mapped onto the typology suggested above. The early period saw trade between coastal and inland African communities and Portuguese merchants in gold, slaves and other commodities. The Portuguese abolition of the slave trade in 1836 disrupted these patterns of trade, and led in the 1840s to a need to consolidate colonial territories in a 'forward policy' that predated the Scramble of the 1870s.[45] We can trace the rudiments of colonial legal policy through these same periods. In the early colonial period, the Portuguese made use of a system of land ownership and settlement (*Prazos da Coroa*), based on the ownership of parcels of land, given to a settler for a period of time and worked by African slaves. As with other empires, tensions developed between the *Prazeiros* and the central power, leading in 1832 to a major reform of the system that limited the *Prazeiros'* law-making powers and abolished slavery.

A key moment in the development of an over-arching system of colonial administration came in 1907 with the initiation of a dual legal system that applied one set of laws to the white settlers and another to the indigents. It is possible to glimpse the dynamics of this system in outline by reference to a provision of the *Lei Organica*, the redrafted code that applied after 1914. Clause 18 stated: 'The indigenous by virtue of his primitive stage of civilisation shall be submitted to a special judicial and political system.' From 1914 to 1961 Africans were denied rights in Portuguese institutions. This separate status can be illustrated by the *Estatuto dos Indigenas* of 1929 that expressly forbade the 'natives' 'political rights', and a law of 1933 that reorganised native authorities. Thus, native populations were organised into divisions (*regedorias*) corresponding to traditional territories. Within *regedorias*, traditional figures could maintain their authority through the jurisdiction of customary law.[46] As with the British Empire, the key to colonial law was not the creation of the native as a subject without rights and without law. Rather, the native is a subject to a different

[44] HS Wilson, *African Decolonisation* (London, Edward Arnold, 1994) 180. This never reached the levels that would allow it to be compared to a settlor economy such as that which developed in Kenya throughout the period of British rule.

[45] M Newitt, *Portugal in Africa: The Last Hundred Years* (London, C Hurst and Co, 1981) 1–20.

[46] MLMM Correia de Matos, *Portuguese Law and the Administration in Mozambique* (University of London PhD thesis, 1969).

form of law. Even after the reforms of 1945, state agencies maintained control of indigenous populations through draconian labour laws that rested on the 'right' of the state to 'oblige all the indigenous people of the colonies to work.'[47]

Resistance to colonial rule took many forms, but one of the major foci was the foundation of a popular front FRELIMO (*Frente de Libertacco de Mozambique*) in 1962. The struggle intensified at the end of the 1960s with the conduct of guerrilla warfare from bases inside Zambia. The collapse of the regime in Mozambique was accelerated by the 'Revolution of the Flowers' in Portugal in 1974, and a precipitous withdrawal from the former colonial territory. FRELIMO occupied the power vacuum and attempted to realise a socialist vision for the newly liberated territories whilst dealing with internal dissent exacerbated by Rhodesian and South African attempts to destabilise the new government. These events made for a very different achievement of a post colonial legal order. However, like Awolowo's imagination of new beginnings, the FRELIMO government pronounced a zero hour; an inbreaking of the future:

> At Zero hour on the 25th June 1975, the Central Committee of the Mozambique Liberation Front (FRELIMO) solemnly proclaimed the total and complete independence of Mozambique and its establishment as the People's Republic of Mozambique.[48]

This passage is the Preamble from the 1990 Constitution and can be read as a testament to a new beginning, a break with the past. The Constitution states a 'Fundamental law', and, as such, announces the identity of the people of Mozambique with a struggle that has given them their freedom. The Constitution will precipitate a democratic future, a 'State of social justice' (Article 1). Law and revolution must be understood in terms of their 'mutual independence' and will lead to 'the total transformation of rural . . . society'.[49] It was necessary to dismantle the colonial structure, and construct a unitary legal system that could coherently apply the newly articulated legal principles. After a period of consultation, the Courts Act of 1978 made for the election at both local and district levels of people's tribunals. People's tribunals were drawn from local communities and empowered to give judgements that were 'in the interests of the people.'[50] These courts were seen as essential to the transforming dynamic of the revolution.

For FRELIMO the issues of law reform and land reform were fundamental to the very nature of revolutionary society. In a directive issued by Samora Machel, the President of FRELIMO, the following passage appeared:

[47] *A Report of the Commission for the Utilization of African Labour* cited in E Martins, *Colonialism and Imperialism in Mozambique* (African Studies, Kastrup Denmark, 1974) 64.

[48] The Constitution of Mozambique.

[49] A Sachs and GH Welch, *Liberating the Law: Creating Popular Justice in Mozambique* (London, Zed Books, 1990) 27.

[50] *Ibid*, 55.

> If I am Nyanja, and cultivate the land alongside an Ngoni, I sweat with him, wrest life from the soil with him, learn with him, appreciating his efforts, and I feel united with him . . . [w]ith him I am destroying tribal, religious and linguistic prejudices, and all that is secondary and divides us. Unity grows with the growing plant, with the sweat and intelligence we both mingle with the soil.[51]

If Awolowo's imagination was seized by Nigeria as a constitutional nation, then, for Machal, labour on liberated land produces the unity of the post-revolutionary Mozambique. Indeed, we could suggest that Machal's directive could be read as a jurisprudence of labour. Communal work on the land has to underlie and underpin any sense of meaningful law. A Constitution may be able to give a legal form to community. But this is nothing if old tribal bonds are not remade as belonging to a nation.

FRELIMO's reforming programme encountered resistance as it ran up against customary legal and governmental structures. These structures had been co-opted by the Portuguese regime into the system of colonial government and were ripe for reform. However, in certain areas they were perceived as legitimately resting on traditional authority. For instance, in Ngoni customary law the village headman or the chief played a central role in the distribution and redistribution of land to both Ngoni and non-Ngoni wishing to settle in Ngoni areas.[52] These issues were acute in relation to both the reform of the court structures, and the essential reforms of land law. The Mozambican Land Law, promulgated by the Peoples' Assembly in 1979, was a second essential intervention into what was seen as the colonial social structure. The whole revolutionary struggle was for title to land to rest with the people of Mozambique rather than the Portuguese colonialists.

Underlying the FRELIMO reforms was the abolition of private ownership of land through its nationalisation. This constitutional measure was further developed by the 1979 Land Law that prohibited the sale or alienation of land and made land use dependent on a grant of permission by the state. The 1979 statute vested land in the state, and gave a right to work the land. However, this law existed alongside customary forms of tenure that allowed both smallholders and communities to continue to enjoy customary rights. At the same time, customary courts lost their jurisdiction over land disputes, which were placed in the hands of courts overseen by FRELIMO cadres.[53] Despite this attempt to compromise with some forms of traditional authority, the new forms of land holding did not meet with universal success. Indeed, the new state faced opposition from different ethnic groupings. For instance, for the Macua: '(l)ocal patterns of land tenure gave the advantage to the lineage which controlled the land on which the communal village was built' and which stood in the face of FRELIMO

[51] S Machel, *Mozambique: Sowing the Seeds of Revolution* (London, Committee for Freedom in Mozambique, Angola and Guinea, 1977) 58.

[52] MLMM Correia de Matos, *Portuguese Law and the Administration in Mozambique*, n 46, 204.

[53] E Lahiff, *The Politics of Land Reform in South Africa* (Sustainable Livelihoods in South Africa Programme, University of Sussex, 2003) 8–9.

land reforms. The relative failure of these reforms is suggested by research in 1999 showing that 'a significant proportion' of land disputes were resolved by traditional means.

FRELIMO's reforms attempted to break down traditional patterns of ownership, but they did not seek to sweep away the past completely. The notion of popular justice that underlay the reforms was founded on the communitarian nature of the differing forms that traditional justice took. To reinvent traditional justice, though, it was necessary to make a distinction between form and content: the feudal content of the traditional had to be stripped away and the form connected to notions of due process.[54] Complete destruction of existing customs would not inculcate respect for the law. At the same time custom must not be fetishised, because it preserves oppressive relations from the past. Development will itself transform custom: one must proceed incrementally, because 'leap[ing] over stages of development sets back rather than advances the revolutionary process.'[55]

This takes us to the central paradox of the revolution: 'the central drama of any revolutionary process, is that the system must be changed while the people remain the same . . . "[t]he people must change themselves."[56] But, what happens when the people refuse to change themselves or refuse to participate in the institutions that the new state has created? An assessment of the effectiveness of social and legal reforms suggests that there is indeed a social 'residue' that resists transformation. Consider the strange *volte face* made by Joaquim Chissano, the Mozambican President, when he announced in 1995 that 'we want traditional authority to exist.'[57] Former '*regulos*' of the Portuguese colonial government greeted this statement with celebrations, and saw it as suggesting that their return to power was imminent. How can we understand the need of a revolutionary government to speak in these terms? Of course, it could be accounted for in terms of pure pragmatics—the need to win over those elements that were sympathetic to counter-revolutionary tendencies. It may also suggest an attempt to undo a mistake that the government had made in opposing the revolutionary and the traditional in such stark terms.

The survival of traditional ways remaining preserved within the transformed returns us to the dilemma of the postcolonial. If there can ever be a jurisprudence of transformation, it needs to engage with this failure of 'zero' hour; or the long shadow that the past casts over the present. Indeed, the very term 'traditional' must be understood as a construction; a 'multi-layered substrate of local histories' where tradition is created and reinterpreted. If this is the case, if

[54] *Mozambique Briefing: Building a New Legal System* (Maputo Information Department, Frelimo Party Central Committee, 1987) 7.

[55] *Ibid*, 71.

[56] A Sachs and GH Welch, *Liberating the Law: Creating Popular Justice in Mozambique*, above n 49, 57.

[57] H West and S Kloeck-Jensen, 'Betwixt and Between: Traditional Authority and Democratic Decentralisation in Post War Mozambique' (1999) 98 *African Affairs* 455, at 457.

Mozambicans must find a common language'[58] then they must settle with their own past in a way that holds together continuity and change.

NATION AND THE FORECLOSED LEGAL SYSTEM

What wider conclusions can we draw about postcolonial legality?

This chapter ends with an image of the fragile nation and an equally fragile notion of a national legal culture. Can we connect this concern with any broader themes in the study of the postcolonial? Consider the following argument:

> Especially in the critique of metropolitan culture, the event of the political independence can be automatically assumed to stand between colony and decolonisation as an unexamined good that operates a reversal. But the political goals of the new nation are supposedly determined by a regulative logic derived from the old colony, with its interest reversed. . .[59]

Although this description of the postcolonial is not specifically directed towards the notion of postcolonial legality, it can perhaps assist us in working through some general orientating themes. An approach to postcolonial legality can, first of all, be conceived of as a 'critique' of 'metropolitan culture' to the extent that it is based on a criticism of the suppositions of a certain jurisprudential tradition. We have seen how these concerns play themselves out with reference to the notion of 'savage culture' in British jurisprudence. Equally as important, though, is the blindness of a way of conceptualising law that ignores history, or, more precisely, the experience of the imposition of the common law as the work of empire.

But the study of the postcolonial is not simply a re-contextualisation of jurisprudence. It is focused upon an 'event'—a problematic and double event. Of course, to refer to the independence of former colonial territories as a single event is far too reductive. The sense of 'event' appeals more to a set of historical singularities that are both peculiar, and which reveal general patterns. Indeed, this chapter has suggested that there is a certain generality to the different ways in which Nigeria and Mozambique gained their independence. Perhaps the central question for the study of postcolonial legality is how the event of independence can be theorised. What sense can we make of the language of 'reversal' in the above quotation? In what sense can we find a 'regulative logic' in the achievement of independence?

The problem faced by the postcolonial nation is one of a colonial legacy. How can law that was used in colonialism be refashioned as the mark of independence? Postcolonial legality leads us to the question of force and of contending forces. After the overthrow of colonialism, there was an attempt to re-fashion

[58] *Ibid*, 469.

[59] GC Spivak, *Outside in the Teaching Machine* (London, Routledge, 1993) 78.

the national legal order either from scratch or incrementally.[60] We have seen that both the constitutional and revolutionary achievements of independence faced difficult tasks. To what extent was it possible to create a new beginning? The difficulty of carrying forward postcolonial reconstruction demands an analytic; a way of conceiving the peculiar nexus of problems.

We could describe this recreation of the legal order of a nation as taking place through a certain foreclosure. Foreclosure can become a way of understanding the continuation of the nation, the adoption and attempted transformation of imposed structures—a way that one continues to think with concepts that are compromised.[61] Foreclosure can be used to theorise the point at which law's symbolic order comes up against a moment when what has been denied erupts and 'marks' it. (The Real is or carries the mark of that expulsion).[62] After this reappearance, the symbolic order will never be the same again. Confronted with the real, it has to redefine itself. This might describe the relationship of the old colonial order to the moment of independence, but, it also indicates another aspect of this problem. The new order has to define itself against a real that has been created by the old order. In its most extended sense, this could describe the way in which the new order is marked by the conflicts of the old. Postcolonial jurisprudence thus studies a colonial legacy; it investigates the struggle with the past, and the very possibility that an independent nation can emerge as a nation of law.

PASSAGES

In the hotel room in Jo'burg I hang my suit from the curtain rail and gaze over the brown smog of the city. I arrange the travelling library. The copy of *The Republic* and *The Inferno*. I just cannot read Dante. I watch the beggars with cardboard signs by the traffic lights. My passport and money are hidden under the bed. When I go out, I will take *The Inferno* with me. If I'm jumped, they can have it.

Later, after the conference, we take a taxi to the airport. I am sitting in the back; tired and bewildered by this manic city; gazing at its madness from the car window. P is by the driver. He's talking in urgent tones: 'this is not the way to the airport. Please turn round. Now.' P has clicked down the lock on his door.

[60] What perhaps stands in the face of the nation are different modes and senses of ethnic belonging that are, more or less, intractable to the secular, modern, liberal nation; or rather, the extent to which this nation exists, is that its existence is qualified or bracketed by different orders. We could, then, speak of the foreclosed nation, or the foreclosed legal order.

[61] In the sense deployed by Freud and, latterly, Lacan, foreclosure theorised a defence mechanism, a form of disavowal, where the ego rejects what is uncomfortable, and attempts to continue as if nothing had troubled it. Of course, the search for what lies behind this mechanism is the proper practice of the analyst. However, this hermeneutic operation is also a trope for the operation of critical theory; indeed, it might be most broadly claimed that the Freud who turns to the use of psychoanalysis as a form of understanding the social, makes use of this very figure.

[62] GC Spivak, *A Critique of Post Colonial Reason* (Cambridge, Mass, Harvard University Press, 1999) 5.

Part 5

Aesthetic Jurisprudence

12

Psychoanalysis Becomes the Law

We are not castrated, so you get fucked. (Feminist Slogan)

THE FIRST SESSION: RATS AND GOVERNMENT

A PSYCHOANALYSIS THAT BECOMES the law raises the issue of a political ethics. It is a matter of asking what kind of psychoanalysis works best for us. What tasks do we want it to fulfill? Our preference is for a way of thinking that can describe the material world of politics, not the bourgeois subject supine on the analyst's couch talking, talking, talking.

Our guiding thread is the question of desire. How does desire relate to the law? Does the law ban or does it produce desire? For St Paul, sin is the creation of the law, while for Hobbes, uncontrollable desire leads to the creation of the all-powerful state of Leviathan and law. What does it mean to say that the subject is produced by desire?

The first section of this chapter will engage with the legal preoccupations of Sigmund Freud. Freud is concerned with the origins of law and its contribution to the creation of the ego and the superego. The family drama and the Oedipal structure set the tone for the encounter between law and psychoanalysis. We will then move to the thought of the celebrated psychoanalyst Jacques Lacan and his jurist follower, Pierre Legendre. Their development of Freudian theory offers a complex picture of the law, the subject and social being. From this perspective, we can explain the persisting and disturbing sense of injustice felt throughout the centuries as the result of an inescapable and insatiable desire.

Lacanian theory offers great insights into the psychic structure of the subject and its implications for law and society. But psychoanalytical jurisprudence must also challenge its basic assumptions. However, it is not as if Lacan's thought can be simply opposed to a 'different' model of the analytical. Read correctly, Lacan problematises his own thought, as, indeed, psychoanalysis constantly problematises itself. We would prefer to follow a certain line out of Lacan, a way of thinking through and against psychoanalysis. Might it be possible to move towards a notion of the unconscious as productive, as resisting the limitations that 'Oedipalisation' imposes upon it? Is that acceptable?

The resistance to Oedipalisation is at the beginnings of a new way of thinking, feeling and living as a subject. This way of thinking plays together a Marxist and psychoanalytic register: desire as production and the production of desire. The subject does not realise herself through a humanistic self discovery of an inner essence, or through the awareness of self as a reflexive process, a creation of 'personhood.' Similarly, communitarian or communist accounts, which identify being with community or class belonging, are equally misleading. The work of French philosophers and activists Gilles Deleuze and Felix Guattari points towards a theory in which power is immanent to the social field. Subjectivity re-appears as intensity and singularity, both defined by, and in opposition to, law and power.

THE SECOND SESSION: WHO'S THE DADDY? FREUD, GUILT, THE LAW

Freud presented the birth of the law as a crime story. The law and the social bond emerge in the bloody aftermath of murder and catastrophe. It is not so much that human nature is considered evil, but that law and morality emerge out of evil deriving from what they will eventually come to condemn and repress. The law is an always belated attempt to fight what led to its own genesis, violence and crime are launched at the heart of the law. So, Freud offers what could be called a genealogy or rather a foundational myth for law's genesis; secondly, Freud discovers the structuring principle of the social bond and is able to understand the reasons why the efforts over three millennia of the finest minds and fieriest hearts, of philosophers, religious leaders and mystics, have left civilisation drowning in its discontent.

We need to tell you a story; a boy's own story.[1]

Freud's 'mythological theory of instincts'[2] and his myth of law's genesis start with the murder of the primordial father by his sons. Desiring the girls for themselves, the sons had come to resent their father's monopolisation of the females of the tribe. The murderers are retrospectively overcome by guilt and remorse, and in legislating against murder they open the field of the morality of interdiction. At the basis of morality thus lies a heinous crime, a patricide. The first and primordial principle through which 'culture begins in opposition to nature'[3] is the prohibition of incest.

[1] His eclectic hypothesis brings together Darwin's 'primal horde' theory with the psychoanalytical explanation of early anthropological evidence in a modern, 'scientific' myth of origins. The hypothesis is a myth, a 'Just-So Story' presented in an openly mythical form, which however has 'left indestructible traces upon the history of human descent'. Freud's story joins in the great myths that bridge religious, apocalyptic and scientific attempts to go back to an *origo*, a time before history and memory that founded the world and law: S Freud, 'Group Psychology and the Analysis of the Ego' in J Starchey (ed), *Civilisation, Society and Religion* (London, Penguin, 1985), above n 1 at 154.

[2] S Freud, 'Why War' in J Strachey (ed), *Civilisation, Society and Religion*, above n 1, 341, 359.

[3] J Lacan, *The Ethics of Psychoanlysis* (London, Routledge 1992) 66–7.

The theory about the foundation of the social bond and law's emergence appears in *Totem and Taboo*. Freud explains the ambivalent attitude of tribesmen towards totemic meals, in which the slaughtering of the animal leads to ritual mourning and lamentation followed by festive and excessive rejoicing. The totemic animal is a substitute for the Oedipal father. At this point, Freud wonders whether this explanation can be used to extrapolate the first form of human organisation. In the later *Group Psychology and the Analysis of the Ego*, Freud abandons the mythical form of the hypothesis of origins, but keeps its main characteristics which are presented as the psychological structure of contemporary groups and society. Groups are naturally and unavoidably divided into the leaders and the led. The primal father was 'the "superman" whom Nietzsche only expected from the future'[4] but who put into operation the principle of violent leadership at the beginning of history and still represents it. The chief, the leader or the hypnotist is very similar to the primal father. He is an individual of superior strength, totally free in his actions and independent of affiliations or affection for the group members. The leader does not love anyone but himself, and uses his subjects to serve his needs. Being free of any emotional, social or ethical ties, the narcissistic leader can offer himself as an object of adoration, with whom the group members identify and turn into a mass brought together in their love for the leader. 'Society', Freud informs us, 'is a unanimous "mass" whose members have set up the same "object" (the "leader" or "Fuhrer") in place of their ego ideal and who, as a result of so doing, identify, reciprocally and among themselves, with each other'.[5]

Freud links his analytical theory with the creation of law more directly in some of his late essays. In *Why War?* he sets out to explain the causes of warfare in response to an invitation by Einstein. His genealogy of the legal institution again starts with the hypothesis of the primal horde. Conflicts were resolved violently when the most powerful member of the horde killed or subjugated his opponents through brute force. The beginning of sociality is untrammeled violence and Freud insists that all law and right comes from violence. The road from the might of the strongest to the legal institution passes through the realisation by the victor that a union of the defeated and weaker members of society could challenge his domination. Law is therefore the replacement of individual violence by the organised violence of the community and is directed against any of its members who resist it. The Hobbesian undertones are striking. Freedom is no gift of civilisation; indeed freedom was much greater, although unenforceable, before the law intervened to protect security. Thus, the desire for freedom is often a remnant of this original untamed personality and expresses resentment and hatred for civilisation's suppression of liberty. The law is the first step in civilisation's long march to restrict the individual satisfaction of instincts and

[4] S Freud, *Why War?*, above n 2, 156.

[5] M Borch-Jacobsen, *The Emotional Tie: Psychoanalysis, Mimesis and Affect*, D Brick (trans), (Stanford, Stanford University Press, 1992) 25.

desires. Freud goes as far as to claim that the 'first requisite of civilization is justice—that is the assurance that a law once made will not be broken in favour of an individual.' But he immediately adds with a sardonic smile that 'this implies nothing as to the ethical value of such law'.[6]

If law and legal institutions are to succeed and persist over time within large social units, they must be recognised as serving communal interests and must help to create and foster emotional ties that will cement the group. But feelings of communal belonging must overcome a difficult obstacle. The members of the community are unequal and these imbalances are reflected in the laws legislated by the powerful and alleged to apply to all. The oppressed try constantly to overthrow their subordination, either by claiming the protection of the law and demanding equal justice or, more often, by rebelling and, if successful, starting a new regime of law that will soon develop the same pathology. Violence—intra or inter-community—cannot be avoided even after the rule of law has been established. Force stands at the origin of law and force is the outcome of the inherent inability of law to resolve conflict in a community that lacks communal feelings. Communities are held together by violence and by shared emotional ties which are not evident on the international level, making the violence of war the main way for resolving conflict. Freud insists again and again that we do not disregard the fact that 'law was originally brute violence and that even to-day it cannot exist without the support of violence'.[7] In the analytical schema, the law helps restrict violence and those urges that militate against civilisation, but at the same time it incorporates the force that it replaces—it is an expression of the powerful and can make no ethical claim other than the—impossible—equal subjection of all to the same rule. Finally, in its attempt to limit desire and aggression—which like their expression, war, seem to be 'quite a natural thing, to have a good biological basis and in practice to be scarcely avoidable'[8]—the law acts unnaturally and its success is inextricably bound with unfailing failure. The law makes the individual discontented by exchanging pre-social fragile happiness for a civilised but pleasureless security. 'The price we pay for our advance of civilisation is a loss of happiness through the heightening of the sense of guilt'.[9]

The only way to combat violence radically is to nurture those 'emotional ties' that Freud keeps mentioning. They are of two types; people may share feelings of love for each other but this is 'more easily said than done'. Or, they may share important interests and concerns, and thus draw closer through their identification with the shared object. There is not much doubt as to the objects of identification that Freud has in mind. The 'innate' and 'ineradicable' inequal-

[6] S Freud, 'Civilisation and its Discontents' in J Strachey (ed), *Civilisation Society and Religion*, above n 1, at 284.

[7] S Freud, 'Why War?', above n 2, 355.

[8] *Ibid*, 360.

[9] S Freud, 'Civilisation and its Discontents', above n 6, 327.

ity of men separates them into leaders and followers who 'stand in need of an authority which will make decisions for them and to which for the most part they offer an unqualified submission. This suggests that more care should be taken than hitherto to educate an upper stratum of men with independent minds . . . whose business it would be to give directions to the dependent masses'.[10] The father-chief-leader is the best supplement to violence and law's best ally.

THE THIRD SESSION: RELAX, THE LAW IS ALWAYS THERE BEFORE YOU

Freud accounted for the law with the myth of patricide: the murder of the primal father. In Lacan's reading, the murdered and cannibalised primal father does not explain the genesis of law. The patricide is a symbol of the internalisation of law that is necessary for the passage from natural survival to socio-cultural identity and adult sexuality. As the patricide and its consequences cannot be proved historically, its basic structure must be presupposed if we are to understand how subjectivity and sexuality come into existence. While Freud—in common with all great system builders and, in particular, his hero Moses—narrates the creation of law—Lacan is closer to the concerns of anthropology, linguistics and structuralism. He emphasises the constitutive operation of law for human identity. Freudian psychoanalysis tries to explain the law as the necessary response of socialised personality to various needs, desires and instincts. Lacanian theory explains the desires, needs and identity of the subject through her subjection to the law. From the genesis of the law—to law the *demiurge*—psychoanalysis proves itself a legal theory—a discourse obsessed with the creation, internal organisation and action of the law.

Lacan's revision of Freud could be seen as starting with a nothing, an impossibility. Subjectivity is seen as founded on the loss of the original union with the maternal object. This loss determines our destinies, but as it comes before the ego, before language and subjectivity, it cannot be represented and remains repressed and forgotten. Lacan calls this lost scene the Real, but it is not reality. The Real must be imagined as the power of creating *ex nihilo* and as the power of *nothing* to challenge being and lead to the extreme form of enjoyment called *jouissance*.

But, we need to move beyond the real. Lacan's motto becomes 'In the beginning (of the subject) is the *Nomos* and the *Logos*'. No subject, no desire, no society can come into being without submission to the symbolic order, which is typically presented as a combination of law and language. The infant enters this order through the encounter with the father, the lawgiver, who initially appears to possess the object of the mother's desire, the phallus. The child wants the absolute love of the mother and therefore desires to become the phallus. But becoming the mother's phallus would stop the child's development into adult.

[10] S Freud, 'Why War?', above n 2, 359.

The father—not as the biological progenitor but as the representative of the law—is now introduced into the dyadic relationship between mother and child. The law's function is to separate the child from the mother through a rival identification with the father. The name of the father, this representative of the symbolic, imposes a double prohibition: on incest—thus stopping the union with the mother—and on patricide—thus leading the male child to identify with the father. The law, the word of the father, confronts the omnipotence of the mother with the power of the word.[11] This separation from the mother and subjection to the law is Lacan's (in)famous 'symbolic castration'.[12]

In castration, the boy child[13] does not identify with the father who is the imaginary phallus of the mother (the primal father or the father of enjoyment) but with the father who has the phallus symbolically through the operation of law and language (the symbolic or dead father). The phallus, elsewhere called the *petit objet a* (the little other object), symbolises the integrity or wholeness which has been lost—both impossible and prohibited through the action of language and law. This little other, the remnant of the Real after its ban by the symbolic, is the inner secret or 'kernel' of the subject: it creates a ceaseless and destructive pressure to return to the primal union (the death drive) which at the same time gives rise to an awesome, obscene enjoyment or *jouissance*.

In Lacan's version therefore, the law creates the ego. The symbolic castration is a question of law and legitimate possession. The mother delivers the boy to the father through a symbolic contract. The boy-child identifies with the father who has the phallus as its legal possessor and does not become the—imaginary—maternal object of desire. He identifies instead with the signifier of the phallus, the 'name of the father', or with the object as prohibited by the paternal interdiction, and thus acquires the phallus. The phallus, this absent, nonexistent master signifier is a legal title or emblem—Lacan calls it a 'sceptre'[14] which the father has acquired through his own castration in order to pass it on according to the law. 'It is in the name-of-the-Father that we must recognise the support of the symbolic function which, from the dawn of history, has identified his person with figure of the law'.[15] The symbolic castration represents the genealogical order by prohibiting imaginary and promoting symbolic

[11] J Lacan, 'The subversion of the subject and the dialectic of desire in the Freudian Unconscious' in *Ecrits: A Selection*, A Sheridan (trans), (London, Routledge, 1977) 292–325.

[12] For Lacan, access to the symbolic order is much easier for the girl-child who, in not having the penis, accepts with less difficulty the interdiction on becoming the mother's imaginary phallus. In this sense, men who harbour the ridiculous hope that the physical organ is identical with the symbolic position are failed women.

[13] For commentary on this process, see J Schroeder, *The Vestal and the Fasces* (Berkeley, University of California Press, 1998) 63–96.

[14] 'If this exchange must be described as androcentric . . . it is, M Levi-Strauss tells us, because of the occurrence of political power that make themselves felt in it, power that falls to men (sic) to exercise. It is therefore because it is also the sceptre that the fallus prevails—in other words because it belongs to the symbolic order.' J Lacan in unpublished Seminar X quoted by M Borch-Jacobsen, *Lacan: The Absolute Master*, D Brick (trans), (Stanford University Press, 1991) 213.

[15] J Lacan, *Ecrits*, above n 11, at 67.

identifications. Without submission to its law, the child cannot be separated from the mother and cannot be introduced to subjectivity. As we will see below, the law, by separating the subject from the love object and introducing it into lack, is also the creator of desire.

When we turn from the law to *logos*, from the father to the linguistic rewriting of the Oedipus drama, legal metaphors proliferate again. Language, both in its structure and action is homologous with the law. 'No-one is supposed to be ignorant of the law; this somewhat humorous formula taken from our Code of Justice nevertheless expresses the truth in which our experience is grounded . . . No man is actually ignorant of it, since the law of man has been the law of language since the first words of recognition.'[16] Again when glossing Levi-Strauss's structural interpretation of kinship and exchange, Lacan insists on the primacy of the law-language order:

> The marriage tie is governed by an order of preference whose law concerning the kinship names is, like language imperative for the group in its forms, but unconscious in its structure . . . The primordial Law is therefore that which in regulating marriage ties superimposes the kingdom of culture on that of nature abandoned to the law of mating . . . This law, then, is revealed clearly enough as identical with an order of language.[17]

And if the order of *logos* as language *is* identical with the order of law, *logos* as speech or discourse *acts* like law. In Lacan's oracular aphorism: It is from somewhere other than the Reality that it concerns that Truth derives its guarantee: it is from Speech. Just as it is from Speech that Truth receives the mark that establishes it in a fictional structure. The first words spoken (*le dit premier*) stand as a decree, a law, an aphorism, an oracle; they confer their obscure authority upon the real other.[18]

The law of desire is neither regularity nor interdiction, neither form nor substance. The law is known in its effects, it structures the ego in its traumatic relationship with desire and the superego. We do not repress desire because we have conscience, but we have conscience because we repress desire. But as our desire is so much structured by repression, the law, too, is desire. We cannot know the law of desire in advance, but we follow the desire of law in its fatal consequences. The unconscious drives one to act, but this action is not fully willed or intended. Psychoanalytical ethics introduces a new responsibility for our desire, a love for telling the truth about something we can never fully know and which is written only in our destinies. All moralistic attempts to achieve the supreme Good must fail, because the lack, the gap opened by the symbolic castration, can never be filled and the subject will always be pursued by his own fate which will befall him in his own history—although this destiny has been articulated in the forgotten past or beyond history in the operation of the

[16] *Ibid*, at 61.
[17] *Ibid*, at 66.
[18] *Ibid*, at 305–6.

elementary structures of personhood. Lacan's Real is our *moira,* our libidinal destiny, the imperative of our *eros,* which we cannot avoid and we cannot avoid betraying.[19]

THE FOURTH SESSION: THE METEOR: LACAN AND JUSTICE

The relevance of a Lacanian approach is not limited to a reading of the law; we will also suggest that one can gain insights into the concern with justice from a psychoanalytic perspective. How does this make for a development of the thesis developed so far in this book?

The central principle of psychoanalytical justice is that the social bond passes through the Thing and is determined not by simple pleasures or pains but by our uncanny dependence on *jouissance.* But for jurisprudence, justice is another name for the various forms of the Good—variously defined as virtue, utility or, belatedly, the law. Freud's great discovery was to understand that the Good is neither an arrangement of virtues and values in the right order of reason—the *orthos logos*—nor the absolute formal law of the deontologists. The Good is the Mother, the Thing, the object of desire which is at the same time the forbidden object. No other Good exists. Indeed, all other goods and resources are distributed and arranged in relation to this Supreme but unattainable Good. Civilisation and culture start with morality, but this is a morality of unfulfilled and unfulfillable desire, and the ego is created in the struggle to satisfy this insatiable and impossible desire that keeps coming back.

All moralistic attempts to define the supreme Good or achieve justice fail because the lack, the gap opened in the subject by the primary separation—the 'symbolic castration'—can never be filled. The self will be pursued by a destiny forged in the forgotten past and operating in the elementary structures of personhood. But if there is no Supreme Good, ethical thought is an ongoing consideration of the relationship between law and desire, and justice becomes an economic operation. The question of the Good is about access, distribution and enjoyment of goods. The Good is double and duplicitous; its bivalence is captured by the double meaning of the classical conception of *praxis. Praxis* means ethical action and practical life in cooperation with others, *synergeia,* but *praxis* also produces *erga*, products and goods. Theories of justice are contemplations on the Good; their operation, however, has always been concerned with goods—the products of labour and the depositories of values that satisfy needs and increase pleasure. History is characterised by the belief that pleasure and pain are the key determinants of the psyche and justice—the public expression of the Good—is a disguised or explicit attempt to arrange the production and distribution of goods. Its various conceptions try to manipulate pain and plea-

[19] J Rajman, *Truth and Eros: Focault, Lacan and the Question of Ethics* (London, Routledge, 1991).

sure and put them at the service of the wider good. In this sense, ethics has always been a hedonism and its history culminates in Bentham. For psychoanalysis, ethical theory proper can only begin when the inquiry into the nature of the Good recognises that the 'law is closely tied to the very structure of desire' and that justice forges a bridge between normal pleasures and intense *jouissance*.[20]

This link explains the inevitable injustice of all theories of justice. The dominant tradition of justice has reduced the Good to the division of goods. Possession of goods that deprives others of their enjoyment and control over goods is control over people. Goods answer need, but they also engender power and intense pleasure through the privation that their ownership creates for others. Our relation to goods is therefore arranged in such a way as to account for the fact that others can deprive me of the Good. Every time the ego chooses to do Good, something beyond justice, 'something completely enigmatic appears and returns to us again and again from our own action—like the ever-growing threat within us of a powerful demand whose consequences are unknown'.[21] The Good brings together an economy of satisfaction and privation in the hands of an imaginary and threatening other, who acts as the depriving agent and bars entry to the locus of *jouissance*.

Despite their differences, both utilitarianism and deontological theories are equally misconceived and counter-productive. Utilitarianism correctly emphasises the key role of the pleasure-seeking emotion and has controlled, exploited and made it productive. But it does not go far enough in acknowledging the privative and destructive element of all theories of the Good. What is uncontrollable and threatening to social stability is the law that structures desire and points to the enjoyment that lies beyond pleasure: the obscene inner law of the superego, the self-tormenting law of conscience, which links transgression with intense asocial pleasure and turns desire into law by marking the performance of duty with intense *jouissance*. These negative forces are joined by moral theories and laws, which in their obsession to turn love into law, miss out its destructive aspect.

The law of Kantianism is even more frightening. Kant separated the law from all consideration of passion and emotion and from all empirical or historical experience. A moral action does not promote the good—common or individual—but is motivated out of pure respect for the law irrespective of rewards or sanctions, calculations and consequences. Moral law does not ally itself with the pleasure principle; it obligates people to apply it freely without fear or passion. Its maxim is found in us and becomes the foundation of freedom, but it acts like a law of nature. We find this law analogically, 'as if' it were a natural law, 'as if' our freedom in applying it came from within us as a natural causation and 'as if' obedience to it was motivated by external fear and internal inclination. But as

[20] J Lacan *The Ethics of Psychanalysis* (London, Tavostock, 1992) at 76.
[21] *Ibid*, 234.

this 'natural' law has no passion and no pathology, it does not touch the empirical world, it has no content and must not be led by impure feelings and inclinations. The only feeling Kant acknowledges is the intense pain produced by obedience to law's demands. Freed from all empirical content, this law can only be pure form—that of universal legislation. Form holds the place of the missing content and the vacated Good.

The wiping out of all content is similar to Lacan's symbolic castration, in which the incestuous maternal object is overthrown from its place as the Supreme Good and the 'paternal law' of symbolic order emerges in the void created through this wiping out. This pure loss changes the status of all objects that fill the void created by it, and which must stand and act against the background of radical absence. Similarly, the emptying of all content from the categorical imperative creates a new kind of object of desire, Lacan's *objet petit a*, and the renunciation of enjoyment gives rise to a certain new surplus enjoyment.[22] Kant's law is experienced as non-economical by the subject, as it has no concern and gives no consideration to the subject's well-being, but at the same time it opens a new vista of enjoyment. For the ethics of duty, self must suffer and the greater the purity of respect for the law, the greater the pain that obedience induces, a pain tinged, however, with obscene pleasure. The categorical imperative is not unlike Sade's law of pleasure inducing pain and Freud's superego. Freud compares the categorical imperative, which works in a 'a compulsive fashion and rejects any conscious motives' with the taboos of primitive tribes.[23] Lacan agrees; when civilisation is based on abstract duty without reference to feeling or passion, the structural law of desire is unleashed and leads to discontent, destruction and death. 'There is a sepulchral mound at the limit of the politics of the good, of the general good, of the good of the community' writes Lacan. 'All life after all is rottenness'.[24] An ethics that does not recognise this basic fact is likely to nourish disenchantment and strengthen the catastrophic tendency of desire on the pretext that it is serving the wider good.

Legal justice also leads to similar problems. Whatever the type of social organisation, psychoanalysis insists that there is a residue, a 'nonlinked thing'[25] or faultline in every community and law, beyond their control and to which they remain hostage. It is analogous to an 'unconscious affect', encountered in the 'sharp and vague feeling that the civilians are not civilised and that something is ill-disposed towards civility', that 'betrays the recurrence of the shameful sickness within what passes for health and betrays the 'presence' of the unmanageable'.[26] The only way of combating this violence is, as we saw above, to nurture 'emotional ties' of love and identification. Justice is one such love

[22] S Zizek, *The Sublime Object of Ideology* (London, Verso, 1991) 231.

[23] S Freud, *Totem and Taboo* (London, The Hogarth Press, 1955) 50.

[24] J Lacan, above n 20, 233, 232.

[25] JF Lyotard, '*A l' Insy* (Unbeknownst)' in Miami Theory Collective (ed), *Community at Loose Ends* (Minnesota, Minnesota University Press, 1991) 42 at 46.

[26] *Ibid*, at 44, 43.

object. It makes people identify with the totality. According to a liberal philosopher, justice makes me feel happy, a member of the tribe: 'I can be happy to be one of We, if We are just, because then We will treat Me as well as reasonably possible; and We will be happy to have Me as one of Us, because We know that I being just, will see things from Our point of view, and will not exclude wider considerations from my assessment of the situation.' In the just society there is no '*stasis*, no dissension . . . no conflict.'[27]

But the Thing always comes back—in xenophobia and racism, in hatred and discrimination—and remains intractable to politics. This original injustice cannot be represented or managed. Politics become a 'politics of forgetting', a forgetting of injustice, a considered strategy which tries to ban whatever questions the legitimacy of the institution and tries to turn the threatening imponderable powers into memory and myth, or into celebration of fictitious unity. The theories of justice are one more failing attempt to forget and exorcise this Thing. This may be the reason why so much intellectual effort has been put into theories of justice and why they are always bound to fail because justice forgets—it must forget—injustice.

But justice is not fully of this world; psychoanalysis reminds us that lack and desire lead to symptoms, often violent and repetitive—the cause of which is forgotten because it never entered consciousness. Justice is these symptoms—nothing more substantial or material—a trace that signifies a past trauma or a future union, always deferred and different. Justice is the name of social desire, and the series of symptoms created by the lack of this foundational and unattainable condition. Injustice, on the other hand, is the way through which people construct this sense of lack, incompleteness or disorder—the name given to the symptoms of social exclusion, domination or oppression. Justice is what society lacks and desires; it has no other definition—or rather justice is the definition of the indefinable, the unconscious of the law. We can only know it through its symptoms, injustice. Theories of justice are therefore a 'fantasy', the Fantastical screen or frame that philosophers, poets and lawyers have erected to shield ourselves and to explain away the unknown desire of the other and of the impossible community. The theory of justice answers the symptoms by negating their cause. But the radical dissymmetry, the abyss of the other's desire and of injustice, will always leave behind a remainder for which neither the law nor fantasy can fully account.

THE FIFTH SESSION: SO THAT'S WHAT IT MEANT: I DREAMT OF THE LAW

Perhaps the most thorough elaboration of Lacan's account of the subject of desire as a juristic structure is that of Pierre Legendre. However, Legendre's work does not specifically engage with the issue of justice. Pierre Legendre's

[27] J Lucas, *On Justice* (Oxford, Clarendon, 1980) 18–19.

contribution to the study of law is his insight into the essentially mythic nature of the legal institution. The positive order of law is profoundly dependent on 'another scene'; a truth to which legal modernity is blind.

Myth describes a function that underlies and founds the social: myth is central to the fashioning of the human subject. It describes an inherently hierarchical or 'stratified' idea of social space where the human world is dependent upon the divine. The divine as such is inaccessible: someone, or some ritual, must 'speak' for it. At this point Legendre's work touches upon those legal histories that see the roots of law as synonymous with a priestly class controlling both legal and religious rituals. Rather than restricting this moment to the prehistory of law, though, Legendre considers law's articulation of social foundations as essential to all social order. This broader understanding is termed dogmatic communication. Dogmatic communication is the transmission of the fundamental social myth, mainly through different types of legality.

In this sense, Legendre turned the ontological power of the Lacanian 'law-speech' into a complete juridical anthropology.[28] For Legendre, the legal system 'institutes life';[29] it forms the 'atomic bond' that binds the 'primary material of man: biology, the social, the unconscious.'[30] The legal institution is functionally homologous to the law of the father or, in another version, it interprets and applies the original interdiction. In the same way that the name of the father introduces the subject into separation, lack and negativity, language and the institution 'separate the subject from the phantasm of being whole.'[31] But this separation needs a guarantor, a 'sacred' inaccessible place that stages the origin or the cause of the subject's being. In pre-modern societies this role was played by totems, religions or mythical references to the just foundations of law. In modernity it is 'the state [which] is the sacred place of the Totem, wherever it takes hold, whatever its constitutional form may be, the religious or mythical space of the discourse called upon to guarantee the foundations without which

[28] The work of Pierre Legendre is quite unprecedented in legal historiography. In his many publications he has opened a new field of legal writing or legal poetics in which the love of the text (of law) and of medieval and patristic sources is accompanied with a highly literary and allusive—almost baroque—style. His genealogy of modern law and of its malady of technocratic rationalism, links the 'revolution of the interpreters' in the 12th century with the incorporation of the key themes of canon law into civil law and challenges many of the assumptions of traditional historiography. Similarly, Legendre's historical and theoretical insight that the law captures the soul, and by attaching body to spirit creates the subject opens a large vista for jurisprudence, and this writer has been considerably influenced by his captivating and seductive theory and prose. But a critical jurisprudence must question the conservative repercussions of his juridical anthropology. In these respects, Legendre joins the climate of the reactionary Catholic response to modernity. Critique of this aspect is indispensable for the development of a critical psychoanalytical jurisprudence, which will profit greatly from an engagement with Legendre's work. See P Goodrich, 'Introduction: Psychoanalysis and Law' in P Goodrich (ed), *Law and the Unconscious: A Legendre Reader* (Macmillan, 1997). For a more critical approach see A Pottage, 'The Paternity of Law' in C Douzinas et al (eds), *Politics, Postmodernity, Critical Legal Studies* (London, Routledge, 1994).

[29] P Legendre, 'The Other Dimension of Law', 943.

[30] *Ibid*, 954.

[31] *Ibid*, 952.

the law would remain unthinkable'.[32] The law stages the totem or the interdiction around the father, more specifically around 'the image of the substance of the Father, which is equivalent to the totemic principle in European civilisation'.[33] The 'juridical montages' of this image, God or Pope, Emperor or King, state or legislator, 'giv[e] consistency to the founding discourse by representing the Other as a concept, in order to spread the effects of the Interdiction, that is to say, the juridically organised effects'.[34] Legendre describes the operation of this interdiction as dogmatic communication.

In the history of the west, dogmatic communication is marked by the conjunction of Classical and Christian cultures. In Roman law terms it describes an inherently hierarchical or 'stratified' idea of social space that sees the human world as dependent upon the divine. The truth of dogmatic communication is the passage of messages from one world to the other, from the divine to the human; it 'constitutes an order of fiction which organises the transmission of words and texts organised between two structurally differentiated levels.' Dogmatic communication must concern the promulgation of both spoken and written texts that define the human space as one that draws upon and is predicated on the divine and inaccessible. In the world view of medieval Christianity, Roman law contributes to the concept of stratified communities united in their devotion to Christ.[35] These terms will be examined in more depth presently, as it is necessary to consider the Legendrian notion of the 'text' to properly appreciate the structures with which this chapter is concerned.

The text represents a 'universal structure'[36] that also includes oral culture. Although in oral cultures the text may not take the form of the written word, it may be present as a particular ritual or set of ritual practices that fulfil a similar structural function. In whatever form it takes, the text returns to the idea that dogmatic communication involves a 'transmission' of messages that are predicated upon reference back to the fundamental truth of the foundational Reference. The transmission of the text is the 'dissemination' of a discourse that, for the society in question, has the status of truth. To engage with the text is to accept its hold, to submit to a 'pre-existent' embodiment of the truth. The text itself bestows on the interpreter the authority to interpret and thus carry forward the function of reference. In other words, the truth of the text is largely a notion of the conditions of its own remembrance, perpetuation and continued dissemination: '*the discourse of truth is the discourse of the reproduction of*

[32] *Ibid.*

[33] *Ibid*, 959.

[34] *Ibid*, 960.

[35] For an elaboration of this notion of society, see St Augustine, *The City of God against the Pagans* (Harmondsworth, Penguin Books, 1972), in particular book *XIX*. For commentary, see HA Deane, *The Political and Social Ideas of St Augustine* (New York, Columbia University Press, 1963) 78–153. For further consideration see N Figgis, *The Political Aspects of Saint Augustine's City of God*, (London, Longmans, 1921) 51–68.

[36] P Goodrich, *Law and the Unconscious: A Legendre Reader* (London, Macmillan, 1997) at 152.

truth.'[37] This theory of hermeneutics is a long way from the idea that it is a particular content of the text that is transmitted. Communication is here no more than a ritual that perpetually stages and re-stages the 'founding reference.'[38] In this way, it is as if Legendre removes any consideration of chronology from his account of interpretation.

The aspect of dogmatic communication that forms the link between the institution and the individual is the interdiction; a term developed within psychoanalysis. However, unlike dogmatic communication, which can be thought of in terms of a content and a form, interdiction is itself an 'empty category'. The interdiction is not the incest taboo; rather it is a space 'between or among', or, 'an utterance which stages speech.'[39] Only after speech has been staged, does the 'normative' content of law become relevant. Interdiction operates on a principle of 'division'. This is a passage through a 'symbolic void'[40] which is the experience of a birth into language. To become a speaking being, the child has to be separated from its mother and realise that language can always summon in words, even if it cannot completely replace the lost object of desire. Learning that language represents is to accept the interdiction, the original separation from the maternal object that re-appears in linguistic representations. Interdiction is thus the Oedipal scene revisited.

Genealogy is directly related to interdiction. If interdiction is a speech that divides the subject and allows it to become a speaker of language, genealogy is an extended notion of the social function of interdiction that exists in the kin group or the community into which the subject is born and positioned more broadly by speech; 'spoken in advance.'[41] In this sense, the origin is always prepared for any individual subject. At this point, Legendre's description of genealogy takes a turn towards the most crudely deterministic as it describes genealogical order as destiny, or *Fata*. However, it must be remembered that this means no more than that the fate of the human subject is to become subject and object in language. Legendre can be defended from accusations of a crude form of determinism. It is in language that the genealogical order functions. The subject occupies a position in a kinship structure, which is preserved by the legal rules that determine succession and inheritance. Switching registers, Legendre begins to speak in terms of the necessity of instituting the 'Third' of language. Genealogy can account for an insertion of the subject into a social order, but to sharpen the analysis there is a necessity for a term which can describe the 'normative' dimension of a law that operates in and through communication.

The void that guarantees the social order—Legendre's Reference—must be transmitted and validated legally, through patrilinear genealogy, juridical

[37] P Goodrich, *Law and the Unconscious: A Legendre Reader* (London, Macmillan, 1997) at 155 [Legendre's italics].
[38] *Ibid*, 156.
[39] *Ibid*, 140.
[40] *Ibid*, at 141.
[41] *Ibid*, at 143.

emblems and the reason of the law. This is the all important but neglected 'other dimension' of law: 'a body of discourses which, within any society, construct the founding image which is the subjects' marching banner . . . These are valorised institutionally; not according to their express content (which is a function of the declared intention of the author), but through the fact of being symbolically accorded a place within society as representations of the reference.'[42] The 'truth' and the function of the institution is therefore produced by 'juridical reason as communicator of this non-juridical dimension of law'.[43]

Legendre's use of Hermes' name to outline the 'dogmatic function' is motivated by the need to recover a mythological dimension which has been lost with the ascendancy of scientific accounts of communication.[44] Politics, as a realisation of social speech at a level more general still than genealogy, has to take this function seriously and effectively provide the means of 'manufacturing' the 'montages' that will sustain social life. Politics is the function of interdiction writ large. Like the enigmatic symbol of the parent, it must be able to provide a foundational scene for the community at large. This means not only that politics can be imagined as a form of speech, but that it must also deal with what is fundamentally absent or lost and evoke it through representations. Politics must speak for the 'absent Object of power.'[45] The object of power is absent, because, as 'dogma' suggests, the whole point of communication is to create a stratified community that draws its being from a divine figure who speaks for it. Alternatively, the 'absent Object' is the 'absolute other'[46] that can only be represented or referred to through images. The role of the messenger is to mediate between this 'alterity'[47] and the institutions that are constructed in the name of the other. Legendre describes this as the 'lynchpin of historical systems of representation'[48] thus suggesting that it is an essential and inescapable function, but it is a function that can only be 'mythical' in that in order to speak, the object from which the subject is divided had to be inaccessible and unapproachable. It can only be mediated through representation. It is what remains presupposed, but absent in every message.

As well as describing universal structures, Legendre's work also concerns itself with a particular history and a specific structure of law. Christianity makes use of Roman law in defining and perpetuating this structure. Roman law has shown itself to be flexible, adapting itself to various historical contexts—from

[42] Legendre, quoted in A Pottage, above n 27 at 165.

[43] *Ibid.*

[44] Legendre's opposition to social science rests on the argument that in a reified social world of 'things', the conventional apologetics of law can do no more than stress efficiency and the monitoring of statistics. It is necessary to recover the sense in which speech, understood as dogmatic communication, can only function as the maintenance of the social bond if it stages interdiction and provides an ongoing sense of being.

[45] *Ibid*, at 146.

[46] *Ibid*, at 147.

[47] *Ibid*, at 147.

[48] *Ibid*, at 146.

its formal use in the development of the common law tradition to the more concrete way in which it provided the axioms for the law of the Holy See. Even when Roman law is most forgotten, or when, as at present, 'science' attempts to usurp its prerogatives, its essential function cannot be replaced or ignored.[49] The law speaks 'in the name of' something or other; law ventriloquises. The voice of the law is that of the Pope or the Emperor, himself an 'alienated body',[50] a representation of the other in whose name the *Pater* speaks. The law is the site that gives the 'space of fiction';[51] the symbolic void which separates signification from its absent source. To approach Roman law is to consider a discourse that allows the truth to appear;[52] it is a logic of messages. Roman law lays down a way of 'staging' functions that psychoanalysis considers as necessary to social being: the institution and reproduction of human life. This is a 'non-negotiable principle'[53] or a 'principle of universal legislation'.[54] Identifying this principle means stripping away the discourses on popular rights that have proved obstructive of the truth of Roman law.

Perhaps all law repeats the truth of Roman law. If it does not, how could psychoanalysis be described differently?

THE SIXTH SESSION: PSYCHOANALYSIS AND OTHER MACHINES

Gilles Deleuze and Felix Guattari's work goes beyond psychoanalysis. But, this 'beyond' is not a rejection; it is, rather, a mutation or transformation of certain psychoanalytic tenets from within the discourse itself. In the hands of these *bricoleurs*, psychoanalysis is put to different uses—becoming more a science of social force than a study of the disembodied bourgeois subject. We will suggest that it is precisely this figure of doubleness, a 'fold' or a re-treat of psychoanalysis that animates its reinvention, and hence also the insights it can give into the operation of law.

To understand Deleuze and Guattari's trajectory, we must appreciate the complicity of psychoanalysis with other forms of thought, other ways of mapping what was once described as the soul. This theme appears clearly in the work of Pierre Legendre. Psychoanalysis is the most recent manifestation of the ancient concern with myth, with the structures that give life meaning. But a twist or a turn must be introduced in the Legendrian project. There is something

[49] That function is the 'mythological' foundation of the social bond. It can be demonstrated by reference to the scholasticism of the middle ages that concerned the reception of Gratian's *Decretals* in around 1140 and the composition of the first glosses and commentaries in the mid thirteen hundreds. Scholasticism developed the materials that allowed the law to speak.

[50] *Ibid*, at 109.

[51] *Ibid*, at 110.

[52] P Legendre, *L'Empire De Verite: Introduction Aux Espaces Dogmatiques Industriels* (Paris, Fayard, 1983) 132.

[53] P Goodrich, *Law and the Unconscious: A Legendre Reader*, above n 28 at 116.

[54] *Ibid*, at 116.

irreducibly modern about the techniques and procedures of psychoanalysis. What were once communal and public rituals have become privatised and predicated on the relationship between the professional analyst and his client/patient, the analysand. This is not to suggest that the contemporary concern with privatisation in economy is necessarily the modernist element of psychoanalysis, rather, that the psychoanalytic relationship is predicated on a contract. As jurists and historians have shown, this is the form that regulates relationships between bourgeois legal subjects, who have left behind the medieval and pre-modern world of status, and entered the modern world of commodities where everything has its price and can be exchanged. Money can buy you a form of happiness; such is the motto inscribed above the door of the analyst, the modern confessor, the priest in the pay of his client. So, despite the importance of the Legendrian concern with the modern presence of myth, its 'form' takes a shape that suggests that psychoanalysis itself is determined by other powerful discourses that come together in organising the social world.

We need to proceed on two fronts. First, we need a critique, or rather a twisting, of the discourse of psychoanalysis. We then need a redefinition of the relationship of psychoanalysis to the question of power. Once we bring these questions together, we can identify the shape of a critical legal psychoanalysis, and a sense of the tasks that lie before it.

To return to the first issue. What are the stakes if we abandon the Lacanian idea of the unconscious or the Real? How might the law appear? Deleuze and Guattari's 'model' is a way of talking about what it means to be in a material world, of approaching the law as a particular manifestation of political desire. The starting point is the idea that the unconscious is—'produced'[55]—an idea that is lost as soon as Oedipus appears. In the prevalent Lacanian schema, the law is related to the symbolic; the law marks entrance into the symbolic by imposing the incest taboo and creating desire through prohibition. Desiring production offers a different account. If desire is not lack, but the social itself, desire for law is part of the production of the real, an organisation of desire, which is never given, and always fluid. Law is not destiny. The question becomes that of how law makes for an organisation of desire, not the fixed and immutable formula law = desire.

Why should it be that Oedipus states the central logic of the unconscious? As we have seen, to become a speaking being in the Lacanian account, is to accept the prohibition, or risk non-being, to fall back into the 'undifferentiated.'[56] The only choice is between 'neurosis and normality.'[57] But Freud himself was aware of the difficulties into which the theory of Oedipus was leading the study of the unconscious: 'Everything unfolds as if the essential were to go beyond the father, as if going beyond the father were always forbidden.'[58] It would appear

[55] G Deleuze and F Guattari, *Anti Oedipus* (London, Athlone, 1983) 25.
[56] *Ibid*, 78.
[57] *Ibid*, 80.
[58] *Ibid*, citing a letter to Romain Rolland 1936.

psychoanalysis is trapped in a contradiction: it is impelled by one sense of its own logic to go beyond the father, beyond Oedipus, but, at the same time, restricted, held back, by other features of its heritage.

The myth of the primal horde can be seen as a response to this impasse. The story of the son's murder of the father begins and ends with Oedipus. The Oedipal bond is established as the reason for the murder, and intensified through internalisation of guilt at the end of the fable. What happens in the period between the murder and the internalisation?

One possible challenge focuses on the unargued premises of the primal horde myth that determine the pathways that psychoanalysis takes. Freud's story of law starts with violence and Lacan's story of the subject begins in separation and lack instituted by the law. But the persistent sense and unceasing critique of injustice indicate that an *eros* precedes and is more primordial than the *thanatos* that the law institutes as the object of desire. Feminist psychoanalysis calls this law before the law the 'primal union with the Mother' (Irigaray)[59] or the 'archaic mother' or 'abject' (Kristeva).[60] In the ethical terms of Levinas, the trauma of the subject is created through its exposure to Otherness, in which the origin of law and language are 'constantly submerged by pre-original substance'.[61] In a paradoxical sense, psychoanalytical jurisprudence can be criticised for not being sufficiently erotic, for being unable fully to understand the nature of the 'emotional ties' that it places at the centre of the social and legal bond. The ethical and critical myth of law reinterprets the primal patrricide and emphasises its erotic aspect. The brothers felt a sense of guilt before law and morality had arisen, because an ethical turning to the Other comes before the law and becomes its ground.[62] In this interpretation, the murder and the eucharistic meal of the dead symbolises not just the narcissistic Oedipal identification with the Father, but the original incorporation of alterity—as Death or the Other—at the heart of subjectivity. It is precisely because the law presupposes ethics that moral guilt could be felt in the absence of the law. This ethical obligation to what in self and society is beyond the ego and the social body, this love for the Other, is what will always infuse the passion for justice in the emotional life of the law.

Deleuze and Guattari's critique shows that after the murder of the father and during the time of the brothers, society is unstable and dangerous. Deleuze and Guattari read the story as suggesting that it is possible to do away with Oedipus, if one sticks to the logic of one's desire. Thus, 'the possibility of living beyond the father's law, beyond all law, is perhaps the most essential possibility brought

[59] L Irigaray, *Speculum for Another Woman: An Ethics of Sexual Difference,* C Burke and G Gill (trans), (London, Athlone, 1993); *I Love to You,* A Martin (trans), (London, Routledge, 1996).

[60] J Kristeva, *The Abject: Powers of Horror,* L Roudiez (trans), (New York, Columbia University Press, 1982); Part II, 'Women, Psychoanalysis Politics' in T Moi (ed), *The Kristeva Reader,* (London, Blackwell, 1986), 137–320.

[61] E Levinas, *Humanisme de l'Autre Homme* (Paris, Montpellier, 1972) 68.

[62] For an elaboration on these themes see C Douzinas and R Warrington, 'A Jurisprudence of Alterity' in *Justice Miscarried* (Edinburgh University Press, 1994) chapters 2 and 4.

forth by Freudian psychoanalysis.'[63] But the way forward is not through the resolving of the Oedipus complex. For Deleuze and Guattari, Oedipus is the wrong way of putting the question of the unconscious.

To understand this radical re-writing of psychoanalysis let us return to one of its key tenets. Why should there be a lost object? Why should the law be our fate? In the Lacanian schema, the ego is always positioned in relation to something that has come before it and that cannot be thought as such, a lost unity, an impossible object. This is a kind of 'totality' or 'unity' from which the subject has to be separated in order to come into being in the first place. The subject, therefore, is based on a constitutive lack, a hole in its being. Indeed, it is this 'lost' something that is common to humanity and allows the 'process of sexuation', the constitution of the sexes, to take place. The move from the pre-Oedipal, from non-being to being is organised by reference to the 'phallus', the 'despotic or master signifier.' In this sense, psychoanalysis always leads back to the same place. The phallus relates to this constitutive absence and leads inescapably to the necessity of law: the law both bans access to the place of primordial unity and makes it impossible. Without law's interdiction, separation from the maternal union, differentiation and individuation cannot take place. Lacanian psychoanalysis takes us back to a kind of beginning; the role of the three orders, the symbolic, the imaginary and the real, is to show how, at this originary point, the unconscious is represented and repressed. This beginning, though, is always also a beyond in which all social relationships will be effectively recorded in advance.

We can ask some further critical questions. Why should we conclude that since an object is forbidden, it was desired in the first place?[64] Freud quotes JG Frazer's remark: the law only forbids men to do what their instincts incline them to do.[65] We would be entitled to suppose, then, that the legal prohibition suggests not a natural distaste for incest, but an urge towards it. Something is prohibited because it is desired. The entire positioning of the law operates through the retrospection: 'I wanted to marry my mother and kill my father. That's what I wanted.' The law is created through a process of 'displacement.'[66] The operation is as follows: the law acts to prohibit 'something that is perfectly fictitious in the order of desire or of the "instincts", so as to persuade its subjects that they have the intention corresponding to the fiction.'[67]

This can be further elaborated. Law is placed at the heart of the family. In other words, the 'beyond' derives from, or is already within, the structure of bourgeois familial relations that becomes so central for the structuring of unconscious desire. As Nietzsche would put it, a cause has been confused with

[63] G Deleuze and F Guattari, *Anti Oedipus* (Minneapolis, University of Minnesota Press, 1980) 81.

[64] *Ibid*, 71.

[65] *Ibid*, 114.

[66] *Ibid*.

[67] *Ibid*, 115.

an effect.[68] However, we need to ask why the unconscious takes the form it does. At one level, it is perhaps suggested by Freud's own background. The idea of the Oedipus complex appeared in his own self-analysis. Looking for a way of understanding this strange discovery, he drew on both the world of 'high' culture with which he was familiar, and the structure of the bourgeois family. The very naming of the complex, with its reference back to Greek theatre and myth already imposes a particular 'representative' form, as indeed does the notion of the familiar relationship: mummy, daddy, me.[69]

Rather than this retrospective re-creation of the familial scene, could law not be thought of as involving an investment of desire in the social? The subject belongs to a family and a tribe, and hence to a community that defines itself through exclusivity. This is indeed a reading, albeit a partial one, of ancient law.[70] Law intervenes with the mask, the tattoo; desire is linked to these marks, it creates signs of belonging that no longer allow free affiliation. But this is not Oedipus, this is a group fantasy. You belong to a people.

Furthermore, the structure of fantasy shows that desire is always already the social. This is not just a narrow technical point about psychoanalytic theory, but a re-working of the entire psychoanalytic theory of law. The individual fantasy turns the social into 'imaginary qualities'[71] that allow the ego to play out a sense of its immortality. In part, this is the Legendrian theory of the law. The individual may die, but the institution will live forever. The effect of this is to associate the ego with the structure of the social, and, to a large degree, to encode and organise desire. Crudely, the fantasy of the juristic ego is to link desire to the legal institution as the only way of perpetuating social being. Indeed, the individual fantasy has a symbiotic relationship with juristic

[68] This can be seen in one of the central texts that establishes Oedipus, 'A Child is Being Beaten' (cited in Deleuze and Guattari, above n 63). Freud is discussing a fantasy where a number of boys are being beaten by a third party in the presence of some young girls. Freud's interpretation imposes a very specific 'reduction' on this strange tale (59), which is required by the form of psychoanalytic theory, rather than the story itself. Firstly, the fantasy is lifted out of the group context, and effectively individualised, so that the ego becomes identified with the child, and the person beating becomes associated with the father; this allows a female fantasy and a male fantasy to be posited. A 'disjuncture' is then posited between the girls and the boys; it is as if the sexes must have something in common, but that something is a lack, whose absence has a differential effect: 'girls' and 'boys' can thus be defined by reference to castration, and the way that castration relates back to the father: 'Castration is at once the common lot—that is, the prevalent and transcendent Phallus, and the exclusive distribution that presents itself in girls as the desire for the penis, and in boys as fear of losing it . . .' (59). The unconscious, it seems, is to be henceforth based on disjuncture and separation understood by reference to the phallus; however: '[t]his something in common, the great Phallus, the Lack . . . is purely mythical . . . it introduces lack into desire and causes exclusive series to emanate, to which it attributes a goal, an origin, and a path of resignation.' (60).

[69] These themes re-appear in Freud's analysis of Judge Shreber's delirium. The text of his breakdown is simply too rich to be adequately explained by reference back to the father; a problem that can be related to the very idea that the unconscious 'expresses' or 'represents' itself through the tropes of myth and religion. The oft repeated notion that psychoanalysis replaces the Church and the confession as the mode in which we moderns come to understand ourselves, creates all too effortlessly an interpretation of psychoanalysis that repeats old patterns and structures.

[70] *Ibid*, 190.

[71] *Ibid*, 62.

structures, since the ego is the correlate of the legal institutions in which it is structured as a legal subject.[72] But this encapturing of desire is only one possible fate. There is a 'revolutionary' aspect to the group fantasy that is realised when institutions are themselves seen as open to change; and change is wrought by desire investing the social space differently. It is as if the subject becomes 'stripped' of an identity, and becomes associated with a point of singularity, a passion that is associated with other singularities. We could perhaps gloss this with the notion of a revolutionary 'subjectivity', an idea to which we shall return. The point is to break through the 'inertia' that law fixes in the social. We need a new language of desire.

We could start by asking the key question: why is desire conceived as lack? For Deleuze, philosophy has badly misunderstood desire. From Plato comes a false choice between desire as production and desire as acquisition.[73] If desire is associated with acquisition, it is thought of primarily as a relation to the object desired; hence to desire is to lack something. What if desire was production?[74] Desire produces the 'real.' In this conception the real is constituted through the conjunction and disjunction of 'units of production.'[75] The process of production has 'parts', but we need to be careful here. The parts can be described as 'desiring machines', elements of a process that operates by coupling or joining together. The machines and the machinery described here are fluid: imagine a vector that coincides with another vector, or a flow where a connection is simultaneously an interruption.

What does this mean? How could it be exemplified? At present I am sitting in an airport waiting room in South Africa. I can hear speech—the production of mouth machines that enters my ear—a hearing machine—interrupting the flow of the reading/writing machine that are my fingers, this pen and this page. As this process is that of desire, the connections between these fragments of my experience, pen, page, voice and thought, are the bringing together of other 'flows and partial objects' that carry on combining their fragments, never achieving a unity other than these manifold and various combinations. For instance, a child is feeding crisps to a dog whose hair has fallen out. The dog keeps creeping into the airport lounge despite the best efforts of the elderly security guard to keep it out. In writing this a combination of objects and desires is brought together, which, on this page, interrupts or combines with your reading, as the desires of the dog and the child, momentarily combined in their own tableau, combine differently in this description, and speed off in their own directions: 'objects' and 'flows.'[76] The object presupposes a combination, a flow, that

[72] *Ibid*, 63.
[73] *Ibid*, 25.
[74] Deleuze credits Kant with this discovery, but it is a skewed account. Although desire can be the cause of objects, Kant understands this process of hallucination and delirium, as a 'psychic reality'. To the extent that there has been a theory of desire as production, it falls back into an understanding of the structure of fantasy as being founded on 'insufficiency' or a 'lack of being'. Wrong again.
[75] *Ibid*, 26.
[76] *Ibid*, 6.

fragments the object. These partial objects, dogs, Africans, page, are brought together by my desire to write this explanation of desire. They become connected with other trajectories, other partial objects, memories, actualities in your life, dear reader, as you attempt to understand this explanation of desire.

How is this thinking relevant? Is it not just a bizarre private language? It certainly reads more like science fiction than philosophy, but, if one follows the logic of its engagement it leads to a novel understanding of the social and law's place within it: indeed, a notion of the immanence of the social field in its entirety. It is moving towards a profound theory of subjectivity as a notion of singularity or intensity. This parts company with the Freudian and Lacanian approaches that we have studied in this chapter. Although psychoanalytic discourse is clearly a study of forces, of energies and the sites that they pass through, it is as if the discourse on the unconscious fails to follow the flow of this question of force or energy. What we need, then, is to understand a wider discourse on power and force and psychoanalysis' place within it, before we can thoroughly understand the notions of subjectivity, law and singularity that remain, at present, so enticingly close to us.

Let us now turn to the relationship between psychoanalysis and power. It is not just 'economics' that influences psychoanalysis. Psychoanalysis is unimaginable without other discourses that structure its mode of operation. These are the clinical, therapeutic, and psychological modes of thought that are so important in creating modern subjectivity. Our concern here is not so much to trace the actual constitution of these discourses on confession, sexuality and therapy, but to try to understand what holds together the contemporary social space—the network of discourses that support and influence the law. In so doing, we hope to elaborate a way of imagining the social that neither rejects psychoanalysis, nor reduces social phenomena to a psychoanalytic discourse that is blind to its own constitution and the role that it plays in the very definition of the social as that which can be known and regulated, either juristically or therapeutically.

We need to return to the question of power. Power is not a property, nor is it 'something' or an ideology that can be owned or determined by a ruling class, as some Marxists would tell us. Power coheres in various strategies, techniques and functions. It is the effect of manifold 'assemblages' of strategic positions.[77] Thus, it would be a mistake to see power as ultimately organised around coherent ideological positions; indeed, there is something in the 'nature' of power that moves towards points of singularity through which it passes. In this approach, the state itself, always seen as the ultimate 'concentration' and 'user' of power, becomes another effect of an assemblage of various networks of power.

Consider the notion that modern societies are characterised by complex relations of discipline and control. There is an essential overlap between Foucault's pioneering insights, and the machinic assemblages described by Deleuze and

[77] G Deleuze, *Foucault* (London, Athlone, 1988) 33.

Guattari. Discipline, in this sense, is not associated with a single institution, apparatus or emanation of the state, but with a power that runs through society in its entirety, taking the forms of manifold technologies dedicated to their own perfection and reproduction. These technologies would, of course, include the traditional manifestations of state power, 'politico-juridical structures' such as prisons and the police, but also, those broader discourses on punishment, rehabilitation and therapeutic normalisation. These institutions and discourses produce complex conjunctions of experts; social workers, doctors, prison wardens, ministers, economists, constables and professors. All these experts are dedicated to the definition, inter-relation and clarification of the respective ways of thinking and acting that constitute the social scientific definitions of the problems that we face. In Deleuze's gnomic statement: 'power is local because it is never global, but it is not local or localisable because it is diffuse.'[78]

This moves beyond the traditional sociological accounts of power that lawyers have always pressed into service. For instance, the Weberian distinction between charismatic and bureaucratic power may allow broad historical periodisations, and a way of thinking about a modern mode of power that does not rely entirely on charismatic authority figures, but also on staffs of experts and autonomous discourses of management. Law is, of course, associated with its own experts and institutions; and plays its role in social regulation and management. Foucault and Deleuze move beyond this rather static model and offer a somewhat different account of 'what' power 'is'.

The machinic 'model' is not concerned with relating power to modes of production or economic instances. These forms of social organisation cannot be seen as privileged, in some way beyond, or as the 'key' to understanding what determines power and its operation. At the same time, though, Deleuze and Guattari's thinking of power would not reject the relevance of economic ideas and prerogatives in the constitution of networks of power. For instance, one could draw correspondences between punitive regimes and systems of production. Modes of punishment in the 18th century were linked to economic ideas about useful labour, and the need to put bodies—whether those of workers or prisoners—to efficient and productive activity. Even those modes of punishment that subjected the prisoner to repetitive and economically worthless tasks, take useful labour as their reference point. So, to sharpen the analysis, these relations of power are not external to the social field, they are not 'super-structural'—they are embedded, always, within the field that they control. In place of a 'pyramidic' structure, then, we are concerned with operations of power that are 'immanent'[79] to the social field; running through factories, schools, hospitals and prisons. Indeed, we could even suggest that the social exists only to the extent that power coheres in various strategies and local manifestations.

[78] *Ibid*, 34.
[79] *Ibid*, 35.

The notion of immanence is central to this analysis. What does it mean for power to be immanent? First, that power is not transcendent, it does not lie above or beyond the social domain. Power is not centralised; it is global to the extent that it is diffused through various techniques and supports that exist in relationships of contiguity, or in series that cannot be referred back to a single logic of organisation. To argue that power is immanent is to suggest that it is not a 'thing' at all; it cannot be possessed, but, rather, creates relationships of subordination and dominance. For Deleuze, power is not an essence, it is an operation;[80] relations of power are the assemblages or associations of forces, or, more precisely, power creates singularities that are relationships of force. Force cannot be understood narrowly as violence, but must be understood as the relationship between forces; thus, we can speak of partitions or shares of force or intensities; compositions of forces. Power or force is creative: it creates the social. Thus, law as force could be understood not so much in terms of legality and illegality, but as a force that imposes a kind of armed peace. Law must be understood in terms not of a binary coding of legal and illegal, but as a series of illegality and law. For Deleuze, the law is always a series of illegalities that are presented as formal legalities. Our immanent analysis of law would suggest, then, that the law is always a form of brute violence, and of a more subtle, but still potent violence that allows it to posit its own formal nature.[81]

If power takes the form of both discourses and the institutions that relate to these discourses, then form is being used in a double sense: power organises materials and gives functions or goals to which institutions and discourses are dedicated. We could thus speak of a 'space of correspondences' between function and form. Consider the celebrated notion of the panopticon. What comes together in the notion of the panopticon is an apparatus arranged around a viewing tower of a circular prison, which makes prisoners visible. This is a new way of organising space and time, a way of creating a field of visibility where objects of power can be arranged, fixed and surveilled. This new form of power could be called diagrammatic; or, rather, an abstract mode of power that can be related to all objects to create the social field as a chart or a map; a map that is 'coextensive'[82] with what it describes. Deleuze calls this an abstract machine, or a machine described by its abstract function. A diagram or abstract machine is a spatio-temporal multiplicity[83] or the mode of disciplinary society, a way of regulating cities and populations.

[80] G Deleuze, *Foucault* (London, Athlone, 1988) 35.

[81] It is necessary to point out at this stage, that immanent thinking can provide a way of reading the liberal jurisprudential tradition that is not simply a rejection, or a crude Marxist approach. The liberal has always had a strong sense of the violence of the law. Hobbes' *Leviathan* presents a choice between violences. The violence of the state of nature, or the violence of the Leviathan whose greater violence can provide a measure of peace. Likewise, the role of the passions of fear and danger in Burke's work, reveals a strong sense of the restrained violence of the law.

[82] *Ibid*, 42.

[83] *Ibid*, 42.

But why does this abstract machine, or this form of immanent power, become associated with, or rather constitutive of, modern social formations? If one looks at societies characterised by sovereignty, one would find a form of power that is not diagrammatic, but whose functioning is somewhat different. Power serves to deduct or withdraw, rather than to combine; it divides up multitudes into estates, or punishes through exile from the body politic. Power as sovereignty does not create zones of detailed control within the body politic itself.

However, we must resist imposing on this way of thinking any simple sense of chronology, and attend to its tensions and disturbances. It would be a mistake to draw certain pessimistic conclusions from this account of power. Certainly, what is no longer sustainable is an idea of the subject as pure interiority, as consciousness of self. The subject is located in the interstices of power. In this sense interiority, or one's sense of self, is constituted by 'exteriority', the power/knowledge conjugations that we have been studying.

The subject, then, is an intensity of force. This is not the humanist essence, the soul; or the process where 'I' truly know myself or discover myself through reason. It is the subject as a site of its own creation of itself; a work on and of itself. Nor is it the 'empty' or the 'elitist' subject of postmodernity.[84] This is the subject as self mastery. How can we explain this point?

Let us return to the distinction between interiority and exteriority, for this might give us the 'formula' for the subject 'after' psychoanalysis. Before psychoanalysis the site of man's interiority was created through moral discourses on the management of one's desires, tastes and appetites. Indeed, psychoanalysis becomes the inheritor of this set of practices. It is not our objective here to follow in detail the path of this research from the ancient Greeks, through to Christianity and into the post-Christian, because we want to determine more thoroughly how the subject can be conceived as a 'fold'. In what sense can we refer to the subject as a fold? The fold allows us to talk of interiority without fetishising the idea of an inner essence. The primary sense of the word relates to a doubling over of fabric or some other material, so that the outside surfaces are brought together to create an inside. The operation thus describes a process where a single plane is folded back on itself to cerate an interior space that did not exist prior to the fold. At a more sophisticated level, this describes the creation of an interiority from an exteriority through a form of self reflection or self relation. It could be extrapolated as follows: one's interior sense of oneself derives from a relationship to others. In this way a moral code creates a self through relating the self and its appetites to others.[85] In other words, if we can see the idea of self mastery as a power that one brings to bear upon oneself then it is simultaneously through this act, and within this power, that one can claim to govern others. This approach to subjectivity takes from more traditional accounts the idea that

[84] See O Feltham and J Clemens, 'An Introduction to Alain Badiou's Philosophy' in O Feltham and J Clemens (trans and eds), *Infinite Thought: Truth and the Return to Philosophy* (London, Continuum, 2003).

[85] G Deleuze and F Guattari, *Anti Oedipus*, above n 63, 100.

behind subjectivity lies reflection. However, to speak in terms of the fold suggests a point where an inside and an outside become caught together for a moment; a moment where a particular conjunction of power/knowledge brings together an arrangement of force that we can call subjectivity.[86]

This approach to subjectivity allows us to refute some of the criticism of the Foucauldian/Deleuzian project.[87] Critics have argued that the account of disciplinary power leaves no room for the subject or agency, and hence for resistance to power: 'If the subject—right down to its most intimate desires, actions and thoughts—is constituted by power, then how can it be the source of independent resistance?' The critics argue that in both Deleuze and Foucault, this resistance comes to be provided by 'an aesthetic project of self authoring.' However, aesthetic self authoring cannot explain 'why . . . some subjects shapes themselves against the grain' and others do not.[88]

We would dispute these arguments. The process of subjectification is both aesthetic and political, as we will show in more detail presently. It is aesthetic only in the sense that it refers to a making of something, and thus does not necessarily refer exclusively to dandyism or a cult of beauty.[89] Furthermore, the subject as fold cannot be divorced from the wider field of antagonistic forces that constitute the social. Why some resist and others succumb is a difficult question to answer, but must relate to the distribution of politically organised forces and ideological processes of identification and subjectification that we have described in chapter 8. Risking banality through compression, we might suggest that what is at stake in the tensions occasioned by Islamic resurgence is precisely this issue of how subjects are to be constituted. Our times are perhaps marked in this way by a clash between secular and religious modes of subjectification. In the most extreme cases, the imposition of the Shari'a code becomes the focus of civil unrest. This can be understood as an attempt to privilege a particular monotheistic ethical code that subjectifies as Moslem or non Moslem.

As much as Moslems may choose to identify as Moslems, non Moslems may take their opposition to civil and political Islamic forms as their own source of identity. We can see this drama playing itself out in different ways. In the north of Nigeria, for instance, there are tensions between Moslems and those who affirm the secular law of the Constitution. The politics of Islam in Europe raises similar issues. To what extent can a national identity, a sense of belonging to a western Christian or post-Christian state, be negotiated with the compelling sense of an international Moslem identity? In France, the Netherlands and the United Kingdom increasingly intense public debate concerns the extent to which secular and religious values can be coordinated. Cultural identity increasingly expresses itself as a kind of political theology of belonging.

[86] G Deleuze and F Guattari, *Anti Oedipus*, above n 63, 101.

[87] Above n 84, at 5.

[88] *Ibid*, 6.

[89] For a greater elaboration of these points, see A Gearey, *Law and Aesthetics* (Oxford, Hart Press, 2001).

Where does this leave us? We are still within a discourse that talks in terms of desire, but desire is now related to the forces that constitute the social field itself. Rather than take us back to an account of the bourgeois subject, and the Oedipal triangle of mummy, daddy and me, we are propelled towards the social field in its entirety before we can talk in terms of subjectivity. Furthermore, we have not turned subjectivity into a matter that only the analyst can speak authoritatively about. We are now within a notion of subjectivity where we are much more concerned with those operations of the self that have to do with defining singularities where powers coalesce. The return to the Greek root may have been necessary to draw attention to a logic, a diagram that we post-moderns had forgotten, but it has immediate purchase. Thus, the gang member who wears a doo rag or a skully is manifesting a subjective singularity that shows where a particular technology of the self manifests itself. Just as the law in its various forms attempts to enforce certain dress codes, from veils to track suits, resistance finds ways of opposing different forces: this is a drama that can be seen playing itself out in *La Republique Francaise*, to the streets of LA, Brixton and Manchester. This, however, remains at a somewhat schematic level. In the next session, we hope to be able to show how the revolutionary singularity, the power against the law, produces itself.

THE SEVENTH SESSION: BIKO

How does the revolutionary create a subjectivity against the law? We will read a text by the South African writer and activist Steve Biko, who gave his life in the struggle against apartheid. Our text is *Black Consciousness and the Quest for a True Humanity*, which we will read as the manifestation of a desire that can mandate a new form of politics and confront the white fantasy that has determined a political terrain. Biko begins by forefronting the scene of thinking as the theatre of praxis: it is a question of what ideas can do. The need is for 'us' to 'think collectively about a problem we never created.'[90] Philosophy is about creating change in the world. It is an expression that produces effects; or, more precisely, philosophical precision is inseparable from a political strategy. The strategy itself combines different arguments, creating points of intensity. 'We' did not create the problem; the address creates an addressee: someone who will become a 'we'; a singularity that will relate to other singularities. How could this argument develop?

Biko presents the 'colour question' as, from the very beginning, a matter of a boundary, a line that separates a privileged minority from an oppressed majority. Biko's text is thus concerned with an economic operation that divides up, and then justifies division and segregation by a logic that inscribes into nature and the social the divisions it has imposed. The contingent is thus passed off as

[90] R Malan (ed), *The Essential Steve Biko* (Cape Town, David Philip Publishers, 1997) 10.

the natural; a political order reinforces itself to the extent that it creates an entire political fantasy, that has to be understood at the level of the group imagining itself, and acting on the basis of its fantasy:

> [t]he racism that we meet does not only exist on an individual basis; it is also institutionalised to make it look like the South African way of life.[91]

And later:

> [t]he overall success of the white power structure has been in managing to bind the whites together in defence of the status quo.[92]

Thus a social structure is created that uses the law to create an apartheid social order. The Population Registration Act of 1950 and the Group Area Act of the same year, created a typology of race—a way of classifying and hierarchising the various ethnic groups that composed South Africa. The classifications defined by the Act were used as the basis for determining employment, residence and other social duties and privileges. These Acts provided the legal basis for the forced resettlement of huge sections of the population and the destruction of homes where people had been settled for generations. If the point of these Acts was to demarcate and limit black and coloured peoples to certain locations, then the Population Registration Act 1949 and the Immorality Act of 1950 created ways of maintaining the separation of the accordingly defined racial groups. Other Acts were aimed at the maintenance of racial boundaries in public facilities, and the operation of an underfunded and massively restricted system of education for those defined as Bantu peoples.

Against this 'racist utopia' is opposed another possibility: 'we have to find out what went wrong-where and when.' To argue that something went wrong, that something fell away, is to posit a point where things were still holding together. This is related to another feature of the question itself:

> we have to find out whether our position is a deliberate creation of God or an artificial fabrication of the truth by power hungry people whose motive is authority, security, wealth and comfort.

The point where things had not yet fallen apart may be an origin, but, it operates here in a way that is not associated with the logic of origins that we have studied in this book. It is not an original emptiness or absence that is to haunt any attempt to posit a political alternative. Establishing its dynamic demands a re-working of history; recovering, or inventing an African spirituality that exists before, alongside and within missionary Christianity, gives rise to a belief in the innocent becomings of man,[93] man's 'inherent goodness' and describes Christ as a 'fighting God' in a black theology of struggle. But this is a theology that pulls together a recovered political history—a connection of intensities and

[91] *Ibid*, 10.
[92] *Ibid*.
[93] *Ibid*, 25.

singularities; the deployment of 'names': 'Shaka, Moshoeshoe Hintsa'[94]and Makana: 'essentially revolutionaries.'[95]

'Black Consciousness' is thus the mark of a particular connective logic that wants to posit humanity itself:

> Black consciousness is an attitude of mind and a way of life . . . Its essence is the realisation by the black man of the need to rally together with his brothers around the causes of their oppression—the blackness of their skin—and to operate as a group to rid themselves of the shackles that bind them to perpetual servitude.[96]

This is a point of force or intensity that can be invoked as an agonistics, to oppose an organisation of force, whose 'motive is authority, security, wealth and comfort.' To the extent that this provides a source for the law, it is not so much an unquestionable prohibition, as an organisation of forces. Likewise, 'God' is here a point immanent to the system of forces. The name is aligned with an intensity; an intensity that poses the question. The invocation of divinity is part of an argument that opposes God and intensity to those sites where intensity has solidified into an 'artificial fabrication.' Indeed, it would appear that the 'Black Consciousness approach' is no more than an arrangement of zones, an organisation of forces in a particular field.

It is a politics of bodies:

> You are either alive and proud or you are dead, and when you are dead, you can't care anyway. And your method of death can be a politicising thing. So you die in the riots. For a hell of a lot of them, in fact, there's really nothing to lose—almost literally, given the kind of situation that they come from. So if you can overcome the personal fear of death, which is a highly irrational thing, you know that you're on the war. And in interrogation the same sort of thing applies . . .[97]

This is not writing that acknowledges the prohibition of the law as the point at which a project stalls or comes to a halt. It is political activism pushed to its extreme point as a life that is lived as struggle. Could we refer to this as the death drive, the urge for personal extinction? Such an approach appears reductive. We need to appreciate that this is a programmatic articulation of desire based on an experience of the body as the thing that must fall, that must be subjected to forces that will destroy it. Biko's writing cannot be described as fantasy because it is not the representation of anything; it causes forces to pass and circulate. Thus Biko's body passes from live body to dead body, but by moving through this process serves a political cause:

> if they beat me up, its to my advantage. I can use it.[98]

[94] *Ibid*, 31.
[95] *Ibid*, 30.
[96] *Ibid*, 21.
[97] *Ibid*, 54.
[98] *Ibid*, 55.

Pain is experienced not as victimhood, as helplessness, but as an intensity of empowerment. On the body is inscribed a truth about the law: it is violence, a practice of violence. It is necessary to identify with and force this to its only possible conclusion:

> . . . if they had meant to give me so much of a beating, and not more, my idea is to make them go beyond what they wanted to give me and to give back as much as I can give so that it becomes an uncontrollable thing.[99]

This appears to suggest a vector, but one that moves in a completely peculiar direction; a moment that pushes a process to its extreme, even to the point of self destruction, and which leaves a remainder which is a kind of writing or token of what a politics must achieve.

THE EIGHTH SESSION

This chapter can have no conclusion, because the energies that it celebrates should not be so limited. Perhaps we can offer a final fold—though, a backward glance over the road we have traveled. We have attempted to trace through the recent history of psychoanalysis a sense in which this kind of thinking can lend itself to both an apologetics for the law, and a more explicitly radical attempt to reshape or oppose the law. Psychoanalysis becomes the law, the encounter between the two was pre-ordained. If classical jurisprudence explains and celebrates the empire of law, classical psychoanalysis insists on law's inevitability. From Freud to Lacan and Legendre, the law is seen as an indispensable controller of self and the organiser and desire. But there is also a counter-move, by thinkers such as Deleuze and Guattari who have attempted to decouple the Oedipal emphasis of psychoanalysis from its potential to determine a particular experience of subjectivity. This does not return to consciousness as the key to subjectivity, and so remains within a psychoanalytic paradigm. However, it sees psychoanalysis as pointing not towards the analysts couch, but towards the social world. This turn of the psychoanalytical has taken us towards the way in which a revolutionary subjectivity can oppose itself to a form of the social and the form of the law. In the intensity of this politics, the body itself becomes a weapon that may be destroyed in the struggle, but offers its defeat as the inspiration—the point of intensity—that will provoke others to action.

PASSAGES

Back at Heathrow in a crumpled suit. Although I use the same taxi company, there is always a different version of my name on the cardboard sign that the

[99] *Ibid*, 55.

driver holds before himself in the foyer. Perhaps this suggests that you always return as a different person; or that those you leave behind have to fool you into thinking that things have changed while you were away. I fall asleep on the M1 in the back of the taxi and wake somewhere near Luton. Could it get much better than this?

13

The Lion for Real: Law and the Demands of Literature

IT IS ONLY AS AN AESTHETIC PHENOMENON THAT THE WORLD CAN BE REDEEMED

LAW AND LITERATURE, as received by the academy, as practiced to date, is another form of restricted jurisprudence.[1] Law and literature could have been an engagement with the subject interpellated by the law; of what it means to be a legal subject. It could have become a general jurisprudence that explicated the law of the law. Instead, it has become limited to a set of *topoi* that make for a restricted sense of the literary.

Law and literature has become infested by a rash of themes that have been generated by a particular set of problems within liberal thinking. The valorisation of the form of the nineteenth century novel by law and literature scholars, and the relative lack of interest in other literary forms, such as poetry, tragic drama and parable, is exemplary of this cast of thought. What lies behind it is a concern with a particular understanding of literary language. The novel is useful if literature is to be put to work, re-inventing public life and discourse; re-invigorating a set of values focused around notions of civility and inclusion in the republic of sensibility. In a wider sense, law and literature as practiced to date is an example of how the aesthetic has been called upon to ground a political order. To this extent, the literary has been called before the law to answer a limited set of questions. The very terms of the interrogation have meant that there was never a chance for a new jurisprudential discourse to develop. The

[1] For a notable exception see the work of Robert Cover which considers the manifold ways in which legal institutions are embedded in broader historical narratives. See R Cover, 'Nomos and Narrative' (1983) 97 *Harvard Law Review* 4. Cover's approach stresses that all narratives are organised into a moral teleology that attempts to shape the world that they describe. Law is always located in a social text, the material world that Cover describes as a *nomos*. Narrative figures in this work as a category of sociological importance; narrative can provide phenomenological insight into law's construction and ordering of the social world. In this tradition, see also A Sarat (ed), *Law, Violence and the Possibility of Justice* (Princeton, Princeton University Press, 2001). This text offers a particularly rich set of readings that relate issues of violence and narrative to constitutional law.

'darker', problematic elements of the literary, the philosophical problem with literature itself, have been downplayed or simply ignored.

We would plead guilty to the charge that we are merely repeating this gesture by privileging a different sense of the literary. However, this is an exemplification of our general theme: that the critical haunts the orthodox, as the dreams of the night haunt the day. Our ambition is merely to show how a kind of dreamwork can reveal the underpinnings of a way of thinking that would rather not know what lies in its own constitution.

Our argument shall develop as follows. After a brief review of the field, we shall offer a historical thesis. Our cast of thought insists on the genealogical. To understand the failures of law and literature, and to recover the sense of promise it may still retain, we need to ask questions of its derivation. We need to locate the present debates within ancient history and an ongoing struggle between kinds of thinking and interpretations of the world. Turning to the law and literature scholarship of the last decade and a half, we will suggest that the limitations of the field are in part due to a failure to take this pedigree into account, and the avoidance of engagement by creating a straw man argument about 'poststucturalism'. This refusal to engage can also be read at a 'methodological' level. Any reference to psychoanalysis, deconstruction or feminism is expunged. To the extent that ethical themes appear, they have been carefully filtered to remove anything that might damage the ability of literary thinking to save the law from its perceived rigidity. However, we will see that an engagement with desire, the body and a politics of eros does emerge from within the belly of the discourse. By means of an extended conclusion, and an exemplification of literary jurisprudence, we turn to a reading of Kafka's parable, *Before the Law*.

We need to begin by asking some general questions about the nature of literary jurisprudence.

THE CLAIMS OF LAW AND LITERATURE

Literary jurisprudence starts from many different perspectives and adopts a variety of theoretical positions, but all agree on two points. First, whatever the differences between judges and storytellers or between practicing and fictional lawyers, they are all united through their use of language. Law's life is predominantly linguistic; language is the material out of which law is made and through which it works on the world. Lawyer and storyteller—despite their differences—are united in their obligation to use language. Whilst the methods and aims of linguistic usage in the two enterprises differ substantially, their practitioners share the aim of shaping language felicitously according to criteria of form and style appropriate to each activity and in their determination to succeed in communicating with their respective audiences. In this general sense, literary jurisprudence can be seen as a sub-species of wider genres and disciplines committed to the study of the organisation, transmission and effects of communication, such as semiotics, hermeneutics or rhetoric.[2] Forensic rhetoric and legal poetics are probably the oldest western theories of legal practice and in the work of Chaim Perelman they have witnessed a long overdue return.[3] Legal semiotics on the other hand has been a moderately popular jurisprudential enterprise for many years and was one of the precursors of the literature school. Literary jurisprudence has incorporated many insights offered by these specialist disciplines, but its contribution is not restricted to the study of legal communication. Law and literature questions the strict generic separation between the two fields, mainly through the use of literary texts and theories for jurisprudential purposes, but its main exponents are not interested in examining the aesthetic and literary qualities of law.

The second and greater influence on literary jurisprudence is the wider movement in legal theory, which challenged the dominant positivised version of law.[4] Positivism, as we have argued, approaches the law as a system of rules, that acquire their legal quality solely through their derivation from a sovereign centre. It is not difficult to develop a highly detailed and delicate account of the linguistic usage of legal terms with the help of analytical philosophy; but it is much harder to answer the criticism that such elegant differentiations and distinctions fail to describe the actual operation of the law and give the impression

[2] B Jackson, *Semiotics and Legal Theory* (London, Routledge, 1985); *Law, Fact and Narrative Coherence* (Liverpool, Deborah Charles Press, 1988). The work of Jackson (1988) provides a theoretically developed account of narrative in the area of adjudication. Jackson argues that narrative is an essential part of legal decision making, picking up and developing themes within schools of both positivist and realist jurisprudence. The theoretical suppositions underlying this work return to the structuralist semiotics of AJ Greimas, which, in turn relies on the notion of a 'semio-narrative' level in the work of Vladimir Propp. Propp's work shows that human action is structured in a narrative fashion. Narrative is understood as a sequence that moves from the setting of goals, the performance of those goals, and the reflection on success or failure. Within this sequence there will be figures who aid or obstruct the subject. In applying this analysis to law, we are concerned with the particular legal forms that these narrative structures take. Based on a semiotic concern with law as a form of communication, this mode of narrative analysis has the potential to develop a sophisticated understanding of the construction of legal meaning. The trial provides a focus for this research. Because analysis of the processes in a courtroom is complex, it is necessary to take an exemplary aspect: witness testimony. Testimony in court can be modelled in Greimasian terms. Imagine that the plaintiff has called a witness. The witness has a helper in the form of counsel for the plaintiff. The witness also has an opponent: counsel for the defence. Whilst counsel for the plaintiff will seek to persuade the jury of the veracity of the witness testimony, counsel for the defence will attempt to cast doubt on the version of events that the witness has given. Of course, if there is a witness who is hostile to the plaintiff's case, counsel for the plaintiff will act as an opponent, and counsel for the defence will act as a helper. Jackson is drawing attention to basic positions that can be occupied by different actors as a narrative develops about the case in the courtroom. At a more general level, the model can also be used to think more broadly about legal reasoning. Jackson's argument is that legal reasoning, which tends to represent itself as scientific, makes use of narrative forms. In summary, what is important in Jackson's work is a conjunction of social psychology and narrative theory as a way of understanding both legal processes and the nature of law in general.

[3] C Perleman and O Tyteca, *The New Rhetoric: A Treatise on Argumentation* (Notre Dame, Notre Dame University Press, 1969).

[4] This challenge is found both in rights jurisprudence, brought to prominence in the work of Ronald Dworkin and his followers, and the neo-naturalism of John Finnis and in the work of the critical legal studies school.

that law is totally unconcerned with the fairness and justice of its operation once the specified criteria of formal validity and efficiency have been met. To its opponents, positivism offers a descriptively inaccurate and ethically impoverished picture. The common law in particular, it is argued, involves the creative and principled retrieval of meanings and values.[5] Such values are said to exist in a nascent state in legal materials and are further specified and developed when courts come to apply them to new situations and circumstances. This reaction to positivism can be broadly termed a hermeneutical jurisprudence, and literary jurisprudence is its main constituent.

Literary jurisprudence claims that literature can give us important insights into the way the law works. World literature has placed disproportionate emphasis on legal questions and themes.[6] Law and legality have competed successfully with other institutions and cultural artefacts for the attention of poets and storytellers; this extensive interest in law makes literature worthy of the attention of lawyers. But literary jurisprudence often makes a stronger point. Both law and literature are involved in the exploration of some of the most important concerns of social life. They address the preconditions and characteristics of the just, peaceful and happy community; the bases of authority, the foundations of the social bond and the related obligation to obey the law. Finally, both law and literature deal with social conflict and with the tension between individual conscience and conventional wisdom or legal imposition. Such dilemmas are at the heart of tragedy but also of law and jurisprudence. In short, both law and literature are preoccupied with the harbingers of justice and the mainsprings of injustice and evil.

If the function of legal education is to give future lawyers a rich, nuanced and pluralistic picture of the role of law and its practitioners in society, literature is a valuable resource. The social sciences have all too often used legal data in their quest for the description and explanation of wider social phenomena. Literary jurisprudence reverses this trend: legal scholars turn to fiction about the law in order to examine the wider cultural understanding and evaluation of legal operations, the world's attitudes to law but also law's internal world, important personal and professional assumptions and characteristics of lawyers not addressed or discussed elsewhere in the legal curriculum.[7] The literary text is

[5] R Dworkin, *Taking Rights Seriously* (London, Duckworth, 1977); *Law's Empire* (Oxford, Hart, 1998); J Finnis, *Natural Law and Natural Rights* (Oxford, Clarendon, 1980).

[6] Weisberg has argued that 'whenever law becomes the dominant cultural and political force, literary art tends to immerse itself in matters legal': RH Weisburg, *The Failure of the Word: The Protagonist as Lawyer in Modern Fiction* (New Haven, Yale University Press, 1984) *x*.

[7] Work to date has considered Holocaust narratives in the courtroom, constitutional law as narrative and the narratives that are at work in criminal trials. A wide-ranging treatment of these themes, with an emphasis on the US scholarship, can be found in P Brooks and P Gewirtz (eds), *Law and Stories: Narrative and Rhetoric in Law* (New Haven, Yale University Press, 1996). This collection also displays a representative concern with the ways in which narrative can problematise legal reasoning. Minow's essay opposes the power of narrative to social science methodologies, in particular law and economics reasoning. Although narrative is linked to the ability to think in new ways, it is still something untrustworthy and can disrupt the categories that legal reasoning depends

approached not as a source of information about the actual workings of a particular legal system,[8] but as a repository of the cultural experiences, narratives and values of law. In a psychoanalytical sense, literature becomes law's dream, which presents some of the unacknowledged and unexplained symptoms of the institution.

But the reverse is also true. The ability of literature to illuminate aspects of law's life is predicated on the special qualities of literary style and its emotional affect. The literary implication between textual form and narrative content points to a similar quality in the legal text and opens the space for a literary reading of law. Traditional jurisprudence has denied that law's language or operations are involved with aesthetic questions. Reading law as a kind of literature does not neglect the distinction between the two types of text and institution, but it warns against an impoverished reading of legal texts and reminds us that more is involved in the organisation and life of law than the simple operation of rules. Legal rules and a certain form of legal language have always been intrinsically linked. Texts of law have historically exhibited a great love of language, an acute awareness of rhetorical figure and trope—both necessary prerequisites for the effective operation and transmission of texts.[9] The doctors of law and the judges of the 'grand' style have personified the spirit of law but they have also been stylists and philologists devoted to the text. It may be that the style of contemporary law is to deny style and to repress its literary qualities. But this does not mean that law is a transparent text that forgoes linguistic virtuosity and semantic richness. On the contrary, if contemporary law's style is its lack of style, literary jurisprudence helps us understand this peculiar stylelessness and explain its effects upon lawyer and lay person alike.

An obvious objection to this approach refers to the difference between the world of law and fictional literature. The law is somehow related to the 'real' world, while literature is the product of imagination and has no referent in reality. But closer reflection on the nature of reference complicates the picture. A text of whatever type or discipline does not and cannot present raw life—life 'in the flesh'—it cannot move directly and without mediation to its referent.

upon. This theme can be linked to an emerging concern with the impact of technology on courtroom narratives. Strictly separate from the interest with fictional representations of lawyers in film studies, this work looks to the impact of television on the forms of legal argument in the wake of cases like Rodney King and OJ Simpson. Prior to the advent of televised trials, legal argument had developed in relative isolation from the wider culture. Instantaneous communications suggest that it will become more difficult to deploy arcane vocabularies to justify the outcome of a trial. Rather, courtroom narrative may have to adapt to the demands of the televisual spectacle: R Sherwin, *When Law Goes Pop* (Chicago, University of Chicago Press, 2000) provides a useful consideration of the scholarship in this area. See also L Moran, E Sandon, I Christie, and E Loizidou (eds), *Law's Moving Image* (London, Cavendish, 2003).

[8] As Posner notes, Kafka's *The Trial* does not give us an accurate picture of the Austro-Hungarian legal system. See R Posner, *Law and Literature: A Misunderstood Relation* (Cambridge, Mass, Harvard University Press, 1998) 21.

[9] P Legendre, *L'Amour du Censeur* (Paris, Seuil, 1974); *L'Inestimable Objet du Transmission* (Paris, Fayard, 1985); P Goodrich, *Languages of Law* (London, Weidenfeld, 1990).

A work of literature makes explicit or implicit choices about life and how it should be lived—it presents life as having a purpose or moving in a certain direction. These choices may be made in the subject matter, in what the text talks about; often however these choices are carried out in the way the text talks, in its form and style. According to Paul Ricoeur, oral communication makes 'ostensive' reference to a common horizon within which the speakers find themselves. Written texts and literature in particular, on the other hand, cannot invoke an immediate situation common to author and reader. In a more technical language, the reference of literature is a world (*Welt*) and not a situation (*Unwelt*). 'Reference is determined by the ability to point to a reality common to the interlocutors.'[10] The interpretation of a work of literature is successful if it creates and projects a world against which the work acquires meaning and significance and, if it incorporates effortlessly the network of related texts. Reading fuses the horizon of the interpreter with the symbolic world projected by the text. This world provides a different 'attitude towards [our situation], a free, distanced attitude which is always realised in language.'[11] But language facilitates the construction of many worlds. Texts, in this sense, by bringing together content and form, concept and expressions, make choices as to the kind of world they want to represent or the type of activity they want to order. Entering the text's world 'light[s] up our own situation, or, if you will, interpolate[s] among the predicates of our own situation all the significations which make a *Welt* out of our *Unwelt*.'[12] The mark of great literature is to combine form and content so that they develop an organic relationship, that illuminates our own world.[13]

Similarly, legal materials do not come to us 'unmediated', free of the need to interpret. If to understand a novel we build a symbolic world using rules, conventions and interpretations, we understand legal texts and practices through an equally elaborate set of conventions and interpretative moves. Fact finding or the presentation of argument before a court is organised by procedural rules and follows narrative expectations and arrangements as much as any reading practice.[14] Legal texts are enmeshed in intricate relations with other texts and project their own world, their explicit or implicit image of what the world should be like and how people should live in it.[15] The worlds projected in literary and legal texts may differ in scope or style, but they are not ontologically

[10] P Ricoeur, *Hermeneutics and the Social Sciences*, JB Thompson (trans), (Cambridge, Cambridge University Press, 1981) 141.

[11] HG Gadamer, *Truth and Method*, W Glen-Doepel (trans), (London, Sheed & Ward, 1975) 403.

[12] P Ricoeur, *Hermeneutics and The Social Sciences*, above n 10, 202.

[13] In Borges's 'Pierre Menard', it would be hard to delete or replace even a single word in *Don Quixote* without damaging the perfection of the original.

[14] B Jackson, *Law, Fact and Narrative Coherence*, above n 2.

[15] C Douzinas and R Warrington with S McVeigh, *Postmodern Jurisprudence* (London, Routledge, 1990) chapter 12; P Goodrich and Y Hachamovitz, 'The Semiotics of the Common Law' in P Fitzpatrick (ed), *Dangerous Supplements* (London, Pluto, 1990).

different. For literary jurisprudence, all form and style—including the alleged absence of style that law claims—is a statement about life. It is therefore part of the literary reading of law to bring to the surface, make conscious and analyse the stylistic conventions, rhetorical devices and other formal arrangements of the legal text in an attempt to understand law's life, and life according to law.

A GENEALOGY OF LAW AND LITERATURE: THE ANCIENT QUARREL AND THE DEMANDS OF THE PRESENT

Law and literature as jurisprudence has to be understood as the outcome of a long historical process of differentiation between legal and literary texts that has resulted in the separation of normative and aesthetic functions. But it should be immediately stressed that the divorce between the two domains was initiated and is still presided over by philosophy, and more specifically, by a philosophical anxiety about aesthetic considerations, rhetorical flourishes, textual embellishments, and the accompanying sensual response and emotional investment by the reader. For philosophy, the senses are inimical to the search for truth, and the emotions are alien to the quest for a just polity.

The separation between the legal and the aesthetic has an old and honourable philosophical pedigree. Plato extended the famous ancient 'quarrel between philosophy and poetry' to the relationship between law and poetry.[16] Marking the difference in function and form, Plato states in *The Laws* that 'when a poet represents men with contrasting characters he is often obliged to contradict himself, and he does not know which of the opposing speeches contains the truth. But for the legislator, this is impossible: he must not let his laws say two different things on the same subject'.[17] For Plato as much as for most contemporary jurisprudence, law must follow a principle of textual parsimony and persist with an unadorned, unambiguous and clear language, which is considered necessary for its consistent interpretation and application. Clarity of language and certainty of purpose allow the incontestable repetition of the rule and minimise the hazards of interpretation.

Similarly, the early modern critical philosophy of Kant insisted on the principles of separation between different intellectual and aesthetic competences. Modernity releases three areas of enquiry and action, the cognitive, the practical and the aesthetic; and the three faculties of knowledge, law and taste are released to develop their own specific, internal rationality, in separate institutions operated by distinct groups of experts.[18] Modern law is born in its

[16] T Gould, *The Ancient Quarrel between Poetry and Philosophy* (Princeton, Princeton University Press, 1990).

[17] Plato, *The Laws* (New York, Penguin, 1977) Bk 2, 91.

[18] For a discussion of the Kantian faculties and their relevance to law and jurisprudence see C Douzinas and R Warrington with S McVeigh, *Postmodern Jurisprudence*, above n 15, chapters 1 and 3.

separation from aesthetic considerations and the aspirations of literature and art. The relationship between art, literature and law, between the aesthetic and the normative, is presented as one between pluralism and unity, between surface openness and deep closure, between figuration and employment. Art is assigned to imagination, creativity and playfulness while law relates to control, discipline and sobriety. There can be no bigger contrast than that between the open texts and abstract paintings of the modernist tradition and the text of statutes, like the Obscene Publications Act or the Official Secrets Act or indeed any other Act. Statutes are supposed to have a true meaning that technical expertise and the correct method will be able to discover.

The self in literature—as author or reader—is free, desiring, corporeal; the literary self has gender and history. The subject of law—as judge or litigant—is constrained, oppressed, censored and ethereal. The legal person is a collection of rights and duties, a point of condensation of capacities and obligations of a general or universal nature,[19] and the judge is at the service of the law of reason which has no history and time—no past or future—but is omnipresent. The legal subject that comes before the law is genderless and contextless, a *persona* or mask placed on the body. Justice must be blindfolded to avoid the temptation to face he who comes before the law and must excise the individual characteristics of the concrete person through the application of law's abstract logic. Finally in an institutional sense, law is presented as the solution to the conflict of values and the plurality of interpretations. Law is therefore functionally and politically differentiated from literature. In a mundane but revealing sense, literature has treated law and lawyers with contempt; a contempt that began in the comedies of Aristophanes and was taken up with vigour by modernist literature. It is clear, however, that while the separation appears today obvious, almost natural, it was philosophy that introduced and policed the generic differentiation.

One of the most important reasons for philosophy's interest in this division concerns the status of language. When truth is presented as mimesis—correspondence or adequation of reality to representation—the distorting effects of the medium must be kept at a minimum. Philosophy's dream has always been to develop a neutral, almost transparent, language and keep at a distance the figures, tropes, devices and argumentative stratagems of literature. An austere and clear language does not need interpretation and dispenses with the difficulties of commentary; the law inscribes itself in the soul without mediation and calls solely for instruction, repetition and exegesis. Rhetorical and beautiful language, on the other hand, deviates from truth and conceals its intentions in tricks and flourishes which cannot yield meaning without interpretation. Adorned speech and oratorical skills may move the emotions, please the soul and influence people but they are not the proper means for the seeker after truth

[19] See generally C Douzinas and R Warrington, *Justice Miscarried: Ethics, Aesthetics and Law* (Hemel Hempstead, Harvester, 1994) chapter 4.

or justice. Art and literature, the proper domains of beautiful speech, have an important role in the city, particularly for the instruction of the young, but their ambition and status is subordinate to philosophy. In the hierarchy of discourses and institutions, law's place is below philosophy, but its importance to a well-governed state makes it imperative that law—as much as philosophy—should keep its language clear, certain and unambiguous.

Despite philosophy's dreams and strictures, however, law and the aesthetic have experienced a close historical relationship. Successful law has always been felicitous language. Instruction into the legal *arcana* has involved an introduction to the power of beautiful speech.[20] The earliest customs and laws of Greece took the form of legends, myths and tales; the earliest judge was a *histor*, and the earliest legislators were storytellers. The first legal form was narrative and the great lawgivers, Solo, Lycurgus, and Plato himself were narrators. This close link between literary form and law continued in the classical period. Legal practice was the mainstay of *rhetors* and orators—a lawyer would be chosen as much for his ability to move an audience as for his mastery of the law. Plato's extreme dislike of the Sophists was partly motivated by their pre-eminent status in Athenian legal and political life. Demosthenes and Cicero were instructed in forensic rhetoric and the felicitous uses of speech and oratorical skill as well as in legal technique and procedure. It may be, as Goodrich has argued, that certain figures and strategies of oration and rhetoric have dominated legal speech in different historical periods, for example figures of exclusion and belonging—the *antirrhetic* and *antithesis*—have been extensively mobilised at times of social and political upheaval and have been solidified into a lawyer resembling a collective legal unconscious.[21]

Throughout history, law has been the performative language *par excellence*, a language whose success is measured by its consequences, by its ability to act on the world and its power to capture the soul. A language that carries the rudiments of order and transmits the commands of the law must act on the emotions and persuade the intellect; it can only be a beautiful language and, despite protestations to the contrary, legal practice and education, consciously or unconsciously, have always understood this point. The link between the performance of law and the love for the text is pervasive in practice. But the greatest impediment to its full recognition has been what we may call the resistance of genre—the belief in the Platonic injunction against poetry and rhetoric and in

[20] Hayden White's essay 'The Value of Narrativity in the Representation of Reality' (1980) 7 *Critical Inquiry* 5 contains some essential insights into the centrality of law for narrative, philosophy, and history. Drawing on Hegel, White sees the existence of a sense in which questions of legitimacy and legality can be posed as a pre-requisite for ordered narrative. Any self-conscious, structured account of history as a realisation of narrative in a modern, sophisticated form must have, as a condition of possibility, structures of legitimacy and right. Ultimately, narrative and law are seen as elements in a broader account of historical being, and the very construction of a world that makes sense and can be judged.

[21] P Goodrich, *Oedipus Lex* (Berkeley, University of California Press, 1995) chapters 3 and 4.

the Kantian separation between the normative and aesthetic—that have acted as the background for the suppression and forgetting of the literary quality of law.

A literary jurisprudence, which is not a sophisticated liberal apologetics, must examine the historical conditions and philosophical presuppositions of this repression. But this is not enough; it must also emphasise the aesthetic qualities of the legal text, which have survived and cannot be erased despite the attempts of theorists and professionals. If the law works through the creation and projection of ordered worlds, attention to style, detail and form will help understand the hidden vision of law and develop alternative worlds and visions, which would derive their legitimacy from law's text, history and tradition.

It may be added, however, that the generic distinction between law and literature may indicate a deeper difference between two drives of the psyche and two aspects of community. One insists that the basis of the social bond—the link between individual and community, freedom and necessity—can be rationally examined and fully understood. In this perspective, a fair and just polity is possible and can be achieved through the combined efforts of reason, institutional existence and tradition. The Platonic dialogues are just such a prolonged quest for a rational and just arrangement of the polity and a long preamble to a constitutional settlement. Benthamite utilitarianism, although at the other end of philosophical speculation, is part of the same philosophical plan to create the city of God on earth. Bentham shares with Plato and Rousseau this legislative ambition, and all three have been actively involved in the legislation of legal codes and constitutions. To legislate justice through the operation of reason was a main urge of philosophy before its modern analytical and linguistic turn; philosophy has historically shared the tasks and aspirations of legislators and of legal and moral systems.

But this philosophical and legal move to control the world and the psyche was always accompanied by an opposed mood and drive associated with popular religion, myth, literature and—belatedly—psychoanalysis. This suggests that the social and psychic world cannot be fully controlled, nor can it become the perfect embodiment of rational schemes. Social injustice, a degree of personal unhappiness, emotional deprivation and material lack are the inescapable conditions of life. Moral and legal systems teach that suffering and injustice are the fault of the sufferer and wrongdoer. These misfortunes should not be blamed on fate, chance or other unknown and uncontrollable forces, but on the acts or omissions of the individual. World literature on the other hand has rarely claimed that perfect justice exists or that it can be achieved in this world.[22] On the contrary, tragedy, in particular, has insisted that misery and injustice are not necessarily caused by their victims and has tried to generate sympathy and compassion for them. This attitude of pity is based on the understanding that there are forces that escape the operation of reason and law. Fate and the furies derive from unconscious forces and determine lives unbeknown.

[22] C Douzinas and R Warrington, *Justice Miscarried*, above n 19 chapter 2.

In modernity, the problem of the social bond has been addressed most systematically by social science and politics, which have replaced philosophy and jurisprudence as the main activities and disciplines in charge of social and individual welfare. But the aspiration remains broadly the same: to organise rationally social interaction and individual behaviour so as to achieve an ordered, just and peaceful community. Academic and professional lawyers accept without difficulty that specific laws may have deviated from their task and that historical institutions may have been imperfect.

But legal discourse is committed to the belief that the world may be ordered according to rational criteria, that the legislator's task is to discover them and the interpreter's is to apply them. It may be that the claims to systematicity and universality associated with the 'science of law' are historically inventions and progeny of Roman law, linked to the empirical conditions and needs of empire. The importation of these principles into the limited and parochial territories of western legal systems, including the common law, raised them from historical constructs to transcendental presuppositions and regulative principles—in short—turned them into categories of an ahistorical, natural, eternal reason.

By exploring the connection of law to the contingency of the world with its petty dominations and major impositions, literary jurisprudence joins the quest for justice but shares with the classical tradition the belief that justice is not fully of this world.

LITERATURE'S ILLUMINATION OF LAW: THE SCHOLARSHIP TO DATE

It will be argued that the dominant version of law and literature is not only unaware of its own derivation, but that it refuses to engage with what it brackets as 'poststructuralism'. Law and literature scholarship has been content to 'translate' into its own terms a jurisprudence from elsewhere, and the opportunity to create an aesthetic jurisprudence has been squandered. To argue that literature can bring an ethics or morality to law is not, in itself, sufficient. We need a more thorough examination of these terms; an examination that would link them to the very question of desire and to the possibility of subjectivity.

One of the earliest texts in law and literature is Posner's book of the same name. The subject is seen as a negotiation between the 'rational methods of inquiry and the non-rational side of human nature'[23] but this is not carried through into any engagement with literature and the 'force of the must.' Posner's criticisms of Derrida's 'view' of literature as 'self referential'[24] are not only simplistic but beg the question of literature's self. To present the 'deconstructionists' as failing to move on from the critical idea that a poem could not

[23] R Posner, *Law and Literature: A Misunderstood Relation*, above n 8, 355.
[24] *Ibid*, 214.

be presented as a paraphrase also shows a failure to engage with Derrida's claims, as does the statement:

> If (as I doubt) he [Derrida] thinks that no writing ever conveys a concept in approximately the form intended by the author, he is, if not barmy, then simply too remote from legal culture to be heeded. Literary texts may or may not be self referential and (if the former) therefore incoherent, but it would not follow that a legal text was self referential and therefore incoherent too; the purposes and techniques of literary texts are different from those of the authors of legal texts.[25]

This is a major misunderstanding of Derrida's work. The deconstructive approach (if there is one) suggests that although a writer is responsible for a text, s/he can never control the contexts in which it will be read and the meanings that will be ascribed to it. As a problem of understanding, this applies to both the literary and to the legal text.[26] To describe this as a problem of self-referentiality obscures the sense in which the meaning ascribed to any text carries with it a destabilising indeterminacy that prevents any guarantee of an unproblematic transmission of 'meaning' from writer to reader.

Posner's work is also representative of wider currents in law and literature scholarship because it is marked by a crude linking of literature with a peculiar reductionism. Richard Posner has argued that literature is by its very nature irrelevant for law as it concerns general, universal themes that transcend the specifics of law. The legal content of novels is merely secondary and provides a background for the great concerns of literature. Thus, it can be asserted that Kafka's *The Trial* is redundant as a jurisprudential text, as it tells us very little about 'Austro Hungarian legal procedure.'[27] *The Trial* is read as a text that concerns the universal existential quest to find meaning in an absurd world. Likewise, *In the Penal Colony* is 'about' the general human problem of failure. This position has drawn fire from a number of writers within the debate. Critics have attacked the focus on a concept of literature that is too narrow and

[25] *Ibid*, 215.

[26] Posner is wrong about the relevance of deconstruction to legal theory in America. Although plotting the rise of deconstructive thought in the American legal academy would be a project in itself, a brief overview can be hazarded. Deconstruction has impacted on the study of doctrinal issues. Clare Dalton in C Dalton, 'An Essay on the Deconstruction of Contract Doctrine' (1994) 94 *Yale Law Journal*, draws on the notion of the dangerous supplement to show how legal discourse has tried to expel disruptive ideas in maintaining the conceptual hierarchies which sustain its world view. This emancipatory project is also apparent in GF Frug, 'The Ideology of Bureaucracy in American Law' (1984) 97 *Harvard Law Review* 1277, which also employs a deconstructive approach to show that justifications of various administrative decisions are contradictory. In a somewhat different field, deconstruction has lent itself to a theorisation of justice. J Balkin's 'Deconstructive Practice and Legal Theory' (1987) 96 *Yale Law Journal* 743 presents deconstruction as motivated by an acknowledgment that to be human is to be marked by a need to evaluate. This forces a realisation that we have to construct an idea of justice in the world of culture. There is a difference; the articulation of the values in culture is different from the values themselves. This is the 'gap' that deconstruction addresses. Transcendental deconstruction is an acknowledgement of the 'interval' between 'the human capacity for judgement' which transcends culture, and 'the prescriptions and evaluations of that culture' that in turn articulate and exemplify 'human values like justice.'

[27] Quoted in I Ward, *Law and Literature* (Cambridge, Cambridge University Press, 1995) 12.

obscures the way in which Kafka's stories concern themselves with moral choices and questions of authority.[28] Overall, Posner's work thus appears crude in both positing a general theory of literature, and relying on a simplistic mimetic model of literary meaning.

Richard Weisberg's work contrasts strongly with that of Posner. It represents a major attempt to 'ground' and bring theoretical order to law and literature scholarship. However, we are not convinced that the theme of *ressentiment* can serve this purpose. In the same way that Posner sees Kafka's stories as being 'about' certain existential or psychological themes, modernist literature is now defined as a critique of 'legalistic proclivity', the modern phenomenon of the need to 'over analyse' beyond the needs for 'accurate perception or action'.[29] In a wider sense, this is part of a general alienation from a moral attitude towards language:

> Modern fiction nowhere expresses better its unity with modern philosophy than in the novelistic interplay of rancour and law. For all our current emphasis on Marxist and Freudian elements in literature, we find a truer source for the novel as form, and as a medium of ideas, in Nietzsche's brilliant aphorisms about *ressentiment*. No phenomenon in recent fiction is as pervasive, none as intricately bound to an understanding of law and language in modern Western Culture. We need to recall and revivify the Nietzschean influence, to drink in iconoclasm, but also to savour the moral absolutism behind his aphoristic offerings.[30]

These references to Freud, Marx and Nietzsche suggest a theoretically sophisticated model of literature; but it is spoiled by the assertion that the theme of *ressentiment* should underpin literature's usefulness for law, a claim reminiscent of Posner's 'revenge' thesis.

Weisberg's prescription for literary jurisprudence goes on to marry together an essentially mimetic understanding of literature with a need for a moral direction:

> Like Mallarme's, our thoughts must leap back to Hamlet to fathom the moral enterprise of modern literary art. In a context of clear injustice, the noble example of his sensitivity wars with the ignoble effects of his wordy investigations. The modern novel, emphasising law, brings to fruition this essential dialectic.[31]

Does this belief in the 'essential dialectic' betray the avowed Nietzschean sympathies? It seems that the radical 'iconoclasm' is to be reintegrated into a moral whole. Literary Jurisprudence is conceived as a form of dialectical thinking; its end is an integration of art and morality. This ethical vision is guided by a notion of fit between the manner of representation and the object represented; literature is to be read for the 'matter' of what it represents, which can 'con-

[28] R West, 'Authority, Autonomy and Choice' (1985) *Harvard Law Review* 84–428.

[29] RH Weisberg, *The Failure of the Word: The Protagonist as Lawyer in Modern Fiction*, above n 6, 4.

[30] *Ibid*, 14.

[31] *Ibid*, 9.

vey[s] deep structural insights about many legal practices.'[32] It is this essential fit between 'style and substance' that grounds Poethics. Poethics is a critical reading method that attempts to read literary materials as having an inherent ethical force. This approach brings to the law a criterion for 'justice' that is derived from the idea of the well-constructed literary expression: in a 'just' statement of law, form and content and the 'craftsmanship' of the judgement will bear out its essential truth:

> Recalling Cardozo's powerful antidote to such beliefs ('the strength that is born of form and feebleness that is born of the lack of form are in truth qualities of the substance.') I would assert that an opinion wrong in its outcome may not at the same time be excellent in its craftsmanship.[33]

The lasting and just judgement will function in some ways like a well-crafted novel. It will attempt to capture the 'human situations' that the law concerns itself with through a humanistic deployment of narrative. Literary judgement recognises that the other should be respected as such. It attempts to 'understand the world from within the other's optic.'[34] Literature can assist the lawyer to open to the world of others, and provides an education in empathy and an antidote to the narrowness of a legal training. This project is indeed marked by a pedagogic programme; literature can teach important lessons about justice that are centred on the need to fathom the 'inner world of others', a fathoming that has to be linked to honest self-criticism—an introspection that can be engaged with in the reading of literature.

The pedagogic orientation of Weisberg's project is also apparent in Nussbaum's work.[35] Her main contribution to the debate concentrates on one text, Charles Dickens' novel *Hard Times*, and builds up a defence of the law-literature project based on Aristotle's *Poetics* and a call to reassess the role of emotions in public reasoning. In Nussbaum's account, literature provides an exemplification of a broader philosophical thesis about the centrality of the emotions in a re-thought version of an Aristotelian practical public life. This philosophical engagement with the idea of literature is developed via a reading of an avowedly Anglo-American utilitarian tradition. Literature appears on the side of the angels; it is a refutation of the self-sufficiency of the objective, neutral dispassionate judge applying a calculus that reduces to the same and ignores a wider, more 'human' form of decision making that takes into account human difference. Literature is distinguished from those other disciplines that simply record 'what happened' by offering the reader some form of emotional engagement. Nussbaum's project is to save this form of 'poetic' reasoning for 'public

[32] *Ibid*, 4.
[33] *Ibid*, 12.
[34] *Ibid*, 46.
[35] See 'Literary Theory and Ethical Theory' in R Cohen (ed), *The Future of Literary Theory* (London, Routledge, 1989) 58–85. This essay is a more detailed development of the thesis in M Nussbaum, *Poetic Justice* (Boston, Beacon Press, 1995).

thinking.'[36] As such, her work shares the explicit pedagogical orientation of the American tradition; literature is to be put to work, saved from pure dilettantism. It is the novel's connection with the contemporary social world that makes it the privileged literary form for this argument: it offers a 'concrete' engagement with man as a social being in a recognisable context which operates not just on the substantive level of the story, but also in the way in which a novel recognises the role of the reader as it attempts to draw him/her into its fictional world. This is developed into a theory of reading that could be seen as having certain correspondences with Weisberg's *Poethics*:

> . . . the novel constructs a paradigm of a style of ethical reasoning that is context specific without being relativistic, in which we get potentially universalisable concrete prescriptions by bringing a general idea of human flourishing to bear on a concrete situation, which we are invited to enter through the imagination. This is a valuable form of public reasoning, both within a single culture and across cultures. For the most part, the genre fosters it to a greater degree than the classical tragic dramas, short stories, or lyric poems.[37]

Once again, it is the marriage of content and form that is the most central feature of the literary, although Nussbaum's point is more specific than Weisberg's. Whereas for Weisburg a well wrought composition appears to be a good in itself, what is important for Nussbaum is the opening of a dialogue between reader and text which unsettles, provokes and entertains, breaking down the reader's solipsism and forcing an engagement with a social world of others. It is this aspect of the novel that is still contemporary, still 'living.' This theory of the novel's ethical worthiness cannot be sustained. The concluding assertion in the paragraph above is hard to substantiate: it could equally be argued, for example, that the lyric trope of *carpe diem* forces a connection with the world of action by showing the reader that all things must pass.

The sense in which a notion of literature is made coherent with a particular political project is apparent in the work of James Boyd White. White argues for an understanding of pluralism, or an other-orientated theory of literary communication. The other is to be included into community, but the other's difference must be respected. It is precisely this respect of the other that literature shows. Legal language can be improved through developing the insights of literature. Central to this view is the assertion that law operates through fixed concepts' whereas literature operates through a notion of text. Literary language is relational and context based, predicated on an awareness of the boundaries of any particular discourse and hence must 'acknowledge'[38] the existence of the other. This is contrasted with the 'aggressive' nature of the 'conceptual talk' on which law is based that seeks to map out and define an area through logic, and to hold to the universal truth claims that a logical process of reasoning arrives at:

[36] M Nussbaum, *Poetic Justice*, above n 35, at 46.
[37] *Ibid*, 8.
[38] JB White, *Justice as Translation* (Chicago and London, University of Chicago Press, 1990) 41.

> The literary method, on the other hand, knows that nothing can be said with certain truth or validity, that no one can be compelled to submit, and that submission is worthless any way. It proceeds on the assumption that our categories and terms are perpetually losing and acquiring meaning; that they mean different things to different people and in different texts. It is not a territorial claim but an invitation to reflection.[39]

The literary becomes the privileged trope for understanding the ethics behind the notion of translation. Translation respects the 'other' as the source of meaning, as the originator of a text that comes from a source other than the self. A characteristic of good translation is this respect, which does not seek to reduce the other to a set of common terms, but seeks to preserve the original difference. The notion of the inherently ethical nature of translation moves beyond the notion of the literary text, and becomes a model of conversation, a form of discourse ethics. Social relationships can be thought of as involving a conversation, where each side has to respect the other. Absolute understanding is not possible, or even desirable; what is necessary is fidelity to the conversation—the need to translate and respond to the terms of the other.

An obvious objection to address to this theory of translation would be to query the very terms that constitute the supposedly shared conversation. There is always the possibility that conversation is inherently coercive. Indeed, Robin West bases her critique of White on this very point. She opposes a reading of Toni Morrison's *Beloved* to White's reading of *Huckleberry Finn*.[40] The opposition of a black woman novelist to the mainstream canonical Twain is essential to West's argument (although now Morrison is equally as canonical as Twain):

> . . . there are other ways in which we form communities, and therefore other ways we might improve them, which White's 'moral textualism' neglects. Like the characters in Beloved, we form communities not just through the reading and criticism of our texts, but also through interacting with others. Our community, defined by the interactive effects we have on others, is considerably larger than the community as defined by our texts.[41]

Central to this critique is a rejection of the usefulness of literary jurisprudence and a call for political action in the 'real world.' As important as West's criticisms of White are, these arguments are pushed to an extreme. If some law and literature scholars can be criticised for a theoretically uninformed model of literature, West can be criticised for underestimating literature. To see literature as a realm that is marked by a separateness from the 'real world' reifies a certain type of literary production. This attitude has a double consequence for her work. Firstly, West's thesis seems close to Weisberg's presentation of *ressentiment*.

[39] *Ibid*, 42.

[40] R West, 'Jurisprudence as Narrative' (1985) 60 *New York University Law Review* 145. In this article West makes use of Frye's work. This inventive piece seems to have had no consideration in literary jurisprudence, and does not even seem to have figured in West's own later work.

[41] *Ibid*, 155.

Whereas Weisberg concludes with a model of the dialectical integration of literature and morality, West, as has been pointed out,[42] abandons literature all together. Her call for a 'truly radical critique of power'[43] draws on a notion of the limitations of literature as a semi-autonomous realm of the aesthetic, and ultimately ignores the ways in which literature could provide a resource for 'critique.'

What has gone wrong? Why has law and literature remained circling around this problematic? Can we read differently? Can we desire a different way of doing things?

NIGHT WORK: DREAM HARDER

Literature, like the dream, can tell us certain things about ourselves: about law and desire. In investigating this line of thought, we turn to the work of Aristodemou.

Aristodemou's thesis begins with the understanding that narrative has always been the way in which our desires have been encoded. From this meridian, Aristodemou can valorise literature against a philosophy that always claimed that its status rested on its ability to speak the truth. Literature is central because it has always told lies. This position is developed by a thesis about literature and ideology. Consider the nineteenth-century novel. It can be read as bolstering the values of the bourgeois world. But this does not exhaust the critical potential of literature. There is another aspect of Aristodemou's argument. It would be wrong to see literature as entirely about morality. Law and literature will not make you a better person. At its best, literature is a laboratory where constructions of the world can be studied; or, to shift metaphors, literature, like the dream is a rebus that offers itself to our interpretation as the very mystery of interpretation itself. The dream, as we know, is a political form, a playing out of unconscious desires that must not be seen as taking place in an intimate or personal space separate from the civic world. It is here that Aristodemou's work reinscribes the famous feminist slogan that the person is political. In Aristodemou's version, this could be read as the dreamer is political. This takes us directly to the quilting point of her discourse: the thinking and feeling of what is best described as an amorous politics in the name of Ariadne.

To build this thesis it is necessary to return to the roots of literature in Greek myth and tragedy. Greek myth offers a point to start again, to recover myths of women's 'origins'[44] and 'women's justice.'[45] Not least, this is a critique of structuralist, poststructuralist and psychoanalytic versions of the social as founded either on an incest taboo, a violent patricide or the exchange of women as objects between male subjects. These ways of thinking have no room for

[42] R West, 'Jurisprudence as Narrative', above n 40 at 11.
[43] *Ibid*, at 11.
[44] M Aristodemou, *Law and Literature* (Oxford, Oxford University Press, 2000) 57.
[45] *Ibid*, 57.

an avowedly utopian imagination of a 'different community . . . founded on cooperation and love and in which women enter as autonomous subjects';[46] a political dream reality that requires its own stories.

Stories of Mothers?

In Aristodemou's reading of the *Oresteia*, the myth is interpreted from the murder and sacrifice of Clytemnestra. It is a counter-reading, aimed at those who would find in tragedy a founding myth of law and order. Connecting with a recurrent theme of the economic, of the circulation of objects and signs, Clytemnestra, and other women in myth, pose the question of a different order of signification and organisation, a re-alignment that is prior to any possible modern discourse. If we cannot escape the symbolic order, we can jam its signals. This testifies to the incompleteness of the symbolic—its control is not total—it is a fixing or ordering of ways of thinking and being that exist alongside each other in hierarchies that can be disturbed and reordered: it plays a Kristevan semiotic against a Lacanian rage for phallic order; it finds the law of the magistrate already circumscribed by the law of love; or to shift again, with reference to a text central to the law and literature canon, Camus' *L'Etranger*, it is the right of the mother to 'give birth to words, to live and die anew'.

A fine exemplification of this is in an engagement with Angela Carter's fairy tales. Aristodemou discovers an important figuring of women as law makers. This turn to Carter is interesting in itself, as her work remains outside the traditional canon of law and literature. This is due to Carter's concern with the 'frivolous' form of the fairy tale, a genre that remains distinct from the 'serious' tradition of the American and the European novel. Carter's re-workings of the fairy tale, though, are an attempt to re-imagine relationships between men and women. What would happen, for instance, if Beauty refused to marry the Beast? This twist in the traditional story raises large questions for the discourse of law. As Aristodemou points out, the idea of marriage, the exchange of women as the foundation of legitimacy and genealogy, is central to law's creation of a world where women are merely objects that seal alliances between men. For Beauty not to marry the beast, though, is not a straightforward refusal of any relationship between women and men. Re-imagining the ending of the story can be read as suggesting that women and men need to relate to each other differently and that this difference is an alternative foundation for notions of legitimacy. This would force a consideration of love, but outside its constructions by the patriarchal tradition. Feminists have drawn attention to a belief and practice of love as indirection, and this is now expressly connected to a female imagination of the law. Even if this is dismissed as a utopian fantasy, it is a provocation to a different imagination and a creation of alternative forms.

[46] *Ibid*, 57.

It would be too easy to reject this talk of mothers and love as an essentialism or a glorifying of heterosexuality. This would misunderstand the way that these themes are deployed and developed. They are figures of production and creative activity. It may be that, given the schizophrenic cultural celebration and denigration of motherhood, there is an interface between these arguments and a political economy of reproduction. This would be to engage with the problematic where one is forced to choose between the family and the civic, home or a career, mother or 'worker'. There is clearly a need for a re-thinking of production and a re-assessment of these activities (a right to universal, free child care?). But in this text, 'motherhood' is a form, if not the form, of a creative politics: 'the father wants to be the mother, to self-generate, to give birth first to his text and through this text, to his law, to his city and to himself.'[47] In a slightly different light, this is a variation of a theme that could be encountered in, say, queer theory, with its sense of self authorship. To put this differently, the mother cannot be limited to a single referent but attests to a notion of creative labour that arguably characterises many aspects of critical thinking, whether explicitly feminist or not.

Where does this lead us? Deeper into the labyrinth?[48]

THE MAN FROM THE COUNTRY: LAW-MAKING LITERATURE

In what sense could we say that a work of poetry, and literature more generally, inaugurates a law? In a different but related sense, how can literature help us understand what it is to be in the law in ways that jurisprudence cannot? We will examine these questions through the reading of an oft-told tale about the

[47] M Aristodemou, *Law and Literature* (Oxford, Oxford University Press, 2000) 59.

[48] See also, the work of Melanie Williams, in particular *One Hundred Years of Law, Literature and Philosophy* (London, Cavendish, 2002). Williams shares with Aristodemou an avowedly feminist approach to law and literature. However, Williams' foundational ideas are drawn from moral philosophy, rather than psychoanalysis. Reading between philosophy and literature, Williams argues that philosophy and literature are held together in the same way that fact and value, individual and community, nature and nurture, male and female: all the great dualities of modern thinking are thus re-assessed. The grounding perspective is the final distinction between men and women. Williams reads this as a glyph to approach numerous 'local' manifestations, rape and pornography, are for example, manifestations of a second over-arching theme—the compromised nature of judgement itself; the repeated failure to adopt any position outside the endless shiftings of the material and the contingent. The response to this is an intellectual 'humility' and a daring approach to a theme that one might have thought had been killed off by the rise of theory: the human as agent. For Williams, the moral life is the acute positing of the theme of the subject as moral actor—as self-reflexive, self-questioning and inescapably anxious. Reason is thought of in these terms: a persistent, uncertain search for what is both necessary and impossible. With the help of Korsgaard, Williams develops a thesis about personhood as the conscious quest for self-understanding, as mediated by one's relations to others (2002). It is linked to a notion of 'person hood entire' which would not encode moral issues, such as abortion, in terms of female nature, and hence a notion of gender as inescapable and essential, but 'to the aspiration of reflexive freedom' (212). Gender is not expelled, but understood from this perspective; only then can the 'intractable' aspects of gender be appreciated.

encounter between a man from the country and the law. Our main concern will be to address the resistance of genre, the repression of the literary and aesthetic aspects of law.

The story initially comes from Jewish legal sources and Hegel narrates a version. The triumvir in Pompeii, curious to know what is the secret behind the closed doors of the tabernacle, entered the innermost part of the Temple. There he looked for a:

> being, an essence offered to his meditation, something meaningful to command his respect; and when he thought he was entering into the secret, before the ultimate spectacle, he felt mystified, disappointed, deceived. He found what he sought in 'an empty space' and concluded from this that the genuine secret was entirely extraneous to them, the Jews; it was unseen and unfelt.[49]

The triumvir was disappointed because his administrative, positivist, literal understanding expected the law to be incarnated in a text or tablet or some other material representation or source. The 'empty space' indicated a lack of comprehension on the part of the Jews; secrets must be hidden from view but they should be somewhere enclosed and in safekeeping.

In later versions, the law is incorporated in the person of the King or the high priest. Respect and veneration for their person and other symbols of their presence is a sign of respect for the incarnate law.[50] The law has a place, it is physically situated in a Temple, court or other building, and to know the law one has to penetrate this holy of holies and come face to face with it. This story finds its most complete, pithy and seemingly frightening formulation in Kafka's *Before the Law*, a short story narrated to Joseph K by the priest in *The Trial*, but also published independently.

A man from the country comes to the Law and asks the doorkeeper to be admitted. The doorkeeper tells him he must wait; the peasant obediently decamps and passes his life sitting in the door of law awaiting admittance. As death approaches, the peasant, in a flash of inspiration, realises that no-one else has been admitted to the law either and asks the doorkeeper why. The doorkeeper answers that the door was only meant for the peasant and no-one else and that now he would close it for good. *Before the Law* is usually interpreted as a parable for the irrationality of the law with its increasingly complex but empty demands, its total disregard for human value and measure—as one more instance of the labyrinthine and bureaucratic legal system so brilliantly portrayed in *The Trial*.

But if the story is a parable of the relation between the modern subject and law, it is also quite literally a case of bringing literature to law and law to literature. Literature comes to law in the sense that literary form, a parable, is used

[49] Our reading is influenced by J Derrida, 'Before the Law' in D Attridge (ed), *Acts of Literature* (New York, Routledge, 1992); and H Cixous, 'Writing the Law' in *Readings* (New York, Harvester, 1992).

[50] See P Goodrich, *Oedipus Lex* (Berkeley, University of California Press, 1995), chapter 8.

to narrate law's nature. The man from the country as well as the literary text in which he appears, approach law's place and secret and try to understand it. The law is not specified as God's law, moral law, state law, aesthetic law or any other type of law; the man wants to see the law behind all types of law, the law of law, the essence of legality. But the story also brings the law before literature. The law must explain itself through the eyes of the man and through the aesthetic considerations of literary form. In a different sense, when we the readers, subjects of law, come before this story and literature more generally, we find ourselves in a position not dissimilar to that of the man from the country: as we approach the great literary texts we feel ignorant as to authorial intention, hesitant as to correct interpretation, willing to read and understand but unable to know fully. The man wants to know what the law is, we to learn how to read and interpret it. Both in the text and beyond the text, both read and reading, before law and literature, the man from the country is a symbol and mask, the *persona* of the contemporary subject.

First, bringing literature to law. How can we read this story justly? The most remarkable thing about *Before the Law* is the urge felt throughout the ages to retell it. The story is repeated and disseminated in slightly different versions; its authors and narrators keep coming back to it like the man from the country. A literary work starts its life as something new and unrepeatable, as the essence of imagination and innovation; but in order to be recognised and to achieve the status of literature it must be repeated, disseminated, even plagiarised and retold in new versions. Repetition and the law paradoxically constitute what is unique and unrepeatable. The law is part of literature in certain obvious senses. A text is considered a work of art, worthy of our attention and critical reading if it meets certain legal requirements. First, it must have an author who is authorised by law to claim authorship, authority and the right of copy over the text and its variations. Literature as much as life, follows the laws of paternity and genealogy that determine the ownership of texts. Next, the text must have a title which, situated in a highly regulated place before or above the text, gives it an identity, makes it proper and unique, and introduces it to the order of legal circulation, financial exploitation and cultural dissemination. The title is for the text what the name is for the person; it guarantees identity through time and various readings, it ensures that while interpretations may differ between places and ages, the text persists over time as the selfsame object. But this is only the beginning. For a text to be recognised as literary and enter the canon, it must follow strict rules and conventions as to genre, style, form, language etc. Literariness is a highly ordered and regulated form of legality. Law is in literature from the very moment of its creation.

The category of literature and its evolution from ancient epics, like *The Iliad* and *Odyssey*, is the result of the creation of rights of attribution and the recognition of original and copy that law brought to writing. Literature as a distinct genre of writing claims its uniqueness only when it can be formally divided from other textual forms and types of writing. Literature needs an authority, an institution and a law, to give it its proper due and its rights but that law, authority and institution cannot exhaust its aesthetic character. This is why literature, the man from the country, comes before the law. He knows that his (and literature's) existence depends on it, that the law was present at his (and its) birth, but he does not know the law and he is desperate to enter it. But his pleas to be allowed admittance to the law go unanswered.

Literature follows the law and exists through its operations, but the law remains unknown and inaccessible, and *Before the Law is* an exemplary instance of its application. The peasant, in not entering the law is obeying the law's command throughout his life, and in this sense, despite his ignorance, he has been already admitted to the law. In awaiting formal admission and begging for an official encounter, the man is deceiving himself or the law is deceiving him. So, too, with literature. The work of art, while following legal and conventional rules, is also an attempt to glimpse at what lies at the other side of law. But the aesthetic law, even when followed, is not fully accessible and the attempt to breach the law is doomed; this failure and deception creates textual desire, pain and pleasure, in other words, literature. Literature can thus be seen as a type of impossible writing and as the writing of the impossible, a writing that follows the law in its breach.

What does literature and *Before the Law* tell us about the condition of law? The inaccessibility of law is not the result of a clear injunction or a prohibitive barrier that blocks its entrance. The guard does not physically stop the man from the country, he even dares him to enter but he intimates that he is only a lowly first official and that many more doors and powerful doorkeepers must be negotiated before coming to the law. The law is not just unknown, it is absent, in the sense that it is not yet before the man in a here-and-now—the law remains temporally and spatially deferred. Law's secret, its essence and principle, is always one door further away, there is always one more guard or judge to persuade. The law is like a coded unreadable text, a tablet written in unknown hieroglyphics, which a scholar spends her whole life trying unsuccessfully to decipher. Before the man, but never facing him or giving its secret away, the law is a vanishing point always still to come, in some other place or in a future time.

According to deconstruction,[51] such temporal deferrals and spatial differentiations are the general characteristics of writing. Their operation makes the meaning of texts inherently unstable and opens them to new and imaginative interpretations. Literature exploits this instability and openness. But the law, too, is caught in the ambiguities of the textual archive, despite the attempts to present it as an enclosed textual machine, a self-interpreting or self-executing system. When the law speaks directly to the spirit or acts itself out on the soul it needs no interpretation or mediation; this is what the man from the country learns before the law. But when it becomes scriptural and institutional the law, like all texts, has no metaphysical guarantees to ensure its uniform reception

[51] J Derrida, *Writing and Difference* (London, Routledge, 1978).

and univocal interpretation. A double absence characterises law; the absence of the future interpreter at the time of its legislation and the absence of the past legislator at the time of its application. What differentiates law from literature is not law's ability to escape the impurities of writing and speak in a single voice, but the Platonic injunction that it should attempt this impossible task and claim some success in achieving it. If literature is the writing of the impossible, law is an injunction to attempt the impossible, to erase textuality, an impossible injunction upon which everything that is possible arises. The crucial space between writing the impossible and impossibly attempting to erase impossibility (in other words, between literature and law) is the space of history, certainly of the history of the legal institution.

At the end of the story the secret of the law is revealed. The man comes to understand that he himself was its only recipient, that the secret of the law is that there is no secret. The law existed and was obeyed in the man's self-prohibition and policing, and his total and voluntary submission acted out law's command. The law is open to everyone, the man insisted at the beginning, only to discover at the end of his law-abiding life that the only universality of the law is its utter uniqueness. What is this strange and inaccessible law that puts the self under its command before it can fully understand its injunction or answer for its actions? *Before the Law* alludes to two laws of this type, the moral law and desire.

For Kant, it is subjection to the law that creates the free subject of modernity. Thought is commanded by the law of reason that formulates universal principles—those concepts, categories and schemas necessary for the regulation and classification of sensuous feelings and the external representations that reach self. The sensuous will that would respond to external stimuli solely according to considerations of pleasure and pain is subordinated to the rational will, which follows universal and necessary categories. A similar situation applies to the moral law that the free subject obeys. Every moral command is an answer or a direction as to what I ought to do or become in a particular situation. But before any formulation of an actual command, the fact that a moral command exists indicates that the law has already taken hold of me. To enquire about what I should do in a particular moral dilemma implies that I already feel that I ought to do something; the feeling of being bound, of having been put under obligation, precedes any particular sense of duty or command. The moral law is already in place, it has captivated me before I know it or follow it. It is always before me like a strange fact which Kant calls the fact of reason. Its specific formulation is the categorical imperative under which we must follow in every action a maxim that could become a principle of universal legislation. This law has no content, it is pure form, the form of the universal; it is the expression of absolute practical necessity and can never become known outside or beyond its sentences. We do not know what the law is, but this lack of knowledge is constitutive of law's operation, in the sense that we must feel duty-bound and obligated before any particular duty or any concrete law is formulated. Absence of cognition and absence to cognition results in continuous deferral; the law is always somewhere else, in the next hall, a vanishing point. Furthermore, this categorical law is accusatory, it takes hold and persecutes the subject, and it leads the self to guilt before it can know it or atone for it.

In following this law we become rational—by subjecting the multitude of chaotic representations and feelings to the coherence of concepts and categories, and we become free—by acting as if we are the legislators of its commands and by suffering from obedience. The modern subject is created in this double movement in which we are subjected to the law while we imagine ourselves as autonomous—as legislating the norms of our subjection. The law arrives with reason—it is pure and without origin or lawgiver. We are given to law, we are before the law, before we know it. *Before the Law* narrates the foundation of the subject in the recognition of the law, in the man's self-prohibition and censorship, in his self-denial and abnegation. The man knows nothing about the law, but he respects this law of nothingness because it is the law and because it says nothing. Thus he can claim that he legislates the law, his own law, the law of freedom, in his decision not to seek the law out, to defer and to wait, to defer in waiting. In legislating his own interdiction, the man from the country becomes the modern, rational man, the free man of rational will, the man who suffers in his respect for the law.

The man fails to reach the law because failure to enter the law is what the law demands, and obedience makes him free. It is not impossible, however, that that the doorkeeper is guarding an empty place, that the representatives of the law stand for nothing, and that law's secret is, exactly as the triumvir discovered, that there is no secret. This dreadful prospect comes to the man at the end of his life. As his sight begins to fail and deceive him, the man discerns a brilliance, an effulgence coming from the door of the law, a visitation or ghost that illuminates his reason at last. All previous images were deceitful, they did not reveal to him either the law or his own fate. It is only this phantasm, this illusion, mirage or symptom that opens his dying eyes. Does the law reveal its secret only to those who are deceived and deceive the law, in other words to literature, law's other? Or is the belief that we can know the law, through the eyes and through vision, through *theoria*, a hopelessly deceptive idea? *Before the Law* ambiguously suggests both answers. 'Before he dies everything he has learnt in the entire time becomes concentrated in his head into one question'. The dying man discovers the right question, not as a knowledge that his mind had possessed and now recalls, but as an unconscious affect that had occupied his body and is being acted out in symptoms, visitations and ghosts. The question of law is about desire, about a desire of the law inscribed on the body.

Freud, like Kant, reminds us that we are subjected to the law and we obey it before any knowledge of its contents. Our subjectivity and ideal image of ourselves comes into being through separation from the mother. This separation is the result of an entrance into the symbolic order and its interdiction upon the primary incestuous desire. But as this loss occurs before the creation of the ego, it cannot be represented and remains repressed and forgotten—it becomes Lacan's Real, the *nihil* from which language and the desire for the Other originate. Our union with the mother subjected us totally to the primordial Other; entry into the symbolic and the law checks the absolute power and whim of the Other and allows the subject to experience pleasure. Thus our *eros* makes us obligated before any particular obligation and subjects us to the law before we can know its demands. But conversely our love confronts us as a necessity, as a fate both pleasurable and painful, structured by the law.

The man's desire is to enter the law; nothing stops him except the doorkeeper's intimation 'it is possible, but not now'. The law works through language and speaking: it prohibits in the name of the law. More accurately, the law works through its name; it is the name 'law' that bars the entrance. And as the door and the doorkeeper are exclusively his own, everything happens internally, for the man's benefit. The secret of the law is that it is empty, just a word, 'the law', but the man desires it fervently, wants to see it and learn it. The law may be just a word, but as soon as the man has spoken it, he has come before law's place and has already put himself under its spell. The law has become part of his self, the voice of the superego. The man's desire is thus split between the law he wants to meet and the law telling him he should not enter; there is a close link between law and desire. Subjection to the law makes pleasure hard to get, but at the same time, as sin feeds on conscience, and transgression is the parasite of the law, so too, desire needs the law. The law represses desire, but it also structures it and gives it direction.

The law appears, therefore, both in Kant and Freud, as an emergent order, absolute and without origins, the very negation of any originality that may have been affected by the impurities of history or the empirical realm. The law is before history; in Kant, it allows the rational person to emerge by subjecting the order of nature to its will, thus opening history. In Freud, the law introduces ego to differentiation and limitation; it frees him from the condition of totally dependent infancy and releases him into an adulthood of controlled desire. Before law's intervention there is no presence or representation, no time or history. The man and we, the readers, are before the law from the beginning, everything is in place, the law is there before us, there is no exit or escape. But while the law claims to have no history, it never stops asking that its history and genealogy be written, that the history of its non-history be told in a narrative fashion as the story and myth of origins. The law happens as an event and as the essence of eventness, but its command is that its happening should be narrated and become the beginning of all narration, literature's birth.

As we have seen, Freud's 'mythological theory of instincts'[52] and his myth of law's genesis starts with the murder by his sons of the primal father who had monopolised the females of the horde. Guilt and remorse retrospectively

[52] S Freud, *Civilisation and its Discontents* (Harmondsworth, Penguin, 1985) 359.

overcome the murderers and in legislating against murder they opened the field of the morality of interdiction. Law acquires its power, not through the presence and strength of the father, but through his absence and memory. Law's force is stronger when the father acts as if he were present, as the conduit of a narrative that repeats, in memory and the superego, the fiction of the murder. If the murder of the father is the origin of morality, it is both a fiction and a myth, the foundation of both law and literature. The origin of law is fictional, literature lies at law's beginning and *Before the Law* is the second great modernist fiction that presents the law as a pure emergent and rational order. But even this pure law needs the fiction of a 'law' that can narrate and the images of sovereignty and legality. Subjection to the word and the images allowed the man to live his life, a life of some disappointment, but also undoubtedly of great hope, expectation and achievement, a life of freedom, of free subjection to the law and autonomous action—in other words—an ordinary life.

The man believed that the law was universal and open to everyone. The vision before his death leads to the discovery that the law was only his own and that law's universality is its utter uniqueness. What type of law is unique in its ability to universalise and remains singular in all its general applications? Two come to mind immediately, aesthetic judgement and death. Kant defines the aesthetic as a 'finality without an end', a 'lawfulness without a law'. Unlike statements of logic or practical judgements which apply a determinant principle or law, aesthetic judgements are reflective. They are examples of the application of the universal law of beauty, but as such a law does not exist, they are applications of a law still to come, instances of a legality in search of its own law. A judgement of taste is subjective and individual but it is carried out in the name of a universal law that has not been determined yet. But if that is the case, law and literature, the normative and the aesthetic, rather than being opposed, are part of each other, and the judgement of taste may be a much better model for law than the moral determinate judgements of the Second Critique.

But it was the man's imminent death that opened his failing eyesight to the reality of his condition, to what his body 'knew' all along as it spent a life of waiting, sitting at the feet of the doorman and observing. Death is our innermost and most owned possibility, our inescapable and imminent fate. This is the one event that will befall all, the most universal of all generalities, but the only universal, the one Other that I cannot share with any other. My death is my own, the only thing that is really mine, that which opens my own individuality and makes my existence unique. The man must be approaching death before he sees the brightness of the law because the law is applied fully in a life driven to death; I am finally and fully subjected to the law when I stop being a legal subject. But my death is imminent here and now; this most unique and unshareable event is also the most alien and unknown both in its (non) meaning and in its timing. The time spent before the law, the time of law's revelation, is the infinitesimal time between in-fancy, absence of law, and entry to the symbolic—always a deferred entry which is being acted out in the whole lifetime.

IN THE PLACE OF A CONCLUSION

We have told *Before the Law* once more, and like many before us, we have attempted to interpret the story. This interpretation, like all others, has tried to explain and decode the meaning of the story and rationalise and theorise its provenance. But to the extent that such attempts succeed, the story enters the annals of literary criticism, and the originality, the strange effects of its law, are lost. Once we have accounted for the story 'fully', we can conclude, like Hegel's triumvir, that the story holds no more secrets and can be vouchsafed to the priests of the literary canon.

Yet it is the alienating, frightening effect of the story that lies behind its repetition. Its law is re-enacted each time the story is narrated or read, and its effects cannot be fully predicted. The law it enacts must be sought in the relationship between the man from the country and us, the narrators and readers—between repetition and originality, law and literature. *Before the Law* brings together the disassociation between law and desire and explores the close link between law and literature, between the moral command 'obey the law' and the aesthetic injunction 'love the text'. *Before the Law* tells us that law is a special type of literature and that literature follows the law that it enacts; that creating meaning is an individual act of will, which is immersed at the same time in the practices and institutions of the written archive—unique and yet imbricated in law and in answer to the law.

Finally we, men from the country or readers, answer the double imperative of a law that deters and of a literature that defers, and the (legal) person is created in the interstices of this double act and its negation as the object of an impossible injunction and as the subject of ever-elusive desire.

The man from the country followed the law against his desire and stayed outside its place; as ideal reader, as the very figure of law and literature, we celebrate literary jurisprudence as the outside within.

PASSAGES

Night is falling. Kafka's man looks from the cover and the manuscript's letters are dancing a crazy gavotte. The light is draining away—a few reluctant stars have appeared. Darkness is erasing all those unwritten words. You have to stop reading; put it away. Your lover is calling you to come to bed. What are your big ideas compared to the body that will be beside you? Perhaps the only law is that of the lovers. Love: the malady and cure of philosophy; law its reluctant handmaiden. Go into the bedroom. It smells of the pomegranates that you gathered earlier. Now, let your mind go blank. If you listen you can hear the wind in the trees, the cicadas singing; although you cannot hear the sea from the house, you can imagine the boats pulled up on the pebbly beach; the soft breaking of the waves. The sheets are warm. This is your reward.

Index